Study Guide

Managerial Economics

ELEVENTH EDITION

Mark Hirschey

University of Kansas

THOMSON

SOUTH-WESTERN

Australia · Brazil · Canada · Mexico · Singapore · Spain · United Kingdom · United States

THOMSON

SOUTH-WESTERN

Study Guide to accompany Managerial Economics, Eleventh Edition
Mark Hirschey

VP/Editorial Director:
Jack W. Calhoun

VP/Editor-in-Chief:
Alex von Rosenberg

Publisher:
Steve Momper

Acquisitions Editor:
Peter Adams

Developmental Editor:
Amy Ray

Marketing Manager:
Brian Joyner

Production Project Manager:
Margaret M. Bril

Manager of Technology, Editorial:
Vicky True

Web Coordinator:
Karen Schaffer

Manufacturing Coordinator:
Sandee Milewski

Printer:
Globus Printing
Minster, OH

Art Director:
Tippy McIntosh

Internal Designer:
Craig Ramsdell, Ramsdell Design

Cover Designer:
Craig Ramsdell, Ramsdell Design

Cover Image(s):
© Digital Vision

For permission to use material from this
text or product, submit a request online
at http://www.thomsonrights.com.

For more information about our
products, contact us at:

Thomson Learning Academic Resource
Center

1-800-423-0563

Thomson Higher Education
5191 Natorp Boulevard
Mason, OH 45040
USA

PREFACE

This *Study Guide* has been prepared to accompany *Managerial Economics*, Eleventh Edition. Use of this *Study Guide* can significantly enhance comprehension of the material presented in *Managerial Economics*, Eleventh Edition and make easier the process of learning the tools and techniques of economic analysis. It is designed as a supplement to the text, and will not substitute for it. Although there are numerous ways in which to incorporate the use of the *Study Guide,* many have found the following four-step approach to be especially beneficial.

1. Read the chapter theme and outline in the *Study Guide* to obtain a quick preview of the material to be presented. This introduction to the chapter alerts students to key concepts being developed.

2. Read the chapter in *Managerial Economics*, Eleventh Edition. Many find that a rapid pass through the chapter, followed by a more careful and deliberate reading, leads to greater comprehension and understanding.

3. Work through the problems in the *Study Guide* and check solutions obtained with those provided. While arriving at correct solutions is certainly important at this stage, real facility in the use of the tools and techniques of economic analysis comes only with an understanding of why the problems were set up and solved as indicated in the *Study Guide* solution. It is crucial to grasp the underlying logic of sample problems and solutions. Only after one has developed such economic intuition does it become possible to transfer the skills demonstrated in the solution of a given problem to other, perhaps more complex, managerial decision problems.

4. Work through the end-of-chapter problems in the textbook. Analysis of why the problem is set up and solved in a particular fashion, as well as an interpretation of the results, enhances both comprehension and the ability to use the concepts developed in real-world applications. You can access and download detailed solutions to the end-of-chapter solved problems at **http://hirschey.swlearning.com.** Check figures for all end-of chapter problems can be found at the end of the text.

This *Study Guide* is designed to make learning managerial economics easier and more fun. It has proven helpful to students in my own classes and the extensive feedback they have provided has led to significant improvements. Of course, comments from many other users--both professors and students alike--have been very helpful over the years, and continue to be welcome. Please let me hear your suggestions for improvement. Finally, I would like to thank Christine Hauschel and Nicholas H. Hirschey for help with proof reading and problem checking.

Mark Hirschey
e-mail: mhirschey@ku.edu
May, 2005

TABLE OF CONTENTS

Chapter 1

NATURE AND SCOPE OF MANAGERIAL ECONOMICS

How do managers make good decisions? What pitfalls must be avoided? When are the characteristics of a market, a line of business, or an industry so attractive that entry becomes appealing? When are these attributes so unattractive that growth is not warranted and exit is preferable to continued operation? Why do some professions continue to pay well, while others offer only minimal financial rewards? How do you effectively motivate employees? All of these questions involve important economic issues that pose a continuing challenge to the managerial decision making process. Providing a logical and consistent framework that can be used to derive an appropriate answer to each of these questions is a task for which managerial economics is ideally suited. Managerial economics tells managers how things should be done to achieve objectives efficiently, and helps them recognize how economic forces affect organizations.

The nature and scope of managerial economics is laid out in this chapter. A primary emphasis of managerial economics is the application of economic theory and methodology to the practice of business decision making. Because managers of not-for-profit and government agencies must also efficiently employ scarce resources, managerial economics is an important tool for them as well. An important secondary emphasis in managerial economics is the study of how managerial decisions are affected by the economic environment. Managerial economics is applied economics; it is the use of economics theory and methodology to solve practical decision problems.

CHAPTER OUTLINE

I.   **HOW IS MANAGERIAL ECONOMICS USEFUL?**

     A.   **Evaluating Choice Alternatives:** Managerial economics links economic concepts with quantitative methods to develop vital tools for managerial decision making.

          1.   Managerial economics identifies ways to efficiently achieve goals.

          2.   Managerial economics can be used to specify pricing and production strategies.

          3.   Managerial economics provides production and marketing rules to help maximize net profits.

     B.   **Making the Best Decision:** To establish appropriate decision rules, managers must understand the economic environment in which they operate.

1.   Once management has set relevant goals, managerial economics can be used to efficiently attain those objectives.

2.   Managerial economics can be used to deduce the underlying logic of company, consumer, and government decisions.

II.   THEORY OF THE FIRM

A.   Expected Value Maximization: Firms exist because they are useful for producing and distributing goods and services.   The basic model of business is called the theory of the firm.

1.   In its simplest version, the firm's owner-manager is assumed to be working to maximize short-run profits.

2.   In a more complete model, the primary goal of the firm is long-term expected value maximization.

3.   The value of the firm is the present value of the firm's expected future net cash flows.

a.   If cash flows are equated to profits for simplicity, the value of the firm today, or its present value, is the value of expected profits or cash flows, discounted back to the present at an appropriate interest rate.

B.   Constraints and the Theory of the Firm: Managerial decisions are often made in light of constraints imposed by technology, resource scarcity, contractual obligations, and government laws and regulations.

1.   To make decisions that will maximize value, managers must consider both short-run and long-run implications and how external constraints affect their ability to achieve organizational objectives.

2.   The value of the firm is given by the equation:

$$\text{Value} = \sum_{t=1}^{n} \frac{TR_t - TC_t}{(1 + i)^t}$$

where TR is total revenue, TC is total cost, and i is a risk-adjusted discount rate, all during period t.

C. **Limitations of the Theory of the Firm:** In practice, it is difficult to determine whether managers actually maximize firm value or merely attempt to satisfy stockholders while pursuing other goals.

1.   Alternative theories, or models, of managerial behavior have added to our understanding of the firm.

a.   Still, the basic value maximization model is a foundation for analyzing managerial decisions.

2.   Vigorous competition in markets for goods and services typically forces managers to seek value maximization in their operating decisions.

3.   Competition in the capital markets forces managers to seek value maximization in their financing decisions.

4.   Managers who pursue their own interests instead of stockholders' interests run the risk of being replaced.

a.   Hostile takeovers are especially unfriendly to inefficient management, which is usually replaced.

5.   What sometimes appears to be satisficing on the part of management can be interpreted as value-maximizing behavior once the costs of information gathering and analysis are considered.

6.   Short-run growth maximization strategies are often consistent with long-run value maximization when the production, distribution, or promotional advantages of large firm size are better understood.

III.   PROFIT MEASUREMENT

A. **Business Versus Economic Profit:** The free enterprise system would fail to operate without profits and the profit motive. Even in planned economies, where state ownership rather than private enterprise is typical, the profit motive is increasingly used to spur efficient resource use.

1.   The general public and the business community typically define profit using an accounting concept.

a.   The amount available to fund equity capital after payment for all other resources the firm uses is called accounting profit, or business profit.

      b.   The risk-adjusted normal rate of return on capital is the minimum return necessary to attract and retain investment.

    2.   Economic profit is business profit minus the implicit costs of capital and other owner-provided inputs used by the firm.

B.   **Variability of Business Profits:** The observed variation in business profits makes it clear that many firms earn significant economic profits or experience meaningful economic losses at any point in time.

    1.   The business profit concept is typically measured in percentage terms by net income divided by the book value of stockholders' equity, or the return on equity (ROE).

IV.   WHY DO PROFITS VARY AMONG FIRMS?

A.   **Disequilibrium Profit Theories:**   Markets are sometimes in disequilibrium because of unanticipated changes in demand or cost conditions.

    1.   Profits are sometimes above or below normal because of factors that prevent instantaneous adjustment to new market conditions.

    2.   Monopoly profits exist when firms are sheltered from competition by high barriers to entry.

        a.   Economies of scale, high capital requirements, patents, or import protection, among other factors, enable some firms to build monopoly positions that allow above-normal profits for extended periods.

B.   **Compensatory Profit Theories:**   Innovation profit theory, describes the above-normal profits that arise following successful invention or modernization.

    1.   As in the case of frictional or disequilibrium profits, innovation profits are susceptible to the onslaught of competition from new and established competitors.

    2.   Compensatory profit theory describes above-normal rates of return that reward firms.

a. Superior firms provide goods and services that are better, faster or cheaper than the competition.

C. **Role of Profits in the Economy:** Each of the preceding theories describe economic profits obtained for different reasons. In some cases, several might apply.

1. Above-normal profits signal that firm or industry output should be increased.

2. Below-normal profits provide a signal for contraction and exit.

V. **ROLE OF BUSINESS IN SOCIETY**

A. **Why Firms Exist:** Business contributes significantly to social welfare.

1. These contributions stem directly from the efficiency of business in serving the economic needs of customers.

B. **Social Responsibility of Business:** Firms exist by public consent to serve the needs of society.

1. The firm can be viewed as a collaborative effort on the part of management, workers, suppliers, and investors on behalf of consumers.

2. Taxes and restrictions on firms are taxes and restrictions on those people associated with the firm.

3. The economic model of the firm emphasizes the close relation between the firm and society, and suggests the importance of business participation in the development and achievement of social objectives.

VI. **STRUCTURE OF THIS TEXT**

A. **Objectives:** This text will help you accomplish the following objectives:

1. Develop a clear understanding of economic theory and methods as they relate to managerial decision making;

2. Acquire a framework for understanding the nature of the firm as an integrated whole as opposed to a loosely connected set of functional departments;

3.   Recognize the relation between the firm and society and the key role of business as a tool for social betterment.

B.   Development of Topics: The value maximization framework is useful for characterizing actual managerial decisions and for developing rules that can be used to improve those decisions.

1.   The basic test of the value maximization model, or any model, is its ability to explain real-world behavior.

2.   This text highlights the complementary relation between theory and practice.

a.   Theory is used to improve managerial decision making.

b.   Practical experience leads to the development of better theory.

VII.   SUMMARY

Chapter 2

ECONOMIC OPTIMIZATION

The purpose of managerial economics is to furnish a systematic framework for problem analysis and solution. This means that the pluses and minuses of various decision alternatives must be carefully measured and weighed. Costs and benefits must be reliably measured; time differences must be accurately reflected. The collection and characterization of relevant information is the most important step of this process. After all relevant information has been gathered, managers must accurately state the goal or goals that they seek to achieve. Without a clear understanding of managerial objectives, effective decision making is impossible. Once all relevant information has been gathered, and managerial objectives have been clearly stated, the managerial decision making process can proceed to the consideration of decision alternatives. Effective managerial decision making is the process of efficiently arriving at the best possible solution to a given problem. If only one solution is possible, then no decision problem exists. When alternative courses of action are available, the decision that produces a result most consistent with managerial objectives is the optimal decision. The process of arriving at the best managerial decision, or best problem resolution, is the focus of managerial economics.

This chapter introduces fundamental principles of economic analysis, which are essential to all aspects of managerial economics and form the basis for describing demand, cost, and profit relations. Once basic economic relations are understood, the tools and techniques of optimization can be applied to find the best course of action.

CHAPTER OUTLINE

I.   **ECONOMIC OPTIMIZATION PROCESS**

      A.   **Optimal Decisions:** The best decision produces the result most consistent with managerial objectives.

           1.   Economic concepts and methodology are used to select the optimal course of action in light of available options and objectives.

      B.   **Maximizing the Value of the Firm:** In managerial economics, the primary objective of management is maximization of the value of the firm. Influences that must be considered include:

           1.   prices and the quantity sold

           2.   cost relations

3.   the appropriate discount rate

II.   EXPRESSING ECONOMIC RELATIONS

A.   **Tables and Equations:** Tables are the simplest and most direct form for presenting economic data. When the underlying relation between economic data is simple, tables and spreadsheets may be sufficient for analytical purposes.

1.   A simple graph or visual representation of the data can provide valuable insight.

2.   Complex economic relations require more sophisticated methods of expression. An equation is an expression of the functional relationship or connection among economic variables.

a.   The variable to the left of the equal sign is called the dependent variable. Its value depends on the size of the variable or variables to the right of the equal sign.

b.   Variables on the right-hand side of the equal sign are called independent variables. Their values are determined independently of the functional relation expressed by the equation.

B.   **Total, Average, and Marginal Relations:** Total, average, and marginal relations are very useful in optimization analysis. A marginal relation is the change in the dependent variable caused by a one-unit change in an independent variable.

1.   When the marginal is positive, the total is increasing; when the marginal is negative, the total is decreasing.

2.   Maximization of any function occurs at the point where the marginal switches from positive to negative.

3.   When the marginal is greater (less) than the average, the average must be increasing (decreasing).

C.   **Graphing Total, Marginal, and Average Relations:** Geometric relations among totals, marginals, and averages provide insight in managerial decision making.

1.   At any point along a total curve, the corresponding average figure is given by the slope of a straight line from the origin to that point.

2.   The marginal rise (or fall) in total profit associated with a one-unit increase in output is the slope of the total profit curve at that point.

D.   Deriving Totals from Marginal and Average Curves: There are simple direct relations among totals, marginals, and averages.

1.   Total profit at any given output level is the sum of marginal profits up to that point.

2.   Total profit is average profit multiplied by the corresponding number of units of output.

III.   MARGINALS AS THE DERIVATIVES OF FUNCTIONS

A.   Concept of a Derivative: A marginal is the change in the dependent variable associated with a one-unit change in an independent variable.

1.   A derivative is a marginal relation.

B.   Derivatives and Slope: The slope of a tangent to any curve $Y = f(X)$ is defined as the derivative, dY/dX.

1.   The derivative of total revenue is a precise measure of marginal revenue at any specific output level.

2.   The derivative of the total cost function at any output level indicates marginal cost at that output.

IV.   MARGINAL ANALYSIS IN DECISION MAKING

A.   Finding Maximums and Minimums: Managerial decision making frequently requires one to find the maximum or minimum value of a function.

1.   Maximization or minimization of a function occurs where its marginal value (slope) is equal to zero. For example, revenue is maximized when $MR = 0$.

B.   Distinguishing Maximums from Minimums: Second derivatives distinguish maximums from minimums.

1.   Maximums occur if the first derivative equals zero, and the second derivative is negative.

2.   Minimums occur if the first derivative equals zero, and the second derivative is positive.

C.   **Maximizing the Difference Between Two Functions:** Total profit is equal to total revenue minus total cost and is equivalent to the vertical distance between these two curves at any output level.

1.   Profit is maximized at the output level where the slopes of the revenue and cost curves are equal.

2.   The slopes of the total revenue and total cost curves measure marginal revenues (MR) and marginal costs (MC). Where these slopes are equal, MR = MC and profit is maximized.

3.   Revenue is maximized where MR = 0.

4.   Average cost is minimized where MC = AC.

V.   **THE INCREMENTAL CONCEPT IN ECONOMIC ANALYSIS**

A.   **Marginal v. Incremental Concept:** Incremental analysis involves examining the impact of alternative managerial decisions on revenues, costs, and profit. It focuses on changes or differences between available alternatives.

1.   The incremental change is the difference resulting from a decision.

2.   Marginal relations measure only the effect associated with *unitary changes* in output.

B.   **Incremental Profits:** Incremental profit is the profit gain or loss associated with a given managerial decision.

1.   When incremental profit is negative, total profit declines.
2.   Incremental profit is positive (and total profit increases) if the incremental revenue associated with a decision exceeds incremental cost.

C.   **Incremental Concept Example:** The incremental concept is important for managerial decision making because it focuses attention on the differences among available alternatives.

1.   Revenues and costs that are unaffected by a decision are irrelevant and should be excluded from analysis.

VI.   **SUMMARY**

PROBLEMS & SOLUTIONS

P2.1 *Marginal Analysis. Characterize each of the following statements as true or false, and explain your answer.*

A. *If marginal revenue is greater than average revenue, the demand curve is downward sloping.*

B. *Profit is minimized when total revenue equals total cost.*

C. *Given a downward-sloping demand curve and positive marginal costs, profit-maximizing firms always sell more output at lower prices than revenue-maximizing firms.*

D. *Marginal cost must be less than average cost for average cost to decline as output expands.*

E. *Marginal profit is the difference between marginal revenue and marginal cost, and always exceeds zero at the profit-maximizing activity level.*

P2.1 **SOLUTION**

A. False. Because average revenue is falling along a downward sloping demand curve, marginal revenue must be less than average revenue for the demand curve to slope downward.

B. False. Profits are maximized when marginal revenue equals marginal cost. Profits equal zero at the breakeven point where total revenue equals total cost. Profits are minimized when the difference between total revenue and total cost is at a maximum.

C. False. Profit maximization involves setting marginal revenue equal to marginal cost. Revenue maximization involves setting marginal revenue equal to zero. Given a downward sloping demand curve and positive marginal costs, revenue maximizing firms charge lower prices and offer greater quantities of output than firms that maximize profits.

D. True. Average cost falls as output expands so long as marginal cost is less than average cost. If this condition is met, average costs decline whether marginal costs are falling, rising or constant.

E.   False. Marginal profit equals marginal revenue minus marginal cost, and equals zero at the profit maximizing activity level.

P2.2   ***Revenue Maximization: Tables.*** *Doug Heffernan is marketing director for Arthur's Bedroom, Inc., a leading retailer. Heffernan has derived the following price/demand information from a market experiment for a new closet-space organizer product called Max Headroom:*

Price	Product Demand
$500	0
475	1
450	2
425	3
400	4
375	5
350	6
325	7
300	8
275	9
250	10
225	11
200	12
175	13
150	14
125	15

A.   *Use a spreadsheet to calculate total and marginal revenue at each level of product demand.*

B.   *At what price level is total revenue maximized? Why?*

P2.2   **SOLUTION**

A.   Total and marginal revenue at each level of product demand are as follows:

Price P	Product Demand Q	Total Revenue TR=P×Q	Marginal Revenue MR=∂TR/∂Q
$500	0	---	---
475	1	$475	$475
450	2	900	425
425	3	1,275	375
400	4	1,600	325
375	5	1,875	275
350	6	2,100	225
325	7	2,275	175
300	8	2,400	125
275	9	2,475	75
250	10	2,500	25
225	11	2,475	(25)
200	12	2,400	(75)
175	13	2,275	(125)
150	14	2,100	(175)
125	15	1,875	(225)

B. At a price level of $250 and product demand of 10 units, total revenue is maximized at a level of $2,500. Prior to that point, the added sales from a decrease in price more than compensate for the loss in revenue from charging current customers a lower price. At prices lower than $250, the loss in revenue from charging current customers a lesser price is greater than the gain in revenues from new customers, and total revenue declines. As seen from the marginal revenue column, total revenue increases so long as marginal revenue is positive, but declines when marginal revenue is negative.

P2.3 *Average Cost Minimization: Tables. Seinfeld Construction, Ltd., has been asked to submit a bid on the projected cost of sophisticated production machinery. To help in the bid development process, Gerry Seinfeld, head of product quality control, has prepared the following schedule of projected volume and production costs:*

Output	Total Cost
0	$50,000
1	51,750
2	54,000
3	56,750
4	60,000
5	63,750
6	68,000
7	73,250
8	79,500
9	86,250
10	93,500
11	102,250
12	111,500
13	122,250
14	134,500
15	150,000

A.   *Use a spreadsheet to calculate the marginal and average cost at each level of production.*

B.   *At what level of production is average cost minimized? Why?*

P2.3   **SOLUTION**

A.   Marginal and average cost at each level of production appear as follows:

Output	Total Cost	Marginal Cost	Average Cost
0	$50,000	---	---
1	51,750	$1,750	$51,750.00
2	54,000	2,250	27,000.00
3	56,750	2,750	18,916.67
4	60,000	3,250	15,000.00
5	63,750	3,750	12,750.00
6	68,000	4,250	11,333.33
7	73,250	5,250	10,464.29
8	79,500	6,250	9,937.50
9	86,250	6,750	9,583.33
10	93,500	7,250	9,350.00
11	102,250	8,750	9,295.45
12	111,500	9,250	9,291.67
13	122,250	10,750	9,403.85
14	134,500	12,250	9,607.14
15	150,000	15,500	10,000.00

B.   Minimum average costs of $9,291.67 are realized at an activity level of 12 units of output. Notice from the marginal cost column that average cost falls so long as marginal cost is less than average cost. Average cost rises so long as marginal cost is greater than average cost. Average cost reaches a minimum when marginal cost switches from being lower than average cost to being greater than average cost.

P2.4   ***Profit Maximization: Spreadsheet Analysis.*** *Roz Doyle, an interior design specialist at Seattle-based Frasier & Niles, Inc., has been asked to project the profit-maximizing activity level for a given design service during the coming period. Relevant demand and cost information are as follows:*

Q	P	TC
0	$1,000	$500
1	960	740
2	920	980
3	880	1,220
4	840	1,460
5	800	1,700
6	760	1,940
7	720	2,180
8	680	2,420
9	640	2,660
10	600	2,900
11	560	3,140
12	520	3,380
13	480	3,620
14	440	3,860
15	400	4,100

A. *Construct a table (or spreadsheet) showing total revenue, marginal revenue, marginal cost, average cost, total profit, marginal profit, and average profit for this product at the various activity levels indicated previously.*

B. *Identify the profit-maximizing activity level.*

C. *Is the profit-maximizing activity level the same activity level as that at which minimum average costs are experienced? Why? or Why not?*

P2.4 **SOLUTION**

A. A table (or spreadsheet) showing total revenue, marginal revenue, marginal cost, average cost, total profit, marginal profit, and average profit for this product at the various activity levels is as follows:

Q	P	TR = P×Q	MR = ∂TR/∂Q	TC	MC = ∂TC/∂Q	AC = TC/Q	π = TR-TC	Mπ = ∂π/∂Q	Aπ = π/Q
0	$1,000	$0	---	$500	---	---	($500)	---	---
1	960	960	$960	740	$240	$740.00	220	$720	$220.00
2	920	1,840	880	980	240	490.00	860	640	430.00
3	880	2,640	800	1,220	240	406.67	1,420	560	473.33
4	840	3,360	720	1,460	240	365.00	1,900	480	475.00
5	800	4,000	640	1,700	240	340.00	2,300	400	460.00
6	760	4,560	560	1,940	240	323.33	2,620	320	436.67
7	720	5,040	480	2,180	240	311.43	2,860	240	408.57
8	680	5,440	400	2,420	240	302.50	3,020	160	377.50
9	640	5,760	320	2,660	240	295.56	3,100	80	344.44
10	600	6,000	240	2,900	240	290.00	3,100	0	310.00
11	560	6,160	160	3,140	240	285.45	3,020	(80)	274.55
12	520	6,240	80	3,380	240	281.67	2,860	(160)	238.33
13	480	6,240	0	3,620	240	278.46	2,620	(240)	201.54
14	440	6,160	(80)	3,860	240	275.71	2,300	(320)	164.29
15	400	6,000	(160)	4,100	240	273.33	1,900	(400)	126.67

B.   Production and sale of 10 units at a price of $600 (or 9 units and a price of $640) is the profit-maximizing activity level. Profits are maximized at a level of $3,100. Prior to this point, the marginal revenue associated with additional sales exceeds their associated marginal cost, marginal profit is positive, and total profit rises with an expansion in output. Subsequent to this point, the marginal revenue associated with additional sales is less than their associated marginal cost, marginal profit is negative, and total profit falls with an expansion in output.

C.   No, the profit-maximizing activity level is not the same activity level as that at which minimum average costs are experienced. In this problem, marginal costs are a constant $240 per unit. With fixed costs of $500, average costs continue to fall as output expands; they approach $240 as a lower limit. Although average costs continue to diminish as output expands, ever lower prices must be offered to generate these added sales. Total profits fall as output expands beyond 10 units because marginal revenues are less than marginal costs beyond that point. It is important to recognize that profit maximization requires a comparison of marginal revenues *and* marginal costs; average cost minimization involves a comparison of marginal cost and average cost relations only (revenue effects are not considered).

P2.5   *Marginal Analysis: Tables. Rachel Green, a student at Minnesota State University, is preparing for final exams and has decided to devote five hours to the study of* managerial economics and finance. Green's goal is to maximize the average grade earned in the two courses, and must decide how much time to spend on each exam. Green realizes that maximizing the average grade in the two courses is equivalent to maximizing the sum of the grades. According to Green's best estimates, the grades achieved will vary according to the schedule shown below.

Managerial Economics		Finance	
Hours of Study	Grade	Hours of Study	Grade
0	25	0	50
1	45	1	62
2	65	2	72
3	75	3	81
4	83	4	88
5	90	5	93

A. Describe the manner in which Green could make use of the marginal concept in managerial economics to assist in determining the optimal allocation of five hours between the two courses.

B. How much time should Green spend studying each subject?

C. In addition to managerial economics and finance, Green is also taking a marketing course. Green estimates that each hour spent studying marketing will result in an eight point increase on the marketing examination score. Green has tentatively decided to spend three hours preparing for the marketing exam. Is Green's attempt to maximize the average grade in all three courses with three hours devoted to marketing and five hours devoted to managerial economics and finance (allocated as in part B) an optimal decision? Why? or Why not?

P2.5 **SOLUTION**

A. An optimal allocation of study time is one that will permit Green to maximize the average grade earned in the managerial economics and finance courses. This maximization will occur when Green allocates each hour of study time to that course where the marginal grade value of study time is greatest.

B. To determine how much time Green should spend studying each subject a table illustrating the marginal grade value of each hour of study time must be constructed. This table reads as follows:

Managerial Economics			Finance		
Hours of Study	**Grade**	**Marginal Grade Value**	**Hours of Study**	**Grade**	**Marginal Grade Value**
0	25	--	0	50	--
1	45	20	1	62	12
2	65	20	2	72	10
3	75	10	3	81	9
4	83	8	4	88	7
5	90	7	5	93	5

With only five hours to study, Green should spend three hours on managerial economics and two hours on finance.

C. No, Green's decision to spend three hours studying for the marketing exam is incorrect if the objective is to maximize the average grade received in managerial economics, finance and marketing. Only two hours should be allocated to studying marketing because an additional hour spent on finance would increase the total grade achieved by nine points; one point more than the eight point gain associated with the third hour spent preparing for the marketing exam, and will lead to a maximum average grade.

P2.6 ***Marginal Analysis: Tables.*** *Monica Geller is a regional media consultant for Friendly Images, Inc., a New York-based media consultant. Geller has gathered the following data on weekly advertising media expenditures and gross sales for a major client, Greenwich Village's Central Perk Coffeehouse.*

	Gross Sales Following Promotion in the Following Media:		
Advertising Expenditure	*Newspaper*	*Radio*	*Television*
$0	*$10,000*	*$10,000*	*$10,000*
100	*12,000*	*14,000*	*13,000*
200	*13,800*	*17,600*	*15,600*
300	*15,400*	*20,200*	*18,000*
400	*16,600*	*22,000*	*18,600*
500	*17,200*	*22,400*	*18,800*

A. Construct a table (or spreadsheet) showing marginal sales following promotion in each media. (Assume here and throughout the problem that there are no synergistic effects across different media.)

B. If the Central Perk Coffeehouse has an advertising budget of $500 per week, how should it be spent? Why?

C. Calculate the profit maximizing advertising budget and media allocation assuming the Central Perk Coffeehouse enjoys an average profit contribution before media expenditures of 6% on store-wide sales. How much are maximum weekly profits (before taxes)?

P2.6 **SOLUTION**

A. A table showing marginal sales generated by promotion in each media appears as follows:

**Marginal Sales Following Promotion in the
Following Media:**

Advertising Expenditure	Newspaper	Radio	Television
$0	---	---	---
100	$2,000	$4,000	$3,000
200	1,800	3,600	2,600
300	1,600	2,600	2,400
400	1,200	1,800	600
500	600	400	200

B. Using the data in part A, and given a $500 advertising budget, gross sales and profit contribution are maximized by allocating $300 to radio and $200 to television advertising. Irrespective of whether the Central Perk Coffeehouse seeks to maximize revenues or profit, this expenditure allocation is optimal.

C. Given an average profit contribution before media expenditures of 6% on store-wide sales, an additional dollar of advertising will be profitable so long as it returns more than $16.67 in additional revenues. That is, the profit contribution on additional revenues of $16.67 is just sufficient to cover media costs of $1 (= $16.67 × 0.06). The profit maximizing advertising budget is $900 per week allocated as: $200 on newspaper, $400 on radio, and $300 on television.

Maximum weekly profits are:

Base sales	$10,000
+ Newspaper sales	3,800
+ Radio sales	12,000
+ Television sales	8,000
	$33,800
× Gross margin	0.06
Gross profit	2,028
- Media costs	900
Net profit	$ 1,128

(before tax)

P2.7   ***Marginal Analysis: Equations.*** *American Idol Products, Inc., has developed a new pocket-sized wireless communications device. This product's reliability level, measured by its failure rate, is a function of the amount of on-site preventive maintenance and warranty work:*

$$Failure\ Rate\ =\ 0.1 - 0.01t + 0.001t^2,$$

$$Marginal\ Failure\ Rate\ =\ \partial F / \partial t = -0.01 + 0.002t,$$

where t represents the amount of time devoted to on-site preventive maintenance and warranty work:

   A.   *Set the marginal failure rate equal to zero to determine the failure rate-minimizing level of on-site preventive maintenance and warranty work.*

   B.   *What is the optimal failure rate?*

P2.7   **SOLUTION**

   A.   Set MF = 0 to find the failure rate-minimizing level of on-site preventive maintenance and warranty work:

$$MF\ =\ -0.01 + 0.002t$$

$$0\ =\ -0.01 + 0.002t$$

$$0.002t\ =\ 0.01$$

$$t\ =\ 5\ hours$$

For this to be a failure-rate minimizing, rather than maximizing, level of on-site preventive maintenance and warranty work, the failure rate must be increasing beyond this point. This is indeed the case, as can be illustrated with a simple numerical example (see part B).

   B.   At t = 5, note that:

$$F\ =\ 0.1 - 0.01t + 0.001t^2$$

$$=\ 0.1 - 0.01(5) + 0.001(5^2)$$

$$=\ 0.075\ (or\ 7.5\%)$$

To confirm that this is failure-rate minimizing level of t, notice that F is increasing for t > 5, e.g., F = 0.076 or 7.6% when t = 6.

P2.8   ***Profit Maximization: Equations.*** *Accounting Temps, Inc., operates with the following revenue and cost functions:*

$$TR = \$100Q - \$0.5Q^2 \qquad \text{(Total Revenue)}$$

$$MR = \partial TR/\partial Q = \$100 - \$1Q \qquad \text{(Marginal Revenue)}$$

$$TC = \$1,500 - \$10Q + \$0.5Q^2 \qquad \text{(Total Cost)}$$

$$MC = \partial TC/\partial Q = -\$10 + \$1Q \qquad \text{(Marginal Cost)}$$

where Q represents the quantity of output produced and sold as measured by thousands of hours of temporary accounting services (000).

A.   *Set $M\pi = MR - MC = 0$ to determine the profit-maximizing price/output combination for ATI.*

B.   *Show that marginal revenue equals marginal cost at this profit-maximizing output level.*

P2.8   SOLUTION

A.   Set $M\pi = MR - MC = 0$ to maximize profits, where:

$$M\pi = MR - MC$$

$$0 = \$100 - \$1Q + \$10 - \$1Q$$

$$2Q = 110$$

$$Q = 55 \ (000)$$

And,

$$P = TR/Q$$

$$= (\$100Q - \$0.5Q^2)/Q$$

$$= \$100 - \$0.5Q$$

$$= \$100 - \$0.05(55)$$

$$= \$72.50$$

B. At Q = 55 (000), note that:

$$MR = \$100 - \$1Q = \$100 - \$55 = \$45$$

$$MC = -\$10 + \$1Q = -\$10 + \$55 = \$45$$

This numerical finding illustrates the general result that if $M\pi = MR - MC = 0$, then MR = MC will always be true.

P2.9 ***Profit Versus Revenue Maximization.*** *West Wing Products, Inc., based in Durham, New Hampshire, produces and sells a wide variety of replacement parts and equipment for light aircraft. Leo McGarry, a product line specialist for the company, is reviewing the company's Internet marketing strategy for a popular flight manual. Demand and cost relations for the guidebook are given by the equations:*

$$P = \$155 - \$0.05Q \qquad\qquad \text{(Demand)}$$

$$MR = \partial TR/\partial Q = \$155 - \$0.1Q \qquad \text{(Marginal Revenue)}$$

$$TC = \$75,000 + \$5Q + \$0.0125Q^2 \qquad \text{(Total Cost)}$$

$$MC = \partial TC/\partial Q = \$5 + \$0.025Q \qquad \text{(Marginal Cost)}$$

where Q is the quantity produced and sold per week.

A. *Calculate the revenue-maximizing price/output combination.*

B. *Calculate the profit-maximizing price/output combination.*

C. *Are the differences in your answers to parts A and B typical or atypical? Explain.*

P2.9 **SOLUTION**

A. Set MR = 0 to find the revenue-maximizing output level:

$$MR = \$155 - \$0.1Q$$

$$0 = \$155 - \$0.1Q$$

$$0.1Q = 155$$

$$Q = 1,550$$

Because total revenue is declining beyond this point, Q = 1,550 is a point of maximum revenues. And,

$$P = \$155 - \$0.05(1,550)$$

$$= \$77.50$$

B.   Set $M\pi = MR - MC = 0$ to find the profit-maximizing output level:

$$M\pi = MR - MC$$

$$0 = \$155 - \$0.1Q - \$5 - \$0.025Q$$

$$0.125Q = 150$$

$$Q = 1,200$$

Because total profit is declining for Q > 1,200, Q = 1,200 is a point of maximum profits. And,

$$P = \$155 - \$0.05(1,200)$$

$$= \$95$$

C.   This is a typical result; so long as the product demand curve slopes downward and marginal cost exceeds zero, revenue maximization results in greater output (here, 1,550 versus 1,200) and lower prices (here, $77.50 versus $95) than is true with profit maximization.

P2.10   ***Profit Maximization Versus Average Cost Minimization.*** *Immensely popular mystery writer Breanna Van De Camp has just published a new book titled "Desperate Housewives." Relevant monthly demand and cost relations for this hard cover title are:*

$$P = \$35 - \$0.00075Q \qquad\qquad (Demand)$$

$$MR = \partial TR/\partial Q = \$35 - \$0.0015Q \qquad\qquad (Marginal\ Revenue)$$

$$TC = \$50,000 + \$5Q + \$0.0005Q^2 \qquad\qquad (Total\ Cost)$$

$$MC = \partial TC / \partial Q = \$5 + \$0.001Q \qquad \textit{(Marginal Cost)}$$

where Q is the number of books produced and sold per month.

A. *Calculate the profit-maximizing price/output combination and profit level.*

B. *Calculate the average cost-minimizing price/output combination and profit level.*

C. *Contrast your answers to parts A and B.*

P2.10   SOLUTION

A. To find the profit-maximizing activity level, set $M\pi = MR - MC = 0$:

$$M\pi = MR - MC$$

$$0 = \$35 - \$0.0015Q - \$5 - \$0.001Q$$

$$0.0025Q = 30$$

$$Q = 12{,}000.$$

$$P = \$35 - \$0.00075(12{,}000)$$

$$= \$26.$$

$$\pi = TR - TC$$

$$= \$35Q - \$0.00075Q^2 - \$50{,}000 - \$5Q - \$0.0005Q^2$$

$$= -\$50{,}000 + \$30Q - \$0.00125Q^2$$

$$= -\$50{,}000 + \$30(12{,}000) - \$0.00125(12{,}000^2)$$

$$= \$130{,}000$$

Because total profit is declining for $Q > 12{,}000$, $Q = 12{,}000$ is a point of maximum profits per month. (*Note*: A publisher's price of $26 is consistent with a bookstore price of roughly $35.)

B. To find the average cost-minimizing activity level, set $MC = AC$:

$$MC = AC = TC/Q$$

$$\$5 + \$0.001Q = (\$50,000 + \$5Q + \$0.0005Q^2)/Q$$

$$\$5 + \$0.001Q = \$50,000/Q + \$5 + \$0.0005Q$$

$$0.0005Q = 50,000/Q$$

$$Q^2 = 100,000,000$$

$$Q = 10,000$$

$$P = \$35 - \$0.00075(10,000)$$

$$= \$27.50$$

$$\pi = -\$50,000 + \$30(10,000) - \$0.00125(10,000^2)$$

$$= \$125,000$$

Because average cost is rising for $Q > 10,000$, $Q = 10,000$ is a point of minimum average costs per month.

C.   Profit maximization involves a comparison of the marginal revenues and marginal costs of production. Average-cost minimization involves a consideration of cost relations only. Therefore, it is not surprising that these two approaches often yield different price/output combinations. In this instance, the added revenues associated with an additional 2,000 units beyond the average cost-minimizing level of 10,000 is so great as to overcome the disadvantage of somewhat higher average costs at the 12,000 units versus 10,000 units activity level.

Chapter 3

DEMAND AND SUPPLY

Nothing is more important to the economic survival of any organization than the need to effectively identify and respond to product demand and supply conditions. In economic terms, demand refers to the amount of a product that people are willing and able to buy under a given set of conditions. Need or desire is a necessary component but must be accompanied by financial capability before economic demand is created. Thus, economic demand requires potential buyers with a desire to use or possess something and the financial ability to acquire it. With vibrant demand for its products, the firm is able to attract the necessary resources to expand and grow. Without demand for a firm's products, no revenues are generated to pay suppliers, workers, and stockholders. Without demand, no amount of efficiency in production can ensure the firm's long-term survival. Without demand, the firm simply ceases to exist.

Once demand for the firm's products has been identified or created, the firm must thoroughly understand supply conditions to efficiently meet customer needs. Supply is the amount of a good or service that firms make available for sale under a given set of economic conditions. Just as demand requires a desire to purchase combined with the economic resources to do so, supply requires a desire to sell along with the economic capability to bring a product to market. Supply increases when additional profits are generated; supply decreases when production results in losses. The concepts of demand, supply, and equilibrium described in this chapter provide the fundamentals for analyzing interactions among buyers and sellers in the markets for all goods and services.

CHAPTER OUTLINE

I.   **BASIS FOR DEMAND**

      A. **Definition:** Demand is the quantity of a good or service that customers are willing and able to purchase during a given period and under a given set of economic conditions.

          1. Demand is created when customers perceive value (have desire) and the financial capability to make purchase decisions.

          2. The success of any organization depends on a clear understanding of the demand and supply conditions for goods and services provided to customers.

      B. **Direct Demand:** Demand for personal goods and services is based on the utility gained through consumption.

          1. Consumers demand products that yield satisfaction.

C.   **Derived Demand:** Demand for inputs that can be used in production is derived from the demand for consumer goods and services.

1.   Firms demand inputs that can be profitably employed.

II.   **THE MARKET DEMAND FUNCTION**

A.   **Determinants of Demand:** A demand function shows the relation between the quantity demanded and all factors that affect it.

1.   Important demand determinants include: price, price of other goods, income, advertising, and so on.

B.   **Industry Demand Versus Firm Demand:** Demand functions can be specified for an entire industry or an individual firm.

1.   Industry Demand: Overall industry demand is subject to general economic influences (population, GDP, interest rates, and so on).

2.   Firm Demand: Firm demand is affected by general economic influences and competitor decisions (prices, advertising, and so on).

III.   **DEMAND CURVE**

A.   **Definition:** A demand curve shows the price-quantity relation, holding constant the effects of all other demand-determining influences.

B.   **Demand Curve Determination:** To derive a demand curve, simply insert values for all nonprice variables into the demand function and determine the price/quantity relation.

C.   **Relation Between the Demand Curve and Demand Function:** A demand curve can be plotted when all variables other than price and quantity in a given demand function are fixed at specific levels.

1.   A change in the quantity demanded reflects movement along a given demand curve following a price change.

2.   A shift in demand occurs when change in a nonprice variable leads to a shift from one demand curve to another.

IV.   **BASIS FOR SUPPLY**

A.   **Definition:** Supply is the quantity of a good or service that producers are willing and able to sell during a given period.

1.   Supply is offered when producers are able to at least cover the marginal cost of production.

B.   **How Output Prices Affect Supply**: Among the factors influencing the supply of a product, the price of the product itself is often the most important.

1.   Higher prices increase the quantity of output producers want to bring to market.

C.   **Other Factors That Influence Supply:** Anything that influences the profitability of production has the potential to influence supply.

1.   Supply determinants include the price of the product itself, prices of competing products, technology, input prices, and weather, among other such factors.

V.   **MARKET SUPPLY FUNCTION**

A.   **Determinants of Supply:** A supply function describes the relation between the quantity supplied and all factors that affect it.

1.   Relevant factors include: price, price of related products, technology, input prices, and so on.

B.   **Industry Versus Firm Supply:** Industry supply is affected by prices, prices of other products, advertising, and macroeconomic conditions.

1.   Firm supply is affected by these factors *and* competitive influences.

2.   Industry supply is the sum total of firm supply.

VI.   **SUPPLY CURVE**

A.   **Definition:** A supply curve shows the price-quantity relation, holding constant the effects of all other supply-determining influences.

B.   **Supply Curve Determination:** To derive a supply curve, simply insert values for all nonprice variables into the supply function and calculate the price/quantity relation.

C.   **Relation Between Supply Curve and Supply Function:** A supply curve can be plotted when all variables other than price and quantity in a given supply function are fixed at specific levels.

   1.   A change in the quantity supplied reflects a movement along a given supply curve following a price change.

   2.   A shift in supply occurs when change in a nonprice variable leads to a switch from one supply curve to another.

VII.   **MARKET EQUILIBRIUM**

A.   **Definition:** Market Equilibrium is perfect balance in demand and supply under a given set of market conditions.

B.   **Surplus and Shortage:** Both of these conditions reflect disequilibrium.

   1.   Surplus is excess supply.

   2.   Shortage is excess demand.

C.   **Comparative Statics: Changing Demand:** Equilibrium will change following a shift in the demand curve (change in demand).

D.   **Comparative Statics: Changing Supply:** Equilibrium will also change following a shift in the supply curve (change in supply).

E.   **Comparative Statics: Changing Demand *and* Supply:** Typically, changes in equilibrium reflect variation in demand and supply.

VIII.   **SUMMARY**

PROBLEMS & SOLUTIONS

P3.1   ***Demand and Supply Concepts****. The market for oil is highly price sensitive. Indicate the effects of each of the following influences on demand and/or supply conditions:*

        A.   *A major oil discovery.*

        B.   *A $5 per barrel tax on oil.*

        C.   *An improvement in oil recovery technology.*

        D.   *An unusually hot summer causing an increase in the demand for air conditioning.*

        E.   *An increase in energy conservation.*

P3.1   **SOLUTION**

        A.   Increase supply/rightward shift in supply curve. A major oil discovery will increase the quantity supplied at every price level.

        B.   Decrease supply/leftward shift in supply curve. A $5 per barrel tax on oil will reduce the share of total oil-related expenditures going to producers, and thus reduce the quantity supplied at every price level.

        C.   Increase supply/rightward shift in supply curve. An improvement in technology will make it possible to supply more oil at every price level.

        D.   Increase demand/rightward shift in demand curve. With an increase in air conditioning demand, electricity usage will rise, as will the demand for oil at every price level.

        E.   Decrease demand/leftward shift in demand curve. Increased energy conservation will cut oil usage at every price level.

P3.2   ***Demand and Supply Concepts****. Describe the effects of each of the following influences on demand and/or supply conditions in the new-hire market for MBAs.*

        A.   *An economic recession (fall in national income).*

        B.   *An increase in MBA graduate salaries.*

        C.   *An increase in the availability of low-cost student loans.*

D.   *A rise in tuition costs.*

E.   *A rise in relative productivity of MBA versus BA/BS job candidates.*

P3.2   **SOLUTION**

A.   Decrease demand/leftward shift in demand curve and increase supply/rightward shift in supply curve. With a fall in national income, the profitability of added employment will fall, thereby causing a decline in the demand for labor. A recession can also reduce job opportunities for BAs and BSs, thereby reducing the income loss incurred while in graduate school, and thus can actually increase the supply of MBAs. Despite this often observed counter-cyclical relation between enrollment and economic activity, recessions can also limit the return to an MBA and thereby limit MBA supply. Thus, the net effect on supply can be uncertain.

B.   Decrease in the quantity demanded/upward movement along demand curve and increase the quantity supplied/upward movement along supply curve. Rising prices cut the quantity demanded while increasing the quantity supplied.

C.   Increase supply/rightward shift in supply curve. An increase in student loan availability will cut the cost of an MBA education, and increase the expected net return, and increase supply at every expected wage level.

D.   Decrease supply/leftward shift in supply curve. A rise in tuition costs increases the cost of an MBA education, cuts the expected net return, and will decrease supply at each expected wage level.

E.   Increase demand/rightward shift in demand. An increase in the relative productivity of MBAs will increase demand for MBAs at every price level.

P3.3   **Surplus and Shortage**. *The following relations describe monthly demand and supply conditions in the market for No. 1 grade cotton blue denim:*

$$Q_D = 100,000 - 40,000P \qquad \text{(Demand)}$$

$$Q_S = -5,000 + 30,000P \qquad \text{(Supply)}$$

where Q is quantity measured in thousands of square yards and P is price per square yard in dollars.

A.   *Complete the following table:*

Price (1)	Quantity Supplied (2)	Quantity Demanded (3)	Surplus (+) or Shortage (-) (4) = (2) - (3)
$2.00			
1.75			
1.50			
1.25			
1.00			

P3.3 **SOLUTION**

A.

Price (1)	Quantity Supplied (2)	Quantity Demanded (3)	Surplus (+) or Shortage (-) (4) = (2) - (3)
$2.00	55,000	20,000	35,000
1.75	47,500	30,000	17,500
1.50	40,000	40,000	0
1.25	32,500	50,000	-17,500
1.00	25,000	60,000	-35,000

P3.4 **Quantity Demanded.** *Tim Taylor is a manager at Tool Time, Inc., a nation-wide supplier of tools and accessories to independent electricians and plumbers. A study of annual demand in several regional markets suggests the following demand function for a popular socket wrench set:*

$$Q = -500 - 10P + 0.001Pop + 0.0125I + 20A$$

where Q is quantity, P is price ($), Pop is population, I is disposable income per person ($), and A is advertising measured in terms of personal selling days per year by Time Tools' sales staff.

A. *Determine the demand curve faced by Tool Time in a typical market where Pop = 1,000,000, I = $40,000, and A = 200 days.*

B. *Calculate the quantity demanded at prices of $250, $275, and $300.*

C. *Calculate the prices necessary to sell 2,000, 3,000, and 4,000 units.*

P3.4   **SOLUTION**

A.   The demand curve can be calculated by substituting each respective variable into the firm's demand function:

$$Q = -500 - 10P + 0.001\text{Pop} + 0.0125I + 20A$$

$$= -500 - 10P + 0.001(1,000,000)$$

$$+ 0.0125(40,000) + 20(200)$$

$$Q = 5,000 - 10P$$

Then, price as a function of quantity can be written:

$$Q = 5,000 - 10P$$

$$5,000 - Q = 10P$$

$$P = \$500 - \$0.1Q$$

B.   At,

$$P = \$250: Q = 5,000 - 10(250) = 2,500$$

$$P = \$275: Q = 5,000 - 10(275) = 2,250$$

$$P = \$300: Q = 5,000 - 10(300) = 2,000$$

C.   At,

$$Q = 2,000: P = \$500 - \$0.1(2,000) = \$300$$

$$Q = 3,000: P = \$500 - \$0.1(3,000) = \$200$$

$$Q = 4,000: P = \$500 - \$0.1(4,000) = \$100$$

P3.5   ***Quantity Demanded.*** *The Montana Steakhouse, Inc., is a rapidly growing chain offering steak sandwiches at popular prices. An analysis of monthly customer traffic at its restaurants reveals the following:*

$$Q = 350 - 500P + 900P_F + 0.02\text{Pop} + 2,000S$$

where Q is quantity measured by the number of customers served per month, P is the average meal price per customer ($), P_F is the average meal price at fast-food restaurants, Pop is the population of the restaurant market area, and S, a binary or dummy variable, equals 1 in summer months and zero otherwise.

A. Determine the demand curve facing the company during the month of December if $P_F = \$6$, Pop $= 300,000$, and $S = 0$.

B. Calculate the quantity demanded and total revenues during the summer month of August if $P = \$16$, and all demand-related variables are as specified above.

P3.5   **SOLUTION**

A. With quantity expressed as a function of price, the firm demand curve can be calculated by substituting the value for each respective variable into the demand function:

$$Q = 350 - 500P + 900P_F + 0.02Pop + 2,000S$$

$$Q = 350 - 500P + 900(6) + 0.02(300,000) + 2,000(0)$$

$$Q = 11,750 - 500P$$

Then, with price as a function of quantity, the firm's demand curve is:

$$Q = 11,750 - 500P$$

$$500P = 11,750 - Q$$

$$P = \$23.5 - \$0.002Q$$

B. The total quantity demanded is found from the demand function:

$$Q = 350 - 500P + 900P_F + 0.02Pop + 2,000S$$

$$= 350 - 500(16) + 900(6) + 0.02(300,000) + 2,000(1)$$

$$= 5,750$$

Thus, total revenue is:

$$TR = P \times Q$$

$$= \$16(5{,}750)$$

$$= \$92{,}000$$

P3.6 **Quantity Supplied.** *A review of industry-wide data for the residential construction industry suggests the following industry supply function:*

$$Q = 1{,}000{,}000 + 5{,}000P - 3{,}500P_L - 30{,}000P_K$$

where Q is housing starts per year, P is the average price of new homes (in \$ thousands), P_L is the average price paid for skilled labor (\$), and P_K is the average price of capital (in percent).

A. *Determine the industry supply curve for a recent year when $P_L = \$40$, and $P_K = 12\%$, show the industry supply curve with quantity expressed as a function of price, and price expressed as a function of quantity.*

B. *Calculate the quantity supplied by the industry at new home prices of \$200 (000), \$300 (000), and \$400 (000).*

C. *Calculate the prices necessary to generate a supply of 1.5 million, 2 million, and 2.5 million new homes.*

P3.6 **SOLUTION**

A. With quantity expressed as a function of price, the industry supply curve can be written:

$$Q = 1{,}000{,}000 + 5{,}000P - 3{,}500P_L - 30{,}000P_K$$

$$= 1{,}000{,}000 + 5{,}000P - 3{,}500(40) - 30{,}000(12)$$

$$Q = 500{,}000 + 5{,}000P$$

With price expressed as a function of quantity, the industry supply curve can be written:

$$Q = 500{,}000 + 5{,}000P$$

$$5{,}000P = -500{,}000 + Q$$

$$P = -\$100 + \$0.0002Q$$

B. Industry supply at each respective price (in thousands) is:

$P = \$200\ (000)$: $Q = 500{,}000 + 5{,}000(200) = 1{,}500{,}000$

$P = \$300\ (000)$: $Q = 500{,}000 + 5{,}000(300) = 2{,}000{,}000$

$P = \$400\ (000)$: $Q = 500{,}000 + 5{,}000(400) = 2{,}500{,}000$

C. The price necessary to generate each level of supply is:

$Q = 1{,}500{,}000$: $P = -\$100 + \$0.0002(1{,}500{,}000) = \$200\ (000)$

$Q = 2{,}000{,}000$: $P = -\$100 + \$0.0002(2{,}000{,}000) = \$300\ (000)$

$Q = 2{,}500{,}000$: $P = -\$100 + \$0.0002(2{,}500{,}000) = \$400\ (000)$

P3.7 **Firm Supply.** *Uniform Supply, Inc., is a uniform rental service. Chandler Bing, company controller, has estimated the following relation between its marginal cost per unit and weekly output:*

$$MC = \partial TC / \partial Q = \$3 + \$0.001Q$$

A. *Calculate marginal costs per unit for 1,000, 2,000, and 3,000 uniform rentals per week.*

B. *Express output as a function of marginal cost. Calculate the level of output when MC = $5, $7.50, and $10.*

C. *Calculate the profit maximizing level of output if prices are stable in the industry at $7.50 per unit and, therefore, P = MR = $7.50.*

D. *Again assuming prices are stable in the industry, derive the company's supply curve. Express price as a function of quantity and quantity as a function of price.*

P3.7 **SOLUTION**

A. Marginal production costs at each level of output are:

$Q = 1{,}000$: $MC = \$3 + \$0.001(1{,}000) = \$4$

$Q = 2{,}000$: $MC = \$3 + \$0.001(2{,}000) = \$5$

$$Q = 3,000: MC = \$3 + \$0.001(3,000) = \$6$$

B.   When output is expressed as a function of marginal cost, one finds that:

$$MC = \$3 + \$0.001Q$$

$$0.001Q = -3 + MC$$

$$Q = -3,000 + 1,000MC$$

The level of output at each respective level of marginal cost is:

$$MC = \$5: Q = -3,000 + 1,000(5) = 2,000$$

$$MC = \$7.50: Q = -3,000 + 1,000(7.5) = 4,500$$

$$MC = \$10: Q = -3,000 + 1,000(10) = 7,000$$

C.   Note from part B that MC = \$7.50 when Q = 4,500. Therefore, when MR = \$7.50, Q = 4,500 will be the profit-maximizing level of output. More formally:

$$MR = MC$$

$$\$7.50 = \$3 + \$0.001Q$$

$$0.001Q = 4.50$$

$$Q = 4,500$$

D.   Because prices are stable in the industry, P = MR. This means that the company will supply output at the point where:

$$MR = MC$$

and, therefore, that:

$$P = \$3 + \$0.001Q$$

This is the supply curve for the company's service, where price is expressed as a function of quantity. When quantity is expressed as a function of price:

$$P = \$3 + \$0.001Q$$

$$0.001Q = -3 + P$$

$$Q = -3,000 + 1,000P$$

P3.8 **Industry Supply.** *Chips Ahoy, Inc., and Nehkdi Trading, Ltd. supply 256MB secure digital cards for MP3's, PDA's, handhelds, digital cameras and digital camcorders that have a secure digital card slot. Confidential cost and output information for each company reveal the following relations between marginal cost and output:*

$$MC_S = \$10 + \$0.0004Q_S \qquad \textit{(Chips Ahoy)}$$

$$MC_N = \$2.50 + \$0.0001Q_N \qquad \textit{(Nehkdi)}$$

The wholesale market for these chips is vigorously price-competitive, and neither firm is able to charge a premium for its products. Thus, P = MR in this market.

A. *Determine the supply curve for each firm. Express price as a function of quantity and quantity as a function of price.*

B. *Calculate the quantity supplied by each firm at prices of $5, $10, and $15. What is the minimum price necessary for each individual firm to supply output?*

C. *Determine the industry supply curve when P < $10.*

D. *Determine the industry supply curve when P > $10. To check your answer, calculate quantity at an industry price of $15 and compare your answer with part B.*

P3.8 **SOLUTION**

A. Each company will supply output to the point where MR = MC. Because P = MR in this market, the supply curve for each firm can be written with price as a function of quantity as:

<u>Chips Ahoy</u>

$$MR_S = MC_S$$

$$P = \$10 + \$0.0004Q_S$$

<u>Nehkdi</u>

$$MR_N \quad = \quad MC_N$$

$$P \quad = \quad \$2.50 + \$0.0001Q_N$$

When quantity is expressed as a function of price:

<u>Chips Ahoy</u>

$$P \quad = \quad \$10 + \$0.0004Q_S$$

$$0.0004Q_S \quad = \quad -10 + P$$

$$Q_S \quad = \quad -25,000 + 2,500P$$

<u>Nehkdi</u>

$$P \quad = \quad \$2.50 + \$0.0001Q_N$$

$$0.0001Q_N \quad = \quad -2.50 + P$$

$$Q_N \quad = \quad -25,000 + 10,000P$$

B. The quantity supplied at each respective price is:

<u>Chips Ahoy</u>

$$P = \$5: Q_S \quad = \quad -25,000 + 2,500(5) = -12,500 \Rightarrow 0$$
$$\text{(because } Q < 0 \text{ is impossible)}$$

$$P = \$10: Q_S \quad = \quad -25,000 + 2,500(10) = 0$$

$$P = \$15: Q_S \quad = -25,000 + 2,500(15) = 12,500$$

<u>Nehkdi</u>

$$P = \$5: Q_N \quad = \quad -25,000 + 10,000(5) = 25,000$$

$$P = \$10: Q_N \quad = \quad -25,000 + 10,000(10) = 75,000$$

$$P = \$15: Q_N \quad = \quad -25,000 + 10,000(15) = 125,000$$

For Chips Ahoy, MC = $10 when $Q_S = 0$. Because marginal cost rises with output, Chips Ahoy will never supply a positive level of output unless a price in excess of $10 per unit can be obtained. Negative output is not feasible. Thus, Chips Ahoy will simply fail to supply output when P < $10. Similarly, $MC_N = 2.50 when $Q_N = 0$. Thus, Nehkdi will never supply output unless a price in excess of $2.50 per unit can be obtained.

C. When P < $10, only Nehkdi can profitably supply output. The Nehkdi supply curve will be the industry curve when P < $10:

$$P = $2.50 + $0.0001Q$$

or

$$Q = -25,000 + 10,000P$$

D. When P > $10, both companies can profitably supply output. To derive the industry supply curve in this circumstance, we simply sum the quantities supplied by each firm:

$$
\begin{aligned}
Q &= Q_S + Q_N \\
&= -25,000 + 2,500P + (-25,000 + 10,000P) \\
&= -50,000 + 12,500P
\end{aligned}
$$

To check, at P = $15:

$$
\begin{aligned}
Q &= -50,000 + 12,500(15) \\
&= 137,500
\end{aligned}
$$

which is supported by the answer to part B, because $Q_S + Q_N = 12,500 + 125,000 = 137,500$.

(*Note*: Some students mistakenly add prices rather than quantities in attempting to derive the industry supply curve. To avoid this problem, it is important to remember that industry supply curves are found through adding up output (horizontal summation), not by adding up prices (vertical summation).)

P3.9   ***Market Equilibrium.*** *The HariKari is a high-mileage subcompact sport utility vehicle (SUV) exported to the U.S. by a leading foreign automobile manufacturer. Demand and supply conditions for the vehicle are as follows:*

$$Q_D = 75,000 - 1.75P \qquad (Demand)$$

$$Q_S = 1.25P \qquad (Supply)$$

where P is average price per unit ($).

A.   *Calculate the HariKari surplus or shortage when the average retail price is $20,000, $25,000, and $30,000.*

B.   *Calculate the market equilibrium price/output combination.*

P3.9   **SOLUTION**

A.   The surplus or shortage can be calculated at each price level:

Price (1)	Quantity Supplied (2)	Quantity Demanded (3)	Surplus (+) or Shortage (-) (4) = (2) - (3)
$20,000	$Q_S = 1.25(20,000)$ = 25,000	$Q_D = 75,000-1.75(20,000)$ = 40,000	-15,000
25,000	$Q_S = 1.25(25,000)$ = 31,250	$Q_D = 75,000-1.75(25,000)$ = 31,250	0
30,000	$Q_S = 1.25(30,000)$ = 37,500	$Q_D = 75,000-1.75(30,000)$ = 22,500	15,000

B.   The equilibrium price is found by setting the quantity demanded equal to the quantity supplied and solving for P:

$$Q_D = Q_S$$

$$75,000 - 1.75P = 1.25P$$

$$75,000 = 3P$$

$$P = \$25,000$$

To solve for Q, set:

$$\text{Demand: } Q_D \quad = \quad 75,000 - 1.75(25,000) = 31,250$$

$$\text{Supply: } Q_S \quad = \quad 1.25(25,000) = 31,250$$

In equilibrium, $Q_D = Q_S = 31,250$.

P3.10   ***Market Equilibrium***. *Industry demand and supply functions for generic (unbranded) 12 ounce cans of cola are as follows:*

$$Q_D \quad = \quad 46,000,000 - 10,000,000P + 2,250,000P_C$$
$$+ \, 2,100Y + 200,000T, \qquad\qquad (Demand)$$

$$Q_S \quad = \quad 4,000,000 + 8,000,000P - 6000,000P_L$$
$$- \, 500,000P_K, \qquad\qquad (Supply)$$

where P is the average price of generic cola ($ per case), P_C is the average wholesale price of name-brand cola beverages ($ per case), Y is income (GNP in $ billions), T is the average daily high temperature (degrees), P_L is the average price of unskilled labor ($ per hour), and P_K is the average cost of capital (in percent).

A.   *When quantity is expressed as a function of price, what are the generic cola demand and supply curves if $P_C = \$8$, $Y = \$10,000$ billion, $T = 75$ degrees, $P_L = \$10$, and $P_K = 12\%$.*

B.   *Calculate the surplus or shortage of generic cola when P = \$5, \$7, and \$9.*

C.   *Calculate the market equilibrium price/output combination.*

P3.10   **SOLUTION**

A.   When quantity is expressed as a function of price, the demand curve for cola soft drinks is:

$$Q_D \quad = \quad 46,000,000 - 10,000,000P + 2,250,000P_C$$

$$+ \, 2,100Y + 200,000T$$

$$= \quad 46,000,000 - 10,000,000P + 2,250,000(8)$$

$$+ \, 2,100(10,000) + 200,000(75)$$

$$Q_D \quad = \quad 100,000,000 - 10,000,000P$$

When quantity is expressed as a function of price, the supply curve for cola soft drinks is:

$$Q_S = 4,000,000 + 8,000,000P - 600,000P_L$$

$$- 500,000P_K$$

$$= 4,000,000 + 8,000,000P - 600,000(10)$$

$$- 500,000(12)$$

$$Q_S = -8,000,000 + 8,000,000P$$

B. The surplus or shortage can be calculated at each price level:

Price (1)	Quantity Supplied (2)	Quantity Demanded (3)	Surplus (+) or Shortage (-) (4) = (2) - (3)
$5	$Q_S = -8,000,000$ $+ 8,000,000(\$5)$ $= 32,000,000$	$Q_D = 100,000,000$ $- 10,000,000(\$5)$ $= 50,000,000$	-18,000,000
$7	$Q_S = -8,000,000$ $+ 8,000,000(\$7)$ $= 48,00,000$	$Q_D = 100,000,000$ $- 100,000,000(\$7)$ $= 30,000,000$	18,000,000
$9	$Q_S = -8,000,000$ $+ 8,000,000(\$9)$ $= 64,000,000$	$Q_D = 100,000,000$ $- 10,000,000(\$9)$ $= 10,000,000$	54,000,000

C. The equilibrium price is found by setting the quantity demanded equal to the quantity supplied and solving for P:

$$Q_D = Q_S$$

$$100,000,000 - 10,000,000P = -8,000,000 + 8,000,000P$$

$$18,000,000P = 108,000,000$$

$$P = \$6$$

To solve for Q, set:

Demand: Q_D = 100,000,000 - 10,000,000($6) = 40,000,000

Supply: Q_S = -8,000,000 + 8,000,000($6) = 40,000,000

In equilibrium $Q_D = Q_S$ = 40,000,000.

Chapter 4

CONSUMER DEMAND

The initial task for any business is to identify or create demand for the goods and services that it offers. Without consumer demand, nothing else matters. The best product quality or cost efficiency doesn't matter unless consumers are willing and eager to buy company products at prices that will yield at least a risk-adjusted normal rate of return on investment.

Therefore, a first step in managerial economics is to assess consumer demand. Managers must understand the factors that underpin consumer demand, and then learn how to respond to the signals provided by customers. This chapter provides the basics of consumer demand theory. It shows how consumer demand stems from the utility, well being or satisfaction derived from consumption. Through the study of utility theory, managerial economics gives a useful framework for understanding how consumers make tradeoffs between the value derived from consumption and the costs entailed with consuming alternative combinations, or market baskets, of goods and services. Because money is scarce, consumers compare the marginal benefits derived from consuming alternative goods and services with the prices, or marginal costs, of those additional items. Every consumer decision involves tradeoffs between price, quantity, quality, timeliness, and a host of related factors. The consideration of such tradeoffs, and the methods used by consumers to make appropriate consumption decisions, is called the study of consumer behavior. It is often difficult to understand the consumer decision making process, but consumer behavior theory is a useful tool for understanding and predicting the results of that process.

CHAPTER OUTLINE

I.   **UTILITY THEORY**

      A.   **Assumptions About Consumer Preferences:** The ability of goods and services to satisfy consumer wants is the basis for consumer demand. Consumer behavior theory rests upon three basic assumptions regarding the utility tied to consumption.

            1.   More is better. All goods and services are desirable in the sense of being able to satisfy consumer wants.

            2.   Preferences are complete. When preferences are complete, consumers are able to compare and rank the benefits tied to consumption of various goods and services.

            3.   Preferences are transitive. When preferences are transitive, consumers are able to rank order the desirability of various goods and services.

    a.   The consumer's understanding of ordinal utility makes possible a rank ordering of preferred goods and services.

    b.   If consumers had understanding of cardinal utility, they would know how much spicy chicken wraps are preferred, say 2:1 or 3:1, over vegetarian wraps. However, that type of detailed information is seldom available.

B.   **Utility Functions:** A utility function is a descriptive statement that relates satisfaction or well-being to the consumption of goods and services.

    1.   Bundles of items desired by consumers are called market baskets because they reflect combinations of goods and services available in the marketplace.

C.   **Marginal Utility:** Marginal utility is the added satisfaction derived from a one-unit increase in consumption of a particular good or service.

    1.   In measuring marginal utility, it is necessary to hold consumption of other goods and services constant.

D.   **Law of Diminishing Marginal Utility:** Marginal utility tends to diminish as consumption increases within a given time interval.

    1.   This law gives rise to a downward-sloping demand curve for all goods and services.

II.   **INDIFFERENCE CURVES**

A.   **Basic Characteristics of Indifference Curves**: Indifference curves represents all market baskets that provide a given consumer the same amount of utility or satisfaction. Indifference curves have four essential properties.

    1.   Higher indifference curves are better. Consumers prefer more to less.

    2.   Indifference curves do not intersect.

    3.   Indifference curves slope downward. The slope of an indifference curve shows the tradeoff involved between goods and services.

    4.   Indifference curves bend inward (are concave to the origin).

B.   Perfect Substitutes and Perfect Complements: Substitutes are goods and services that can be used to fulfill a similar need or desire. Goods and services that become more desirable when consumed together are called complements.

    1.   Perfect substitutes are goods and services that satisfy the same need or desire.

    2.   Perfect complements are goods and services consumed together in the same combination.

III.   BUDGET CONSTRAINTS

A.   Basic Characteristics of Budget Constraints: A budget constraint represents all combinations of products that can be purchased for a fixed amount.

    1.   The slope of the budget constraint is equal to $-P_X/P_Y$ and, therefore, is a measure of the relative prices of the products being purchased.

    2.   Change in the budget level B leads to a parallel shift in the budget constraint, whereas change in the relative prices of items being purchased causes the slope of the budget constraint to rotate.

B.   Effects of Changing Income and Changing Prices: The effect of a budget increase is to shift a budget constraint outward and to the right. The effect of a budget decrease is to shift a budget constraint inward and to the left.

    1.   A fall in the price of goods or services permits an increase in consumption and consumer welfare.

    2.   If all prices fall by a given percentage, a parallel rightward shift in the budget constraint occurs that is identical to the effect of an increase in budget.

C.   Income and Substitution Effects: When product prices change, the consumer is affected in two ways.

    1.   The income effect of a price change is the increase in overall consumption made possible by a price cut, or decrease in overall consumption that follows a price increase.

a. The income effect shifts buyers to a higher indifference curve following a price cut or shifts them to a lower indifference curve following a price increase.

2. The substitution effect of a price change describes the change in relative consumption that occurs as consumers substitute cheaper products for more expensive products.

a. The substitution effect results in an upward or downward movement along a given indifference curve.

3. The total effect of a price change on consumption is the sum of income and substitution effects.

IV. INDIVIDUAL DEMAND

A. **Price-consumption Curve:** If income and the prices of other goods and services are held constant, a reduction in the price of a given consumption item causes consumers to choose different market baskets.

1. The price-consumption curve depicts how the optimal consumption of both goods and services are affected by changing prices for services (or goods).

2. It shows how the quantity demanded of services (goods) rises in a response to a fall in the price for services (goods).

B. **Income-consumption Curve:** The income-consumption curve portrays the utility-maximizing combinations of goods and services at every income level.

1. It is worth emphasizing that price-consumption curves and income-consumption curves focus on different aspects of demand.

a. Price-consumption curves show how optimal consumption is affected by changing prices, or movements along the demand curve.

b. Income-consumption curves show how optimal consumption is affected by changing income. Income-consumption curves illustrate the effects of shifts in demand due to changing income.

C. **Engle Curves:** A plot of the relationship between income and the quantity consumed of a good or service is called an Engle curve, named after economist Ernst Engle who popularized their study.

1.   Engle curves are closely related to income-consumption curves.

2.   If consumers have a tendency to buy more of a product as their income rises, such products are called normal goods.

      a.   This is true for most goods and services.

3.   If consumers tend to buy less of a product following an increase in income, such products are called inferior goods.

V.   DEMAND CURVES AND CONSUMER SURPLUS

A.   Graphing the Demand Curve: Demand curves slope downward indicating an increase in quantity demanded as the price of a product falls.

B.   Consumer Surplus: Consumer surplus is the value of purchased goods and services above and beyond the amount paid to sellers.

1.   Consumer surplus arises because individual consumers place different values on goods and services.

C.   Consumer Surplus and Two-Part Pricing: A common two-part pricing technique is to charge all customers a fixed "membership" fee per month or per year, plus a per-unit usage charge.

1.   The seller must enjoy at least some market power in order to institute any two-part pricing scheme.

D.   Consumer Surplus and Bundle Pricing: When significant consumer surplus exists, profits can be enhanced if products are purchased together as a single package or bundle of goods or services.

1.   The optimal bundle price is simply a lump sum amount equal to the total area under the demand curve at that activity level.

VI.   CONSUMER CHOICE

A.   Marginal Utility and Consumer Choice: The best allocation of a budget is the allocation that maximizes the utility, or satisfaction, derived from consumption.

1.   The optimal market basket lies directly on the budget line.

2.   The optimal market basket reflects consideration of marginal benefits and marginal costs.

B.   **Revealed Preference:** If a given consumer consistently chooses a specific market basket over another market basket, and if the chosen market basket is more expensive that the alternative, then the consumer has a revealed preference for the chosen market basket.

1.   A revealed preference is a documented desire for a given good or service over some other less expensive good or service.

VII.   OPTIMAL CONSUMPTION

A.   **Marginal Rate of Substitution:** The marginal rate of substitution is the change in consumption of Y (goods) necessary to offset a given change in the consumption of X (services) if the consumer's overall level of utility is to remain constant.

1.   The marginal rate of substitution (MRS) typically diminishes as the amount of substitution increases.

2.   The slope of an indifference curve is directly related to the concept of diminishing marginal utility.

     a.   The marginal rate of substitution is equal to -1 times the ratio of the marginal utility derived from the consumption of each product (MRS $= -1(MU_X/MU_Y)$, which is the slope of an indifference curve.

B.   **Utility Maximization:** The optimal market basket maximizes a consumer's utility for a given budget expenditure.

1.   Optimal market baskets of goods and services are indicated by points of tangency between respective indifference curves and budget constraints.

2.   At each point where goods and services are combined optimally, there is a tangency between the budget constraint and the indifference curve; hence, their slopes are equal.

3.   For optimal consumption combinations, the price ratios for goods and services must equal the ratios of their marginal utilities.

VIII.   **SUMMARY**

PROBLEMS & SOLUTIONS

P4.1   **Budget Allocation.** *Consider the following data:*

	Goods (G)		Services (S)
Units	**Total Utility**	**Units**	**Total Utility**
0	0	0	0
1	50	1	100
2	90	2	185
3	120	3	255
4	140	4	310
5	150	0	350

A.   *Construct a table showing the marginal utility derived from the consumption of goods and services. Also show the trend in marginal utility per dollar spent (the MU/P ratio) if $P_G = \$5$ and $P_S = \$12.50$.*

B.   *If consumption of two units of goods is optimal, what level of services consumption could also be justified?*

C.   *If consumption of four units of services is optimal, what level of goods consumption could also be justified?*

D.   *Calculate the optimal allocation of a $25 budget. Explain.*

P4.1   **SOLUTION**

    A.

	Goods				Services		
Units	**Total Utility**	**Marginal Utility**	**MU/P = MU/$5**	**Units**	**Total Utility**	**Marginal Utility**	**MU/P = MU/$12.5**
0	0	--	--	0	0	--	--
1	50	50	10	1	100	100	8.0
2	90	40	8	2	185	85	6.8
3	120	30	6	3	255	70	5.6
4	140	20	4	4	310	55	4.4

| 5 | 150 | 10 | 2 | 5 | 350 | 40 | 3.2 |

B. S = 1. When 2 units of goods are purchased, the last unit consumed generates 40 utils of satisfaction at a rate of 8 utils per dollar. Consumption of 1 unit of services could also be justified on the grounds that consumption at that level would also generate 8 utils per dollar spent on services.

C. G = 3. When 4 units of services are purchased, the last unit consumed generated 55 utils of satisfaction at a rate of 4.4 utils per dollar. Consumption of 3 units of goods could be justified on the grounds that consumption at that level would generate 6 utils per dollar spent on goods. At that consumption level, goods remain a relative bargain. Consumption of a fourth unit of goods could not be justified because it would generate only 4 utils per dollar spent.

D. G = 2 and S = 1.2. The optimal allocation of a $25 budget involves spending according to the highest marginal utility generated per dollar of expenditure. First, one unit of goods would be purchased since it results in 10 utils per dollar spent. Then, one additional unit of goods and one unit of services would be purchased, each yielding 8 utils per dollar. With 2 units of goods and one unit of services, a total of $10 dollars will have been spent on goods and $12.50 on services. This totals $22.50 in expenditures, and leaves $2.50 unspent from a $25. budget. Assuming that partial units can be consumed, $2.50 is enough to buy an additional 0.2 units of services.

P4.2 **Individual Demand Curve.** *Gabrielle Solis loves to munch on boxes of Hot Tamales, a popular candy. The following table shows the relation between the number of boxes of Hot Tamales consumed per month and the total utility Solis derives from consumption:*

Boxes of Hot Tamales per Month	Total Utility
0	0
1	60
2	110
3	150
4	180
5	200

A. *Construct a table showing Solis' marginal utility derived from baseball game consumption.*

B. *At an average price of $2.50 per box, Solis can justify consuming only two boxes per month. Calculate Solis's cost per unit of marginal utility derived from Hot Tamale consumption at this activity level.*

C. *If the cost/marginal utility trade-off found in part B represents the most Solis is willing to pay for Hot Tamales, calculate the prices at which Solis would buy 1-5 boxes per month.*

D. *Plot Solis' Hot Tamale demand curve.*

P4.2 **SOLUTION**

A.

Boxes of Hot Tamales Per Month	Total Utility	Marginal Utility
0	0	--
1	60	60
2	110	50
3	150	40
4	180	30
5	200	20

B. At two boxes of Hot Tamales per month, MU = 50. Thus, at a $2.50 price per box, the cost per unit of marginal utility derived from Hot Tamales consumption is P/MU = $2.50/50 = $0.05 or 5¢ per util.

C. At a maximum acceptable price of 50¢ per util, Solis' maximum acceptable price for Hot Tamales varies according to the following schedule:

Boxes of Hot Tamales Per Month	Total Utility	Marginal Utility $MU = \partial U/\partial G$	Maximum Acceptable price at 50¢ per MU
0	0	--	--
1	60	60	$3.00
2	110	50	2.50

3	150	40	2.00
4	180	30	1.50
5	200	20	1.00

D.   Solis' Hot Tamales demand curve is:

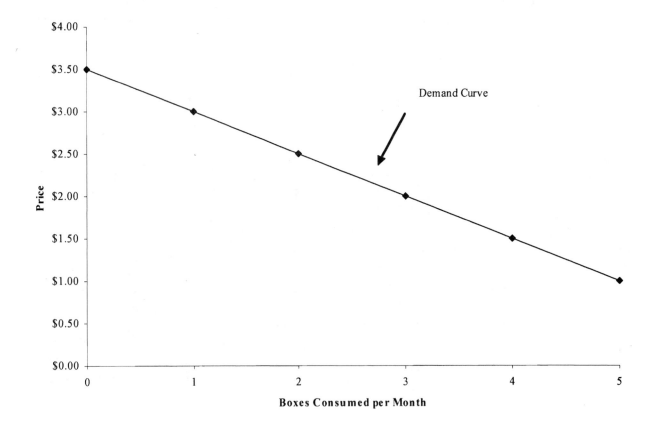

P4.3   ***Utility Theory.*** *Determine whether each of the following statements is true or false. Explain why.*

A.   *If preferences are complete, consumers know by how much they prefer one product over another.*

B.   *The ability of goods and services to satisfy consumer wants is the basis for consumer demand.*

C. *Because consumers do in fact become sated, the nonsatiation principle flies in the face of reality.*

D. *Indifference implies equivalence in the eyes of the consumer.*

E. *Marginal utility measures change in the consumer's overall level of satisfaction derived from consumption activities*

P4.3 **SOLUTION**

A. False. When preferences are complete, consumers are able to simply compare and rank the benefits tied to consumption of various goods and services. Consumers know that A is preferred to B, but they do not know if A is better than B.

B. True. The ability of goods and services to satisfy consumer wants is the basis for consumer demand.

C. False. At any specific place and time, consumers do become sated. Therefore, the nonsatiation principle involves a certain amount of abstraction from these considerations. It is best considered within the context of money income where more money brings additional satisfaction or well-being. To the extent that consumers always crave more income, the nonsatiation principle is a useful abstraction from reality.

D. True. If two products provide the same amount of satisfaction or utility, the consumer is said to display indifference between the two. Indifference implies equivalence in the eyes of the consumer.

E. True. Whereas total utility measures the consumer's overall level of satisfaction derived from consumption activities, marginal utility measures the added satisfaction derived from a one-unit increase in consumption of a particular good or service, holding consumption of other goods and services constant.

P4.4 *Law of Diminishing Marginal Utility. Indicate whether each of the following statements is true or false. Explain why.*

A. *The law of diminishing marginal utility states that as an individual increases consumption of a given product within a set period of time, the added utility gained from consumption eventually declines.*

B. *When prices are held constant, a diminishing marginal utility for consumption increases the cost of each marginal unit of satisfaction.*

C. *Marginal utility measures the added satisfaction derived from a one-unit increase in consumption, holding consumption of other goods and services constant.*

D. *The law of diminishing marginal utility is based upon the cardinal utility concept.*

E. *The law of diminishing marginal utility is inconsistent with an upward-sloping demand curve for all goods and services.*

P4.4   SOLUTION

A. True. In general, the law of diminishing marginal utility states that as an individual increases consumption of a given product within a set period of time, the added or marginal utility gained from consumption eventually declines.

B. True. When prices are held constant, a diminishing marginal utility for consumption increases the cost of each marginal unit of satisfaction.

C. True. Whereas total utility measures the consumer's overall level of satisfaction derived from consumption activities, marginal utility measures the added satisfaction derived from a one-unit increase in consumption of a particular good or service, holding consumption of other goods and services constant.

D. False. The law of diminishing marginal utility has nothing to do with the cardinal utility concept. If consumers had an understanding of cardinal utility, they would know how much spicy chicken wraps are preferred, say 2:1 or 3:1, over vegetarian wraps. However, that type of detailed information is seldom available. That's not a problem because nobody has to know how much more desirable spicy chicken wraps are compared to vegetarian wraps in order to make a simple choice between the two. All that's necessary is to know that one product is preferred to another product.

E. True. This law gives rise to a downward-sloping demand curve for all goods and services.

P4.5   *Substitutes and Complements.* *Suggest briefly whether each of the following statements about substitutes and complements is true or false and defend your answer.*

A. *The law of diminishing marginal utility states that as an individual increases consumption of any complement good or service within a set period of time, the marginal utility gained from consumption eventually declines.*

B. *To a greater or lesser degree, suits and dry cleaning services can be described as substitutes.*

C. *Perfect substitutes are goods and services that satisfy the same need or desire.*

D. *Perfect complements are goods and services consumed together in the same combination.*

E. *Good examples of near-perfect complements are provided by Visa debit cards and Visa credit cards, generic and branded drugs, drive-through and dine-in service at your favorite fast-food restaurant, and DVD and video movie rentals.*

P4.5 **SOLUTION**

A. True. The law of diminishing marginal utility states that as an individual increases consumption of any product within a set period of time, the marginal utility gained from consumption eventually declines. This includes both complements and substitutes.

B. True. To a greater or lesser degree, goods and services can be substituted for one another. For example, a consumer may own many suits and dry clean each suit only occasionally. Alternatively, a consumer may own only a few suits but dry clean each one frequently. In the first instance, the consumer has bought a market basket with a high proportion of total expenditures devoted to suits (goods) and relatively little devoted to dry cleaning services. The latter market basket is weighted less toward goods and more toward services.

C. True. Perfect substitutes are goods and services that satisfy the same need or desire. Perfect complements are goods and services consumed together in the same combination.

D. True. Substitutes are goods and services that can be used to fulfill a similar need or desire. Goods and services that become more desirable when consumed together are called complements. Perfect complements are goods and services consumed together in the same combination.

E. False. Good examples of near-perfect substitutes are provided by *Visa* debit cards and *Visa* credit cards, generic and branded drugs, drive-through and dine-in service at your favorite fast-food restaurant, and DVD and video movie rentals.

P4.6   ***Budget Constraints.*** *Holding all else equal, indicate how each of the following changes would affect a budget constraint that limits consumption of food (Y) and clothing (X). Explain your answer.*

    A.   *A federal income tax increase.*

    B.   *An increase in the cost of transportation costs caused by a jump in gasoline prices.*

    C.   *Poor weather that reduces food supply and increases the price of food, but leaves the price of clothing unchanged.*

    D.   *A tax cut that boosts the level of disposable income.*

    E.   *Government-mandated health care coverage for all workers that boosts the price of everything by 10%.*

P4.6   **SOLUTION**

    A.   A federal income tax increase reduces the amount of after-tax net income available for the purchase of food and clothing, and results in a parallel leftward (inward) shift in the budget constraint. Higher federal income taxes reduce the amount of food and clothing that consumers can buy with a fixed amount of before-tax income. This harmful impact on consumption is similar to that following a decrease in income.

    B.   A jump in gasoline prices that leads to a similar increase in the price of all goods and services results in a parallel leftward (inward) shift in the budget constraint. Holding income constant, higher gasoline prices reduce the amount of food and clothing that consumers can buy with a fixed amount of spending. This harmful impact on consumption is similar to that following a decrease in income, or a rise in income taxes.

    C.   Poor weather that reduces food supply and increases the price of food, but leaves the price of clothing unchanged results in an inward rotation of the budget constraint along the food (Y) axis. After such a change, the budget line intersects the Y axis at a lower point, indicating that a lesser amount of food can be purchased with a fixed budget. The amount of clothing that can be purchased for a fixed amount is unaffected by such a change, and the X intercept (clothing axis) of the budget constraint is unaffected by such a change.

> **D.** A tax cut that boosts the level of disposable income results in a parallel rightward (outward) shift in the budget constraint. Holding prices constant, growing income makes it possible for consumers to buy more food and clothing with the same total amount of spending. This beneficial impact on consumption is similar to that following deflation that drops the price of all goods and services.
>
> **E.** Government-mandated health care coverage for all workers that boosts the price of everything by 10% will have a negative impact on consumption of both food and clothing. Government-mandated health care coverage for all workers will cause a parallel leftward (inward) shift in the budget constraint. If all prices rise by 10%, consumers will be unable to afford as much food and clothing, and the resulting decline in consumption will be similar to that seen following an unexpected increase in inflation.

P4.7   ***Consumer Surplus.*** *Indicate whether each of the following statements is true or false and support your response.*

> ***A.*** Consumer surplus is the value of purchased goods and services above and beyond the amount paid to sellers.
>
> ***B.*** A fair price is paid if the amount required is just equal to the total benefit gained through consumption.
>
> ***C.*** A bargain exists if an individual consumer is able to buy something for less than the maximum amount they are willing to pay.
>
> ***D.*** The value obtained by consumers from consumption is captured by the total area under the demand curve.
>
> ***E.*** No transaction occurs if the price charged exceeds the total benefit from consumption perceived by the consumer.

P4.7   **SOLUTION**

> **A.** True. Consumer surplus is the value of purchased goods and services above and beyond the amount paid to sellers.
>
> **B.** False. A fair price is paid if the amount required is just equal to the added benefit gained through consumption.
>
> **C.** True. A bargain exists if an individual consumer is able to buy something for less than the maximum amount they are willing to pay.

D. True. The value obtained by consumers from consumption is captured by the total area under the demand curve.

E. False. No transaction occurs if the price charged exceeds the marginal benefit from consumption perceived by the consumer.

P4.8 **Consumer Surplus**. *Just minutes from Mexico's Puerto Vallarta International Airport, Paradise Village is well known among discriminating travelers for its world-class amenities including a championship golf course, beautiful beaches, a modern shopping mall, and a full service marina. Assume that weekly demand and marginal revenue curves for a two-bedroom suite during spring break can be written for a typical customer as:*

$$P = \$2,000 - \$250Q,$$

$$MR = \partial TR/\partial Q = \$2,000 - \$500Q,$$

where P is the price of a single week of vacation time, and Q is the number of weeks of vacation time purchased during a given year. For simplicity, assume that the resort's marginal cost for a week of vacation time is \$1,000, and that fixed costs are nil. This gives the following total and marginal cost relations:

$$TC \quad = \quad \$1,000Q,$$

$$MC \quad = \quad \partial TC/\partial Q = \$1,000.$$

A. *Calculate the profit-maximizing price and output levels assuming a single fixed price per week is charged each customer.*

B. *Calculate the amount of consumer surplus enjoyed by the typical customer*

P4.8 **SOLUTION**

A. If a single per unit price is charged, the profit-maximizing price is found by setting MR = MC, where

$$MR \quad = \quad MC$$

$$\$2,000 - \$500Q \quad = \quad \$1,000$$

$$500Q \quad = \quad 1,000$$

$$Q = 2$$

At the profit-maximizing quantity of two weeks, the optimal single unit price is $1,500 per week because:

$$P = \$2,000 - \$250(2)$$

$$= \$1,500$$

B.   The value of consumer surplus at a standard per unit price is equal to the region under the demand curve that lies above the profit-maximizing price of $1,500. Because the area of such a triangle is one-half the value of the base times the height, the value of consumer surplus equals:

$$\text{Consumer Surplus} = \tfrac{1}{2}\,[2 \times(\$2,000 - \$1,500)]$$

$$= \$500 \text{ per customer}$$

In words, this means that at a single per unit price of $1,500 per week, a typical customer would choose 2 weeks of vacation time at the resort, resulting in total revenues of $3,000 per customer for the resort facility. The fact that consumer surplus equals $500 means that the typical vacationer would have been willing to pay an additional $500 for this two weeks of vacation time. This is an amount above and beyond the $3,000 paid. The customer received a real bargain. Graphically, this relationship can be shown as follows:

Paradise Village Demand

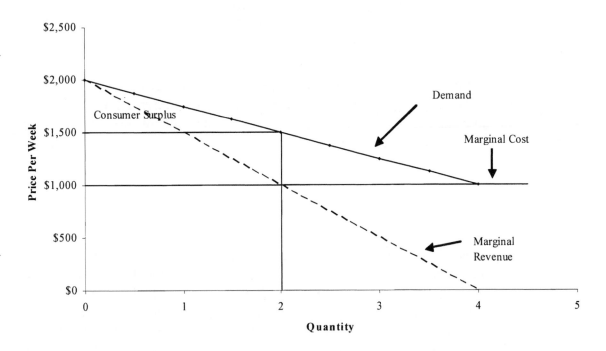

P4.9   ***Two-part Pricing.***   *Like many vacation resorts, the Lawai Beach Resort on the beautiful island of Kauai in Hawaii has discovered the advantages of offering its services on an annual membership or "time-sharing" basis. To illustrate, assume that an individual vacationer's weekly demand and marginal revenue curves can be written:*

$$P = \$4{,}000 - \$1{,}000Q,$$

$$MR = \partial TR / \partial Q = \$4{,}000 - \$2{,}000Q,$$

where P is the price of a single week of vacation time, and Q is the number of weeks of vacation time purchased during a given year. For simplicity, assume that the resort's marginal cost for a week of vacation time is \$2,000, and that fixed costs are \$1 million per year. This gives the following total and marginal cost relations:

$$TC = \$1{,}000{,}000 + \$2{,}000Q,$$

$$MC = \partial TC / \partial Q = \$2{,}000.$$

A. Calculate the profit-maximizing price and consumer surplus levels per customer assuming that the same per unit price is charged each customer.

B. Calculate the profit-maximizing price, output and profit level assuming a two-part pricing strategy is adopted for each customer. Assume that 600 time-share customers ("owners") are attracted when an optimal two-part pricing strategy is adopted.

P4.9 **SOLUTION**

A. If a single per unit price is charged, the profit-maximizing price is found by setting MR = MC, where

$$MR = MC$$

$$\$4,000 - \$2,000Q = \$2,000$$

$$2,000Q = 2,000$$

$$Q = 1$$

At the profit-maximizing quantity of 1, the optimal single unit price is $3,000 because:

$$P = \$4,000 - \$1,000(1)$$

$$= \$3,000$$

The value of consumer surplus at a standard per unit price is equal to the region under the demand curve that lies above the profit-maximizing price of $3,000. Because the area of such a triangle is one-half the value of the base times the height, the value of consumer surplus equals:

$$\text{Consumer Surplus} = \frac{1}{2} [1 \times (\$4,000 - \$3,000)]$$

$$= \$500 \text{ per customer}$$

In words, this means that at a single per unit price of $3,000 per week, a typical individual would choose to use 1 week of vacation time at the resort. The fact that consumer surplus equals $500 means that the typical vacationer would have been willing to pay an additional $500 for this one week of vacation time. This is an amount above and beyond the $3,000 paid. The customer received a real bargain.

B.   As an alternative to charging a single-unit price of $3,000 per week, consider the profits that could be earned using a two-part pricing scheme. To maximize profits, the resort would choose to charge a per-unit price that equals marginal cost, plus a fixed fee equal to the amount of consumer surplus received by each consumer at this price. Remember, the value of consumer surplus is equal to the region under the demand curve that lies above the per-unit price. When the per-unit price is set equal to marginal cost, P = $2,000 and Q = 2 because

$$P \ = \ MC$$

$$\$4{,}000 - \$1{,}000Q \ = \ \$2{,}000$$

$$Q \ = \ 2$$

$$P \ = \ \$4{,}000 - \$1{,}000(2)$$

$$= \ \$2{,}000$$

At the per unit price of $2,000 and output level of 2, the value of consumer surplus equals:

$$\text{Consumer Surplus} \ = \ \tfrac{1}{2}\,[2 \times (\$4{,}000 - \$2{,}000)]$$

$$= \ \$2{,}000 \text{ per customer}$$

Thus, $2,000 is the maximum time-share or annual membership fee that the typical vacationer would pay to spend 2 weeks at the resort when a modest additional "use" charge of $2,000 per week was paid for each week spent at the resort. It follows that the profit-maximizing two-part pricing scheme is to charge an annual time-share or membership fee of $2,000 per year plus weekly fees of $2,000 per week. Resort revenues of $6,000 [= $2,000 + (2 × $2,000)] per customer represent the full value derived from a typical customer staying 2 weeks per year, cover marginal costs of $4,000 (= 2 × $2,000), and result in a $2,000 (= $6,000 - $4,000) profit contribution per customer for the resort.

     If the number of paying time-share subscribers is 600 per year, and fixed costs total $1 million per year, then total net profits equal:

$$\pi \ = \ \text{Total revenue - Marginal cost - Fixed cost}$$

$$= 600 \times [\$2,000 + \$2,000(2)] - 600 \times [\$2,000(2)] - \$1,000,000$$

$$= \$200,000 \text{ per year}$$

Lawai Beach Resort

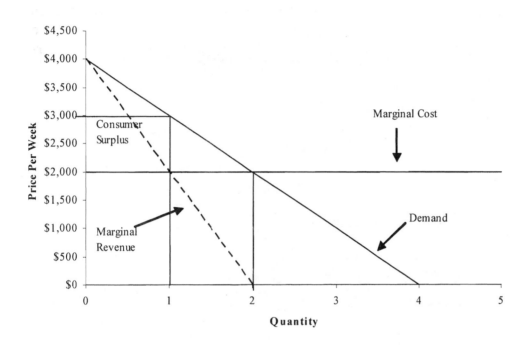

It is interesting to note that time-shares and annual memberships are so profitable that such marketing arrangements have largely replaced pay-as-you-go resorts at many popular vacation destinations.

P4.10 **Revealed Preference.** *During the summer months, Mary Young sells low-carb fruit smoothies from a portable stand on the beach. Young rents the stand for $800 per week and is responsible for covering all of the variable costs associated with units sold. Last week, Young sold 650 smoothies at a price of $4. This week, sales fell to 600 smoothies when Young raised the price to $4.25.*

Using these two price/output combinations, the relevant linear demand and marginal revenue curves can be estimated as:

$$P = \$7.25 - \$0.005Q \text{ and } MR = \$7.25 - \$0.01Q$$

A.   *Set MR = 0 and solve for Q to calculate the revenue-maximizing price/output combination and profit level. How much are these maximum revenues?*

B.   *If marginal cost is $1.25 per unit, calculate the profit-maximizing price/output combination. Also calculate revenues and profits at this profit-maximizing activity level. (Remember MR = MC at the profit-maximizing activity level.)*

P4.10   **SOLUTION**

A.   To find the revenue-maximizing price/output rental rate, set MR = 0, and solve for Q. Because

$$TR = P \times Q$$

$$= (\$7.25 - \$0.005Q)Q$$

$$= \$7.25Q - \$0.005Q^2$$

$$MR = \partial TR/\partial Q$$

$$MR = \$7.25 - \$0.01Q = 0$$

$$0.01Q = 7.25$$

$$Q = 725$$

At Q = 725,

$$P = \$7.25 - \$0.005(725)$$

$$= \$3.625$$

$$\pi = TR - TC$$

$$= \$3.625Q - \$1.25Q - \$800$$

$$= \$3.625(725) - \$1.25(725) - \$800$$

$$= \$921.88 \text{ per week}$$

Total revenue at a price of $3.625 is:

$$TR = P \times Q$$

$$= \$3.625 \times 725$$

$$= \$2,628.13 \text{ per week}$$

(*Note:* $\partial^2 TR/\partial Q^2 < 0$. This is a revenue-maximizing output level because total revenue is decreasing for output beyond $Q > 725$ hours.)

B. To find the profit-maximizing output level analytically, set MR = MC, or set Mπ = 0, and solve for Q. Because

$$MR = MC$$

$$\$7.25 - \$0.01Q = \$1.25$$

$$0.01Q = 6$$

$$Q = 600$$

At $Q = 600$,

$$P = \$7.25 - \$0.005(600)$$

$$= \$4.25$$

Total revenue at a price of $4.25 is:

$$TR = P \times Q$$

$$= \$4.25 \times 600$$

$$= \$2,550 \text{ per week}$$

$$\pi = TR - TC$$

$$= \$4.25Q - \$1.25Q - \$800$$

$$= \$4.25(600) - \$1.25(600) - \$800$$

$$= \$1,000 \text{ per week}$$

(*Note*: $\partial^2\pi/\partial Q^2 < 0$, This is a profit maximum because total profit is falling for Q >600.)

Chapter 5

DEMAND ANALYSIS

Demand analysis and estimation is the most vital responsibility of management. No matter how efficient the firm's production process, and regardless of overall managerial skill, it is impossible to operate profitably unless product demand exists or can be created. If any firm enjoys robust sales revenue growth, they possess the opportunity to capture a strong and growing level of profitability. If sales revenue growth is anemic, or worse yet if sales are falling, even dramatic restructuring and corporate downsizing seldom leads to higher profits. Successful stock-market investors have learned that over the long-run there is a 100% correlation between earnings growth and stock prices. Similarly, successful managers have learned that, again in the long-run, there is a 100% correlation between the growth in product demand and the firm's ability to enjoy high and expanding profitability.

Because demand is a fundamental determinant of profitability, management must have accurate information about demand conditions to make effective short-run operating decisions and strategic long-run planning decisions. To price the firm's products effectively, managers must know how changing prices affect the quantity demanded. Similarly, they must understand how advertising and credit terms affect demand to appraise the attractiveness of current or proposed credit and promotional strategies. Dependable estimates of the sensitivity of demand to changes in both population and income are helpful in the analysis of the firm's growth potential and, therefore, in the long-range planning process.

CHAPTER OUTLINE

I. **MEASURING MARKET DEMAND**

    A. **Graphing the Market Demand Curve:** The market demand curve shows the total amount of a specific good or service customers are willing to buy at various prices under present market conditions.

    B. **Evaluating Market Demand:** Market demand is the sum of demand for each customer group at each specific market price.

II. **DEMAND SENSITIVITY ANALYSIS: ELASTICITY**

    A. **Elasticity Concept:** Elasticity measures the percentage change in a dependent Y-variable caused by a one percent change in an independent X-variable.

        1. Demand analysis focuses on the percentage change in quantity sold due to a one percent change in some demand related factor X.

$$\text{Elasticity} = \frac{\%\Delta Q}{\%\Delta X} = \frac{\Delta Q/Q}{\Delta X/X} = \frac{\Delta Q}{\Delta X} \times \frac{X}{Q}.$$

where Δ designates change.

2. Endogenous factors are demand-related influences controlled by the firm.

3. Exogenous factors are demand-related influences outside the control of the firm.

B. **Point Elasticity and Arc Elasticity:** Elasticity can be measured in two different ways.

1. Point elasticity is a measure of elasticity at a given spot along a demand function:

$$\varepsilon = \frac{\partial Q}{Q} \div \frac{\partial X}{X} = \frac{\partial Q}{\partial X} \times \frac{X}{Q}$$

Point elasticities are useful in predicting the sales effect of "small" changes in X (i.e., $\partial X/X < 5\%$).

2. Arc elasticity is a measure of average elasticity over a range of the demand function:

$$E = \frac{Q_2 - Q_1}{(Q_2 + Q_1)/2} \div \frac{X_2 - X_1}{(X_2 + X_1)/2} = \frac{Q_2 - Q_1}{X_2 - X_1} \times \frac{X_2 + X_1}{Q_2 + Q_1}$$

Arc elasticities are useful in predicting the sales effect of "big" changes in X (i.e., $\Delta X/X \geq 5\%$).

C. **Advertising Elasticity Example:** Managers are sometimes concerned with the impact of substantial changes in a demand-determining factor, such as advertising. In these instances, the point elasticity concept suffers a conceptual shortcoming.

1. A problem sometimes occurs because elasticities are not typically constant but vary at different points along a given demand function.

2. To overcome the problem of changing elasticities along a demand function, the arc elasticity formula was developed to calculate an average elasticity for incremental as opposed to marginal changes.

III. PRICE ELASTICITY OF DEMAND

A. **Price Elasticity Formula:** The price elasticity of demand, or "own" price elasticity, measures the responsiveness of the quantity demanded to changes in price, holding constant all other variables in the demand function.

1. Because demand curves slope downward, price increases cause the quantity demanded to fall, and price decreases cause the quantity demanded to rise.

2. It follows that own price elasticities always have a negative sign.

3. Because the negative sign on own price elasticities is obvious, it is often ignored for convenience.

B. **Price Elasticity and Total Revenue:** Depending upon the degree of price elasticity, a given change in price will result in an increase, decrease, or no change in total revenue.

1. Total revenue is unaffected by changes in price if elasticity is unitary:

$$|\varepsilon_p| = 1.$$

2. Total revenue declines with price increases and rises with price decreases if demand is elastic:

$$|\varepsilon_p| > 1.$$

3. Total revenue rises with price increases and declines with price decreases if demand is inelastic:

$$|\varepsilon_p| < 1.$$

C. **Uses of Price Elasticity Information:** Price elasticity information is very useful.

1. A profit-maximizing firm would never choose to lower its prices in the inelastic range of the demand curve. Such a price decrease would decrease total revenue and at the same time increase costs, because the quantity demanded would rise. A dramatic decrease in profits could result.

2. The profitability of a price cut in the elastic range of the demand curve depends on whether the marginal revenues generated exceed the marginal cost of added production.

3. Price elasticity of demand information has a multitude of useful applications, including: inventory control, production planning, optimal pricing policy.

IV. PRICE ELASTICITY AND MARGINAL REVENUE

A. **Varying Elasticity at Different Points on a Demand Curve:** The price elasticity of demand varies along a given demand curve.

1. As price increases, the price elasticity of demand also increases.

2. As price decreases, the price elasticity of demand also decreases.

B. **Price Elasticity and Price Changes:** The revenue impact of a price change depends upon the price elasticity of demand.

1. In the elastic portion of the demand curve, $|\varepsilon_p| > 1$ and marginal revenue is greater than zero. Total revenue increases with reductions in price because this leads to a greater than proportional increase in quantity sold.

2. When $|\varepsilon_p| = 1$, marginal revenue equals 0 and total revenue is maximized.

3. In the inelastic range of the demand curve, $|\varepsilon_p| < 1$ and marginal revenue is negative. When price is reduced, output increases but revenue declines.

V. PRICE ELASTICITY AND OPTIMAL PRICING POLICY

A. **Optimal Price Formula:** Profits are maximized when MR = MC. Price elasticity estimates represent vital information because these data reveal the marginal revenue tied to price changes.

1. There is a simple direct relation between marginal revenue, price and the price elasticity of demand:

$$MR = P(1 + \frac{1}{\varepsilon_p}).$$

2. Because profits are maximized when MC = MR, the optimal or profit-maximizing price is:

$$P^* = \frac{MC}{(1 + \frac{1}{\varepsilon_p})}.$$

B. **Optimal Pricing Policy Example:** Optimal prices can be easily calculated on the basis of marginal cost and point price elasticity of demand information.

C. **Determinants of Price Elasticity:** Demand tends to be less (more) elastic when:

1. A good is considered to be a necessity (nonessential).

2. Few (many) substitutes exist.

3. A small (large) proportion of income is spent on the product.

VI. **CROSS-PRICE ELASTICITY OF DEMAND**

A. **Substitutes and Complements:** The responsiveness of demand for one product to changes in the price of some other product, holding all other variables constant, is the cross-price elasticity of demand:

$$\varepsilon_{PX} = \frac{\partial Q_Y}{Q_Y} \div \frac{\partial P_X}{P_X} = \frac{\partial Q_Y}{\partial P_X} \times \frac{P_X}{Q_Y}$$

1. If $\varepsilon_{PX} > 0$, goods are substitutes and the price of one good and demand for another move in the same direction.

2. If $\varepsilon_{PX} < 0$, goods are complements and the price of one good and demand for another move in opposite directions.

3. If $\varepsilon_{PX} = 0$, goods are unrelated.

B. **Cross-Price Elasticity Example:** Cross-price elasticity information is useful for a number of purposes.

a.   Pricing strategy is dependent on how demand is affected by changes in the prices of other goods.

b.   Cross-price elasticity data is used in industry studies to define markets.

VII.   INCOME ELASTICITY OF DEMAND

A.   **Normal Versus Inferior Goods:** Income elasticity measures the responsiveness of demand to changes in income, holding all other variables constant:

$$\varepsilon_I = \frac{\partial Q}{Q} \div \frac{\partial I}{I} = \frac{\partial Q}{\partial I} \times \frac{I}{Q}.$$

1.   If $\varepsilon_I > 0$, products are normal or superior goods, and demand rises with rising personal income and economic growth.

2.   If $\varepsilon_I < 0$, products are inferior goods, and demand falls with rising personal income and economic growth.

B.   **Types of Normal Goods:**

1.   Noncyclical normal goods display $0 < \varepsilon_I < 1$; producers of such products do not share proportionally in economic growth.

2.   Cyclical normal goods are characterized by $\varepsilon_I > 1$; producers of such products gain (lose) more than a proportionate share of increases (decreases) in income.

VIII.   SUMMARY

PROBLEMS & SOLUTIONS

P5.1   ***Basic Demand Concepts.*** *A recent study of the Fargo, North Dakota market by Chemyard, Inc., found that the local demand for weed control and fertilizer services is described by the following elasticities: price elasticity = -1.5, cross-price elasticity with department store fertilizer = 2, income elasticity = 5, TV advertising elasticity = 3. Indicate whether each of the following statements is true or false, and explain your answer.*

    A.   *A price reduction for Chemyard services will increase both the number of units demanded and Chemyard revenues.*

    B.   *A 15% reduction in Chemyard prices would lead to a 10% increase in unit sales.*

    C.   *The cross-price elasticity indicates that a 10% increase in Chemyard prices would lead to a 20% increase in department store fertilizer demand.*

    D.   *The demand for Chemyard services is price elastic and typical of noncyclical normal goods.*

    E.   *A 4% increase in TV advertising would be necessary to overcome the negative effect on Chemyard sales caused by a 6% decrease in department store fertilizer prices.*

P5.1   **SOLUTION**

    A.   True. Quantity demanded always rises following a price reduction. In the case of elastic demand (here $|\varepsilon_P| = 1.5 > 1$), the percentage increase in quantity will be greater than the percentage decrease in price, and total revenue will rise.

    B.   False. Given $\varepsilon_P = -1.5$, a 15% reduction in Chemyard prices would lead to a 22.5% increase in unit sales.

    C.   False. The $\varepsilon_{PX} = 2$ indicates that a 10% reduction in department store fertilizer prices would lead to a 20% reduction in the demand for Chemyard services.

    D.   False. The demand for Chemyard services is price elastic, but $\varepsilon_I = 5 > 1$ indicates that service demand is cyclical.

    E.   True. A 4% increase in TV advertising would increase service demand by 12%. Conversely, a 6% decrease in department store prices would decrease service demand by 12%. Therefore, these changes would be mutually offsetting.

P5.2   ***Demand Analysis.*** *Mike Delfino, owner-manager of The Perfect Sleeper, Inc., has estimated the following demand and marginal revenue relations for the deluxe Edie Britt model waterbed:*

$$P = \$500 - \$0.25Q \qquad \text{(Demand)}$$

$$MR = \$500 - \$0.5Q \qquad \text{(Marginal Revenue)}$$

where Q is quantity (in units).

A.   *Plot the demand, marginal, and total revenue curves.*

B.   *At what price would the firm fail to sell any waterbeds?*

C.   *What is the maximum quantity that the firm could give away?*

D.   *What is the maximum revenue that the firm could receive?*

E.   *For a given percentage change in price, what would be the percentage change in quantity demanded at the output level Q = 600?*

F.   *What is the arc price elasticity of demand for the quantity range of 600-700 units?*

P5.2   **SOLUTION**

A.   Note that:

Demand Curve = P = $500 - $0.25Q

Total Revenue Curve = TR = P × Q = $500Q - $0.25Q^2

Marginal Revenue Curve = MR = ∂TR/∂Q = $500 - $0.5Q

Q	P	Total Revenue = P × Q
0	$500	$0
400	400	160,000
800	300	240,000
1,000	250	250,000
1,200	200	240,000
1,600	100	160,000
2,000	0	0

The Perfect Sleeper, Inc.

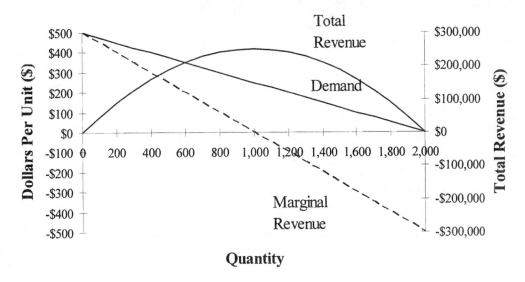

Quantity

B.   At P = $500, Q = 0 because P = $500 - $0.25(0) = $500.

C.   At a price of $0, Q = 2,000 - 4P = 2,000 - 4(0) = 2,000 units.

D.   Total revenue is maximized when MR = 0, provided that total revenue is falling as output increases. Here, revenue is maximized when Q = 1,000 because:

$$MR \quad = \quad \partial TR/\partial Q = \$500 - \$0.5Q$$

$$0 \quad = \quad \$500 - \$0.5Q$$

$$0.5Q \quad = \quad 500$$

$$Q \quad = \quad 1,000$$

At Q = 1,000, TR = $250,000, because:

$$TR \quad = \quad P \times Q$$

$$= \quad \$500Q - \$0.25Q^2$$

$$= \quad \$500(1,000) - \$0.25(1,000)^2$$

$$= \$250,000$$

(This is a maximum because marginal revenue is negative for Q > 2,000.)

E.   First, determine $\partial Q/\partial P$ as:

$$P = \$500 - \$0.25Q$$

$$Q = 2,000 - 4P$$

$$\partial Q/\partial P = -4$$

Then, at Q = 600 and P = 350:

$$\varepsilon_P = \partial Q/\partial P \times P/Q$$

$$= -4 \times (\$350/600)$$

$$= -2.33$$

The percentage change in quantity demanded is -2.33 times the percentage change in price. The point price elasticity is -2.33.

F.   Because P = $500 - $0.25Q,

At Q = 600: P = $500 - $0.25(600) = $350

At Q = 700: P = $500 - $0.25(700) = $325

Therefore:

$$\text{Arc Price Elasticity} = \frac{Q_2 - Q_1}{P_2 - P_1} \times \frac{P_2 + P_1}{Q_2 + Q_1}$$

$$= \frac{700 - 600}{\$325 - \$350} \times \frac{\$325 + \$350}{700 + 600}$$

$$= -2.1$$

As is typical, the price elasticity of demand is decreasing in absolute terms, here from $\varepsilon_P = -2.33$ to $\varepsilon_P = -2.1$, as price decreases.

P5.3 ***Demand Curve Determination.*** *Security Systems, Inc., markets electronic surveillance equipment used to control inventory "shrinkage" (shoplifting, employee theft) at retail clothing stores. The demand function for a new portable tag sensor is:*

$$Q = 100 - 20P + 0.4A + 0.025I$$

where Q = quantity demanded, P = price, A = advertising expenditures, and I = disposable income per family.

 A. *Assuming A = $6,000, and I = $60,000, what is the demand curve for the tag sensor?*

 B. *What are the total and marginal revenue functions for the tag sensor?*

 C. *What is the point price elasticity of demand, and the point income elasticity of demand under the assumptions in part A and if P = $150?*

P5.3 **SOLUTION**

 A. The demand curve for the tag sensor is simply:

$$
\begin{aligned}
Q \ &= \ 100 - 20P + 0.4A + 0.025I \\
&= \ 100 - 20P + 0.4(6,000) + 0.025(60,000) \\
&= \ 4,000 - 20P
\end{aligned}
$$

or

$$P \ = \ \$200 - \$0.05Q$$

 B.
$$
\begin{aligned}
TR \ &= \ P \times Q \\
&= \ (\$200 - \$0.05Q)Q \\
&= \ \$200Q - \$0.05Q^2
\end{aligned}
$$

$$MR \ = \ \partial TR / \partial Q = \$200 - \$0.1Q$$

 C. Note that:

$$Q \ = \ 100 - 20P + 0.4A + 0.025I$$

$$= 100 - 20(150) + 0.4(6,000) + 0.025(60,000)$$

$$= 1,000$$

Thus, the own price elasticity is:

$$\varepsilon_P = \partial Q/\partial P \times P/Q$$

$$= -20 \times (\$150/1,000)$$

$$= -3$$

The income elasticity of demand is:

$$\varepsilon_I = \partial Q/\partial I \times I/Q$$

$$= 0.025 \times (\$60,000/1,000)$$

$$= 1.5$$

Because $\varepsilon_I = 1.5 > 0$, the tag sensor is a cyclical normal good.

P5.4   ***Arc Price Elasticity.*** *During September, in an effort to reduce end-of-the-model-year inventory, Newark Mercedes-Benz offered a $12,000 discount from the $120,000 sticker price on the Mercedes CL600 2-door coupe. Due to the success of the promotion, monthly sales rose from 15 to 23 units.*

A. *Calculate the arc price elasticity for the CL600 2-door coupe.*

B. *Calculate the sticker price reduction necessary to eliminate Newark's remaining inventory of 27 units during the month of October.*

P5.4   SOLUTION

A. $$E_P = \frac{\Delta Q}{\Delta P} \times \frac{P_2 + P_1}{Q_2 + Q_1}$$

$$= \frac{23 - 15}{\$108,000 - \$120,000} \times \frac{\$108,000 + \$120,000}{23 + 15}$$

$$= -4$$

B. The new price P_2 required to sell 27 units during October can be calculated from the arc price elasticity formula:

$$E_P = \frac{\Delta Q}{\Delta P} \times \frac{P_2 + P_1}{Q_2 + Q_1}.$$

$$-4 = \frac{27 - 15}{P_2 - \$120,000} \times \frac{P_2 + \$120,000}{27 + 15}$$

$$-4 = \frac{12(P_2 + 120,000)}{42(P_2 - 120,000)}$$

$$-168P_2 + 20,160,000 = 12P_2 + 1,440,000$$

$$180P_2 = 18,720,000$$

$$P_2 = \$104,000$$

A new $P_2 = \$104,000$ implies a sticker price reduction of $16,000 because:

$$\Delta P = P_2 - P_1$$

$$= \$104,000 - \$120,000$$

$$= -\$16,000$$

P5.5 **Cross-Price Elasticity.** *The Van De Camp Paper Company conducted a research study to determine how the demand for high strength paper boxes, product X, is affected by price changes of paper towels, product Y. Research staff member Bree Cross estimates the relation between sales of X and the price of Y, holding other things constant, as:* $Q_Y = 1,000 - 0.6P_X$.

A. *How would you classify the relation between X and Y: substitute, complement, or independent?*

B. *Determine the quantities demanded of Y for the following prices of X:* $P_X = \$100$, $\$80$, $\$60$, $\$40$.

C. *Determine the point cross-price elasticity of demand at* $P_X = \$80$ *and at* $P_X = \$40$.

D.   *Determine the arc cross-price elasticity for these price ranges:* $P_X = \$100$ *to* $\$80$; $\$60$ *to* $\$40$

P5.5   **SOLUTION**

A.   X and Y are complement products. A rise in P_X causes a decrease in the demand for Y. Apparently, Adirondack's customers are more likely to buy its paper boxes if they are already a paper towel customer.

B.   Given the functional relation $Q_Y = 1,000 - 0.6P_X$:

P_X	Y(units)
$100	940
80	952
60	964
40	976

C.   At $P_X = 80$,

$$\varepsilon_{PX} = \partial Q_Y/\partial P_X \times P_X/Q_Y$$

$$= -0.6 \times (\$80/952)$$

$$= -0.05$$

At $P_X = 40$,

$$\varepsilon_{PX} = -0.6 \times (\$40/976)$$

$$= -0.02$$

D.   For the range $100 to $80:

$$E_{PX} = \frac{Y_2 - Y_1}{P_{X2} - P_{X1}} \times \frac{P_{X2} + P_{X1}}{Y_2 + Y_1}$$

$$= \frac{952 - 940}{\$80 - \$100} \times \frac{\$80 + \$100}{952 + 940}$$

$$= -0.06$$

For the range $60 to $40:

$$E_{PX} = \frac{964 - 976}{\$60 - \$40} \times \frac{\$60 + \$40}{964 + 976}$$

$$= -0.03$$

P5.6   ***Cross-Price Elasticity.*** *Laguna Sporting Goods sells Roller-Ball roller skates at a wholesale price of $120 per pair. Last year, its sales volume was 10,000 pairs. This year, a competitor, Oceanside Sports, cut the wholesale price of Roller-Ball skates from $130 to $110 per pair. As a result, Laguna sales fell to only 8,000 pairs of skates.*

    A.   *Determine the arc cross-price elasticity of demand between Laguna's and Oceanside's roller skates. (Assume that Laguna's price is held constant.)*

    B.   *Assume that the arc price elasticity for Laguna's skates is $E_p = -2$. Assume also that Oceanside keeps the price of its skates at $110. What price cut must be made by Laguna in order to increase its annual sales volume back to 10,000 pairs?*

P5.6   **SOLUTION**

    A.   Using the arc cross-price elasticity formula:

$$E_{PX} = \frac{Q_2 - Q_1}{P_{X2} - P_{X1}} \times \frac{P_{X2} + P_{X1}}{Q_2 + Q_1}$$

$$= \frac{8,000 - 10,000}{\$110 - \$130} \times \frac{\$110 + \$130}{8,000 + 10,000}$$

$$= 1.33$$

Because $E_{PX} > 0$, a substitute good relation exists between Laguna and Oceanside roller skates (as expected).

    B.   Using the formula for arc price elasticity of demand:

$$E_P = \frac{Q_2 - Q_1}{P_2 - P_1} \times \frac{P_2 + P_1}{Q_2 + Q_1}$$

$$-2 = \frac{10,000 - 8,000}{P_2 - \$120} \times \frac{P_2 + \$120}{10,000 + 8,000}$$

$$-2 = \frac{2,000}{18,000} \times \frac{P_2 + 120}{P_2 - 120}$$

$$-18 = \frac{P_2 + 120}{P_2 - 120}$$

$$2,160 - 18P_2 = P_2 + 120$$

$$19P_2 = 2,040$$

$$P_2 = \$107.37$$

Thus, $107.37 is the price required to again sell 10,000 pairs. This involves a $12.63 price reduction because,

$$\Delta P = P_2 - P_1$$

$$= \$107.37 - \$120$$

$$= -\$12.63$$

P5.7 **_Optimal Pricing Policy._** *Captain Video, Inc., sells DVD recordings of recent movies and blank DVDs for home recording use. During recent years, Captain Video has run a Christmas special on its products, reducing average prices of first-run movie videos from $19.99 to $14.99, and 25-packs of blank DVDs from $12.69 to $9.99. Captain Kirk, manager of a new Captain Video outlet, questions the wisdom of this pricing policy in light of a recent trade association study that reports point price elasticity estimates of $\varepsilon_P = -2.5$ for first-run movie DVDs, and $\varepsilon_P = -4$ for blank DVDs.*

A.   *Is a price reduction likely to increase unit sales of movie DVDs and blank DVDs?*

B.   *What is the likely impact on total revenues of the Christmas price reductions?*

C.   *Determine optimal average prices if movie DVDs cost Captain Video $9 and five-packs of blank DVDs cost $7.50?*

D.   *Is the Christmas special pricing policy desirable?*

P5.7 **SOLUTION**

    A. Yes, price reductions will always increase unit sales.

    B. Given $|\varepsilon_P| > 1$ for both movie DVDs and blank DVDs, demand is elastic and price reductions will increase both units sold and total revenues.

    C. Because MC = MR at the profit-maximizing level of output, the optimal pricing formula is:

$$P = \frac{MC}{\left(1 + \dfrac{1}{\varepsilon_P}\right)}.$$

<u>Movie DVDs</u>

$$P = \frac{MC}{\left(1 + \dfrac{1}{\varepsilon_P}\right)}$$

$$\$14.99 \overset{?}{=} \frac{\$9}{\left(1 + \dfrac{1}{-2.5}\right)}$$

$$\$14.99 \overset{\checkmark}{=} \$15 \text{ (or } \$14.99)$$

<u>Blank DVDs</u>

$$P = \frac{MC}{\left(1 + \dfrac{1}{\varepsilon_P}\right)}$$

$$\$9.99 \overset{?}{=} \frac{\$7.50}{\left(1 + \dfrac{1}{-4}\right)}$$

$$\$9.99 \overset{\checkmark}{=} \$10 \text{ (or } \$9.99)$$

D.   Given these data, Kirk is wrong to question the Christmas special pricing policy. At P = \$14.99, MR = MC for movie DVDs. Similarly, prices for blank DVDs will maximize profits when P = \$9.99 for blank DVDs. Captain Video's pricing policy is optimal.

P5.8   ***Arc Income Elasticity.*** *Kitchen Art, Ltd., sells its basic food processor for \$300. The company's experience indicates that sales volume is affected by changes in consumers' income as well as by the price of the product. Specifically, the market research department estimates that the arc price elasticity of demand is -9, whereas the arc income elasticity is 4. These relations are expected to remain stable in the near future over the contemplated range of price and incomes.*

Last year, sales volume for the food processor was 100,000 units, and disposable income per capita was \$37,500.

A.   *Using the arc elasticity of demand formula, and holding all else equal, calculate the effect on sales of a rise in disposable income per capita from \$37,500 to \$42,500.*

B.   *Using the arc price elasticity of demand formula, and holding all else equal, estimate the quantity effect of a \$50 price reduction.*

C.   *Based on your answers to parts A and B, calculate the total effect on unit sales of a \$37,500 to \$42,500 increase in disposable income per capita and a \$50 price reduction.*

P5.8   SOLUTION

A.   Using the arc income elasticity of demand formula to find Q:

$$E_I = \frac{Q_2 - Q_1}{I_2 - I_1} \times \frac{I_2 + I_1}{Q_2 + Q_1}$$

$$4 = \frac{Q_2 - 100{,}000}{\$42{,}500 - \$37{,}500} \times \frac{\$42{,}500 + \$37{,}500}{Q_2 + 100{,}000}$$

$$4 = \frac{Q_2 - 100{,}000}{Q_2 + 100{,}000} \times \frac{80{,}000}{5{,}000}$$

$$4Q_2 + 400{,}000 = 16Q_2 - 1{,}600{,}000$$

$$12Q_2 = 2,000,000$$

$$Q_2 = 166,667 \text{ units}$$

B. Using the arc price elasticity of demand formula to find Q:

$$E_P = \frac{Q_2 - Q_1}{P_2 - P_1} \times \frac{P_2 + P_1}{Q_2 + Q_1}$$

$$-9 = \frac{Q_2 - 100,000}{\$250 - \$300} \times \frac{\$250 + \$300}{Q_2 + 100,000}$$

$$-9 = \frac{Q_2 - 100,000}{Q_2 + 100,000} \times \frac{550}{(-50)}$$

$$-9Q_2 - 900,000 = -11Q_2 + 1,100,000$$

$$2Q_2 = 2,000,000$$

$$Q_2 = 1,000,000 \text{ units}$$

C. To estimate sales when disposable income per capita rises from $37,500 to $42,500 and price falls from $300 to $250, simply calculate the price effect from the Q = 166,667 base, or the income effect from the Q = 1,000,000 base.

Using the first approach:

$$E_P = \frac{Q_2 - Q_1}{P_2 - P_1} \times \frac{P_2 + P_1}{Q_2 + Q_1}$$

$$-9 = \frac{Q_2 - 166,667}{\$250 - \$300} \times \frac{\$250 + \$300}{Q_2 + 166,667}$$

$$-9 = \frac{Q_2 - 166,667}{Q_2 + 166,667} \times \frac{550}{(-50)}$$

$$-9Q_2 - 1,500,000 = -11Q_2 + 1,833,337$$

$$2Q_2 = 3,333,337$$

$$Q_2 = 1,666,667 \text{ units}$$

Using the second approach:

$$E_I = \frac{Q_2 - Q_1}{I_2 - I_1} \times \frac{I_2 + I_1}{Q_2 + Q_1}$$

$$4 = \frac{Q_2 - 1,000,000}{\$42,500 - \$37,500} \times \frac{\$42,500 + \$37,500}{Q_2 + 1,000,000}$$

$$4Q_2 + 4,000,000 = 16Q_2 - 16,000,000$$

$$12Q_2 = 20,000,000$$

$$Q_2 = 1,666,667 \text{ units}$$

P5.9   ***Arc Cross-Price Elasticity.*** *B.B. Lean, Inc., is a catalog retailer offering quality outdoor and travel apparel for the entire family. In an audit of Christmas season sales data, the company noted that sales of its popular $276 Harris Tweed sports jacket fell to 2,000 units from the 5,000 units sold last season. Apparently, this sales downturn was caused by department store competitors who reduced their average price on similar items from $300 to $225 per unit.*

A.   *Calculate the arc cross-price elasticity of demand for this product.*

B.   *Calculate B.B. Lean's arc price elasticity of demand for this product if sales rebounded from 2,000 to 4,000 units following a price reduction to $241.50 per unit.*

C.   *Calculate the additional price reduction B.B. Lean must offer on this item to fully recover lost sales (i.e., regain a volume of 5,000 units).*

P5.9   **SOLUTION**

A. $$E_{PX} = \frac{Q_{Y2} - Q_{Y1}}{P_{X2} - P_{X1}} \times \frac{P_{X2} + P_{X1}}{Q_{Y2} + Q_{Y1}}$$

$$= \frac{2,000 - 5,000}{\$225 - \$300} \times \frac{\$225 + \$300}{2,000 + 5,000}$$

$$= 3 \text{ (substitutes)}$$

B. $E_P = \dfrac{Q_2 - Q_1}{P_2 - P_1} \times \dfrac{P_2 + P_1}{Q_2 + Q_1}$

$$= \dfrac{4{,}000 - 2{,}000}{\$241.50 - \$276} \times \dfrac{\$241.50 + \$276}{4{,}000 + 2{,}000}$$

$$= -5 \text{ (Elastic)}$$

C. $E_P = \dfrac{Q_2 - Q_1}{P_2 - P_1} \times \dfrac{P_2 + P_1}{Q_2 + Q_1}$

$$-5 = \dfrac{5{,}000 - 4{,}000}{P_2 - \$241.50} \times \dfrac{P_2 + \$241.50}{5{,}000 + 4{,}000}$$

$$-5 = \dfrac{P_2 + \$241.50}{9(P_2 - \$241.50)}$$

$$-45P_2 + \$10{,}867.50 = P_2 + \$241.50$$

$$46P_2 = \$10{,}626$$

$$P_2 = \$231$$

Thus, \$231 is the price required to again sell 5,000 units. This involves a further price reduction of \$10.50 because,

$$\Delta P = P_3 - P_2$$

$$= \$231 - \$241.50$$

$$= -\$10.50$$

P5.10   ***Other Demand Elasticities.*** *Last year, a 1% increase in overall economic activity (GDP) caused a 5% increase in equipment sales at Empire State Manufacturing. George Costanza, executive vice-president, believes that during the coming year the anticipated 1% downturn in GDP will require a 2.5% increase in advertising to maintain current sales.*

A.   *Calculate the point income elasticity of demand for Empire State's products.*

B.   *Calculate the point advertising elasticity assumption underlying Costanza's projection.*

P5.10   SOLUTION

A. $\varepsilon_I = \dfrac{\text{Percentage Change in Q}}{\text{Percentage Change in I}}$

$= \dfrac{0.05}{0.01}$

$= 5$ (A cyclical normal good)

B.   All else equal, a 1% decrease in income would cause a 5% decrease in equipment demand because:

$$\varepsilon_I = \dfrac{\text{Percentage Change in Q}}{\text{Percentage Change in I}}$$

Percentage Change in Q $= \varepsilon_I \times$ (Percentage Change in I)

$= 5(-0.01)$

$= -0.05$ or -5%

If this income effect is to be offset by a 2.5% increase in advertising, the relevant advertising elasticity is:

$$\varepsilon_A = \dfrac{\text{Percentage Change in Q}}{\text{Percentage Change in Advertising}}$$

$= \dfrac{0.05}{0.025}$

$= 2$

Chapter 6

DEMAND ESTIMATION

Accurate estimation of demand relations is among the most challenging responsibilities that managers must meet in a dynamic economic environment. Demand is difficult to measure because consumers often react in unexpected ways to price changes, innovative advertising campaigns, changes in the pace of economic activity, and so on. Derived demand for intermediate products is similarly difficult to characterize because corporate customers frequently shift from one supplier to another on the basis of modest changes in product price and quality characteristics. Most firms simply don't have the resources to continuously monitor all current and potential customers. Others that closely monitor customer purchase decisions and perceptions are stymied by customers that have neither the time nor inclination to respond to detailed surveys. For both of these reasons, demand estimation is a difficult task.

In this chapter, three approaches to demand estimation are explored, including: consumer interviews, market experiments, and regression analysis. Consumer interviews and market experiments yield best results when skilled interviewers deal with carefully selected samples. An advantage of both techniques is that they can glean meaningful information from only limited data; a drawback to each is that they simulate actual customer decisions only imperfectly. With the present revolution in personal computing and user-friendly software, regression analysis and the statistical analysis of demand relations is now within the domain of even the smallest organization. Managers are often directly responsible for the design and execution of statistical studies, and the material contained in this chapter helps one become skillful at these tasks.

CHAPTER OUTLINE

I.   **DEMAND CURVE ESTIMATION**

      A.   **Simple Linear Demand Curves**: The best technique for estimating the market demand curve is the method that provides a necessary level of accuracy at minimum cost.

            1.   Nobody employs expensive, time consuming, and complicated demand estimation techniques when inexpensive and simple methods work just fine.

      B.   **Using Simple Linear Demand Curves**: Simple linear market demand curves give the firm a powerful tool that can be profitably employed in its production, pricing, and promotion decisions.

II.   **IDENTIFICATION PROBLEM**

A. **Changing Nature of Demand Relations:** Demand estimation is sometimes relatively simple, especially in the case of stable short-run demand relations. In most situations, however, the changing nature of demand relations makes it difficult to compile accurate short-run estimates.

   1. More difficult still is the problem of determining the effect on demand of changes in specific variables such as price, advertising expenditures, credit terms, prices of competing products, and so on.

   2. The unpredictable nature of general economic conditions makes demand estimation difficult for many products. When the income elasticity of demand is high, demand tends to vary more than the parallel change in economic activity.

B. **Interplay of Demand and Supply:** It is sometimes difficult to obtain accurate estimates of demand relations because linkages exist among most economic variables.

   1. To plot a demand curve, it is necessary to vary price to obtain data on the price/quantity relation, while keeping fixed the effects of all factors in the demand function.

C. **Shifts in Demand and Supply:** If the demand curve has not shifted but the supply curve *has* shifted, price/quantity data can be utilized to estimate demand relations.

   1. If sufficient information exists to determine how demand and supply curves shift between data observations, both curves can be estimated.

D. **Simultaneous Relations:** At any point in time, a simultaneous relation, or coincident association, exists between demand and supply.

   1. The problem of estimating any given economic relation in the presence of important simultaneous relations is the identification problem.

   2. To separate shifts in demand or supply from changes or movements along a single curve, it is necessary to have more than just price/quantity data.

   3. Advanced statistical techniques, such as two-stage least squares (2SLS) or seemingly unrelated regression (SUR) analysis, are sometimes required to solve the identification problem.

III. INTERVIEW AND EXPERIMENTAL METHODS

A. **Consumer Interviews:** The consumer interview, or survey, method requires questioning customers or potential customers to estimate demand relations.

   1. Unfortunately, the quantity and quality of survey information are typically limited because consumers are often unable or unwilling to provide accurate answers to hypothetical questions.

B. **Market Experiments:** Market experiments examine consumer behavior in actual "test" markets or in laboratory settings.

   1. Market experiments are expensive and usually undertaken on a scale too small to allow high levels of confidence in the results.

   2. Market experiments are seldom run for sufficiently long periods to indicate the long-run effects of various price, advertising, or packaging strategies.

   3. Controlled laboratory experiments have the advantages of lower cost and greater control of extraneous factors. However, the value of consumer clinics or laboratory experiments suffers because such tests often distort shopper buying habits.

IV. REGRESSION ANALYSIS

A. **What Is a Statistical Relation?:** A statistical relation exists between two economic variables if the average of one is related to another, but it is impossible to exactly predict the value of one based on the value of another.

   1. A deterministic relation is an association between variables that is known with certainty.

   2. Regression analysis is a powerful technique used to describe the statistical relation among important economic variables.

      a. A time series of data is a daily, weekly, monthly, or annual sequence of data on an economic variable such as price, income, cost, or revenue.

      b. A cross section of data is a group of observations on an important economic variable at any given point in time.

3.   The simplest and most common means for analyzing a sample of historical data is to plot and visually study the data.

    a.   A scatter diagram is a plot of data where the *dependent* variable is plotted on the vertical axis (Y axis), and the *independent* variable is plotted on the horizontal axis (X axis).

B.   **Specifying the Regression Model:** The first step in regression analysis is to specify the variables to be included in the regression equation or model. The second step in regression analysis is to obtain reliable estimates of the variables. Once variables have been specified and the data have been gathered, the functional form of the regression equation must be determined.

1.   The most common specification is a linear model where unit demand is assumed to change in a straight-line fashion with changes in each independent variable.

    a.   Linear models imply a constant marginal effect on the Y variable due to one-unit changes in the various independent X variables.

    b.   Elasticity varies along linear demand functions.

2.   Another common regression model form is the multiplicative model where the marginal effect of each independent variable depends on the value of all independent variables.

    a.   Multiplicative models can be transformed into a linear relation using logarithms and then estimated by the least squares technique.

    b.   Multiplicative models imply a changing absolute effect on the Y variable due to one-unit changes in the various independent X variables.

    c.   Multiplicative demand functions implicitly assume constant elasticities.

    d.   The specific form of any regression model--linear, multiplicative, or otherwise--must be consistent with economic theory.

C.   **Least Squares Method:** Regression equations are typically estimated, or "fitted," by the method of least squares. This method fits the regression line that minimizes the sum of the squared deviations between the best-fitting line and the set of original data points.

1. The minimization of squared deviations avoids the problem of having positive and negative deviations cancel one another out.

V.   MEASURES OF REGRESSION MODEL SIGNIFICANCE

A. **Standard Error of the Estimate:** A very useful measure for examining the accuracy of any regression model is the standard error of the estimate (SEE), or the standard deviation of the dependent Y variable after controlling for the influence of all X variables.

1. The standard error of the estimate increases with the amount of scatter about the sample regression line.

2. If each data point were to lie exactly on the regression line, then the standard error of the estimate would equal zero because each $\hat{Y}_t$ would exactly equal Y_t.

3. The standard error of the estimate is used to determine a range within which the dependent Y variable can be predicted with varying degrees of statistical confidence based on the regression coefficients and values for the X variables.

    a. The best estimate of the tth value for the dependent variable is $\hat{Y}_t$, as predicted by the regression equation.

    b. There is a 95% probability that observations of the dependent variable will lie within the range $\hat{Y}_t \pm (1.96 \times \text{SEE})$, or within roughly 2 standard errors of the estimate.

    c. The probability is 99% that any given $\hat{Y}_t$ will lie within the range $\hat{Y}_t \pm (2.576 \times \text{SEE})$, or within roughly 3 standard errors of its predicted value.

B. **Goodness of Fit, r, and R^2:** In a simple regression model with only one independent variable, the correlation coefficient, r, measures goodness of fit. In multiple regression models where more than one independent X variable is considered, the coefficient of determination, or R^2, shows how well a multiple regression model explains changes in the value of the dependent Y variable.

1. R^2 is the proportion of total variation in the dependent variable that is explained by the full set of independent variables.

   a. If $R^2 = 0$, the regression model is unable to explain *any* variation in the dependent Y variable.

   b. If $R^2 = 1$, the regression model is able to explain *all* variation in the dependent Y variable.

   c. In judging R^2, the type of analysis conducted and the anticipated use of statistical results must be considered.

C. **Corrected Coefficient of Determination, $\bar{R}^2$:** R^2 always equals 100% when the number of estimated coefficients equals or exceeds the number of observations because each data point can then be placed exactly on the regression line. The corrected coefficient of determination, denoted by the symbol $\bar{R}^2$, is an adjustment to R^2 based upon the number of observations (data points) and the number of estimated coefficients.

1. The downward adjustment to R^2 is large when n, the sample size, is small relative to k, the number of coefficients being estimated.

2. The downward adjustment to R^2 is small when n is large relative to k.

D. **F Statistic:** The F statistic provides evidence on whether a statistically significant proportion of total variation in the dependent variable has been explained by the regression model.

1. Like $\bar{R}^2$, the F statistic is adjusted for sample size and coefficient number.

2. The F test is used to determine whether a given F statistic is statistically significant.

   a. Performing F tests involves comparing F statistics with critical values from a table of the F distribution.

b. If a given *F* statistic *exceeds* the critical value from the *F* distribution table, the hypothesis of no relation between the dependent *Y* variable and the set of independent *X* variables can be rejected.

VI. MEASURES OF INDIVIDUAL VARIABLE SIGNIFICANCE

A. **t statistic:** The *t* statistic (or test statistic) has an *approximately* normal distribution with a mean of zero and a standard deviation of 1. It describes the difference between an estimated coefficient and some hypothesized value in terms of "standardized units," or by the number of standard deviations of the coefficient estimate.

   1. It is rare to find a calculated *t* statistic that falls outside the bounds ±1.96, or roughly ±2, when the true value of *t* = 0. This occurs less than 5% of the time.

   2. It is very rare to find a calculated *t* statistic that falls outside the bounds ±2.576, or roughly ±3, when the true value of *t* = 0; this happens less than 1% of the time.

B. **Two-Tail *t* Tests:** In regression analysis, the most common *t*-test is performed to learn if an individual slope coefficient estimate *b* = 0. If *X* and *Y* are unrelated, then the *b* slope coefficient for a given *X* variable equals zero.

   1. If the *b* = 0 hypothesis can be rejected, then it is possible to infer that *b* ≠ 0 and that a relation exists between *Y* and a given *X* variable.

      a. Calculated *t* statistics greater than 2 usually permits rejection of the hypothesis that there is no relation between the dependent *Y* variable and a given *X* variable with 95% confidence.

      b. A calculated *t* statistic greater than 3 typically permits rejection of the hypothesis that there is no relation between the dependent *Y* variable and a given *X* variable with 99% confidence.

   2. Critical *t* values are adjusted upward when sample size is small in relation to the number of estimated coefficients.

      a. Precise critical *t* values can be obtained from a *t* table, such as that found in Appendix C.

b. If the calculated t statistic is greater than the relevant critical t value, the $b = 0$ hypothesis can be rejected.

c. If the calculated t statistic is not greater than the critical t value, it is not possible to reject the $b = 0$ hypothesis. In that case, there is no evidence of a relation between Y and a given X variable.

3. Tests of the hypothesis $b = 0$ are referred to as two-tail t tests because either very small negative t values or very large positive t values can lead to rejection.

C. **One-Tail t tests:** Some managerial questions go beyond the simple matter of whether X influences Y. Tests of direction (positive or negative) or comparative magnitude are called one-tail t tests.

1. In a two-tail t test, rejection of the null hypothesis occurs with a finding that the t statistic is not in the *region around zero*.

2. In one-tail t tests, rejection of the null hypothesis occurs when the t statistic is in one specific tail of the distribution.

VII. **SUMMARY**

PROBLEMS & SOLUTIONS

P6.1 **Demand Concepts.** *Identify each of the following as true or false and explain why.*

A. *The effect of a one-unit change in advertising is constant along a linear demand curve.*

B. *An increase in income increases the quantity demanded for normal goods and services.*

C. *A demand curve is revealed if prices fall while demand conditions are held constant.*

D. *The price elasticity of demand is constant along a linear demand curve.*

E. *A rise in price tends to reduce the quantity demanded.*

P6.1 **SOLUTION**

A. True. The effect of a one-unit change in advertising is constant, but the advertising elasticity of demand varies along a linear demand curve.

B. False. An increase in income causes an upward shift in the demand curve for normal goods and services.

C. True. A demand curve is revealed if prices fall while demand conditions are held constant.

D. False. The effect of a one-unit change in price is constant, but the elasticity of demand varies along a linear demand curve.

E. True. A rise in price causes an upward movement along the demand curve and a decrease in the quantity demanded.

P6.2 **Regression Analysis.** *Identify each of the following as true or false and explain why.*

A. *A parameter is a sample characteristic.*

B. *A one-tail F test is used to indicate whether or not the independent variables as a group explain a significant share of demand variation.*

C. *The estimated demand relation can be used to derive a predicted value for demand.*

D. *A two-tail t test is an appropriate means for testing whether or not individual independent variables have an influence on the dependent variable.*

E. *The coefficient of determination shows the share of total variation in demand that can be explained by the regression model.*

P6.2 ***SOLUTION***

A. False. A parameter is a population characteristic that is estimated by a coefficient derived from a sample of data.

B. True. An *F* test is used to indicate whether or not the independent variables as a group explain a significant share of demand variation.

C. True. Given values for independent variables, the estimated demand relation can be used to derive a predicted (or fitted) value for demand.

D. True. A two-tail t test is an appropriate means for tests concerning the influences of independent variables on *Y*.

E. True. The coefficient of determination (R^2) shows the share of total variation in demand that can be explained by the regression model.

P6.3 ***Demand Curve Analysis.*** *Game-Gear, Inc., is a leading supplier of video games for hand-held video game players. Average wholesale price and unit sales data for the "Game-Gear Football" over the past five-month period are shown in the table.*

	June	*July*	*August*	*Sept.*	*Oct.*
Price ($)	*$36*	*$34*	*$33*	*$35*	*$34*
Units sold	*350,000*	*400,000*	*425,000*	*375,000*	*400,000*

A. *Complete the following table, and use these data to derive intercept and slope coefficients for a linear demand curve.*

Month	Price	Quantity	∂Price	∂Quantity	Slope = ∂P/∂Q
June	$36	350,000	---	---	---
July	34	400,000			
August	33	425,000			
Sept.	35	375,000			
Oct.	34	400,000			

B.   *Assuming that demand conditions are held constant, use the preceding data to plot a linear demand curve.*

P6.3   **SOLUTION**

A.   A linear demand curve is based on the assumption that a one-unit change in price leads to a constant change in the quantity demanded. From the monthly price/output data note that:

Month	Price	Quantity	∂Price	∂Quantity	Slope = ∂P/∂Q
June	$36	350,000	---	---	---
July	34	400,000	-$2	50,000	-0.00004
August	33	425,000	-1	25,000	-0.00004
Sept.	35	375,000	2	-50,000	-0.00004
Oct.	34	400,000	-1	25,000	-0.00004

When a linear demand curve is written as:

$$P = a + bQ$$

a is the intercept and b is the slope coefficient. By definition, slope equals ∂P/∂Q. From the above data note:

$$b = \partial P / \partial Q = -0.00004$$

Therefore,

$$P = a - \$0.00004Q$$

Under the assumption of a liner demand relation, each of the data points given in the table fall exactly along the linear demand curve. The value of the intercept term can therefore be easily calculated using data for any of the data points given in the table. For example, using the June data point where P = $36 and Q = 350,000,

$$P = a - \$0.00004Q$$

$$\$36 = a - \$0.00004(350,000)$$

$$\$36 = a - \$14$$

$$a = \$50$$

Therefore, in general:

$$P = \$50 - \$0.00004Q$$

or

$$Q = 1,250,000 - 25,000P$$

B. The linear demand curve can be plotted as:

Game Gear, Inc.

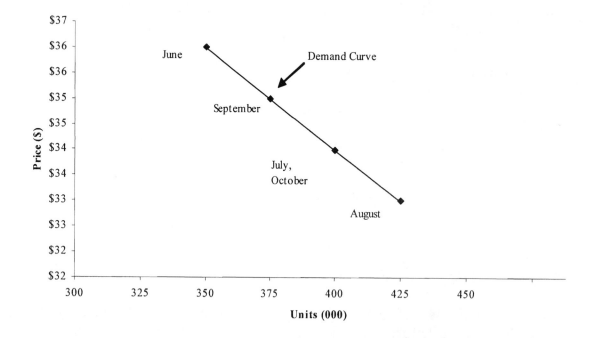

P6.4   ***The Identification Problem.*** *Complex Circuits, Inc., is a small but rapidly growing supplier of analog/digital circuits and systems used for measurement and control. The average price received by CCI for the XKE device, and the number sold (output) per quarter over the past five years given in the table.*

	Year				
	1	*2*	*3*	*4*	*5*
Price	$100	$110	$120	$130	$140
Quantity	500	600	700	800	900

Annual demand and supply curves for CCI services are:

$$Q_D = 625 - 2.5P + 125T \qquad \text{(Demand)}$$

$$Q_S = -500 + 10P \qquad \text{(Supply)}$$

where Q is output (000), P is price, T is a trend factor, and T = 1 during Q-1 and increases by one unit per quarter.

A.   *Express each demand and supply curve in terms of price as a function of output.*

B.   *Plot the quarterly demand curves for the last six quarterly periods. (Hint: Let T=1 to find the Y-intercept for Q-1, T = 2 for Q-2, and so on.)*

C.   *Plot the CCI supply curve on the same graph.*

D.   *What is this problem's relation to the identification problem?*

P6.4   **SOLUTION**

A.   Demand

$$Q_D = 625 - 2.5P + 125T$$

$$2.5P = 625 - Q_D + 125T$$

$$P = \$250 - \$0.4Q_D + \$50T$$

                             Supply

$$Q_S = -500 + 10P$$

$$10P \ = \ 500 + Q_S$$

$$P \ = \ \$50 + \$0.1Q_S$$

B.,C.

Demand Curve Analysis for Complex Circuits, Inc (Y1 to Y5)

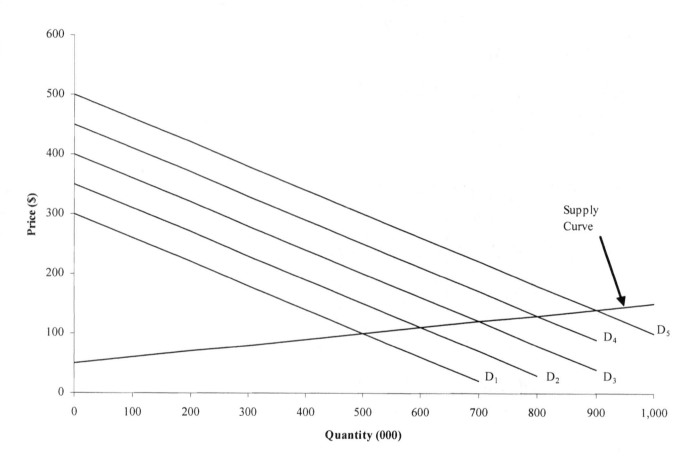

D. This example illustrates the identification problem. If we know that either the demand or supply function is shifting while the other is stable, then the price/output data can be used to trace out the stable curve. Here the supply curve is stable while demand is growing rapidly (shifting to the right). Therefore, the price/output data given in the problem can be used to trace out the relevant supply curve.

P6.5   **Regression Statistics.** *The Travel Company, Inc., has hired a management consulting firm to analyze demand in 26 regional markets for one of its major spring break tours. A preliminary report from the consultant contained the following regression results (standard errors in parentheses):*

$$Q = 260 + 2A + 6.4I + 3P_X - 4P$$
$$(400)\ (0.4)\ (2.4)\ (0.9)\ (1.2)$$

$$R^2 = 90\%$$

Standard Error of the Estimate = 10

Here, Q is the annual demand for the tour in question, P is the price charged by TTC in dollars, A is thousands of dollars of advertising expenditures, P_X is the average price of another product (unidentified), also measured in dollars, and I is thousands of dollars of disposable income per family in the market area.

A.   *Interpret the demand equation and explain the use of the regression statistics provided.*

B.   *Assume that the consultant is not available and the management of TTC is unsure whether the P_X variable in the equation is the price of a complementary or competing product. (Both were used in different regression runs and, because of a mixup in labeling, the P_X variable is unidentified.) Can you determine at the 99% confidence level whether X is a complement or a substitute? Why or why not? If so, which is it?*

C.   *Assuming that the current price is $400, advertising expenditures are $20,000, P_X is $500, and disposable income per family is $62,500, what is the point price elasticity of demand? Would a reduction in price result in an increase in total revenues? Why?*

D.   *Given the data in part C, what is the point cross-price elasticity between the tour and product X?*

E.   *If TTC wished to use this equation for forecasting purposes, what is the size of the 99% confidence interval for predicting Q?*

P6.5   **SOLUTION**

A.   The regression equation relates the number of tours sold annually to the value of four variables: advertising expenditures, A, per family income, I, the average price of the unidentified product, P_X, and the price charged by TTC, P. More specifically, the expected sales quantity for any year is equal to 260 plus 2 times the advertising expenditures (measured in thousands of dollars), plus 6.4 times the per family income in the market area (in thousands of dollars), plus 3 times the average price of another unidentified product (in dollars), minus 4 times the price charged by TTC (also measured in dollars).

The individual coefficients of the equation provide estimates of the marginal relationships between the annual number of tours sold and each of the independent variables in the model. All of the other information provided relates to the accuracy of the empirical estimation of the demand equation. $R^2 = 90\%$ is the coefficient of determination. It measures the proportion of the total variation in the annual number of tours sold that has been explained by the regression model as a whole. That is, it measures the percentage of total variation in Q that has been accounted for by variation in A, I, P_X and P taken together.

The standard error of the estimate provides information about the level of accuracy one can expect when using the equation for forecasting purposes. The standard error of the estimate corresponds to the standard deviation of a probability distribution and thus can be used to develop a confidence interval for sales predictions.

Letting $\hat{Q}_t$ represent the sales forecast for a given set of values for A, I, P_X and P, there is approximately a 95% probability that actual sales, Q_t, will fall in the range $Q_t = \hat{Q}_t \pm 2.08$ standard errors (where $t^*_{26 - 5 = 21, \alpha = 0.05} = 2.08$), and a 99% probability that $Q_t = \hat{Q}_t \pm 2.831$ standard errors of the estimate (where $t^*_{26 - 5 = 21, \alpha = 0.01} = 2.831$).

For simplicity, these critical t values are often rounded off to $t = 2$ (for 95% confidence), and $t = 3$ (for 99% confidence).

The standard errors of the coefficient estimate provide information about the level of accuracy with which the individual relationships between the independent variables and sales of the tour have been estimated. The standard errors of the coefficients can be used to estimate confidence intervals within which the true parameter relating each independent variable to sales will lie with varying degrees of probability. For example, there is a 95% probability that the true parameter relating price to quantity sold lies in the interval -1.5 (= - 4 + 2.08(1.22)) to -6.5 (= - 4 - 2.08(1.22)) which is the estimated parameter -4 ± 2.08 times the coefficient standard error of 1.22. Thus, the smaller the relative size of a coefficient's standard error, the greater the level of accuracy that can be ascribed to the parameter estimate.

B.   The fact that the coefficient of P_X is positive indicates that there is a substitute relation between tours and product X. As the price of X increases so too does the demand for the tour in question. In order to conclude that product X is in fact a substitute, one must be able to reject $H_0: b_{P_X} < 0$ (one-tail test).

At the 99% confidence level, this hypothesis can be rejected because:

$$t = \frac{b - 0}{\sigma_b} = \frac{3}{0.9} = 3.33 > 2.518 = t^*_{21, \alpha = 0.01}$$

Thus, a substitute relation exists between X and tours.

(*Remember*: the *t* table at the back of the text shows rejection regions for *two*-tail tests. Thus, the $\alpha = 0.1$ column shows critical *t* values for $\alpha = 0.1$ (one-tail) *and* for $\alpha = 0.05$ (two-tail). Here t* = 2.518 because the relevant hypothesis involves a one-tail test and $\alpha = 0.01$ or 99% confidence).

C. To calculate the point price elasticity one must first substitute the values of the independent variables into the demand model to obtain $\hat{Q}$.

$$\hat{Q} = 260 + 2A + 6.4I + 3P_X - 4P$$

$$= 260 + 2(20) + 6.4(62.5) + 3(500) - 4(400)$$

$$= 600$$

Therefore,

$$\varepsilon_P = \partial Q / \partial P \times P/Q$$

$$= -4 \times (\$400/600)$$

$$= -2.67$$

A price reduction would increase total revenue because demand is elastic ($|\varepsilon_P| > 1$).

D. Using the point cross-price elasticity formula:

$$\varepsilon_{PX} = \partial Q_Y / \partial P_X \times P_X / Q_Y$$

$$= 3 \times (\$500/600)$$

$$= 2.5$$

Because $\varepsilon_{PX} = 2.5 > 0$, a substitute good relation exists between X and tours. This is consistent with the individual coefficient analysis of Part B.

E.   The 99% confidence interval for Q is $\hat{Q} \pm 2.831$ times the standard error of the estimate (where $t^*_{26-5=21,\alpha=0.01} = 2.831$). Given the current values for A, I, P_X and P, the 99% confidence interval would be $Q = 600 \pm 2.831(10) = 600 \pm 28$.

P6.6   ***Elasticity Estimation.*** *The Washington Life Insurance Company offers a wide variety of insurance products, including whole-life and term policies. The company has compiled the following data concerning policy sales during recent years:*

Year	Whole-life		Term	
	Price*	Quantity	Price*	Quantity
2001	$2.00	240,000	$1.50	100,000
2002	2.00	200,000	1.45	130,000
2003	1.90	230,000	1.45	150,000
2004	1.80	280,000	1.40	200,000
2005	1.80	238,000	1.33	270,000

*Price is quoted in terms of cost per $1,000 of coverage.

A.   *Calculate the point price elasticity of demand for whole-life insurance?*

B.   *Calculate the point price elasticity of demand for term insurance?*

C.   *Evaluate the percentage change in whole-life demand given a 1% change in the price of term insurance. Is term insurance a substitute for whole-life?*

P6.6   **SOLUTION**

A.   To evaluate the point price elasticity of demand for whole-life insurance, one must only consider years when the price of whole-life changed but the price of term remained constant. Therefore, only the 2002-03 period is relevant.

$$\varepsilon_P \;=\; \partial Q/\partial P \times P/Q$$

$$=\; \frac{230,000 \,-\, 200,000}{\$1.90 \,-\, \$2} \;\times\; \frac{\$2}{200,000}$$

$$=\; -3 \text{ (Elastic)}$$

B. To evaluate the point price elasticity of demand for term insurance, one must only consider years when the price of term changed, but the price of whole-life remained constant. Therefore, only the 2001-02 and 2004-05 periods are relevant.

<u>2001-02</u>

$$\varepsilon_P = \partial Q/\partial P \times P/Q$$

$$= \frac{130,000 - 100,000}{\$1.45 - \$1.50} \times \frac{\$1.50}{100,000}$$

$$= -9$$

<u>2004-2005</u>

$$\varepsilon_P = \partial Q/\partial P \times P/Q$$

$$= \frac{270,000 - 200,000}{\$1.33 - \$1.40} \times \frac{\$1.40}{200,000}$$

$$= -7$$

<u>Average:</u> $\varepsilon_P = (-9 + -7)/2 = -8$ (Highly elastic)

C. To evaluate the relevant cross-price elasticity of demand, it is necessary to consider periods when only the price of term insurance changed.
Thus, only the 2001-02 and 2004-05 periods are relevant.

<u>2001-02</u>

$$\varepsilon_{PX} = \partial Q_Y/\partial P_X \times P/Q$$

$$= \frac{200,000 - 240,000}{\$1.45 - \$1.50} \times \frac{\$1.50}{240,000}$$

$$= 5$$

<u>2004-05</u>

$$\varepsilon_{PX} = \partial Q_Y/\partial P_X \times P/Q$$

$$= \frac{238,000 - 280,000}{\$1.33 - \$1.40} \times \frac{\$1.40}{280,000}$$

$$= 3$$

Average: $\varepsilon_{PX} = (5 + 3)/2 = 4$ (Substitutes)

Yes, term insurance appears to be a substitute for whole-life insurance.

P6.7   ***Standard Error of the Estimate***. *Body Fit, Inc., runs a California-based chain of health clubs featuring aerobic exercise, racket sports, swimming and weight training facilities. An in-house study of monthly sales by three outlets during the past year (a total of 36 observations) revealed the following (standard errors in parentheses):*

$$Q_Y \;=\; 410 - 20P_Y + 12P_X + 8A + 50T - 5W$$
$$\quad\;\; (250)\;(7.5)\;\;(7)\;\;(3.5)\;(10)\;\;(2.8)$$

$$R^2 \;=\; 96\%$$

Standard Error of the Estimate = 10

Here Q_Y = membership sales (in units), P_Y = average membership price (in dollars), P_X = average membership price charged by competitors (in dollars), A = advertising expenditures (in hundreds of dollars), T = time (in months of continuous operation), W = weather (in average monthly temperature).

A.   *What share of overall variation in membership sales is explained by the regression equation? What share is left unexplained?*

B.   *Using a 95% confidence level criterion, which independent factors have an influence on membership sales?*

C.   *During this period, the San Diego outlet's average monthly price was $150, the average competitor's monthly price was $100, advertising was $6,750, the outlet had been in operation for 3 years, and the average temperature was 70°. Assuming this was a typical observation included in the study, derive the relevant demand curve for Body Fit memberships.*

D.   *Assume the model and data given above are relevant for the coming period. Calculate the range within which you would expect to find actual monthly sales revenue with 95% confidence.*

P6.7   **SOLUTION**

   A. $R^2 = 96\%$ means that 96% of the total variation in demand is explained by the regression model.   This implies that 4% of demand variation remains unexplained.

   B.   With a sample size $n = 36$ and a model featuring $k = 6$ coefficients, the relevant number of degrees of freedom is $d.f. = n - k = 30$. Roughly speaking, this means that a coefficient estimate more than twice as large as the coefficient's standard deviation, or a t-statistic of more than two, is necessary before we can conclude that a given independent variable influences Q at the 95% confidence level (assuming a two-tail test).
   More precisely, $t^*_{30,\alpha = 0.05} = 2.042$. Therefore, from the regression equation:

	Variable	Influence
Price:	$t = \dfrac{b_{P_Y}}{\sigma_{P_Y}} = \dfrac{20}{7.5} = 2.67 > t^*_{30,\alpha=0.05}$	Yes.
Competitor Price:	$t = \dfrac{b_{P_X}}{\sigma_{P_X}} = \dfrac{12}{7} = 1.71 \ngtr t^*_{30,\alpha=0.05}$	No.
Advertising:	$t = \dfrac{b_A}{\sigma_A} = \dfrac{8}{3.5} = 2.29 > t^*_{30,\alpha=0.05}$	Yes.
Time:	$t = \dfrac{b_T}{\sigma_T} = \dfrac{50}{10} = 5.00 > t^*_{30,\alpha=0.05}$	Yes.
Weather:	$t = \dfrac{b_W}{\sigma_W} = \dfrac{5}{2.8} = 1.79 \ngtr t^*_{30,\alpha=0.05}$	No.

   C.   The demand curve for Body Fit memberships is given by the expression:

$$Q_Y = 410 - 20P_Y + 12P_X + 8A + 50T - 5W$$

$$= 410 - 20P_Y + 12(100) + 8(67.5) + 50(36) - 5(70)$$

$$= 3,600 - 20P_Y$$

   D.   Given a monthly membership price $P_Y = \$150$, the estimated value for membership demand (in units) is:

$$\hat{Q} = 3,600 - 20(150)$$

$$= 600$$

Therefore, using the standard error of the estimate SEE = 10, the 95% confidence region for membership sales (in units) is:

$$Q_Y = \hat{Q} \pm t_{30,\alpha = 0.05} \times SEE \text{ (with 95\% confidence)}$$

$$= 600 \pm 2.042(10)$$

$$= 600 \pm 20.42, \text{ or } 579.58 \text{ to } 620.42$$

Finally, given a membership price P_Y = $150, the 95% confidence region for annual sales revenue is:

$$579.58 \times \$150 \text{ to } 620.42 \times \$150$$

or

$$\$86{,}937 \text{ to } \$93{,}063$$

P6.8   ***Demand Curve Estimation.*** *Z-Box, Inc. produces and sells computer games. An empirical demand function for the Sims Tycoon, one of the firm's games, has just been estimated over the last 21 quarters using regression analysis. The demand function is:*

$$Q_Y = -800 - 500P_Y + 24A + 15I + 200P_X$$
$$\quad (600) \quad (100) \quad (12) \quad (30) \quad (80)$$

$$R^2 = 91\%$$

Standard Error of the Estimate = 50

Here Q_Y is quantity (measured in units) of Product Y demanded in the current period, A is hundreds of dollars of advertising ($00), I is thousands of dollars of disposable income per capita ($000), and P_X is the price ($) of another toy manufactured by ABC. The terms in parentheses are the standard errors of the coefficients.

A.   *How would you characterize the ability of this empirical demand function to explain demand for Product Y?*

B.   *Currently, P_Y = $8, advertising is $20,000, disposable income per capita is $40,000 and P_X = $7. What are expected sales of Y in this period, and what* *range of sales would you specify for the current period if you wanted to establish a 99% confidence interval?*

C. *What is the demand curve currently facing Z-Box for Product Y? (Note: Be careful to properly account for the units in which advertising and income appear in the estimated demand function.)*

D. *What is the point price elasticity of demand for Y at the current price?*

E. *Given the current price elasticity of demand, would a price reduction increase Z-Box profits? Explain.*

F. *What demand curve would Z-Box face for Product Y if it raised advertising expenditures to $30,000?*

P6.8 **SOLUTION**

A. The regression equation appears to explain the relation between demand for the product and the independent variables quite well. The coefficient of determination $R^2 = 91\%$ indicating that 91% of the variation in sales has been explained by the variation in the independent variables.

B. Note that:

$$\hat{Q}_Y = -800 - 500P_Y + 24A + 15I + 200P_X$$

$$= -800 - 500(8) + 24(200) + 15(40) + 200(7)$$

$$= 2,000 \text{ units}$$

The 99% confidence interval for Q is $\hat{Q} \pm 2.921$ times the standard error of the estimate (where $t^*_{21 - 5 = 16, \alpha = 0.01} = 2.921$). Given the current values for P_Y, A, I, and P_X, the 99% confidence interval is:

$$Q = \hat{Q} \pm 2.921 \times \text{SEE}$$

$$= 2,000 \pm 2.921(50)$$

$$= 2,000 \pm 146 \text{ units}$$

C. The relevant demand curve is found by noting:

$$Q_Y = -800 - 500P_Y + 24A + 15I + 200P_X$$

$$= -800 - 500P_Y + 24(200) + 15(40) + 200(7)$$

$$= 6,000 - 500P_Y$$

$$P_Y = 12 - 0.002Q_Y$$

D. Using the point price elasticity formula, it is obvious that:

$$\varepsilon_{P_Y} = \partial Q_Y/\partial P_Y \times P_Y/Q_Y$$

$$= -500 \times (8/2,000)$$

$$= -2$$

E. With $|\varepsilon_P| > 1$, the relative change in quantity is greater than that of price so a price reduction will lead to an increase in total revenue. However, to determine whether such a price reduction is appropriate, one would need information concerning the marginal cost of increased output. In other words, the marginal revenue of added sales is positive, but one can't know whether $MR > MC$. Thus, although revenue would be increased with a price reduction, profits might be reduced. Without further information, no recommendation concerning the profit implications of a price reduction can be made.

F. With an increase in advertising of \$15,000, the demand curve for product Y becomes:

$$Q_Y = -800 - 500P_Y + 24A + 15I + 200P_X$$

$$= -800 - 500P_Y + 24(300) + 15(40) + 200(7)$$

$$= 8,400 - 500P_Y$$

or

$$P_Y = \$16.8 - \$0.002Q_Y$$

P6.9 ***z-Statistics***. *Martin's Footware, Inc., of Boston, Massachusetts has retained you to aid the firm in an evaluation of its marketing strategy. Martin's "Happy Feet" running shoes are marketed through local retail outlets in the eastern United States. A move* to extend Martin's market to midwestern and western states is currently being contemplated.

A marketing research group conducted an empirical analysis of demand for Martin's "Happy Feet" during 2005 in thirty-six regional markets and found the following (standard errors in parentheses):

$$Q = 982 - 10P + 12.5I + 5W - 0.5CA + 5A$$
$$(240)\ (1.3)\quad (8.6)\quad (2.8)\quad (0.4)\quad (2.5)$$

$$R^2 = 85\%$$

Standard error of the estimate = 200

$cov(I,W) = 3.5,\ cov(I,CA) = 8.6,\ cov(I,A) = 2.8$

where Q = quantity sold (in pairs of shoes), P = wholesale price (in dollars), I = disposable income per capita (in thousands of dollars), W = weather measured by average temperature (in degrees), CA = competitor advertising (in thousands of dollars), A = Martin's "own" advertising (in thousands of dollars).

A. Fully evaluate and interpret the empirical results reported above on an overall basis. Include in your analysis a discussion of:

    (i) R^2

    (ii) $\bar{R}^2$

    (iii)   F statistic

    (iv)   Standard error of the estimate

B. Will a recession hurt sales?

C. Is demand more dependent on local income than on weather conditions?

D. Champaign-Urbana, Illinois is a potential Midwestern market with economic characteristics typical of those eastern markets included in the empirical analysis. In Champaign-Urbana, expected levels are: disposable income per household of $60,000, average temperature of 54°, competitor advertising of $64,000, and Martin's advertising of $6,000. Given these data,

    (i)   Derive the demand curve for the Champaign-Urbana market.

       (ii)   *Calculate the probability of Martin's generating at least $35,525 in revenues in the Champaign-Urbana market given a wholesale price of $25 per pair.*

P6.9   **SOLUTION**

A.   (i)   Coefficient of determination = R^2 = 85% implying that 85% of demand variation is explained by the regression model.

       (ii)   Corrected coefficient of determination = $\overline{R}^2$ = $R^2 - (k-1/n-k)(1-R^2)$ = $0.85 - (5/30)(1 - 0.85) = 0.825$ implying that 82.5% of demand variation is explained by the regression model when both coefficient number, k, and sample size, N, are controlled for.

       (iii) F statistic = $F = (n-k/k-1)(R^2/1-R^2) = (30/5)\,(0.85/0.15) = 34 > F^{*}_{5,30,\alpha}$ $_{=0.01} = 3.70$ implying that we can reject null hypothesis $H_0{:}b_1 = b_2 = ... = b_5 = 0$ and conclude with 99% confidence that the independent variables as a group explain a significant share of demand variation.

       (iv)   Standard error of the estimate = SEE = 200 implying that:

$$Q = \hat{Q} \pm 2.042 \times 200 \text{ with 95\% confidence.}$$

$$Q = \hat{Q} \pm 2.750 \times 200 \text{ with 99\% confidence.}$$

(Note: Here d.f. = $n - k = 36 - 6 = 30$).

B.   To learn whether a recession will hurt sales, one must ask is $b_1 > 0$? At first this may seem counter intuitive, but we must remember that a recession is associated with a fall in income, just as "hurting" sales is associated with a fall in sales. The only way falling income could cause sales to fall is if $b_1 > 0$. If $b_1 < 0$, then evidence exists that a fall in income would increase sales. For testing purposes, the null hypothesis which one seeks to reject is the converse of the initial question:

$$H_0{:}b_1 < 0 \quad \text{(One-tail test)}$$

where

$$t = \frac{b_1}{\sigma_{b_1}} = \frac{12.5}{8.6} = 1.453 > 1.31 = t^{*}_{30,\alpha=0.1}$$

which means that we can reject $H_0:b_I < 0$ with 90% confidence and conclude that yes, a recession will hurt sales.

C. For demand to be more dependent upon income than upon weather conditions the coefficient for I would have to be larger than the coefficient for W. Therefore, the relevant question is $|b_I| > |b_W|$ or is $|b_I| - |b_W| > 0$? If $|b_I| > |b_W|$, then a change in local income will have a bigger affect on demand than will a change in weather conditions. Absolute values are considered in the questions above because either positive or negative impacts on demand are possible. For testing purposes, the null hypothesis which one seeks to reject is the converse of the above question:

$$H_0:|b_I| < |b_W| \text{ or } H_0:|b_I| - |b_W| < 0 \text{ (One-tail test)}$$

where,

$$t = \frac{|b_I| - |b_W|}{\sigma|b_i| - |b_W|} = \frac{12.5 - 5}{\sqrt{8.6^2 + 2.8^2 - 2(3.5)}}$$

$$= \frac{7.5}{\sqrt{74.8}} = 0.867 \not> 1.13 = t^*_{30,a=0.10}$$

which means that we cannot reject $H_0:|b_I| < |b_W|$ nor $H_0:|b_I| - |b_W| < 0$ with even 90% confidence and conclude that no, there is no evidence that demand is more sensitive to changes in income than to changes in weather conditions.

D. (i) The demand curve for the Champaign-Urbana market is found simply by substituting relevant independent variable values into the demand function.

$$Q = 982 - 10P + 12.5I + 5W - 0.5CA + 5A$$

$$= 982 - 10P + 12.5(60) + 5(54) - 0.5(64) + 5(6)$$

$$= 2,000 - 10P$$

(ii) At a price of \$25, the estimated value of Q is:

$$\hat{Q} = 2,000 - 10P$$

$$= 2,000 - 10(25)$$

$$= 1,750$$

and the estimated value of total revenues is:

$$T\hat{R} = P\hat{Q}$$

$$= \$25(1,750)$$

$$= \$43,750$$

To generate revenues of $35,525, Martin's would have to sell $Q = TR/P = 35,525/25 = 1,421$ pairs of shoes in the Champaign-Urbana market.

Because expected sales are $\hat{Q} = 1,750$, there is a greater than 50/50 chance of reaching the target sales level of $Q = 1,421$. To learn the exact probability, note that $Q = 1,421$ is $\hat{Q} = 1,750$ minus 1.645 standard deviations because:

$$z = \frac{x - \hat{Q}}{S.E.E.}$$

$$= \frac{1,421 - 1,750}{200}$$

$$= -1.645$$

where z is the relative distance from $\hat{Q}$ (or standard normal), x is the point of interest, $\hat{Q}$ is the expected value or mean, SEE is the standard error of the estimate or standard deviation.

With $z = -1.645$, only 0.05 or 5% of the total area under the normal curve will lie to the left of or below $Q = 1,421$. Thus, there is a 95% chance that actual Q in Champaign-Urbana will meet or exceed $Q = 1,421$, and generate at least $35,525 in revenues.

P6.10   ***Multiplicative Model Estimation***. *A study of the demand for imported motorcycles recently appeared in an industry newsletter. According to the study, demand for motorcycle imports is described by the function:*

$$Q_Y = 1.5P_Y^{-4}P_X^{3}A_Y^{2}A_X^{2}P^{3}$$

$$R^2 = 95\%$$

Standard error of the estimate = 30

Here Q_Y is the quantity of motorcycles imported (000), P_Y is average motorcycle price ($), P_X is the average price of imported compact cars, A_Y is motorcycle industry advertising ($000,000), A_X is industry advertising of compact cars ($000,000), and I is average disposable family income ($000). The standard errors of the exponents in the multiplicative demand function above are:

$$b_{P_Y} = 1, \ b_{P_X} = 1.5, \ b_{A_Y} = 0.8, \ b_{A_X} = 1.5, \ b_I = 1.2$$

And finally, this demand function was estimated using two years of monthly data (24 observations).

A.   Is the demand for imported motorcycles elastic with respect to price?

B.   Are imported motorcycles a normal good?

C.   Are motorcycles and compact cars substitutes?

D.   Given your answer to part A, can you explain why the coefficients for both A_Y and A_X are positive?

P6.10   **SOLUTION**

A.   The exponents of multiplicative demand functions are elasticity estimates. Therefore, motorcycle demand is elastic with respect to price provided:

$|b_{P_Y}| > 1$ or $|b_{P_Y}| - 1 > 0$. For testing purposes, the null hypothesis to reject is: $H_0 : |b_{P_Y}| < 1$ or $|b_{P_Y}| - 1 < 0$ (One-tail test)

where:

$$t = \frac{|b_{P_Y}| - 1}{\sigma|b_{P_Y}|} = \frac{4 - 1}{1} = 3 > 2.552 = t^*_{18, \alpha = 0.01}$$

meaning one can reject H_O with 99% confidence and conclude that motorcycle demand is elastic with respect to price.

B.   Because exponents in multiplicative models are elasticity estimates, motorcycles will be a normal good provided $b_I > 0$. For testing purposes, the null hypothesis to reject is:

$$H_O: \ b_I < 0 \qquad \text{(One-tail test)}$$

where

$$t = \frac{|b_I|}{\sigma|b_{P_I}|} = \frac{3}{1.2} = 2.5 > 1.734 = t^*_{18,\alpha=0.05}$$

meaning one can reject H_O with 95% confidence and conclude motorcycles are a normal good.

C.   Because exponents here are elasticity estimates, motorcycles and compact cars will be substitutes provided $b_{P_X} > 0$, and complements if $b_{P_X} < 0$. To test the substitute good hypothesis, the hypothesis to reject is:

$$H_0: b_{P_X} < 0 \quad \text{(One-tail test)}$$

where

$$t = \frac{b_{P_X}}{\sigma b_{P_X}} = \frac{3}{1.5} = 2 > 1.33 = t^*_{18,\alpha=0.1}$$

meaning one can reject H_0 with 90% confidence, and conclude motorcycles and compact cars are substitutes.

D.   Recall that an increase in price by a competitor leads to an increase in units sold, and that a decrease in price by a competitor leads to a decrease in units sold. From the perspective of the firm's demand curve, units sold and the price moves of competitors are inversely related. Similarly, in most instances an increase in "own advertising" leads to an increase in sales revenue and profits, whereas an increase in competitor advertising leads to a decrease in sales revenue and profits. In fact, it is common to consider such negative influences as *prima facie* evidence that another firm is in fact a competitor.

Both "own" and compact car advertising appear to increase sales. Although relatively uncommon, this is not a rare occurrence. Advertising of substitutes can sometimes raise sales for competitor products due to beneficial spillover effects following increased customer awareness regarding, for example, the quality of foreign-produced goods.

Chapter 7

FORECASTING

Success in business depends on management's ability to develop and execute long-range strategic plans that take advantage of the organization's comparative strengths. This planning process involves a number of important related activities. Management must decide the range of products that the firm will offer customers, and then forecast the level of demand under assorted conditions. Typically, the effects of pricing policy, promotional activity, competition, and general economic conditions must all be considered. In addition to compiling a range of demand forecasts, management must also forecast costs of producing different levels of output in light of changing technology, wage rates, and raw materials prices. After all relevant data have been collected and analyzed, managers must pick and choose from among a range of reasonable decision scenarios to select the value-maximizing operating plan.

If forecasts about demand, the cost of inputs, technology, and other planning considerations are seriously in error, operating plans will be of little practical value. When forecast errors have the potential to adversely affect the realization of planning objectives, the control phase of the planning process must allow for necessary changes and modifications. At the same time, the planning and control process must be sufficiently structured to facilitate the realization of firm objectives. Managerial economics has developed a number of forecasting techniques that have proven successful in a variety of real-world applications. The purpose of this chapter is to help students understand how managers can make better forecasts.

CHAPTER OUTLINE

I.   **FORECASTING APPLICATIONS**

      A.   **Macroeconomic Applications:** Macroeconomic forecasting involves predicting aggregate measures of economic activity at the international, national, regional, or state level.

              1.   In the case of macroeconomic forecasting, uncontrollable factors loom large in influence.

      B.   **Microeconomic Applications:** Microeconomic forecasting involves the prediction of desegregate or partial economic data at the industry, firm, plant, or product level.

              1.   Trained and experienced analysts often find it easier to accurately forecast microeconomic trends, like the demand for new cars, than macroeconomic trends in the overall economy, such as GDP growth.

2.   Microeconomic forecasts abstract from the profusion of variables and variable interrelationships that determine the macroeconomy.

3.   When the influence of uncontrollable factors is significant, as in macroeconomic forecasting, it is prudent to allow for large forecast error.

C.   **Forecast Techniques:** Multiple forecasting tools are available; their strengths and weaknesses must be understood if accurate forecasts are to be obtained. Common methods of forecasting include:

1.   Qualitative analyses,

2.   Trend analysis and projection,

3.   Exponential smoothing,

4.   Econometric methods.

II.   **QUALITATIVE ANALYSES**

A.   **Expert Opinion:** When quantitative information is not available, qualitative analysis must be relied upon to prepare required forecasts. Prevalent qualitative forecast methods include:

1.   Personal insight from a knowledgeable individual.

2.   Panel consensus from a group of informed individuals.

3.   The Delphi method in which an independent expert tries to elicit the unspoken consensus from a panel of informed individuals.

B.   **Survey Techniques:** Accurate forecasting using survey techniques requires the careful selection of a sample that is fully representative of the entire population, as well as a skillful interpretation of sample results.

1.   Samples may be drawn in a random fashion, or stratified in an explicit attempt to match overall population characteristics.

2.   Advantages: Surveys based on mailed questionnaires or individual interviews can be a low cost way of adding valuable background and depth to the sometimes superficial data available for statistical analyses.

3. Limitations: Unlike "hard" market transactions data, survey data can be "soft" if consumers are unwilling or unable to reveal true preferences prior to actual purchase decisions.

III. TREND ANALYSIS AND PROJECTION

A. **Trends in Economic Data:** Trend projection assumes that economic relations will be maintained subject to historical patterns of variability. There are a number of causes of historical variability.

1. Secular trends reflect long-run growth or decline.

2. Cyclical fluctuations show rhythmic variations from boom to recession.

3. Seasonal variations are caused by weather or custom.

4. Irregular or random influences often result in unpredictable variation.

B. **Linear Trend Analysis:** Linear trend analysis assumes a constant *unit* change in an important economic variable over time.

1. Accurate forecasts can sometimes be obtained from linear trend analysis because some economic variables display roughly constant change per period.

2. Exogenous shocks to the economic system (such as oil embargoes) have unanticipated consequences and reduce the accuracy of trend forecasts.

C. **Growth Trend Analysis:** Growth trend analysis assumes constant *percentage* change in an important economic variable over time.

1. Growth trend analysis often gives a realistic view of economic growth patterns.

D. **Linear and Growth Trend Comparison:** Both methods offer useful insight concerning the economic growth.

1. Both methods suffer from a failure to incorporate the effects of exogenous shocks.

IV. BUSINESS CYCLE

A. **What is the Business Cycle?:** The business cycle is a rhythmic pattern of contraction and expansion in the overall economy.

    1. Many important economic time series are also subject to additional variation caused by weather and custom.

B. **Economic Indicators:** Series of data that successfully describe the pattern of projected, current, or past economic activity are called economic indicators.

    1. A composite index is a weighted average of leading, coincident, or lagging economic indicators.

C. **Economic Recessions:** An economic recession is a significant decline in activity spread across the economy that lasts more than a few months.

    1. In the United States, economic recessions are defined by the National Bureau of Economic Research (NBER), a private nonprofit research organization.

        a. Recessions are rare and brief, usually less than a year in duration.

    2. Economic expansion is a period of rising economic activity.

        a. Expansion is the typical state of the U.S. economy. Expansions typically last roughly four years.

D. **Sources of Forecast Information:** Forecasts of economic trends are regularly reported by the U.S. government, industry trade groups, and the business press.

    1. The world-wide web features a plethora of relevant sites. For example, check out the *USA Today* money section at http://www.usatoday.com

V. **EXPONENTIAL SMOOTHING**

A. **Exponential Smoothing Concept:** Exponential smoothing is a method for forecasting time series of data.

    1. This technique identifies historical trends in the data series one wishes to forecast, and then extrapolates these patterns forward into the forecast period.

2. Its accuracy depends on the degree to which established patterns of change are operative and consistent over time.

B. One-Parameter (Simple) Exponential Smoothing: In one-parameter (simple) exponential smoothing, the sole regular component is the level of the forecast data series.

1. It is implicitly assumed that the data consist of irregular fluctuations around a constant or very slowly changing level.

2. Simple exponential smoothing is appropriate for forecasting sales in mature markets with stable activity.

3. Simple exponential smoothing is not appropriate for forecasting data that exhibit trends.

C. Two-Parameter (Holt) Exponential Smoothing: In two-parameter (Holt) exponential smoothing, the data are assumed to fluctuate around a level that is changing with some constant or slowly drifting linear trend.

1. Two-parameter exponential smoothing is appropriate for forecasting sales in established markets with stable growth.

2. It is inappropriate in either stable or rapidly growing markets.

D. Three-Parameter (Winters) Exponential Smoothing: The three-parameter (Winters) exponential smoothing method extends the two-parameter technique by including a smoothed multiplicative index to account for seasonal behavior.

1. Because much economic data involves both growth trend and seasonal considerations, three-parameter exponential smoothing is one of the most commonly used forecasting methods employed in business today.

2. Three-parameter exponential smoothing is best suited for forecasting problems that involve rapid and/or changing rates of growth combined with seasonal influences.

3. Three-parameter exponential smoothing is suitable for forecasting sales in both rapidly growing markets and in rapidly decaying markets with seasonal influences.

E.   Practical Use of Exponential Smoothing: In practical application various exponential smoothing methods are typically used in tandem with other forecast techniques.

VI.   ECONOMETRIC FORECASTING

A.   Advantages of Econometric Methods: Econometric forecasting relies on theoretically derived economic relations as the basis for statistical forecasts.

1.   Econometric methods benefit from insights provided by economic theory.

2.   Forecast error information can also be used to improve subsequent forecasts.

B.   Single Equation Models: Single equation econometric models offer a simple but powerful technique for regression-based forecasts.

1.   Forecasting with a single-equation model consists of evaluating the equation with specific values for the independent variables.

C.   Multiple Equation Systems: Multiple equation systems offer a means for considering interrelated influences among a variety of dependent *Y*-variables and independent *X*-variables.

1.   Although forecasting problems can often be analyzed with a single-equation model, complex relations among economic variables sometimes require use of multiple-equation systems.

   a.   Variables whose values are determined within such a model are *endogenous*, meaning originating from within.

   b.   Variables determined outside, or external to, the system are referred to as *exogenous*.

2.   Identities express relations that are true by definition (e.g., $\pi = TR - TC$).

3.   Behavioral equations may indicate how individuals and institutions are expected to react to various stimuli (e.g., $Q = a - bP$).

VII.   JUDGING FORECAST RELIABILITY

A. **Tests of Predictive Capability:** To test predictive capability, a model generated from one set of data is used to predict a second set of data.

1. Data used to generate a forecast model are called the test group.

2. Data used to examine a forecast model are called the forecast group.

B. **Correlation Analysis:** The simple correlation between actual and forecast values provides an attractive index of forecast accuracy:

$$r = \frac{\sigma_{fx}}{\sigma_f \sigma_x},$$

where *r* is the correlation coefficient, σ_{fx} is the covariance between the forecast and actual series, and σ_f and σ_x are the standard deviations of the forecast and actual series, respectively.

1. Generally speaking, when $r \geq 0.95$ or 0.99 (95 or 99%), a high level of forecast accuracy has been achieved in terms of predicting variation in an important series.

C. **Sample Mean Forecast Error Analysis:** This index of forecast reliability, denoted by U, provides valuable insight regarding the absolute level of forecast accuracy:

$$U = \sqrt{\frac{1}{n}\sum_{i=1}^{n}(f_i - x_i)^2},$$

where *n* is the number of sample observations, f_i is a forecast value, and x_i is the corresponding actual value.

1. Generally speaking, when the mean or average forecast error is a small fraction, 0.05 or 0.01 (5 or 1%), of actual values, a high level of absolute forecast accuracy has been achieved.

VIII. **CHOOSING THE BEST FORECAST TECHNIQUE**

A. **Data Requirements:** Complex forecasting methods require extensive data.

1. Limited data mandates use of simple techniques.

B.   **Time Horizon Considerations:**   Very long-term forecasts often require qualitative insight.

   1.   Quantitative methods work best for monthly or annual forecast problems.

C.   **Role of Judgment:** Don't dismiss the importance of informed judgment.

   1.   Experienced professionals often achieve enviable results with simple forecast techniques.

   2.   The objective of economic forecasting is to improve on the subjective judgments made by managers.

   3.   All managers forecast; the goal is to make better forecasts.

IX.   **SUMMARY**

PROBLEMS & SOLUTIONS

P7.1   **Sales Trend Analysis.** *The following figures show the trend in annual sales for Josh Bartlet's Steak House over the 1995-2005 period.*

Year	Sales
1995	$284,000
1996	266,000
1997	287,000
1998	315,000
1999	353,000
2000	384,000
2001	427,000
2002	462,000
2003	520,000
2004	575,000
2005	568,000

A.   *Calculate the rate of growth in sales for 1995-2005 using the constant rate of change model with annual compounding. (Note: $t = 0$ in 1995).*

B.   *Forecast Sales for 2010 and 2015.*

P7.1   **SOLUTION**

A.

$$S_t = S_0(1 + g)^t$$

$$\$568,000 = \$284,000(1 + g)^{10}$$

$$568,000/284,000 = (1 + g)^{10}$$

$$2 = (1 + g)^{10}$$

$$\ln 2 = 10 \times \ln(1 + g)$$

$$0.693/10 = \ln(1 + g)$$

$$e^{0.0693} = 1 + g$$

$$g = 0.0718 \text{ or } 7.18\%$$

B.   5-year Forecast

$$S_t = S_0(1 + g)^t$$

$$= \$284,000(1 + 0.0718)^{15}$$

$$= \$284,000(2.829)$$

$$= \$803,436$$

10-year Forecast

$$S_t = S_0(1 + g)^t$$

$$= \$284,000(1 + 0.0718)^{20}$$

$$= \$284,000(4.002)$$

$$= \$1,136,568$$

P7.2   ***Growth Rate Estimation.*** *Durable Products, Inc., is a leading manufacturer and distributor of polyethylene liners for pickup truck beds. Annual sales revenue has grown rapidly from \$30 million to \$60 million during the past five-year period.*

A.   *Calculate the five-year growth rate in sales using the constant rate of change model with annual compounding.*

B.   *Calculate the five-year growth rate in sales using the constant rate of change model with continuous compounding.*

C.   *Compare your answers to parts A and B, and discuss any differences.*

P7.2   **SOLUTION**

A. $$S_t = S_0(1 + g)^t$$

$$\$60 = \$30(1 + g)^5$$

$$2 = (1 + g)^5$$

$$\ln(2) = 5 \times \ln(1 + g)$$

$$0.693/5 = \ln(1 + g)$$

$$e^{0.139} = 1 + g$$

$$1.149 - 1 = g$$

$$g = 0.149 \text{ or } 14.9\%$$

B. $$S_t = S_0 e^{gt}$$

$$\$60 = \$30 e^{5g}$$

$$2 = e^{5g}$$

$$\ln(2) = 5g$$

$$g = 0.693/5$$

$$= 0.139 \text{ or } 13.9\%$$

C. If annual sales revenue doubles from \$30 million to \$60 million over a five-year period, a 14.9% rate of sales growth is indicated when annual compounding is assumed. With continuous compounding, a 13.9% rate of growth leads to a doubling in sales over a five-year period. The difference, of course, is the amount of "interest-on-interest." Either method can be employed to measure the rate of growth, the analyst must simply be sure to make growth comparisons using a consistent basis.

P7.3   ***Growth Rate Analysis***. *The Coat Factory Warehouse, Inc., is a leading retailer of off-price women's clothing, predominately outer wear. Ross Geller, general sales manager for the company, is concerned about the company's erratic revenue pattern during recent years.*

   A.   *Complete the following table showing annual sales data for the Coat Factory during the 2000-05 period.*

Year (1)	Sales ($ millions) (2)	Current Sales/Previous Period Sales (3)	Growth Rate (4)=[(3)-1]×100
2000	$50	--	--
2001	40		
2002	80		
2003	100		
2004	100		
2005	50		

B.   *Calculate the geometric average annual rate of growth for the five-year 2000-05 period. (Hint: Calculate this growth rate using sales from 2000 and 2005.)*

C.   *Calculate the arithmetic average annual rate of growth for the five-year 2000-05 period. (Hint: This is the average of column (4) figures.)*

D.   *Discuss any differences in your answers to parts B and C.*

P7.3   **SOLUTION**

A.

Year (1)	Sales ($ millions) (2)	Current Sales/Previous Period Sales (3)	Growth Rate (4)=[(3)-1]×100
2000	$50	--	--
2001	40	0.80	-20%
2002	80	2.00	100
2003	100	1.25	25
2004	100	1.00	0
2005	50	0.50	-50

B.   From column (3) of part A, the geometric average rate of return is calculated as:

$$\bar{g} = \left[\prod_{t=1}^{n} (1 + g_t) \right]^{\frac{1}{n}} - 1$$

$$= [(0.80)(2.00)(1.25)(1.00)(0.50)]^{1/5} - 1$$

$$= 1^{1/5} - 1$$

$$= 0 \text{ or } 0\% \text{ (No growth)}$$

Alternatively, the geometric average rate of return is:

$$S_t = S_0(1 + g)^t$$

$$\$50,000,000 = \$50,000,000(1 + g)^5$$

$$1 = (1 + g)^5$$

$$g = 0 \text{ or } 0\% \text{ (No growth)}$$

C. From column (4) of part A, the arithmetic average rate of return is calculated as:

$$\bar{g} = \frac{1}{n}\sum_{t=1}^{n} g_t$$

$$= \frac{1}{5}(-20 + 100 + 25 + 0 - 50)$$

$$= 11\%$$

D. The zero geometric average rate of growth is consistent with the zero growth in sales observed for the Coat Factory over the 2000-05 period. The arithmetic average rate of return of 11% is greater than the geometric (true) mean. This is always the case, and results from the changing base used from one period to another. Note that when sales increase from $50,000,000 to $100,000,000 (a 100% gain), but then fall back to $50,000,000 (a 50% loss), the arithmetic average growth is 25% (= (100% - 50%)/2) despite the fact that no net growth has occurred. As a result, when compound growth rates are considered, managers rely on the geometric average rather than the arithmetic average rate of return.

P7.4   ***Cost Forecasting***. *Dr. Linda Abbott is a quality-control supervisor for Rocket Merchandise, Inc. Abbott is concerned about unit cost increases for imported components. Costs for components imported from Germany have increased from $10* to $12.21 per unit over the last two years. Abbott thinks that buying from domestic suppliers at a cost of $16.49 per unit may soon be desirable.

A.   Calculate the company's unit cost growth rate during the past two years using the constant rate of change model with continuous compounding.

B.   Forecast when costs for imported units are expected to equal $16.49, the domestic supplier cost.

P7.4   **SOLUTION**

A. $C_t = C_0 e^{gt}$

$$\$12.21 = \$10 e^{2g}$$

$$1.221 = e^{2g}$$

$$\ln(1.221) = 2g$$

$$g = 0.1997/2$$

$$= 0.1 \text{ or } 10\%$$

B.   Domestic Cost $= C_0 e^{gt} =$ Forecast Cost

$$\$16.49 = \$12.21 e^{(0.1)t}$$

$$1.35 = e^{(0.1)t}$$

$$\ln(1.35) = 0.1t$$

$$t = 0.3/0.1$$

$$= 3 \text{ years}$$

P7.5   **Unit Sales Forecast Modeling**. The change in the quantity of product A demanded in any given year is inversely proportional to the change in sales of product B in the previous year. That is, if sales of B rose by X% last year, sales of A can be expected to fall by X% this year.

A. Write the equation for next year's sales of A, using the symbols A = sales of product A, B = sales of product B, and t = time. Assume that there will be no shortages of either product.

B. Last year, 500 units of A and 400 units of B were sold. Two years ago, 250 units of product B were sold. What would you predict the sales of A to be this year?

P7.5 **SOLUTION**

A.
$$A_t = A_{t-1} + \Delta A_{t-1}$$

$$A_t = A_{t-1} - \left(\frac{B_{t-1}}{B_{t-2}} - 1 \right) A_{t-1}$$

B. For A_t, forecast sales are:

$$A_t = A_{t-1} - \left(\frac{B_{t-1}}{B_{t-2}} - 1 \right) A_{t-1}$$

$$= 500 - \left(\frac{400}{250} - 1 \right) 500$$

$$= 500 - 300$$

$$= 200$$

P7.6 **Unit Sales Forecast Modeling.** *The quantity demanded of product A in any given week is inversely proportional to the sales of product B in the previous week. That is, if sales of B rose by X% last week, sales of A can be expected to fall by X% this week.*

A. Write the equation for next week's sales of A, using the symbols A = sales of product A, B = sales of product B, and t = time. Assume there will be no shortages of either product.

B. Two weeks ago, 200 units of product A and 150 units of product B were sold. Last week, 160 units of A and 180 units of B were sold. What would you predict sales of A to be this week?

C. What is the significance of the error term? What property must the error term have to allow use of regression results in forecasting?

P7.6   **SOLUTION**

    A.   An equation for next week's sales of A is:

$$A_t = A_{t-1} + \Delta A_{t-1}$$

$$= A_{t-1} - \left(\frac{B_{t-1}}{B_{t-2}} - 1 \right) A_{t-1}$$

    B. A_t is forecast as follows:

$$A_t = A_{t-1} - \left(\frac{B_{t-1}}{B_{t-2}} - 1 \right) A_{t-1}$$

$$= 160 - \left(\frac{180}{150} - 1 \right) 160$$

$$= 128 \text{ units}$$

    C.   The error term represents the "margin of error" in forecasting. For forecasting to be viable, the average value of the error term must be zero or $E(u) = 0$.

P7.7   ***Sales Forecasting.*** *Jing-Mei Chen, manager of the Beijing Garden Restaurant, knows that sales of Egg Rolls appetizers average 40 orders per day. Recently, however, sales declined to 20 orders per day. During this period, Beijing was running a special that reduced the price on Crab Rangoons appetizers, a competing product, from $5 to $4.*

    A.   *What is the arc cross-price elasticity between Egg Rolls and Crab Rangoons?*

    B.   *What level of Egg Rolls sales would you forecast if the regular price on Crab Rangoons were raised from $5 to $6?*

P7.7   **SOLUTION**

    A. $E_{PX} = \dfrac{\Delta Q}{\Delta P_X} \times \dfrac{P_{X2} + P_{X1}}{Q_2 + Q_1} = \dfrac{(20 - 40)}{(\$4 - \$5)} \times \dfrac{(\$4 + \$5)}{(20 + 40)} = 3$

    B. $E_{PX} = \dfrac{\Delta Q}{\Delta P_X} \times \dfrac{P_{X2} + P_{X1}}{Q_2 + Q_1}$

$$3 = \frac{Q_2 - 40}{(\$6 - \$5)} \times \frac{(\$6 + \$5)}{(Q_2 + 40)}$$

$$3(Q_2 + 40) = 11(Q_2 - 40)$$

$$3Q_2 + 120 = 11Q_2 - 440$$

$$8Q_2 = 560$$

$$Q_2 = 70 \text{ units}$$

(*Note*: The arc cross-price elasticity formula is used in this problem given the large percentage changes in price being considered).

P7.8 **Sales Forecast Modeling.** *Gil Grissom, president of CSI, Inc., in Las Vegas, Nevada, believes that sales in the coming year are closely related to disposable income.*

A. *Write an equation for next year's sales, using the symbols S = sales, Y = income, t = time, a_0 = constant term, a_1 = regression slope coefficient, and u = random disturbance term.*

B. *Now assume that sales in the coming year increase by the same percentage as income increased during the past year. Write an equation for predicting next year's sales.*

C. *This year, sales totaled $1.4 million, while income per capita in Las Vegas increased from $35,000 to $36,050. Forecast next year's sales using your forecast equation from part B.*

P7.8 **SOLUTION**

A. A forecast equation for next year's sales is:

$$S_{t+1} = a_0 + a_1 Y_t$$

B. A forecast equation relating percent changes in sales and income is:

$$S_{t+1} = S_t + \Delta S$$

$$= S_t + \left(\frac{Y_t}{Y_{t-1}} - 1 \right) S_t$$

$$= \left(\frac{Y_t}{Y_{t-1}} \right) S_t$$

C.   Next year's sales are:

$$S_{t+1} = (\$36{,}050/\$35{,}000)\$1{,}400{,}000$$

$$= \$1{,}442{,}000$$

P7.8   ***Sales Forecast Modeling.*** *Dr. Kerry Weaver, sole proprietor of the Westwood Physical Therapy Center, would like to generate a sales forecast. Based on the assumption that next-period sales are a function of current-period local disposable income, own advertising, and advertising by a competing hospital:*

A.   *Specify a general demand equation, assuming that sales rise with income and own advertising but fall with competitor advertising.*

B.   *Write an equation for predicting sales if you assume that the percentage growth (or decline) in sales is twice as large as the sum of the current period's percentage changes in local disposable income and own advertising, minus one-half of the current period's percentage change in competitor advertising.*

C.   *Forecast sales if current period sales total $900,000, average disposable income per household is $82,800, own advertising is $33,000, and competitor advertising is $63,000. Previous period levels were $80,000 for disposable income, $30,000 for own advertising, and $60,000 for competitor advertising.*

P7.8   **SOLUTION**

A.   A general demand equation can be written:

$$S_{t+1} = b_0 + b_1 Y_t + b_2 A_t + b_3 A_{Xt}$$

B. $S_{t+1} = S_t + \Delta S$

$$= S_t + 2 \left(\frac{Y_t}{Y_{t-1}} - 1 \right) S_t + 2 \left(\frac{A_t}{A_{t-1}} - 1 \right) S_t$$

$$- \frac{1}{2} \left(\frac{A_{Xt}}{A_{Xt-1}} - 1 \right) S_t$$

$$= S_t + 2S_t\left(\frac{Y_t}{Y_{t-1}}\right) - 2S_t + 2S_t\left(\frac{A_t}{A_{t-1}}\right) - 2S_t$$

$$- \frac{1}{2}S_t\left(\frac{A_{Xt}}{A_{Xt-1}}\right) + \frac{1}{2}S_t$$

$$= 2S_t\left(\frac{Y_t}{Y_{t-1}}\right) + 2S_t\left(\frac{A_t}{A_{t-1}}\right) - \frac{1}{2}S_t\left(\frac{A_{Xt}}{A_{Xt-1}}\right)$$

$$- 2.5S_t$$

C. Forecast sales are:

$$S_{t+1} = 2(\$900,000)(1.035) + 2(\$900,000)(1.1)$$

$$- \frac{1}{2}(\$900,000)(1.05) - 2.5(\$900,000)$$

$$= \$1,120,500$$

P7.10 **Simultaneous Equations.** *Macrosoft, Inc., is a leading provider of software and technical services to business and government. The company has found that demand for its products tends to be closely related to aggregate economic activity. The company has collected the following data in order to forecast economic activity during the coming year:*

Last Year's Corporate
Profits, P_{t-1} = $1,100

This Year's
Federal Government
Spending, G = $2,400

Annual Consumption
Expenditures, C = $2,175 + 0.7Y

Annual Investment
Expenditures, I = $550 + 1.5P_{t-1}

Annual Federal Tax Receipts, T = *0.25 GDP*

Income, Y = *GDP - T*

Net Exports, X = *$1,350 - 0.15 GDP*

Gross Domestic Product, GDP = *C + I + G + X*

Assuming that all random disturbances average out to zero, forecast each of the above variables through the simultaneous relations expressed in the multiple equation system. All dollar values are in billions of dollars.

P7.10   SOLUTION

Investment

$$I = \$550 + 1.5P_{t-1}$$

$$= \$550 + 1.5(\$1,100)$$

$$= \$2,200 \text{ billion}$$

Gross Domestic Product (GDP)

$$GDP = C + I + G + X$$

$$GDP = \$2,175 + 0.7(GDP - T) + \$2,200 + \$2,400 + \$1,350 - 0.15GDP$$

$$GDP = \$8,125 + 0.7(GDP - (0.25GDP)) - 0.15GDP$$

$$GDP = \$8,125 + 0.375GDP$$

$$0.625GDP = \$8,125$$

$$GDP = \$13,000 \text{ billion}$$

Consumption

$$C = \$2,175 + 0.7Y$$

$$= \$2,175 + 0.7(GDP - T)$$

$$= \$2{,}175 + 0.7(\text{GDP} - 0.25 \text{ GDP})$$

$$= \$2{,}175 + 0.525 \text{ GDP}$$

$$= \$2{,}175 + 0.525(\$13{,}000)$$

$$= \$9{,}000 \text{ billion}$$

Taxes

$$T = 0.25 \text{ GDP}$$

$$= 0.25(\$13{,}000)$$

$$= \$3{,}250 \text{ billion}$$

Income

$$Y = \text{GDP} - T$$

$$= \$13{,}000 - \$3{,}250$$

$$= \$9{,}750 \text{ billion}$$

Net Exports

$$X = \$1{,}350 - 0.15 \text{ GDP}$$

$$= \$1{,}350 - 0.15(\$13{,}000)$$

$$= -\$600 \text{ billion (which implies a trade deficit)}$$

Chapter 8

PRODUCTION ANALYSIS AND COMPENSATION POLICY

Given product demand conditions, how does a firm determine the optimal level of output during any given production period? When several alternative production methods are available, how does a firm choose the best one? How will investment in new manufacturing equipment affect worker productivity and the unit costs of production? If the firm undertakes an expansion program to increase productive capacity, will cost per unit be higher or lower after the expansion? Each of these questions can be critically important to firm success. Valuable insights and further questions that make ultimate answers obvious are provided by the study of production.

Production concepts have broad application and are equally relevant to the manufacture of physical goods and to the provision of services. In each instance, production analysis focuses on the efficient use of inputs to create outputs that meet the demonstrated demand of customers. Technical and economic characteristics of production methods used in the manufacture of both goods and services are studied to determine the low-cost means of meeting specific customer needs. It is worth emphasizing that the study of production involves much more than the simple physical transformation of resources. Production involves all the activities associated with providing goods and services. The hiring of workers (from unskilled labor to top management), personnel training, and the organizational structure adopted to maximize efficiency are all part of the production process. The efficient employment of capital resources is also part of production, as are the design and use of appropriate accounting and management information systems.

CHAPTER OUTLINE

I.   **PRODUCTION FUNCTIONS**

        A.   **Properties of Production Functions:** A production function specifies the maximum output that can be produced from a given combination of inputs; or alternatively, the minimum quantity of inputs necessary to produce a given level of output.

                1.   Production functions are determined by technology, equipment, and input prices.

                2.   Discrete production functions have distinct or "lumpy" input patterns.

                3.   Continuous production functions have the potential to employ inputs in small increments.

B.   Returns to Scale and Returns to a Factor: Returns to scale and returns to a factor measure the effects of changes in inputs on output.

   1.   The relation between changes in output and a percentage change in *all* inputs is the returns to scale attribute of a production function.

   2.   The relation between changes in output and change in a *single* input identifies the factor returns attribute of a production function.

II.   TOTAL, MARGINAL AND AVERAGE PRODUCT

A.   Total Product: Total product is the quantity of output that results from employing a specific level of resources in a production system.

B.   Marginal Product: Marginal product is the change in output caused by a unit change in a given input, holding all else constant:

$$MP_X = \frac{\partial Q}{\partial X}.$$

   1. MP_X is the slope of the total product curve.

      a.   Total product rises when $MP_X > 0$, and falls when $MP_X < 0$.

      b.   When $MP_X = 0$, total product is maximized.

C.   Average Product: Average product is simply total product divided by the amount of input employed:

$$AP_X = \frac{Q}{X}.$$

   1.   Average product rises when $MP_X > AP_X$, and falls when $MP_X < AP_X$.

   2.   When $MP_X = AP_X$, average product is maximized.

III.   LAW OF DIMINISHING RETURNS TO A FACTOR

A.   **Diminishing Returns to a Factor Concept:** If use of a given variable factor input rises while all other inputs are held constant, the marginal product of that factor (MP_X) eventually diminishes.

   1.   Diminishing returns imply positive but falling marginal products.

        a.   *Negative* marginal products are never observed because it would be irrational to expand input use if doing so causes total output to fall.

   2.   Diminishing returns exist for each factor in every known production system.

B.   **Illustration of Diminishing Returns to a Factor:** Input combinations in the range of diminishing returns are commonly observed.

   1.   Theoretically, when input usage is very low, increased specialization and better utilization of other factors in the production process allow factor productivity to grow.

   2.   In practice it is very rare to see input combinations that exhibit increasing returns for any factor. With increasing returns to a factor, an industry would come to be dominated by one very large producer--and this is seldom the case.

IV.   INPUT COMBINATION CHOICE

A.   **Production Isoquants:** An isoquant curve shows all possible input combinations which, when used efficiently, produce a given quantity of output.

   1.   Technical efficiency is achieved when output is produced in a least-cost fashion.

B.   **Input Factor Substitution:** The shape of an isoquant indicates the degree of substitutability among input factors.

   1.   A straight line isoquant implies perfect substitutability.

   2.   Isoquants that are made up of two straight lines perpendicular to each other (L-shaped) imply complete non-substitutability.

   3.   C-shaped or curved isoquants imply limited substitutability.

C. **Marginal Rate of Technical Substitution:** The marginal rate of technical substitution (MRTS$_{XY}$) measures the amount of one input factor (X) that must be substituted for some other input factor (Y) to hold output constant.

1. MRTS$_{XY}$ can be thought of as the marginal productivity of X relative to the marginal productivity of Y:

$$\text{MRTS}_{XY} = -\frac{\text{MP}_X}{\text{MP}_Y}$$

2. MRTS$_{XY}$ is -1 times the slope of an isoquant drawn on a graph where X is on the horizontal axis and Y is on the vertical axis:

$$\text{MRTS}_{XY} = -\frac{\text{MP}_X}{\text{MP}_Y}$$

$$= -\frac{\partial Q/\partial X}{\partial Q/\partial Y}$$

$$= -\frac{1/\partial X}{1/\partial Y}$$

$$= -\frac{\partial Y}{\partial X}$$

D. **Rational Limits of Input Substitution:** Ridge lines show the rational limits on resource use.

1. Activity will never be observed the range where MP$_X$ < 0 or MP$_Y$ < 0.

2. Outside the ridge lines, output can be increased by reducing use of the relatively more abundant factor employed.

V. **MARGINAL REVENUE PRODUCT AND OPTIMAL EMPLOYMENT**

A. **Marginal Revenue Product:** Optimal input use requires a careful consideration of productive capability and economic cost.

1.   Marginal Revenue Product (MRP) is the revenue gain to increasing input *X* usage by one unit.

   a.   Algebraically,

$$MRP_X = MP_X \times MR_Q$$

$$= \frac{\partial Q}{\partial X} \times \frac{\partial TR}{\partial Q}$$

$$= \frac{\partial TR}{\partial X}$$

where X is any single input and Q is output.

B.   Optimal Level of a Single Input: The profit-maximizing level of usage is at the point where the marginal revenue product of the last input unit employed is equal to input price.

1.   Algebraically,

$$\begin{array}{ccc} \text{Marginal} & = & \text{Marginal} \\ \text{Input Revenue} & & \text{Input Cost} \end{array}$$

$$\frac{\partial TR}{\partial X} = \frac{\partial TC}{\partial X}$$

$$MRP_X = P_X$$

VI.   Illustration of Optimal Employment: Firm employment is optimal when it equates the marginal revenue product and marginal cost of each input.

1.   Economic efficiency is achieved in the overall economy when all firms employ resources so as to equate each input's marginal revenue product and marginal cost.

VII.   OPTIMAL COMBINATION OF MULTIPLE INPUTS

A.   Budget Lines: The optimal input combination occurs at the point of tangency between a budget (isocost) line and a production isoquant.

1.   The least-cost combination of inputs requires that the marginal-product-to-price ratio be equal for all inputs (or relative marginal products equal relative price):

$$\frac{MP_X}{P_X} = \frac{MP_Y}{P_Y} \quad \text{or} \quad \frac{MP_X}{MP_Y} = \frac{P_X}{P_Y}$$

B.   Expansion Path: The expansion path depicts optimal input combinations as the scale of production expands.

1.   For optimal input combinations, the ratio of input prices must equal the ratio of input marginal products.

C.   Illustration of Optimal Input Proportions: Optimal input proportions are employed when an additional dollar spent on any input yields the same increase in output.

1.   No other input combination that can be purchased for the same cost produces as much output.

2.   When input proportions are optimal, a given level of output is produced efficiently. However, this does not ensure than an optimal *total amount* of output is produced.

VIII.   OPTIMAL LEVELS OF MULTIPLE INPUTS

A.   Optimal Employment and Profit Maximization: Profits are maximized when inputs are employed so that price equals marginal revenue product for each input.

1.   Algebraically, for all inputs X and Y:

$$MRP_X = P_X$$

$$MRP_Y = P_Y$$

2.   When optimal levels of multiple inputs are employed, output is produced efficiently and the optimal *total amount* of output is produced.

B.   Illustration of Optimal Levels of Multiple Inputs: At the optimal employment level, marginal revenue product equals marginal for each input.

1.   At the optimal employment level, an optimal combination of inputs is employed.

2.   At the optimal employment level, optimal levels of each input are employed.

3.   At the optimal employment level, a profit-maximizing level of output is produced.

IX.   RETURNS TO SCALE

A.   **Evaluating Returns to Scale:** Returns to scale are measured in terms of the output response to a given percentage increase in *all* inputs.

1.   If the percentage increase in output is greater than the percentage increase in inputs, increasing returns prevail.

2.   If the percentage increase in output is precisely equal to the percentage increase in inputs, constant returns prevail.

3.   If the percentage increase in output is less than the percentage increase in inputs, decreasing returns prevail.

4.   Returns to scale can be evaluated graphically by considering the distance between consecutive isoquants.

   a.   If the distance between successive isoquants diminishes, then doubling output requires less than a doubling of inputs, and increasing returns are indicated.

   b.   If the distance between isoquants for successive output quantities is constant, then output doubles when input usage doubles, and constant returns prevail.

   c.   If the distance between successive isoquants increases, then doubling output requires more than a doubling of inputs, and diminishing returns are indicated.

B.   **Output Elasticity and Returns to Scale:** Output elasticity, ε_Q, is the percentage change in output associated with a 1% increase in all inputs.

1.   By definition:

$$\varepsilon_Q = \frac{\partial Q}{Q} \div \frac{\partial X}{X} = \frac{\partial Q}{\partial X} \times \frac{X}{Q}$$

where $\underline{X}$ represents all inputs (capital, labor, etc.). Possibilities include:

    a. $\varepsilon_Q > 1$ implies increasing returns to scale.

    b. $\varepsilon_Q = 1$ implies constant returns to scale.

    c. $\varepsilon_Q < 1$ implies diminishing returns to scale.

C. **Returns to Scale Estimation:** In most instances, returns to scale can be easily estimated.

    1.   If a 1% increase in all inputs causes more than a 1% increase in output, returns to scale are increasing.

    2.   If a 1% increase in all inputs causes a 1% increase in output, returns to scale are constant.

    3.   If a 1% increase in all inputs causes less than a 1% increase in output, returns to scale are diminishing.

X.   **PRODUCTION FUNCTION ESTIMATION**

A. **Cubic Production Functions:** Cubic production functions exhibit stages of first increasing and then diminishing returns to scale.

B. **Power Production Functions:** The power (or multiplicative) function is probably the most popular structural form employed.

    1.   Power functions allow the marginal productivity of individual inputs to vary depending upon employment levels for all inputs.

XI.   **PRODUCTIVITY MEASUREMENT**

A. **How is Productivity Measured?:** Studies of output per hour in individual industries and the overall economy have been a responsibility of the Bureau of Labor Statistics (BLS) since the 1800s.

    1.   Productivity growth is the rate of increase in output per unit of input

2.   Labor productivity refers to the relationship between output and the worker time used to generate that output.

   a.   It is the ratio of output per worker hour.

3.   In multifactor productivity measures, output is related to combined inputs of labor, capital and intermediate purchases.

B.   Uses and Limitations of Productivity Data: Measures of output per hour are useful for analyzing trends in labor costs across industries, comparing productivity progress among countries, examining the effects of technological improvements, and analyzing related economic and industrial activities.

1.   Productivity measures of output per hour may not fully take into account changes in the quality of goods and services produced.

2.   Year-to-year changes in output per hour are sometimes irregular and not indicative of basic changes in long-term trends.

XII.   SUMMARY

PROBLEMS & SOLUTIONS

P8.1   ***Production Function Concepts****. Indicate whether each of the following statements is true or false. Explain why.*

   A.   *The law of diminishing returns states that returns to scale are diminishing in all known production systems.*

   B.   *Decreasing returns to scale and increasing average costs are indicated when $\varepsilon_Q > 1$.*

   C.   *Straight line-shaped isoquants describe production systems in which inputs are perfect substitutes.*

   D.   *The marginal rate of technical substitution is not affected by a given percentage decrease in the marginal productivity of all inputs.*

   E.   *Returns to a factor describe the percentage change in output relative to a percentage change in all inputs.*

P8.1   **SOLUTION**

   A.   False. The law of diminishing returns states that as the quantity of any *single* variable input increases, holding other inputs constant, the marginal product of that single input eventually decreases. Returns to scale are often constant or increasing over limited ranges of output.

   B.   False. When $\varepsilon_Q > 1$, the percentage change in output is greater than a given percentage change in all inputs. Thus, increasing returns to scale and decreasing average costs are indicated.

   C.   True. Straight line-shaped production isoquants reflect a perfect substitute relation among inputs.

   D.   True. The marginal rate of technical substitution is measured by the relative marginal productivity of input factors. This relation is unaffected by a commensurate decrease in the marginal productivity of all inputs.

   E.   False. Returns to scale describe the percentage change in output relative to a percentage change in *all* inputs.

P8.2   ***Returns to Scale Estimation.*** *Determine whether the following production functions exhibit constant, increasing or decreasing returns to scale.*

A. $Q = 0.6X + 20Y + 10Z$

B. $Q = 200 + 4L$

C. $Q = 20L + 16K + 10LK$

D. $Q = 2A^2 + 3AB + 5B^2$

E. $Q = 20L^{0.25}K^{0.70}$

F. $Q = \sqrt{3X^2 + 2Y^2 + 15Z^2}$

P8.2   **SOLUTION**

A.   Returns to scale can be determined by evaluating the percentage increase in output which follows any given percentage increase in inputs. Answers to parts A, B and C reflect this approach. Alternatively, returns to scale can be evaluated using the more general algebraic approach of parts D, E and F. Both approaches work; use the one that is easiest for you.

If $X = Y = Z = 100$, then:

$$Q_1 = 0.6X + 20Y + 10Z$$

$$= 0.6(100) + 20(100) + 10(100)$$

$$= 3,060$$

Increasing each input by 1% yields:

$$Q_2 = 0.6(101) + 20(101) + 10(101)$$

$$= 3,090.6$$

which implies a 1% increase in output ($Q_2/Q_1 = 3,090.6/3,060 = 1.01$), and therefore the function exhibits constant returns to scale.

B.   If $L = 100$, then:

$$Q_1 = 200 + 4L$$

$$= 200 + 4(100)$$

$$= 600$$

Increasing labor by 2% yields:

$$Q_2 = 200 + 4(102)$$

$$= 608$$

which implies a 1.3% increase in output ($Q_2/Q_1 = 608/600 = 1.013$, and therefore the function exhibits diminishing returns to scale. (Note: $Q = 200$ even though $L = 0$ could be descriptive of an agricultural production function).

C. If $L = K = 100$, then:

$$Q_1 = 20L + 16K + 10LK$$

$$= 20(100) + 16(100) + 10(100)(100)$$

$$= 103,600$$

Increasing each input by 3% yields:

$$Q_2 = 20(103) + 16(103) + 10(103)(103)$$

$$= 109,798$$

which implies a 5.98% increase in output ($Q_2/Q_1 = 109,798/103,600 = 1.0598$), and therefore the function exhibits increasing returns to scale.

Alternatively, for a k proportionate increase in all inputs (where $k > 1$):

$$Q = 20L + 16K + 10LK$$

$$hQ = 20(kL) + 16(kK) + 10(kL)(kK)$$

$$= k^1(20L + 16K + 10kLK)$$

$$= k^1(Q^*)$$

Here, returns to scale would be constant if $Q^* = Q$. However, because $k > 1$, it is clear that $Q^* > Q$. This implies that returns to scale for this production function are increasing (as before).

D.   For a k proportionate increase in all inputs:

$$Q = 2A^2 + 3AB + 5B^2$$

$$hQ = 2(kA)^2 + 3(kA)(kB) + 5(kB)^2$$

$$= k^2(2A^2 + 3AB + 5B^2)$$

$$= k^2Q$$

$$h = k^2$$

Therefore, $h > k$ and the production function demonstrates increasing returns to scale.

E.   For a k proportionate increase in all inputs:

$$Q = 20L^{0.25}K^{0.70}$$

$$hQ = 20(kL)^{0.25}(kK)^{0.70}$$

$$= k^{0.25 + 0.70}(20L^{0.25}K^{0.70})$$

$$= k^{0.95}Q$$

$$h = k^{0.95}$$

Because $h < k$, the production function exhibits diminishing returns to scale.

F.   For a k proportionate increase in all inputs:

$$Q = \sqrt{3X^2 + 2Y^2 + 15Z^2}$$

$$hQ = \sqrt{3(kX)^2 + 2(kY)^2 + 15(kZ)^2}$$

$$= \sqrt{k^2(3X^2 + 2Y^2 + 15Z^2)}$$

$$= k\sqrt{3X^2 + 2Y^2 + 15Z^2}$$

$$= kQ$$

$$h = k$$

Therefore, h = k and the production function demonstrates constant returns to scale.

P8.3   ***Marginal and Total Product.*** *The patient insurance record processing department for St. Eligius Hospital has a production function described by the relation:*

$$Q = 0.4K^2 + 0.2KL + 0.3L^2$$

where Q is output in records processed, K is capital in terms of the number of computer hours, and L is the number of labor hours employed.

Assume a weekly rate of use where K = 40 computer hours and L = 150 labor hours.

A.   *What is total product per week?*

B.   *What are the marginal products for computer hours and for labor hours?*

P8.3   **SOLUTION**

A. $Q = 0.4K^2 + 0.2KL + 0.3L^2$

$$= 0.4(40^2) + 0.2(40)(150) + 0.3(150^2)$$

$$= 8{,}590 \text{ records processed}$$

B.   Marginal product of computer time $= MP_K = \partial Q / \partial K$

$$= 0.8K + 0.2L$$

$$= 0.8(40) + 0.2(150)$$

$$= 62 \text{ records processed}$$

Marginal product of labor $= MP_L = \partial Q / \partial L$

$$= 0.2K + 0.6L$$

$$= 0.2(40) + 0.6(150)$$

$$= 98 \text{ records processed}$$

P8.4   ***Optimal Wages***. *Shortcuts, Inc., is a regional chain offering walk-in haircut services at popular prices. The company currently has two employee job classifications. Inexperienced haircutters (I) have six months or less job experience, and, on average, are able to cut a customer's hair in 20 minutes. Experienced haircutters (E), employees with more than six months experience, can provide one haircut in 15 minutes.*

   A.   *If inexperienced haircutters are readily available at a wage of $10 per hour, what is the maximum hourly wage that could be justified for experienced haircutters?*

   B.   *What would be your employment recommendation to the company if experienced haircutters can be readily employed at a wage of $12 per hour?*

P8.4   **SOLUTION**

   A.   The rule for optimal relative employment of inexperienced (I) and experienced (E) haircutters is:

$$\frac{MP_I}{P_I} = \frac{MP_E}{P_E} \quad \text{or} \quad \frac{MP_I}{MP_E} = \frac{P_I}{P_E}$$

Because inexperienced haircutters can provide one haircut in 20 minutes, or 1/3 hour, their marginal product per hour is $MP_I = 3$. Because experienced haircutters can provide one haircut in 15 minutes, or 1/4 hour, their marginal product per hour is $MP_E = 4$. Therefore, given $P_I = \$10$ per hour, the maximum hourly wage that could be justified for experienced haircutters is:

$$\frac{MP_I}{MP_E} = \frac{P_I}{P_E}$$

$$\frac{3}{4} = \frac{\$10}{P_E}$$

$$P_E = \$13.33 \text{ per hour}$$

B. If experienced haircutters can be readily employed at a wage of $12 per hour, then relative to inexperienced haircutters, the experienced haircutters represent an employment bargain. Whereas the labor cost per haircut with inexperienced haircutters is $3.33 (= P_I/MP_I), the labor cost per haircut with experienced haircutters is only $3 (= P_E/MP_E). The superior productivity of experienced haircutters more than compensates for their higher wages. Shortcuts should employ relatively more experienced haircutters. Indeed, if the marginal productivity of each employment class is independent, experienced haircutters would be employed exclusively.

P8.5 ***Marginal Rate of Technical Substitution.*** *Bush's Broccoli Farm is a moderate-sized Connecticut broccoli grower. Bush's estimates that broccoli output would increase by 600 bushels with an additional 1,000 gallons of water provided to its irrigation system. Alternatively, broccoli output could be increased by 500 bushels with an additional 2 tons of lime fertilizer.*

A. *Estimate the marginal products of water and fertilizer.*

B. *What is the marginal rate of technical substitution between these inputs?*

C. *Assuming the cost of water is 6¢ per gallon and the cost of fertilizer is $25 per ton, is Bush's currently using an optimal combination of fertilizer and water?*

P8.5 **SOLUTION**

A.

$$\text{Marginal product of water} = MP_W = \frac{\partial Q}{\partial W}$$

$$= \frac{600}{1,000}$$

$$= 0.6 \text{ bushels per gallon}$$

$$\text{Marginal product of fertilizer} = MP_F = \frac{\partial Q}{\partial F}$$

$$= \frac{500}{2}$$

$$= 250 \text{ bushels per ton}$$

B. Marginal rate of technical substitution

$$\text{MRTS} = -\frac{MP_W}{MP_F}$$

$$\frac{\partial Q/\partial W}{\partial Q/\partial F} = -\frac{0.6}{250}$$

$$\frac{\partial F}{\partial W} = -0.0024$$

which implies:

$$\partial F = -0.0024\partial W \text{ or } \partial W = -416.6\partial F$$

C. Yes, Bush's current combination of water and fertilizer is optimal because:

$$\frac{MP_W}{MP_F} = \frac{P_W}{P_F}$$

$$\frac{0.6}{250} \overset{?}{=} \frac{\$0.06}{\$25}$$

$$0.0024 \overset{\checkmark}{=} 0.0024$$

P8.6 **Optimal Input Mix.** *Lockheart Laboratories, Inc., offers medical tests to private employers and government agencies. To better serve the rapidly growing demand for its services, LLI is considering hiring a new lab technician, leasing new testing equipment, or both. The cost of hiring a new lab technician is $8,000 per month (including fringes); the cost of leasing additional testing equipment is $10,000 per month. A new lab technician would allow LLI to increase output from 60,000 to 62,000 tests per month; a new piece of testing equipment is capable of increasing current staff output by 2,500 tests per month.*

A. *Does MLI's current employment of lab technicians and testing equipment reflect an optimal mix of labor and equipment?*

B. *If each test provides a $6 net marginal revenue before labor and capital costs, is expansion advisable?*

P8.6 **SOLUTION**

A. The rule for an optimal mix of labor and capital is:

$$\frac{MP_L}{P_L} = \frac{MP_K}{P_K} \quad \text{or} \quad \frac{MP_L}{MP_K} = \frac{P_L}{P_K}$$

On a monthly basis, the relevant question is:

$$\frac{MP_L}{P_L} \stackrel{?}{=} \frac{MP_K}{P_K}$$

$$\frac{2,000}{\$8,000} \stackrel{?}{=} \frac{2,500}{\$10,000}$$

$$0.25 \stackrel{\checkmark}{=} 0.25$$

Therefore, the marginal effect on output of one dollar spent on either labor technicians or capital equipment is 0.25 tests. This indicates an *optimal mix* of labor and capital because output could not be increased by changing the relative usage of labor and capital.

B. Yes, expansion would be profitable. The rule for an optimal level of input employment is:

$$MRP = MP \times MR_Q = \text{Input Price}$$

In this instance, for each input:

$$MRP_L = MP_L \times MR_Q \stackrel{?}{=} P_L$$

$$2,000 \times \$6 \stackrel{?}{=} \$8,000$$

$$\$12,000 > \$8,000$$

$$MRP_K = MP_K \times MR_Q \stackrel{?}{=} P_K$$

$$2,500 \times \$6 \stackrel{?}{=} \$10,000$$

$$\$15,000 > \$10,000$$

Both inputs generate net marginal revenues in excess of marginal costs. As a result, expansion would be profitable.

P8.7   ***Optimal Input Level***. *Enron Natural Resources, Ltd., is a leading energy provider with vast coal holding in western states. The company is in the process of negotiating a new labor agreement, and is relying upon an engineering analysis that suggests the following production and marginal product relations:*

$$Q = 1,000L^{0.5}K^{0.5}$$

$$MP_L = \partial Q/\partial L = 500L^{-0.5}K^{0.5}$$

$$MP_K = \partial Q/\partial K = 500L^{0.5}K^{-0.5}$$

where

Q = *Coal output (in thousands of tons).*

L = *Labor (in hundreds of employees).*

K = *Capital (in billions of dollars).*

MP_L = *Marginal product of labor (in hundreds of employees).*

MP_K = *Marginal product of capital (in billions of dollars).*

Enron employs 10,000 workers and maintains a $16 billion capital investment. Coal output is sold in competitive markets at an expected price of $33.75 per ton.

A.   *Determine and interpret returns to scale.*

B.   *Determine and interpret returns to each factor input.*

C.   *What is the maximum annual salary Enron is willing to pay a labor force of 10,000 employees?*

D.   *How many workers would Enron willingly employ at a $75,000 annual salary?*

(Note: Interpret your units of measurement carefully!)

P8.7   **SOLUTION**

A.
$$Q = 1,000L^{0.5}K^{0.5}$$

$$hQ = 1,000(kL)^{0.5}(kK)^{0.5}$$

$$= k^{0.5 + 0.5}(1,000L^{0.5}K^{0.5})$$

$$= k^1Q$$

$$h = k^1$$

Therefore, h = k and the above production exhibits constant returns to scale.

B. Returns to each factor can be determined by looking at how each marginal product changes with increased input usage.

<u>Returns to Labor:</u>

$$\text{Marginal product of labor} = MP_L = \partial Q/\partial L = 500L^{-0.5}K^{0.5}$$

$$= \frac{500(16^{0.5})}{100^{0.5}}$$

$$= 200$$

Because $\partial^2 Q/\partial L^2 = -250L^{-1.5}K^{0.5} < 0$, MP_L is decreasing beyond this point, and returns to the labor factor are diminishing.

<u>Returns to Capital:</u>

$$\text{Marginal product of capital} = MP_K = \partial Q/\partial K = 500L^{0.5}K^{-0.5}$$

$$= \frac{500(100^{0.5})}{16^{0.5}}$$

$$= 1,250$$

Because $\partial^2 Q/\partial K^2 = -250L^{0.5}K^{-1.5} < 0$, MP_K is decreasing beyond this point, and returns to the capital factor are diminishing.

C. The optimal employment rule, $P_i = MRP_i$, is used to determine the maximum annual salary that Enron would willingly pay 10,000 employees.

$$\frac{\text{Price}}{\text{of labor}} = \frac{\text{Marginal revenue}}{\text{product of labor}}$$

$$P_L = MP_L \times MR_Q$$

$$= (500L^{-0.5}K^{0.5})(\$33.75 \times 1{,}000)$$

$$= \frac{500K^{0.5}}{L^{0.5}} \times 33{,}750$$

$$= \frac{500(16^{0.5})}{100^{0.5}} \times 33{,}750$$

$$= \$6{,}750{,}000 \text{ per hundred workers or } \$67{,}500 \text{ per worker}$$

These numerical calculations must reflect the fact that Q is in thousands of tons, L is in hundreds of employees, and K is in billions of dollars of capital. Given that coal sells for \$33.75 per ton, the $MR_Q = \$33{,}750$ because Q is one thousand tons of coal. Similarly, the P_L derived above is for one hundred employees because the MP_L is also for one hundred employees. At first, making such unit adjustments may seem confusing. With practice, however, you will become able to deal with "units problems" and be able to interpret and use productivity studies compiled by subordinates, consultants, government agencies, and others.

D. Again, using the optimal employment rule:

$$\frac{\text{Price}}{\text{of labor}} = \frac{\text{Marginal revenue}}{\text{product of labor}}$$

$$P_L = MP_L \times MR_Q$$

$$\$75{,}000 \times 100 = (500L^{-0.5}K^{0.5})(\$33.75 \times 1{,}000)$$

$$7{,}500{,}000 = \frac{500K^{0.5}}{L^{0.5}} \times 33{,}750$$

$$7,500,000 = \frac{500(16^{0.5})}{L^{0.5}} \times 33,750$$

$$7,500,000 = \frac{67,500,000}{L^{0.5}}$$

$$L^{0.5} = \frac{67,500,000}{7,500,000}$$

$$L^{0.5} = 9$$

$$L = 81(00) \text{ or } 8,100 \text{ workers}$$

At a salary of \$75,000, Enron would be willing to employ only 8,100 workers.

P8.8 ***Optimal Employment.*** *Both Senior Claims Analysts and Junior Claims Analysts process claims at the Wakarusa Insurance Company. Senior Claims Analysts earn \$30 while processing an average of 5 claims per hour. Junior Analysts earn \$16 while processing an average of 2 claims per hour.*

A. *Calculate the marginal labor cost per claim processed by Senior and Junior Analysts.*

B. *Is the firm operating efficiently? Explain.*

C. *Should Wakarusa increase or decrease the relative number of Senior Analysts? Explain.*

D. *Holding all else unchanged, what Senior Analyst wage would make the current ratio of Senior Analysts to Junior Analysts optimal?*

P8.8 **SOLUTION**

A. The marginal labor cost per claim processed is given by the ratio:

$$\text{Marginal labor cost per unit} = \frac{P_L}{MP_L} = \frac{\text{Labor cost per hour}}{\partial Q \text{ per hour}}$$

Therefore, for senior (SA) and junior (JA) claims analysts:

$$MC_{SA} = \frac{P_{SA}}{MP_{SA}} = \frac{\$30}{5} = \$6 \text{ per claim}$$

$$MC_{JA} = \frac{P_{JA}}{MP_{JA}} = \frac{\$16}{2} = \$8 \text{ per claim}$$

B.   No, the firm is employing an inefficient combination of senior and junior analysts. The marginal labor cost per claim processed is only $6 for senior analysts, but $8 per claim processed by junior analysts. To be optimal, the employment of senior and junior analysts should be such that the marginal labor processing costs are equal for each type of employee.

C.   Increase. If relatively more senior analysts are hired the firm will reduce its average labor processing cost per claim. Holding the number of junior analysts constant, additional senior analysts will be employed until the marginal product of senior analysts falls to 3.75 claims per hour. At that point, the marginal labor cost of claims processed by senior analysts would equal $8 per claim (= $30/3.75). If the number of senior analysts is held constant, the number of junior analysts should be reduced until the marginal product of junior analysts rises to 2.67 claims per hour. At that point, the marginal labor cost of claims processed by junior analysts would equal $6 (= $16/2.67).

   In either case, the marginal labor processing costs would become equal across employee classifications, as is required for input proportions to be optimal.

D.   Senior analysts are 2.5 (= MP_{SA}/MP_{JA} = 5/2) times as productive as junior analysts, while earning only 1.875 (= P_{SA}/P_{JA} = $30/$16) times as much pay. Given their relative productivity, a senior analyst pay level of $40 per hour or 2.5 times that of junior analysts can be justified. At that wage,

$$MC_{SA} = \frac{P_{SA}}{MP_{SA}} = \frac{\$40}{5} = \$8 \text{ per claim}$$

Optimality would be reached because, at that higher wage for senior analysts,

$$\frac{P_{SA}}{MP_{SA}} = \frac{P_{JA}}{MP_{JA}}$$

Therefore, a $10 per hour raise (= $40 - $30) for senior analysts could be justified.

P8.9 **Power Production Functions**. *Data Analysis, Inc., has engaged Ray Barone, a recent MBA graduate, to recommend a hiring policy for its soon to be opened office in Long Island, New York. Barone has conducted a statistical study of operations at twelve similar-sized DAI offices and found the following (standard errors in parentheses):*

$$\ln Q = 0.50 \ln L + 0.25 \ln C + 0.25 \ln B$$
$$\qquad\quad (0.13) \qquad (0.06) \qquad (0.11)$$

$$R^2 = 87\%$$

Q = data processing output.

L = labor hours for data processing staff.

C = computer time-sharing hours for data processing.

B = office building space in hundreds of square feet.

A. *Describe the economic logic underlying Barone's choice of the above log-linear production relation as opposed to, say, a linear relation.*

B. *Based on the above analysis, Barone projects the following marginal products for each input:*

$$MP_L = \partial Q / \partial L = 0.5 L^{-0.5} C^{0.25} B^{0.25}$$

$$MP_C = \partial Q / \partial C = 0.25 L^{0.5} C^{-0.75} B^{0.25}$$

$$MP_B = \partial Q / \partial B = 0.25 L^{0.5} C^{0.25} B^{-0.75}$$

Determine the optimal relation between total expenditures for L and C.

C. *Barone projects computer time-sharing costs of $225 per hour, and anticipates needing to pay $90,000 per year to attract and retain data processing personnel. If a total labor and computer time budget of $1,350,000 has been established for the Long Island office, and staff members work 2,000 hours per year, how many staff members should be hired and how much computer time should be purchased?*

P8.9 SOLUTION

A. Log-linear (or power) production relations are appropriate when the marginal products of individual inputs depend upon the levels of all inputs employed.

Although many other functional forms (quadratic and cubic, for example) also enjoy this feature, log-linear forms are easy to estimate and results are easily interpreted.

B. The optimal combination rate for L and C is determined by the relation:

$$\frac{MP_L}{MP_C} = \frac{P_L}{P_C}$$

$$\frac{0.5L^{-0.5}C^{0.25}B^{0.25}}{0.25L^{0.5}C^{-0.75}B^{0.25}} = \frac{P_L}{P_C}$$

$$\frac{2C}{L} = \frac{P_L}{P_C}$$

which implies an optimal relation between total expenditures for L and C of:

$$2C \times P_C = P_L \times L$$

$$2 \times \begin{array}{c} \text{Expenditures} \\ \text{on computer time} \end{array} = \begin{array}{c} \text{Expenditures} \\ \text{on labor} \end{array}$$

Thus, expenditures on labor will be twice the total level of expenditures on computer time. Alternatively, expenditures on computer time will be one-half total expenditures on labor.

C. From part B it is clear that:

$$\begin{array}{c} \text{Total} \\ \text{budget} \end{array} = \begin{array}{c} \text{Labor} \\ \text{expenditures} \\ \text{(two thirds)} \end{array} + \begin{array}{c} \text{Computer} \\ \text{expenditures} \\ \text{(one third)} \end{array}$$

Given a salary of $90,000 per employee and assuming 2,000 worker hours per year, a wage of $90,000/2,000 = $45 per hour is implied. The number of staff members to be hired is determined as follows:

$$\text{Labor expenditures} = \$900,000$$

$$P_L \times L = 900,000$$

$$45 \times L = 900,000$$

$$L = 20,000$$

If each programmer works 2,000 hours per year, then:

$$\frac{\text{New}}{\text{programmers}} = \frac{20,000}{2,000}$$

$$= 10 \text{ employees}$$

Similarly, the amount of computer time to be purchased is determined as:

$$\frac{\text{Computer time}}{\text{expenditures}} = \$450,000$$

$$P_C \times C = 450,000$$

$$225 \times C = 450,000$$

$$C = 2,000 \text{ hours}$$

P8.10 **Marginal Product Analysis.** *Kenny Kramer, head of the engineering department of the Automatic Switch Company, estimates the following production and marginal product functions for assembly of the K-2 switch:*

$$Q = 30X + 2XY - 0.5X^2 - 0.5Y^2$$

$$MP_X = 30 + 2Y - X$$

$$MP_Y = 2X - Y$$

where Q = total output of K-2 switches, X = worker hours, and Y = machine tool hours.

A. *Assume a weekly rate of use where X = 70 worker hours and Y = 30 machine tool hours. What is total product per week?*

B. *Calculate the marginal product for each input at this rate of usage.*

C. *Calculate the marginal revenue product for each input at these usage levels, assuming K-2 switches are sold at a competitive market price of 50¢ each.*

D. *Are these input usage levels optimal in light of wage costs of $25 per hour and machine tool costs of $40 per hour? If so, why? If not, calculate optimal input levels and explain your answer.*

P8.10   **SOLUTION**

A.   At $X = 70$ and $Y = 30$,

$$Q = 30X + 2XY - 0.5X^2 - 0.5Y^2$$

$$= 30(70) + 2(70)(30) - 0.5(70^2) - 0.5(30^2)$$

$$= 3,400$$

B.   In general,

$$MP_X = \partial Q / \partial X = 30 + 2Y - X$$

$$= 30 + 2(30) - 70$$

$$= 20$$

$$MP_Y = \partial Q / \partial Y = 2X - Y$$

$$= 2(70) - 30$$

$$= 110$$

C.   In general,

$$MRP_X = MP_X \times MR_Q$$

$$= (30 + 2Y - X)(\$0.5)$$

$$= \$15 + Y - \$0.5X$$

$$= \$15 + \$30 - \$0.5(70)$$

$$= \$10$$

$$MRP_Y = MP_Y \times MR_Q$$

$$= (2X - Y)(\$0.5)$$

$$= X - \$0.5Y$$

$$= \$70 - \$0.5(30)$$

$$= \$55$$

D. Input usage levels of $X = 70$ and $Y = 30$ will be optimal provided $MRP_i = P_i$. Here, usage of neither X nor Y is optimal because:

$MRP_X = \$10 < \$25$ and X usage should be reduced.

$MRP_Y = \$55 > \$40$ and Y usage should be expanded.

Optimal input usage will be achieved only when $MRP_X = P_X$ and $MRP_Y = P_Y$:

$$(1)\ MRP_X = \$15 + Y - \$0.5X = \$25 = P_X$$

$$(2)\ MRP_Y = X - \$0.5Y = \$40 = P_Y$$

This constitutes a system of two equations with two unknowns to be solved simultaneously. Taking equation (1) plus two times (2) yields:

$$(1) \qquad 15 + Y - 0.5X = 25$$

$$+ 2 \times (2) \qquad \underline{\qquad 2X - Y = 80 \qquad}$$

$$15 + 1.5X = 105$$

$$1.5X = 90$$

$$X = 60$$

And substituting $X = 60$ into (1) yields:

$$(1) \qquad 15 + Y - 0.5X = 25$$

$$15 + Y - 0.5(60) = 25$$

$$Y = 40$$

Chapter 9

COST ANALYSIS AND ESTIMATION

Corporate restructuring typically involves eliminating nonstrategic operations to redeploy assets and strengthen core lines of business. When nonessential assets are disposed of in a depressed market, there is often no relation between low "fire sale" proceeds and book value, historical cost, or replacement cost. Conversely, when assets are sold to others who can more effectively use such resources, sale proceeds can approximate replacement valuations and greatly exceed historical costs and book values. Even under normal circumstances, the link between economic and accounting values can be tenuous. Economic worth as determined by profit-generating capability, rather than accounting value, is always the most relevant consideration when determining the cost and use of specific assets. In cost analysis and estimation, historical accounting information provides a valuable starting point for evaluation. Nevertheless, these data must be constantly monitored and adjusted, when necessary, to reflect economic reality.

This chapter focuses on how costs and output are related on a conceptual level, and how practical knowledge about such relations can be used to accurately estimate cost relationships. Cost analysis and estimation plays an essential role in managerial economics because virtually every managerial decision requires a careful comparison between costs and benefits. Central to all economic analysis is the notion that relevant cost determination depends on a careful consideration of applicable decision alternatives.

CHAPTER OUTLINE

I.   **WHAT MAKES COST ANALYSIS DIFFICULT?**

      A.   **Link Between Accounting and Economic Valuations:** Cost analysis is made difficult by the effects of unforeseen inflation, unpredictable changes in technology, and the dynamic nature of input and output markets.

          1.   Divergences between economic costs and accounting valuations are common.

          2.   Accurate cost analysis involves careful consideration of all relevant decision alternatives.

      B.   **Historical Versus Current Costs:** The term *cost* can be defined in a number of ways; the correct definition varies from situation to situation.

          1.   For tax purposes, historical cost, or actual cash outlay, is the relevant cost.

2.   Current costs are typically more relevant than historical costs.

    a.   Current cost is the amount that must be paid under prevailing market conditions.

C.   Replacement Cost: Replacement cost is the cost of duplicating productive capability using current technology.

1.   In assessing the cost of using productive assets, the appropriate measure is the replacement cost.

II.   OPPORTUNITY COSTS

A.   Opportunity Cost Concept: Opportunity cost is value foregone with current rather than next-best use of a given asset.

1.   Opportunity cost is determined by the highest-valued *opportunity* that must be foregone to allow current use.

B.   Explicit and Implicit Costs: Resource costs often involve out-of-pocket expenses, or explicit costs, and other noncash expenses, called implicit costs.

1.   Wages, utility expenses, raw materials costs, interest expenses, and rent are all examples of explicit expenses.

2.   Implicit costs do not involve cash expenditures and can be wrongly overlooked in decision analysis.

III.   INCREMENTAL AND SUNK COSTS IN DECISION ANALYSIS

A.   Incremental Cost: The change in cost associated with a given managerial decision is called the incremental cost.

1.   Marginal cost involves a one-unit change in output; incremental cost can involve a multiple-unit change in output.

B.   Sunk Costs: Any cost that does not vary across decision alternatives is a sunk cost.

1.   Sunk costs arise from past decisions that are irreversible.

2.   Sunk costs are irrelevant for current and future decisions.

IV.   SHORT-RUN AND LONG-RUN COSTS

    A.   Cost Functions: A cost function is the functional relation between cost and output.

        1.   Technology, or the manner in which inputs are converted to output, plays a role in determining costs.

        2.   The level and rate of change in input prices also affect costs.

    B.   How is the Operating Period Defined?: The short run is the time-frame within which operating decisions are made. The long run is the time-frame within which planning decisions are made.

        1.   At least one input is fixed in supply during the short run.

        2.   Firms have complete input flexibility in the long run.

    C.   Fixed and Variable Costs: Fixed costs do not vary with output. Variable costs differ according to output.

        1.   Fixed costs exist in the short-run only; all costs are variable in the long-run.

V.   SHORT-RUN COST CURVES

    A.   Short-Run Cost Categories: Total, average, and marginal costs in short-run cost functions are described as:

        1.   Total Cost (TC) = Fixed Costs (TFC) + Total Variable Costs (TVC)

        2.   Average Fixed Cost (AFC) = TFC/Q.

        3.   Average Variable Cost (AVC) = TVC/Q.

        4.   Average Cost (or Average Total Cost) (AC) = TC/Q.

        5.   Marginal Cost (MC) = $\partial TC/\partial Q = \partial TVC/\partial Q$.

    B.   Short-Run Cost Relations: A short-run cost curve shows the minimum cost impact of output changes for a specific plant in a given operating environment.

1. The slope of the total cost curve is identical to the slope of the total variable cost curve.

    a. A change in fixed costs merely shifts the total cost curve to a different level.

    b. Marginal costs are independent of fixed costs.

2. Assuming constant input prices, the shape of the total variable cost curve is determined by the productivity of variable input factors employed.

VI. LONG-RUN COST CURVES

A. **Long-Run Total Costs:** All long-run cost curves are based on the assumption that an optimal scale of plant is used to produce any given output level.

1. If input prices are held constant, there is a direct relation between cost and production.

2. Long-run total cost functions and production functions both provide returns to scale information.

B. **Economies of Scale:** The impact on total cost of a percentage change in output is the returns to scale attribute of a cost function.

1. Returns to scale are increasing, constant, or diminishing depending upon the relation between long-run total costs and output.

2. Economists often use the term economies of scale as synonymous with increasing returns to scale.

C. **Cost Elasticities and Returns to Scale:** Cost elasticity, ε_C, measures the percentage change in total cost associated with a 1% change in output. By definition:

$$\varepsilon_C = \partial C/C \div \partial Q/Q = \partial C/\partial Q \times Q/C.$$

The relation between cost elasticity and returns to scale is straightforward.

1. If $\varepsilon_C < 1$, returns to scale are increasing.

2.   If $\varepsilon_C = 1$, returns to scale are constant.

3.   If $\varepsilon_C > 1$, returns to scale are decreasing.

D.   Long-Run Average Costs: The long-run average cost curve is the envelope (or border) of the short-run average cost curves for various plant sizes.   Given constant input prices and unchanging technology, there is a direct relation between long-run average costs and returns to scale.

1.   If LRAC are falling, returns to scale are increasing.

2.   If LRAC are constant, returns to scale are constant.

3.   If LRAC are rising, returns to scale are decreasing.

VII.   MINIMUM EFFICIENT SCALE

A.   Competitive Implications of Minimum Efficient Scale: The minimum efficient scale concept has important implications for competition.

1.   Minimum efficient scale is the plant size at which long-run average cost is first minimized.

a.   MES is the minimum point of a "U-shaped" LRAC curve.

b.   MES is the "corner" point of an "L-shaped" LRAC curve.

2.   Competition tends to be most vigorous when:

a.   MES is small in absolute terms.

b.   MES is a small share of industry output.

c.   The cost disadvantage to less than MES operation is minor.

B.   Transportation Costs and MES: High transportation costs can offset the cost advantages of MES-size operation.

1.   Transportation costs include terminal, line-haul, and inventory charges associated with moving output from production facilities to customers.

    a.   Terminal charges or loading and unloading expenses do not vary with the distance of shipment.

    b.   Line-haul expenses, including equipment, labor, and fuel costs, vary directly with the distance shipped.

    c.   The inventory cost component of transportation costs relates to the time element involved in shipping goods.

2.   When transportation costs are high, even small, relatively inefficient local competitors can survive, if not prosper.

3.   When transportation costs are low, markets are national or international in scope and significant economies of scale can cause output to be produced at only a few large plants.

VIII. FIRM SIZE AND PLANT SIZE

    A.   **Multiplant Economies and Diseconomies of Scale:** Multiplant economies are cost savings that arise from operating multiple facilities in the same line of business or industry.

1.   Multiplant diseconomies are cost disadvantages that arise from the difficulty of coordinating multiple locations.

2.   If long-run average costs decline, multiplant economies exist, and multiplant firms are more efficient than single-plant operations.

3.   Constant average costs for multiplant operations indicate that there are no economies or diseconomies in combining plants.

4.   If average costs first decline and then rise, economies of scale for the multiplant firm dominate initially, but eventually diseconomies result.

    B.   **Economics of Multiplant Operation: An Example:** This example illustrates the effects of multiplant economies on firm size.

1.   Multiplant production is preferable to centralized production when it allows the firm to concentrate production at the minimum point on the single-plant U-shaped average cost curve.

C.   **Plant Size and Flexibility:** In choosing a plant to produce a certain output, the firm should select the plant with the lowest expected average total cost over the range of possible output levels.

IX.   **LEARNING CURVES**

A.   **Learning-Curve Concept:** Learning curves illustrate the predictable decrease in average production costs that often accompanies greater production experience.

1.   Like any technical innovation, learning results in an inward (leftward) shift in the firm's LRAC curve.

B.   **Learning-Curve Example:** The rate of learning is typically expressed in terms of the average cost reduction percentage following a doubling in total production.

C.   **Strategic Implications of the Learning-Curve Concept:**   Early in the development of important industries featuring new products and/or new production techniques, learning curve advantages have allowed industry leaders to enhance their relative cost advantage over nonleading firms.

1.   To play an important role in competitive strategy, learning must be significant. Cost savings of 20% to 30% as cumulative output doubles must be possible.

2.   If only modest effects of learning are present, product quality or customer service often plays a greater role in determining firm success.

X.   **ECONOMIES OF SCOPE**

A.   **Economies of Scope Concept:** Economies of scope exist when it is cheaper on a per unit basis to produce and/or deliver goods or services in tandem rather than individually.

1.   With scope economies, firms sell multiple outputs (e.g., copier machines and copier service).

2.   Without scope economies, firms specialize (e.g., gourmet ice cream shops).

B.   **Exploiting Scope Economies:** Scope economies are often an important element of competitive strategy for new products with standard characteristics where price is a key consideration.

XI.   **COST-VOLUME-PROFIT ANALYSIS**

    A.   **Cost-Volume-Profit Charts:** Cost-volume-profit (or breakeven) analysis is an analytical technique used to study relations among costs, revenues, and profits.

         1.   The object of the analysis is to discover the output quantities where profit targets are realized.

         2.   Cost-volume-profit charts and electronic spreadsheets depict cost and revenue categories as a function of the quantity produced and sold.

             a.   The point where total revenue equals total costs is the breakeven output level.

    B.   **Degree of Operating Leverage:** The degree of operating leverage is the percentage change in profit that results from a 1% change in units sold.

         1.   When price and variable costs per unit are constant, DOL is:

$$DOL = \frac{Q(P - AVC)}{Q(P - AVC) - TFC},$$

where P is price, AVC is average variable cost, and TFC is total fixed costs.

         2.   Because profit contribution equals total revenue minus total variable cost, DOL is the profit contribution to net profit ratio.

         3.   DOL is also the elasticity of profit with respect to output.

XII.   **SUMMARY**

PROBLEMS & SOLUTIONS

P9.1   ***Cost Concepts.*** *Holding all else equal, describe the decline in average costs caused by each of the following as due to economies of scale, economies of scope, or learning curve advantages. Explain.*

       A.   *Increased worker specialization as output expands.*

       B.   *Growing levels of output per period.*

       C.   *Product line extension.*

       D.   *Better labor-management coordination over time.*

       E.   *Growing practical experience in production.*

P9.1   **SOLUTION**

       A.   Economies of Scale. Increased worker specialization as output expands is a prime cause of increasing returns to scale in production.

       B.   Economies of Scale. As output per period expands, increased worker specialization and other advantages of large size become operative. As in Part A, this involves a downward movement along the average cost curve.

       C.   Economies of Scope. Product line extension allows a firm to extend to related products the special productive capabilities and marketing skills gained in the production and sale of a given product. The cost savings which result are due to economies of scope.

       D.   Learning curve advantages. Better labor-management coordination over time is an example of how production experience can lead to substantial cost savings. Because such advantages are a function of time (cumulative output), they can be described as learning curve advantages.

       E.   Learning curve advantages. Growing practical experience in production is a prime source of learning curve advantages.

P9.2   ***Cost Concepts.*** *Determine whether each of the following is true or false. Explain why.*

       A.   *Average cost exceeds marginal cost at the minimum efficient scale of plant.*

B. *An increase in fixed cost will typically cause a reduction in the break-even activity level.*

C. *If $\varepsilon_C > 1$, increasing returns to scale and increasing average costs are indicated.*

D. *When long-run average cost is increasing, it can pay to operate larger plants with some excess capacity rather than smaller plants at their peak efficiency.*

E. *An increase in minimum efficient scale will typically increase the degree of operating leverage.*

P9.2 **SOLUTION**

A. False. The point of minimum average cost identifies the minimum efficient scale of plant. By definition, average and marginal costs are equal at this point.

B. False. The breakeven activity level is where $Q = TFC/(P - AVC)$. As total fixed cost (TFC) increases, this ratio and the breakeven activity level will increase.

C. False. When $\varepsilon_C > 1$, the percentage change in cost exceeds a given percentage change in output. This describes a situation of increasing average costs and diminishing returns to scale.

D. False. When long-run average costs are increasing, it can pay to operate smaller plants at above-minimum costs rather than larger plants at their peak efficiency.

E. True. An increase in minimum efficient scale is typically associated with an increase in fixed costs and the degree of operating leverage.

P9.3 **Cost Curve Analysis.** *Indicate whether each of the following involves an upward or downward shift in the long-run average cost curve, or instead involves a leftward or rightward movement along a given curve. Also indicate whether each will have an increasing, decreasing, or uncertain effect on the level of average cost.*

A. *A fall in wage rates*

B. *A rise in output*

C. *An labor-saving technical change*

D. *A rise in interest rates*

  E. *An increase in scope economies*

P9.3 **SOLUTION**

  A. A fall in wage rates causes a downward shift in the LRAC curve, and decrease LRAC.

  B. A rise in output is reflected in a rightward movement along a given LRAC curve, and involve an uncertain effect on the level of LRAC.

  C. Labor saving technical change causes a downward shift in the LRAC curve, and decrease LRAC.

  D. A rise in interest rates gives rise to a upward shift in the LRAC curve, and an increase in LRAC.

  E. Like any beneficial technical change or innovation, an increase in scope economies causes a downward shift in the LRAC curve, and decrease LRAC.

P9.4 **Incremental Analysis.** *One year ago, Will Truman quit a promising career with a major Manhattan-based law firm to set up his own law practice. Truman was a valued member of the firm, and his former employer has been persistent in its efforts to get Truman to return. They have offered Truman a promotion to the rank of partner with a starting salary of $150,000 per year. Truman has asked your opinion as to whether or not it would be financially wise to do so, and has provided the following data on his own law practice:*

Income Statement

<u>Revenues</u>		$315,000
<u>Expenses</u>:		
Materials, exhibits, etc.	$25,000	
Labor	90,000	
Rent, misc.	<u>40,000</u>	<u>155,000</u>
		$ 160,000

Balance Sheet

<u>Assets</u>:	
Accounts Receivable	$85,000
Office Equipment, etc.	65,000

Automobile	*40,000*	*$190,000*
Liabilities:		
Accounts Payable	*$5,000*	
Note Payable	*15,000*	*20,000*
Net Book Value		*$170,000*

After making a few phone calls, you find out that Truman's office equipment and company car can be sold for 75% of book value, while a local factor will purchase Truman's accounts receivable for 90% of face value. In addition, a local real estate firm has offered to sublet Truman's office space, effectively letting Truman out of his office lease of $2,500 per month. As an alternative to dissolving Truman's law practice, Truman's former employer has offered to absorb the practice and pay Truman $175,000 for his interest.

A. *Determine the economic value before taxes of the dissolution sale versus sale as ongoing concern alternatives.*

B. *If Truman sells his practice for more than its net book value he must pay a state plus federal capital gains tax of 40% on his profit. In light of this fact, what rate of return on investment of the sale proceeds would make Truman financially indifferent to selling his practice and returning to his former employer, versus continuing his solo career? (Note: Labor expenses itemized in the income statement do not include a salary for Truman.)*

P9.4   SOLUTION

A.   The economic value of the dissolution sale versus sale as ongoing concern alternatives can be determined as follows:

Dissolution Sale Proceeds	
Accounts Receivable (0.9 × $85,000)	$76,500
Office Equipment, Car (0.75 × $105,000)	78,750
Gross Proceeds	155,250
Debts	(20,000)
Net Proceeds	$135,250
Ongoing Concern Sale Proceeds	
Offer	$175,000

Thus, the sale as an ongoing concern dominates the dissolution sale alternative, and constitutes a measure of the economic value of the firm.

B. The before tax interest rate necessary for Truman to be indifferent between selling his own law practice and returning to his former employer is calculated by comparing current profits with the current economic value of his own practice.

Actual profits can be obtained by adjusting reported profits to reflect Truman's employment opportunity costs.

Reported profits	$160,000
Truman's employment opportunity cost	(150,000)
Adjusted business profits	$10,000

The after-tax economic value of Truman's own practice is:

Sale Proceeds	$175,000
Capital gains tax 0.4($175,000 - $170,000)	(2,000)
	$173,000

Therefore, Truman's effective current rate of return on the realizable economic value of his own law practice is:

$$\frac{\$10,000}{\$173,000} = 0.058 \text{ or } 5.8\%$$

This means that Truman would be indifferent between the two alternatives of maintaining his own law practice versus returning to his former employer if investments with taxable returns and similar risks currently yield 5.8%. If they yield more, he would realize an economic gain from selling out and returning to his former employer. This problem points out the importance of considering the cost of owner-supplied capital. Capital isn't free, even when it's your own.

P9.5 ***Incremental Analysis.*** *Flintstones, Inc., markets a small solid cylinder of a spark-producing alloy used to ignite the fuel in residential and commercial furnaces. Currently, the company's products are sold to other manufacturers who then incorporate it in their merchandise. The yearly volume of output is 5,000 units produced and sold. The selling price and cost per unit are:*

Selling Price	*$250*
Costs:	

Direct material	$40	
Direct labor	60	
Variable overhead	30	
Variable selling expenses	25	
Fixed selling expenses	_20_	_175_
Unit profit before tax		$ 75

Barney Rubble, marketing director for Flintstones, is considering whether or not the company should use the Internet to market its product directly to end-users for $300 per unit. Although no added investment in productive facilities is required, there are additional costs for further packaging and marketing. Rubble estimates these costs as:

Direct labor	$20 per unit
Variable overhead	$5 per unit
Variable selling expenses	$2 per unit
Fixed selling expenses	$20,000 per year

Should Flintstones market its product directly to end-users?

P9.5   **SOLUTION**

This problem deals with the preferable extent of product marketing and packaging, and must be answered through incremental profit analysis. The analysis deals only with the incremental revenues and costs associated with the decision to market directly to end-users.

Incremental revenue per unit ($300 - $250)	$50
Incremental variable cost per unit ($20 + $5 + $2)	_27_
Incremental profit contribution per unit	$23
Yearly output volume in units	× 5,000
Incremental variable profit per year	$115,000
Incremental fixed cost per year	20,000
Yearly incremental profit	$ 95,000

Because incremental profit is positive, the decision to market directly to end-users is preferable to continuing the present operating policy.

P9.6 **_Learning or Experience._** *Grace Adler Designs, Inc., has successfully completed a $2 million interior decorating project for the headquarters of a Silicon valley-based high tech firm. Adler believes that experience gained on the project will allow the company to now complete a similar job for $1.9 million.*

    A.   *In percentage terms, what is the learning or experience rate projected by Adler? (Hint: Learning rates are expressed as a cost savings percentage).*

    B.   *Assuming Adler's learning rate estimate is accurate, how would you explain actual costs of $1.95 million on a second project?*

P9.6 **SOLUTION**

    A.   In this problem, the learning rate projection is made using total costs because the project is the relevant scale of output.

$$\text{Learning rate} = \left(1 - \frac{\text{Cost}_2}{\text{Cost}_1}\right) \times 100$$

$$= \left(1 - \frac{\$1.9}{\$2.0}\right) \times 100$$

$$= 5\%$$

    B.   If actual costs were $1.95 million, or $500,000 above the $1.9 million projection, then one of two possible explanations could be offered. A first possibility is that the second project may not have been as efficiently carried out. The same level of operating efficiency must be achieved in both periods if learning curve advantages are to be fully realized. Secondly, higher costs could be due to increases in wage or interest rates, higher material costs, poorer weather conditions, etc. Learning curve calculations are made based on the assumption that all else is held equal in terms of operating conditions.

P9.7 **_Profit Contribution Analysis._** *Cleo Finch, sales manager of Medical Supply, Inc., has informed the company president that if the price of MSI's disposable syringe is reduced, sales and profits will both increase. Currently, sales are 100,000 units per month, variable costs are 40% of total revenue, allocated fixed costs are 50% of total revenue, with profits making up the remaining 10%. The current syringe price is $2. According to Finch, a price reduction of 10% will result in profits one and one-half times what they are now. The firm has large amounts of excess capacity and, therefore, no increase in* *overhead is expected to accompany an increase in output. Unit variable costs are also expected to remain constant.*

A. *How many units must be sold at the new price for Finch to be correct?*

B. *What point price elasticity is implicit in Finch's forecast?*

P9.7   SOLUTION

A. Currently,

$$TR = P \times Q = \$2(100,000) = \$200,000$$

$$\pi = 0.1(\$200,000) = \$20,000$$

$$TFC = 0.5(\$200,000) = \$100,000$$

$$TVC = 0.4(\$200,000) = \$80,000$$

$$AVC = \frac{TVC}{Q} = \frac{\$80,000}{100,000} = \$0.80$$

The projected profit is 150% of current profit, or:

$$\pi_P = 1.5(\$20,000)$$

$$= \$30,000$$

The new price is 90% of the current price, therefore:

$$P_P = 0.9(\$2)$$

$$= \$1.80$$

The unit profit contribution of the product is price minus variable cost, thus:

$$\pi_C = \$1.80 - \$0.80$$

$$= \$1$$

Dividing fixed costs plus the projected profit by the unit profit contribution determines the projected sales quantity:

$$Q_P = \frac{TFC + \pi_P}{\pi_C}$$

$$= \frac{\$100,000 + \$30,000}{\$1}$$

$$= 130,000 \text{ units}$$

B. Following a price decline from $2 to $1.80, the quantity purchased is projected to increase from 100,000 to 130,000. Therefore, the sales manager is projecting:

$$\varepsilon_P = \partial Q / \partial P \times P/Q$$

$$= \frac{\$130,000 - 100,000}{\$1.80 - \$2} \times \frac{\$2}{100,000}$$

$$= -3 \text{ (Elastic)}$$

P9.8 ***Multiplant Operation.*** *Jack McFarland is CEO of the Cola King Bottling Company, a small regional producer operating in the Pacific Northwest. McFarland is considering two alternative expansion proposals:*

1. *Construct a single bottling plant in Phoenix, Arizona with a capacity of 40,000 cases per month, at a monthly fixed cost of $20,000 and a variable cost of $2.50 per case.*

2. *Construct 3 plants, 1 each in Phoenix, Arizona; Las Vegas, Nevada; and Albuquerque, New Mexico, with capacities of 15,000, 14,000 and 13,000 respectively; and monthly fixed costs of $11,000, $10,000 and $9,000 each. Variable costs would be only $2.30 per case due to lower distribution costs, but sales from each plant would be limited to demand within the home state. The total estimated monthly sales volume in the southwestern states, 37,000 cases, is distributed as: Arizona, 15,000 cases; Nevada, 14,000 cases; and New Mexico, 8,000 cases.*

    A. *Using a wholesale price of $4 per case in each state, calculate the breakeven output quantities for each alternative.*

    B. *Which alternative expansion scheme should Cola King follow?*

C.   *If sales increase to production capacities, which alternative would prove to be more profitable?*

P9.8   **SOLUTION**

A.   Single-plant alternative

$$Q = \frac{TFC}{P - AVC}$$

$$= \frac{\$20,000}{\$4 - \$2.50}$$

$$= \frac{20,000}{1.5}$$

$$= 13,333 \text{ cases}$$

Multiple-plant alternative

$$\text{Phoenix: } Q = \frac{\$11,000}{\$4 - \$2.30}$$

$$= \frac{11,000}{1.70}$$

$$= 6,471 \text{ cases}$$

$$\text{Las Vegas: } Q = \frac{\$10,000}{\$1.70}$$

$$= 5,882 \text{ cases}$$

$$\text{Albuquerque: } Q = \frac{\$9,000}{\$1.70}$$

$$= 5,294 \text{ cases}$$

Thus, the breakeven quantity for the multiple-plant option would be:

$$6,471 + 5,882 + 5,294 = 17,647 \text{ cases}$$

Of course, this assumes that the demand is distributed among the states in amounts equal to the breakeven quantities for the individual plants.

B.   Single-plant alternative

$$\pi = TR - TC$$

$$= P(Q) - TFC - AVC(Q)$$

$$= \$4(37,000) - \$20,000 - \$2.50(37,000)$$

$$= \$35,500$$

Multiple-plant alternative

$$\pi = TR - TC$$

$$= P(Q) - TFC - AVC(Q)$$

$$= \$4(37,000) - \$30,000 - \$2.30(37,000)$$

$$= \$32,900$$

Management should elect the single-plant alternative because of its larger profit.

C.   Single-Plant at Full Capacity

$$\pi = TR - TC$$

$$= P(Q) - TFC - AVC(Q)$$

$$= \$4(40,000) - \$20,000 - \$2.50(40,000)$$

$$= \$40,000$$

Multiple-Plant at Full Capacity

	P(Q)	−	TFC	−	AVC(Q)	=	Profit
Phoenix Plant	$4(15,000)	−	$11,000	−	$2.30(15,000)	=	$14,500
Las Vegas Plant	$4(14,000)	−	$10,000	−	$2.30(14,000)	=	13,800
Albuquerque Plant	$4(13,000)	−	$9,000	−	$2.30(13,000)	=	13,100
					π	=	$41,400

In this case, management should select the multiple-plant alternative because of its larger profit potential.

P9.9   ***Cost-Volume-Profit Analysis.*** *Karen Walker is CFO of Rosario Products, Inc., a New England-based manufacturer of electrical components. RPI is currently producing and selling 40,000 units of output. Unfortunately, plant capacity is also 40,000 units and potential orders are being turned down. As a result, Walker is considering expanding capacity to 50,000 units. RPI's product sells for $6 per unit, and Walker expects to maintain that price if capacity is expanded. Currently, output has a variable cost of $2 per unit and fixed costs are $80,000. Expansion of capacity to 50,000 units will increase fixed costs by 50% to $120,000, but variable costs per unit will decline by 40% to $1.20.*

   A.   *What is RPI's current breakeven output level?*

   B.   *What is RPI's current degree of operating leverage at 40,000 units?*

   C.   *Considered by itself (that is, assuming that variable cost per unit remains at $2), would the increase in fixed costs associated with expansion increase, decrease, or leave unchanged the degree of operating leverage at 40,000 units?*

   D.   *Considered by itself (that is, assuming that fixed costs remain at $80,000), would the decrease in variable costs associated with expansion increase or leave unchanged the degree of operating leverage at 40,000 units?*

   E.   *What is the importance of analyzing operating leverage in a decision problem such as this one?*

P9.9   **SOLUTION**

   A.   The breakeven quantity is:

$$Q = \frac{TFC}{P - AVC} = \frac{\$80,000}{\$6 - \$2} = 20,000 \text{ units}$$

B.   The degree of operating leverage formula is:

$$DOL = \frac{Q(P - AVC)}{Q(P - AVC) - TFC}$$

$$= \frac{40,000(\$6 - \$2)}{40,000(\$6 - \$2) - 80,000}$$

$$= 2$$

C.   Because,

$$DOL = \frac{Q(P - AVC)}{Q(P - AVC) - TFC}$$

If TFC increases while Q, P and AVC remain constant, then DOL will increase. Proof:

$$DOL = \frac{Q(P - AVC)}{Q(P - AVC) - TFC}$$

$$\frac{\partial DOL}{\partial TFC} = \frac{[Q(P - AVC) - TFC] \times (0) - Q(P - AVC)(-1)}{(Q(P - AVC) - TFC)^2}$$

$$= \frac{Q(P - AVC)}{(Q(P - AVC) - TFC)^2} > 0$$

D.   If AVC decreases while holding Q, P and TFC constant, then DOL will decrease. Proof:

$$DOL = \frac{Q(P - AVC)}{Q(P - AVC) - TFC}$$

$$= \frac{Q(P) - Q(AVC)}{Q(P) - Q(AVC) - TFC}$$

$$\frac{\partial DOL}{\partial AVC} = \frac{[Q(P) - Q(AVC) - TFC](-Q) - [Q(P) - Q(AVC)](-Q)}{[Q(P) - Q(AVC) - TFC]^2}$$

$$= \frac{Q(TFC)}{(Q(P - AVC) - TFC)^2} > 0$$

E. The study of operating leverage is important for operating and planning purposes. For example, the level of operating leverage can have an important effect on changes in operating profits, especially when projected changes in output are substantial. Remember:

$$DOL = \frac{\partial\pi/\pi}{\partial Q/Q}$$

$$\partial\pi/\pi = DOL \times \partial Q/Q$$

If the expected $\partial Q/Q$ over the next couple of years is positive, then one would want the highest DOL possible, thus achieving the highest $\partial\pi/\pi$. Unfortunately, it is seldom possible to know for certain that changes in output will be positive. A severe recession, for example, can cause output to fall. If this were the case and DOL were high, then a large negative change in operating profits would result. Because the expected change in output has an element of uncertainty attached to it in the real world, the desired level for DOL depends on the risk attitude of the managers and owners of the firm. By changing fixed and variable costs, the level of DOL can be changed to the desired level.

P9.10 ***Breakeven Analysis.*** *Korean Motor Works , Inc., recently converted an unused assembly plant in Pennsylvania to produce budget-priced compact sport-utility vehicles, thus adding to the number of foreign-owned auto makers in the United States. KMW's analysis indicate that variable production costs can be described by the function:*

$$TVC = \$13,500Q + \$10Q^2$$

Where TVC = total variable costs in thousands of dollars, and Q = output in thousands of SUVs. KMW's SUVs have been enthusiastically accepted in the market given their surprisingly good quality and low average price of $18,000 per unit.

Calculate the breakeven level of yearly output for KMW, assuming that fixed costs are $500 million.

P9.10 **SOLUTION**

From the breakeven formula:

$$Q = \frac{TFC}{P - AVC}$$

$$Q = \frac{\$500{,}000}{\$18{,}000 - \left(\dfrac{\$13{,}500Q + \$10Q^2}{Q} \right)}$$

$$500{,}000 = (18{,}000 - 13{,}500 - 10Q)(Q)$$

$$0 = -10Q^2 + 4{,}500Q - 500{,}000$$

This is a quadratic equation in the form:

$$aQ^2 + bQ + c = 0$$

where $a = -10$, $b = 4{,}500$ and $c = -500{,}000$. Its two roots can be obtained from the quadratic formula:

$$Q = \frac{-b \pm \sqrt{b^2 - 4ac}}{2a}$$

$$= \frac{-4{,}500 \pm \sqrt{4{,}500^2 - 4(-10)(-500{,}000)}}{2(-10)}$$

$$= \frac{-4{,}500 \pm 500}{-20}$$

$$= 200\ (000) \text{ or } 250\ (000)$$

Thus, there are dual breakeven points of 200,000 and 250,000 cars. A "unit's problem" may be encountered if one isn't careful in the solution to this problem. All dollar and output values must reflect the fact that TVC is in thousands of dollars and Q is in thousands of cars. Here, a P = $18,000 per car becomes $18,000,000 per unit of Q when expressed in dollars, and $18,000 per unit of Q when expressed in thousands of dollars. Thus, P = $18,000 is used in the breakeven formula.

Chapter 10

COMPETITIVE MARKETS

To this point, managerial decisions have been studied without attention to market structure considerations. In practice, the competitive environment or market structure faced by the firm is a factor of utmost importance. Market structure analysis is so important that this text devotes five full chapters to this topic. This chapter considers market structure, firm conduct, and economic performance in vigorously competitive markets. The economic model of perfect competition describes sectors of the economy in which widespread price competition drives equilibrium profits to a level just sufficient to maintain required investment. Agriculture, mining, and stock trading are good examples of final product markets that can be described as perfectly competitive. The unskilled labor market, commodity and raw material markets are good examples of intermediate product markets that can be described as vigorously competitive. Despite energetic competition, significant disequilibrium profits or losses are sometimes earned in competitive markets when unanticipated changes in demand or supply conditions cause unpredictable changes in prices and/or costs. In competitive markets, any disequilibrium profits tend to be fleeting as entry by new competitors and/or expansion by established firms causes supply to rise and prices to fall back to normal levels. Conversely, when disequilibrium losses are experienced, industry supply tends to fall and prices rise following the exit of weak competitors and/or output contraction by established firms. In both cases, normal profits tend to be quickly reestablished in long-run equilibrium. In competitive markets, dynamic competition ensures that consumer prices reflect the marginal costs of production by firms that efficiently produce output in a cost-minimizing fashion.

CHAPTER OUTLINE

I. **COMPETITIVE ENVIRONMENT**

    A. **What is Market Structure?** The competitive environment in the market for any product is the market structure faced by the firm.

        1. Market structure is measured in terms of the number of actual buyers and sellers plus potential entrants, barriers to entry and exit, capital requirements, nonprice competition, and so on.

    B. **Vital Role of Potential Entrants:** Potential entrants pose a sufficiently credible threat of entry to affect price/output decisions of incumbents.

II. **FACTORS THAT SHAPE THE COMPETITIVE ENVIRONMENT**

A.   Product Differentiation: The extent of product differentiation is an important determinant of the competitive environment.

    1.   Product differentiation includes all of the methods used by firms to distinguish their products from those produced by rivals.

        a.   R&D, advertising, innovative product design, and imaginative customer service are all valuable means of product differentiation.

    2.   Price competition tends to diminish when products are highly differentiated..

    3.   When distribution costs are low, broad geographic markets and active competition are possible.

B.   Production Methods: Industries with production functions that exhibit increasing returns to scale are sometimes characterized by less competition than are industries with constant or decreasing returns.

C.   Entry and Exit Conditions: When entry and exit are easy, the threat of potential entry can effectively limit prices and profits for current competitors.

    1.   A barrier to entry is any advantage for industry incumbents over new rivals.

    2.   A barrier to exit is any limit on asset redeployment.

III.   COMPETITIVE MARKET CHARACTERISTICS

A.   Basic Features: Perfect competition exists when individual producers in a market have no influence over prices. Basic requirements for perfect competition are:

    1.   Large number of buyers and sellers.

    2.   Product homogeneity.

    3.   Free entry into and exit from the market.

    4.   Perfect dissemination of information.

B.   Examples of Competitive Markets: Many big agricultural product markets, the unskilled labor market, and much of retailing can be described as vigorously competitive, if not perfectly competitive.

1.   Many prominent markets for intermediate goods and services are perfectly competitive.

2.   The unskilled labor market in many medium- to large-size cities fits this description because unskilled workers often have a ready market for their services at the going wage rate.

IV.   PROFIT MAXIMIZATION IN COMPETITIVE MARKETS

A.   **Profit Maximization Imperative:** In competitive markets, firms must be vigilant to produce the goods and services consumers want in a cost-effective manner.

    1.   Maximum profits result when market price is set equal to marginal cost for firms in a perfectly competitive industry.

    2.   Normal profit, defined as the rate of return necessary to attract and retain capital investment, is included as part of the financing costs included in total costs.

    3.   Economic profit represents an above-normal rate of return.

    4.   The firm incurs economic losses whenever it fails to earn a normal profit.

B.   **Role of Marginal Analysis:** Profit is maximized when the difference between marginal revenue and marginal cost, called marginal profit, equals zero.

    1. $MR = MC$ when $M\pi = MR - MC = 0$.

    2.   For profit maximization, total profits must be decreasing beyond the point where $MR = MC$.

V.   MARGINAL COST AND FIRM SUPPLY

A.   **Short-Run Firm Supply Curve**: The competitive market price (P) is shown as a horizontal line because competitive firms are price takers and, hence, $P = MR$.

    1.   The firm's marginal-cost curve shows the amount of output the firm would be willing to supply at any market price.

    2.   The marginal cost curve is the competitive firm's short-run supply curve so long as $P > AVC$.

B.   Long-run Firm Supply Curve: To ensure long-term viability, the competitive firm must cover all necessary costs of production and earn a profit sufficient to provide an adequate rate of return to the firm's stockholders.

1.   In the short-run, if P > AVC, the firm's operating losses will decrease as output expands and firms will proceed to offer supply at the profit-maximizing, or loss-minimizing, point where P = MR = MC.

2.   Given the need to cover all fixed costs and earn a fair rate of return, the marginal cost curve is the competitive firm's long-run supply curve so long as P > ATC.

VI.   COMPETITIVE MARKET SUPPLY CURVE

A.   Market Supply With a Fixed Number of Competitors: In the short run, the amount supplied in a competitive market is simply the sum of output produced by all established competitors.

B.   Market Supply With Entry and Exit: In the long run, markets are dynamic rather than static.

1.   Entry expands the number of firms in the industry, increases the quantity of goods and services supplied, shifts the supply curve rightward, and drives down prices and profits.

2.   Exit reduces the number of firms in the industry, decreases the quantity of goods and services supplied, shifts the supply curve leftward, and allows prices and profits to rise for remaining competitors.

VII.   COMPETITIVE MARKET EQUILIBRIUM

A.   Balance of Supply and Demand: Competitive market prices and quantities are determined by the interplay of market demand and market supply.

B.   Normal Profit Equilibrium: At the profit-maximizing output level, MR = MC and individual firm profits are maximized.

1.   Given the horizontal market demand curve facing individual competitive firms, marginal revenue and price are also equal, MR = P.

2.   In competitive market equilibrium P = MR = MC = ATC.
      a.   In competitive market equilibrium, there are no economic profits.

b. All firms earn a risk-adjusted, fair, or normal, rate of return.

VIII. SUMMARY

PROBLEMS & SOLUTIONS

P10.1   ***Competitive Markets Concepts.*** *Indicate whether each of the following statements is true or false, and explain why.*

A.   *In long-run equilibrium, the marginal firm or most likely potential entrant in a perfectly competitive industry earns zero profit.*

B.   *Goods and services must have unique characteristics in order for firms to have price-setting ability.*

C.   *In long-run equilibrium, competitive market output is seldom produced at the point where P = AC and AC is minimized.*

D.   *Profit maximization always requires that firms operate at the output level at which marginal revenue and marginal cost are equal.*

E.   *The existence of economic profit is a theoretical concept that cannot be measured in practical terms.*

P10.1   ***SOLUTION***

A.   False. In long-run equilibrium, the marginal firm or most likely potential entrant in a perfectly competitive industry earns zero economic profit. For long-term viability, firms in competitive markets must earn a normal rate of return on investment.

B.   True. Perfect competition exists in a market when individual customers and individual firms have no influence over price. In such markets, both customers and firms take prices as given. Goods and services must have unique characteristics in order for firms to have price-setting ability.

C.   False. In long-run equilibrium, competitive market output is produced at the point where $P = AC$ and AC is minimized. Because competitive firms are price takers, $P = MR$ in competitive markets. Because competitive firms also operate at the point where $MC = AC$ and average costs are minimized, it follows that $P = MR = MC = AC$ in competitive markets.

D.   True. Profit maximization always requires that firms operate at the output level at which marginal revenue and marginal cost are equal.

E. False. Normal profit is defined as the rate of return necessary to retain and attract needed capital investment. Economic profit represents an above-normal rate of return. The firm incurs economic losses whenever it fails to earn a normal profit. If economic profits can be earned by the marginal firm or most likely potential entrant, market entry or expansion by existing firms will be observed. Conversely, if economic losses are earned by the marginal firm, market exit or contraction by existing firms will be observed. Therefore, the presence of economic profits or losses can be inferred from entry and exit decisions.

P10.2 **Firm v. Market Equilibrium.** *Specify whether each of the following statements is true or false and demonstrate why.*

A. *Competitive market equilibrium results when the intersection of industry demand and supply curves occurs at a point where long-run average costs are declining.*

B. *In long-run equilibrium, every firm in a perfectly competitive industry earns zero profit.*

C. *Perfect competition exists in markets where the firm demand curve is horizontal.*

D. *Downward-sloping industry demand curves characterize competitive markets.*

E. *The price elasticity of demand would rise following an increase in product standardization.*

P10.2 **SOLUTION**

A. False. Competitive market equilibrium only occurs in constant cost industries. This means that the market clearing price, or price where Demand (Price) = Supply (Marginal Cost), occurs at an output level where long-run average costs are constant.

B. False. In long-run equilibrium, every firm in a perfectly competitive industry earns zero economic profit. However, firms can expect to earn a normal rate of return on investment in competitive markets.

C. True. Perfect competition exists in a market when individual firms have no influence over price. Such firms take industry prices as a given, and MR = P.

D. True. Downward sloping demand curves follow from the law of diminishing marginal utility and characterize competitive market structures.

E. True. An increase in the price elasticity of demand would result following an increase in product standardization and a reduction in the firm's price-setting ability.

P10.3 ***Demand and Supply Concepts.*** *The retail market for unleaded gasoline is extremely price competitive. Describe the effects of each of the following influences on demand and/or supply conditions in this fiercely competitive market.*

A. *An economic recession (fall in national income).*

B. *An increase in EPA-mandated mileage requirements for automobiles.*

C. *An increase in environmental restrictions on domestic oil and gas exploration.*

D. *A reduction in the global risk of terrorist attacks.*

E. *An increase in refining costs to reduce air pollution in major cities.*

P10.3 **SOLUTION**

A. Decrease demand/leftward shift in demand curve. With a fall in national income, consumers and business people will have less money to spend on transportation and the demand for unleaded gasoline can be expected to fall.

B. Decrease demand/leftward shift in demand curve. With a rise in EPA-mandated mileage requirements for automobiles, consumers and business people will demand less gasoline at every price level and the demand for unleaded gasoline can be expected to fall.

C. Decrease supply/leftward shift in supply curve. An increase in environmental restrictions on domestic oil and gas exploration will reduce the availability of unleaded gasoline by increasing the marginal costs of production at every price level.

D. Increase supply/rightward shift in supply curve. A decrease in the global risk of terrorist attacks will increase supply at every price level by reducing the marginal costs of production at every price level.

E. Decrease supply/leftward shift in supply curve. An increase in refining costs to reduce air pollution in major cities will reduce the availability of unleaded gasoline by increasing the marginal costs of production at every price level.

P10.4 ***Perfectly Competitive Equilibrium.*** *Fuel costs have risen sharply during recent years as consumption, refining and production costs have risen sharply. Demand and Supply conditions in the perfectly competitive domestic crude oil market are:*

$$Q_S = -3.33 + 0.833P \qquad (Supply)$$

$$Q_D = 50 - 0.5P \qquad (Demand)$$

where Q is quantity in millions of barrels per day, and P is price per barrel.

A. *Graph industry supply and demand curves.*

B. *Determine both graphically and algebraically the equilibrium industry price/output combination.*

P10.4 **SOLUTION**

A.

Crude Oil Market

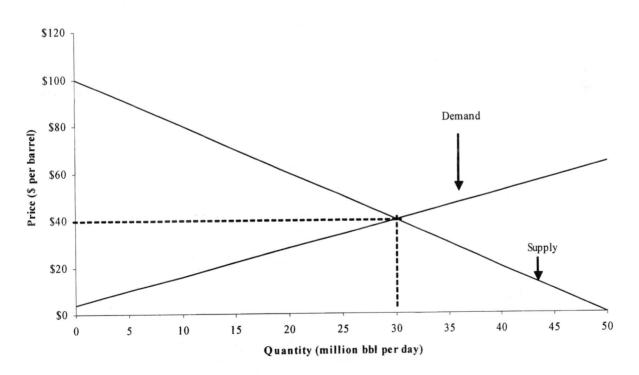

B. From the graph, it is clear that $Q_D = Q_S = 30(000,000)$ at a price of \$40 per barrel. Thus, P = \$40 and Q = 30(000,000) is the equilibrium price/output combination.

Algebraically,

$$Q_D = Q_S$$

$$50 - 0.5P = -3.33 + 0.833P$$

$$1.33P = 53.33$$

$$P = \$40$$

Both demand and supply equal 30(000,000) because:

Demand: $Q_D = 50 - 0.5(40) = 30(000,000)$
Supply: $Q_S = -3.33 + 0.833(40) = 30(000,000)$

P10.5   ***Perfectly Competitive Firm Supply.*** *The market price for 512MB PC2100 DDR SODIMM memory chips used in computers and "intelligent" electronics fluctuates widely depending on changes in world-wide demand and supply conditions in this perfectly competitive industry. Market prices for a recent seven-month period were as follows:*

Month	Price
January	*\$29.00*
February	*30.00*
March	*33.50*
April	*35.50*
May	*42.50*
June	*37.50*
July	*35.00*

Marginal cost conditions in the industry are:

$$MC = \$25 + \$0.0001Q$$

where MC is marginal cost and Q is output (in thousands).

A. What is the minimum price necessary before domestic firms will supply chips?

B. Calculate the domestic supply of chips per month.

P10.5 ***SOLUTION***

A. $25. Given MC = $25 + $0.0001Q, a minimum price of $25 must be obtained before any domestic supply would be forthcoming.

B. In a perfectly competitive industry, P = MC. Therefore, when price is expressed as a function of output, the industry supply curve equals the marginal cost curve:

$$P = MC = \$25 + \$0.0001Q$$

To express quantity as a function of price, note that:

$$P = \$25 + \$0.0001Q$$

$$0.0001Q = -25 + P$$

$$Q = -250,000 + 10,000P$$

Therefore, domestic supply per month is:

Month	Supply (000)
January	Q = -250,000 + 10,000(29) = 40,000
February	Q = -250,000 + 10,000(30) = 50,000
March	Q = -250,000 + 10,000(33.5) = 85,000
April	Q = -250,000 + 10,000(35.5) = 105,000
May	Q = -250,000 + 10,000(42.5) = 175,000
June	Q = -250,000 + 10,000(37.5) = 125,000
July	Q = -250,000 + 10,000(35) = 100,000

P10.6 ***Perfectly Competitive Firm and Industry Supply.*** *Solar Systems, Inc., produces and sells solar heat panels for hot water heaters in a perfectly competitive industry and has the following total and marginal cost functions:*

$$TC = \$500Q - \$10Q^2 + Q^3$$

$$MC = \partial TC/\partial Q = \$500 - \$20Q + \$3Q^2$$

where TC is total cost (in thousands of dollars) and Q is output (in thousands of units). Included in this cost function is a normal return of 15% on invested capital.

A. *Assuming that the firm and the industry are in equilibrium, what is the price charged by Solar Systems for its product?*

B. *What is the value of economic profits, average cost, and marginal cost at this equilibrium price?*

C. *Graph the marginal revenue, marginal cost, and average cost curves.*

D. *What is the supply function for Solar Systems' output?*

P10.6 **SOLUTION**

A. If the firm and the industry are in equilibrium, then P = AC where average costs are minimized. To find the point of minimum average costs, set MC = AC where:

$$MC = AC$$

$$\$500 - \$20Q + \$3Q^2 = \frac{\$500Q - \$10Q^2 + Q^3}{Q}$$

$$500 - 20Q + 3Q^2 = 500 - 10Q + Q^2$$

$$2Q^2 = 10Q$$

$$2Q = 10$$

$$Q = 5 \,(000)$$

At Q = 5 (000),

$$AC = 500 - 10Q + Q^2$$

$$= 500 - 10(5) + 5^2$$

$$= \$475$$

Therefore, because P must equal AC:

$$P = AC$$

$$= \$475$$

(*Note*: $\partial AC/\partial Q = -10 + 2Q > 0$ for $Q > 5$, so AC is rising beyond that point and $Q = 5$ is a point of minimum average costs.)

B. In equilibrium, economic profits equal zero, and average cost equals marginal cost.

$$\pi = TR - TC$$

$$= P \times Q - 500Q + 10Q^2 - Q^3$$

$$= \$475(5) - \$500(5) + \$10(5^2) - \$1(5^3)$$

$$= \$0$$

$$AC = \$500 - \$10Q + Q^2$$

$$= 500 - 10(5) + 5^2$$

$$= 500 - 50 + 25$$

$$= \$475$$

$$MC = \$500 - \$20(5) + \$3(5^2)$$

$$= \$475$$

C.

Solar Systems, Inc.

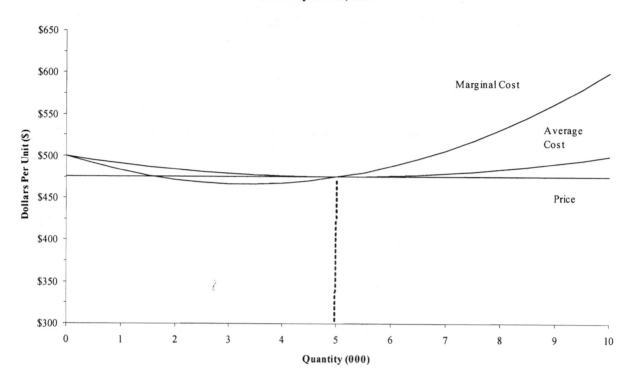

D.   A competitive firm's supply function is defined by that portion of the marginal cost curve lying above the average variable cost curve. Because Solar Systems' total cost function does not contain a fixed cost component, average costs and average variable costs are identical. Thus, Solar Systems' supply curve would be that portion of its marginal cost curve lying above the average cost curve.

P10.7   ***Competitive Market Supply***. *The Merry Maids, Inc. and Kwickie Kleaners, Ltd., offer housecleaning services in the Chicagoland area. Confidential cost and output information for each company reveal the following relations between marginal cost and output:*

$$MC_M = \$8 + \$0.00032Q_M \qquad (Merry\ Maids)$$

$$MC_K = \$15 + \$0.00008Q_K \qquad (Kwickie\ Kleaners)$$

The wholesale market for these housecleaning services is vigorously price-competitive, and neither firm is able to charge a premium for its products. P = MR in this market and Q is hours of housecleaning services provided.

A.   *Determine the supply curve for each firm. Express price as a function of quantity and quantity as a function of price.*

B.   *Calculate the quantity supplied by each firm at prices of $8, $15, and $20. What is the minimum price necessary for each individual firm to supply output?*

C.   *Determine the industry supply curve when P < $15.*

D.   *Determine the industry supply curve when P > $15. To check your answer, calculate quantity at an industry price of $20 and compare your answer with part B.*

P10.7   SOLUTION

A.   Each company will supply output to the point where MR = MC. Because P = MR in this market, the supply curve for each firm can be written with price as a function of quantity as:

<u>Merry Maids</u>

$$MR_M \;=\; MC_M$$

$$P \;=\; \$8 + \$0.00032Q_M$$

<u>Kwickie Kleaners</u>

$$MR_K \;=\; MC_K$$

$$P \;=\; \$15 + \$0.00008Q_K$$

When quantity is expressed as a function of price:

<u>Merry Maids</u>

$$P \;=\; \$8 + \$0.00032Q_S$$

$$0.00032Q_S \;=\; -8 + P$$

$$Q_S \;=\; -25{,}000 + 3{,}125P$$

<u>Kwickie Kleaners</u>

$$P = \$15 + \$0.00008Q_K$$

$$0.00008Q_K = -15 + P$$

$$Q_K = -187{,}500 + 12{,}500P$$

B.   The quantity supplied at each respective price is:

Merry Maids

$$P = \$8: Q_M = -25{,}000 + 3{,}125(8) = 0$$

$$P = \$15: Q_M = -25{,}000 + 3{,}125(15) = 21{,}875$$

$$P = \$20: Q_M = -25{,}000 + 3{,}125(20) = 37{,}500$$

Kwickie Kleaners

$$P = \$8: Q_K = -187{,}500 + 12{,}500(8) = -87{,}500 \Rightarrow 0$$
$$\text{(because } Q < 0 \text{ is impossible}$$

$$P = \$15: Q_K = -187{,}500 + 12{,}500(15) = 0$$

$$P = \$20: Q_K = -187{,}500 + 12{,}500(20) = 62{,}500$$

For Merry Maids, $MC = \$8$ when $Q_s = 0$. Because marginal cost rises with output, Merry Maids will never supply a positive level of output unless a price in excess of $8 per unit can be obtained. Negative output is not feasible. Thus, Merry Maids will simply fail to supply output when $P < \$8$. Similarly, $MC_K = \$15$ when $Q_K = 0$. Thus, Kwickie Kleaners will never supply output unless a price in excess of $15 per unit can be obtained.

C.   When $P < \$15$, only Merry Maids can profitably supply output. The Merry Maids supply curve will be the market curve when $P < \$15$:

$$P = \$8 + \$0.00032Q$$

or

$$Q = -25{,}000 + 3{,}125P$$

D.   When $P > \$15$, both companies can profitably supply output. To derive the industry supply curve in this circumstance, we simply sum the quantities supplied by each firm:

$$Q = Q_M + Q_K$$

$$= -25,000 + 3,125P + (-187,500 + 12,500P)$$

$$= -212,500 + 15,625P$$

To check, at $P = \$20$:

$$Q = -212,500 + 15,625(20)$$

$$= 100,000$$

which is supported by the answer to part B, because $Q_M + Q_K = 37,500 + 62,500 = 100,000$.

(*Note*: Some students mistakenly add prices rather than quantities in attempting to derive the industry supply curve. To avoid this problem, it is important to remember that industry supply curves are found through adding up output (horizontal summation), not by adding up prices (vertical summation).)

P10.8   ***Short-run Firm Supply.*** *AccountTemps, Inc., provides remote bookkeeping, CPA, and professional tax accounting services on a national basis. Because services are provided at the home or office of the service provider and transmitted to clients over the Internet, the market for AccountTemps' basic bookkeeping services can be regarded as perfectly competitive.*

$$MC = \$30 + \$0.000025Q$$

Where Q is ours of services provided.

   A.   *Calculate the industry price necessary to induce short-run firm supply of 200,000, 300,000, and 400,000 hours of service. Assume that MC > AVC at every point along the firm's marginal cost curve and that total costs include a normal profit.*

   B.   *Calculate short-run firm supply at industry prices of \$35, \$37.50, and \$40 per hour.*

P10.8   ***SOLUTION***

   A.   The marginal cost curve constitutes the short-run supply curve for firms in perfectly competitive industries provided that price exceeds average variable cost.

Because P = MR, the price necessary to induce short-run firm supply of a given amount is found by setting P = MC, assuming P > AVC. Here:

$$MC = \partial TC/\partial Q = \$30 + \$0.000025Q$$

Therefore, at:

$$Q = 200,000: P = MC = \$30 + \$0.000025(200,000) = \$35$$

$$Q = 300,000: P = MC = \$30 + \$0.000025(300,000) = \$37.50$$

$$Q = 400,000: P = MC = \$30 + \$0.000025(400,000) = \$40$$

B. When quantity is expressed as a function of price, the firm's supply curve can be written:

$$P = MC = \$30 + \$0.000025Q$$

$$0.000025Q = -30 + P$$

$$Q = -1,200,000 + 40,000P$$

Therefore, at:

$$P = \$35: Q = -1,200,000 + 40,000(\$35) = 200,000$$

$$P = \$37.5: Q = -1,200,000 + 40,000(\$37.50) = 300,000$$

$$P = \$40: Q = -1,200,000 + 40,000(\$40) = 400,000$$

P10.9 **Short-run Market Supply.** *New Deli Credit Card Services, Inc., provides account balance and credit card information over the phone to credit card users in the United States. New Deli is a medium-sized service provider with the following total and marginal cost relations:*

$$TC = \$25,000 + \$2.50Q + \$0.000125Q^2$$

$$MC = \partial TC/\partial Q = \$2.50 + \$0.00025Q$$

where Q is the number of phone inquiries answered per month. Assume that MC > AVC at every point along the firm's marginal cost curve, and that total costs include a normal profit.

A.   *Derive the firm's supply curve, expressing quantity as a function of price.*

B.   *Derive the market supply curve if New Deli is one of 400 competitors.*

C.   *Calculate market supply per month at a market price of $8.75 per inquiry.*

P10.9   SOLUTION

A.   The perfectly competitive firm will supply output so long as it is profitable to do so. Because P = MR in perfectly competitive markets, the firm supply curve is given by the relation:

$$P = MC = \partial TC/\partial Q = \$2.50 + \$0.00025Q$$

when quantity is expressed as a function of price, the firm supply curve is:

$$P = \$2.50 + \$0.00025Q$$

$$0.00025Q = -2.50 + P$$

$$Q_s = -10{,}000 + 4{,}000P$$

(*Note*: Variable Cost = $\$2.50Q + \$0.000125Q^2$, and AVC = $\$2.50 + \$0.000125Q$, so MC > AVC at each point along the firm's short-run supply curve.)

B.   If the company is one of 400 such competitors, the industry supply curve is found by simply multiplying the firm supply curve derived in part A by 400. This is equivalent to a horizontal summation of all 400 individual firm supply curves. When quantity is expressed as a function of price:

$$Q_s = 400 \times (-10{,}000 + 4{,}000P)$$

$$= -4{,}000{,}000 + 1{,}600{,}000P$$

When price is expressed as a function of quantity:

$$Q_s = -4{,}000{,}000 + 1{,}600{,}000P$$

$$1{,}600{,}000P = 4{,}000{,}000 + Q_s$$

$$P = \$2.50 + \$0.0000006Q_s$$

C. Q_S = -4,000,000 + 1,600,000P

                              = -4,000,000 + 1,600,000($8.75)

                              = 10,000,000

P10.10   ***Dynamic Competitive Equilibrium.*** *COX-2 inhibitors are drugs used to combat pain and inflammation by selectively blocking the COX-2 enzyme. Blocking this enzyme impedes the production of the chemical messengers (prostaglandins) that cause pain and swelling for arthritis sufferers.   Suppose the following total and marginal revenue relations are relevant for a single producer of COX-2 inhibitors:*

$$TR = \$15Q - \$0.001Q^2$$

$$MR = \partial TR / \partial Q = \$15 - \$0.002Q$$

Total costs (TC) and marginal costs (MC) for research and development, production and distribution are:

$$TC = \$30,400 + \$0.25Q + \$0.000475Q^2$$

$$MC = \partial TC / \partial Q = \$0.25 + \$0.00095Q$$

and Q is the number of doses (in millions). Costs are measured in million of dollars and include a normal profit.

A.   *Use the marginal revenue and marginal cost relations given above to calculate output, price, and economic profits at the profit-maximizing activity level for the period during which a single company enjoys an exclusive patent on this medicine.*

B.   *Calculate optimal output, price, and profit levels in the period following expiration of patent protection based on the assumption that a competitive market where P = MR = MC = AC and minimum AC are achieved.   Is this a stable equilibrium?*

P10.10   SOLUTION

A.   Set MR = MC to find the profit-maximizing activity level:

$$MR = MC$$

$$\$15 - \$0.002Q = \$0.25 + \$0.00095Q$$

$$0.00295Q = 14.75$$

$$Q = 5,000 \text{ (million)}$$

$$P = TR/Q$$

$$= (\$15Q - \$0.001Q^2)/Q$$

$$= \$15 - \$0.001Q$$

$$= \$15 - \$0.001(5,000)$$

$$= \$10 \text{ per dose}$$

$$\pi = TR - TC$$

$$= \$10(5,000) - \$30,400 - \$0.25(5,000) - \$0.000475(5,000)^2$$

$$= \$6,475 \text{ (million)}$$

B.   In a perfectly competitive industry, $P = MR = MC = AC$ in equilibrium. To find minimum AC, set

$$MC = AC$$

$$\$0.25 + \$0.00095Q = (\$30,400 + \$0.25Q + \$0.000475Q^2)/Q$$

$$\$0.25 + \$0.00095Q = \$30,400/Q + \$0.25 + \$0.000475Q$$

$$\$0.000475Q = \$30,400/Q$$

$$Q^2 = 30,400/0.000475$$

$$Q = (30,400/0.000475)^{0.5}$$

$$= 8,000 \text{ (million)}$$

$$P = MC$$

$$= \$0.25 + \$0.00095(8,000)$$

$$= \$7.85$$

$$\pi \; = \; TR - TC$$

$$= \; \$7.85(8,000) - \$30,400 - \$0.25(8,000) - \$0.000475(8,000)^2$$

$$= \; \$0$$

Because only normal profits are being made, this is a stable equilibrium in the market for COX-2 inhibitors and there will be no incentive for entry nor exit.

Chapter 11

PERFORMANCE AND STRATEGY IN COMPETITIVE MARKETS

Society in general has an enormous interest in the performance of the overall economy. When business is functioning efficiently, a growing amount of desired goods and services are produced in a least-cost fashion. In a poorly functioning economy, businesses produce too little of what consumers want, and/or charge them prices that are above and beyond the levels necessary to maintain a fair and reasonable profit. Inefficiency and waste, and an inequitable allocation of economic resources, are characteristic of a poorly functioning economy. Because the economic well being of society is closely tied to the economic performance of business, society in general has an important interest in making sure that the economic environment of business encourages efficiency, innovation, and growing economic betterment. From the perspective of individual businesses, economic performance is measured in terms of expanding revenues, profits, and high-wage employment opportunities. From the firm's perspective, competitive strategy is the relentless pursuit of economic betterment. In a biological sense, individual species compete for resources and habitat. Species grow in importance when they are well-suited to meeting the demands and opportunities presented by the natural environment. Species flourish when they have superior characteristics; they wither and die when they possess inferior characteristics. Competitive firms prosper when they offer goods and services that customers crave in a cost-efficient manner. Successful competitive firms have superior characteristics that allow them to produce goods and services that are cheaper, faster, and better than the competition.

CHAPTER OUTLINE

I.   **COMPETITIVE MARKET EFFICIENCY**

      A.   **Why is it Called Perfect Competition?** Perfectly competitive markets are typically described as an ideal form of market structure that creates an exact balance between supply and demand that maximizes social welfare.

            1.   In competitive market equilibrium, social welfare is measured by the sum of net benefits derived by consumers and producers.

      B.   **Deadweight Loss Problem:** Any real imperfection in competitive markets or government policy has the potential to affect consumer demand, producer supply, and competitive market equilibrium.

            1.   A deadweight loss is any loss suffered by consumers or producers that is not transferred, but is instead simply lost as a result of market imperfections or government policies.

2.   The total deadweight loss is simply the sum of deadweight losses suffered by consumers and producers and is described as the welfare loss triangle.

C.   **Deadweight Loss Illustration:** To find the market equilibrium levels for price and quantity, simply set the market supply and market demand curves equal to one another so that $Q_S = Q_D$.

1.   Deadweight losses arises due to variation from the competitive market equilibrium.

II.   MARKET FAILURE

A.   **Structural Problems:** In some competitive markets, a small group of sellers is able to exert undue influence by unfairly increasing prices and restricting supply.

1.   Above-normal profits are unwarranted if they reflect the raw exercise of market power, and do not reflect superior efficiency or exceptional capability.

2.   Market failure occurs when competitive market outcomes fail to sustain socially desirable activities or to eliminate undesirable ones.

3.   Failure by market structure can occur when markets do not have many sellers (producers) and buyers (customers), or at least the ready potential for many to enter.

B.   **Incentive Problems:** Problems occur in competitive markets when some of the benefits and costs tied to production or consumption are not reflected in market prices.

1.   Differences between private and social costs or benefits are called externalities.

a.   A negative externality is a cost of producing, marketing, or consuming a product that is not borne by the product's producers or consumers.

b.   A positive externality is a benefit of production, marketing, or consumption that is not reflected in the product pricing structure and, hence, does not accrue to the product's producers or consumers.

2.   Failure by incentive is a risk in markets where social values and social costs differ from the private costs and values of producers and consumers.

III. **ROLE FOR GOVERNMENT**

A. **How Government Influences Competitive Markets:** Government affects what and how firms produce, influences conditions of entry and exit, dictates marketing practices, prescribes hiring and personnel policies, and imposes a host of other requirements on private enterprise.

1. Although all sectors of the U.S. economy are regulated to some degree, the method and scope of regulation vary widely.

2. From an economic efficiency standpoint, a given mode of tax or economic regulation is desirable to the extent that benefits exceed costs.

3. Social equity, or fairness, criteria must also be carefully weighed when social considerations bear on the tax or regulatory decision-making process.

B. **Broad Social Considerations:** Competition promotes efficiency by giving firms incentives to produce the types and quantities of products that consumers want.

1. Preservation of consumer choice or consumer sovereignty is an important feature of competitive markets.

a. Public policy can be a valuable tool with which to control unfairly gained market power, and restore control over price and quantity decisions to the public.

2. Another social purpose of taxation or regulatory intervention is to limit concentration of economic and political power.

IV. **SUBSIDY AND TAX POLICY**

A. **Subsidy Policy:** Government sometimes responds to positive externalities by providing subsidies.

1. Subsidy policy can be indirect, like government construction and highway maintenance grants that benefit the trucking industry.

2. Subsidy policy can be direct, like agricultural payment-in-kind (PIK) programs, special tax treatments, and government-provided low-cost financing.

        a.   Tradable emission permits are pollution licenses granted by the government to firms and individuals.

B.   **Deadweight Loss From Taxes:** Public policy makers must consider the full range of consequences of negative externalities to create appropriate and effective incentives for pollution control.

    1.   Taxes cause deadweight losses because they reduce the amount of economic activity in competitive markets, and thereby prevent buyers and sellers from realizing some of the gains from trade.

    2.   Many prefer tax policy to subsidies as a method for pollution reduction on the grounds that it explicitly recognizes the public's right to a clean and safe environment.

V.   **TAX INCIDENCE AND BURDEN**

A.   **Role of Elasticity:** The question of who pays the economic cost of taxation can seldom be determined merely by identifying the taxed, fined, or otherwise regulated party.

    1.   In general, who pays the economic burden of a tax or operating control regulation depends on the elasticities of supply and demand for the final products of affected firms.

    2.   Elasticity also has implications for the amount of social welfare lost due to the deadweight loss of taxation.

        a.   Holding the elasticity of demand constant, the deadweight loss of a tax is small when supply is relatively inelastic.

            (1)   When supply is relatively elastic, the deadweight loss of a tax is large.

        b.   Holding supply elasticity constant, the deadweight loss of a tax is small when demand is relatively inelastic.

            (1)   The deadweight loss of a tax is large when demand is relatively elastic.

B.   **Tax Cost Sharing Example:** State and local authorities find it difficult to tax or regulate firms that operate in highly competitive national markets.

1.   Such taxes and regulations usually are initiated at the national level.

VI.   PRICE CONTROLS

A.   **Price Floors:** The most famous price support program, or price floor, in the United States is administered by the U.S. Department of Agriculture (USDA).

1.   A complex system of price floors, crop loans, production subsidies, and land set aside programs has evolved to counteract the effects of rising agricultural productivity in the face of generally inelastic demand for foodstuffs.

2.   Costly government-set price floors in agriculture products have persisted because politicians remain highly sensitive to rural voters and powerful special interest groups.

B.   **Price Ceilings:** A price ceiling is a costly and seldom used mechanism for restraining excess demand.

1.   Despite convincing evidence that price ceilings are an ineffective means for restraining excess demand, some large cities continue to use price ceilings in an effort to make housing more affordable.

2.   Like surplus, shortage results in significant economic costs and represents a serious economic problem in that it signifies a significant loss in social welfare.

VII.   BUSINESS PROFIT RATES

A.   **Return on Stockholders' Equity:** Business profit rates are best evaluated using the accounting rate of return on stockholders' equity (ROE).

1.   ROE is net income divided by the book value of stockholders' equity, where stockholders' equity is total assets minus total liabilities.

2.   ROE also equals the firm's profit margin multiplied by the total asset turnover ratio, all multiplied by the firm's leverage ratio:

$$ROE = \frac{Net\ Income}{Equity}$$

$$= \frac{Net\ Income}{Sales} \times \frac{Sales}{Total\ Assets} \times \frac{Total\ Assets}{Equity}$$

$$= Profit\ Margin \times \frac{Total\ Asset}{Turnover} \times Leverage.$$

3. Profit margin is accounting net income expressed as a percentage of sales revenue and shows the amount of profit earned per dollar of sales.

   a. When profit margins are high, robust demand or stringent cost controls, or both, allow the firm to earn a significant profit contribution

   b. Holding capital requirements constant, profit margin is a useful indicator of managerial efficiency in responding to rapidly growing demand and/or effective measures of cost containment.

4. Total asset turnover is sales revenue divided by the book value of total assets.

   a. When total asset turnover is high, the firm makes its investments work hard in the sense of generating a large amount of sales volume.

5. Leverage is often defined as the ratio of total assets divided by stockholders' equity.

   a. It reflects the extent to which debt and preferred stock are used in addition to common stock financing.

   b. During economic booms, leverage can dramatically increase the firm's profit rate. During recessions and other economic contractions, leverage can just as dramatically decrease realized rates of return, or lead to losses.

B. **Typical Profit Rates:** For successful large and small firms in the United States and Canada, ROE averages roughly 15% to 20% during a typical year, before deducting extraordinary items.

1. After extraordinary items, ROE averages about 10% to 15% per year for highly successful companies.

2. This average ROE is comprised of a typical profit margin on sales revenue of approximately 5 to10%, a standard total asset turnover ratio of 1.0 times, and a common leverage ratio of about 2:1 or 5:1:

$$\frac{\text{Typical}}{\text{ROE}} = \text{Profit Margin} \times \frac{\text{Total Asset}}{\text{Turnover}} \times \text{Leverage}$$

$$= 5 \text{ to } 10\% \times 1.0 \times 2 \text{ to } 5$$

$$= 10 \text{ to } 15\%.$$

3. If ROE consistently falls below 10-15%, sources of financing tend to dry up and the firm withers and dies.

4. If ROE consistently exceeds 10-15%, new debt and equity financing are easy to obtain, and growth by new and established competitors is rapid.

VIII. MARKET STRUCTURE AND PROFIT RATES

A. Profit Rates in Competitive Markets: In a perfectly competitive market, profit margins are low.

1. During periods of weak economic activity, such as during 2002-2003, many firms in competitive markets earn meager profits or suffer temporary losses.

B. Mean Reversion in Profit Rates: In long-run equilibrium, profit rates in competitive markets reflect only a risk-adjusted normal rate of return.

1. Over time, entry and nonleading firm growth in highly profitable competitive markets cause above-normal profits to regress toward the mean.

2. Bankruptcy and exit allow the below-normal profits of depressed competitive markets to rise toward the mean.

3. In competitive markets, the tendency of firm profit rates to converge over time towards long-term averages is called reversion to the mean.

IX. COMPETITIVE MARKET STRATEGY

A.   **Short-run Firm Performance:** In the short run, above-normal profits in perfectly competitive industries are sometimes simply disequilibrium profits.

1.   Disequilibrium profits are above-normal returns earned in the time interval that exists between when a favorable influence on industry demand or cost conditions first transpires and the time when competitor entry or growth finally develops.

2.   Disequilibrium losses are below-normal returns suffered in the time interval between when an unfavorable influence on industry demand or cost conditions first transpires and the time when exit or downsizing finally occurs.

3.   Firms in some competitive markets enjoy above-normal returns stemming from economic luck, or temporary good fortune due to some unexpected change in industry demand or cost conditions.

B.   **Long-run Firm Performance:** In long-run equilibrium, the typical firm in a perfectly competitive market only has the potential for a normal rate of return on investment.

1.   Above-normal profits in perfectly competitive industries are usually transitory and typically reflect disequilibrium conditions.

a.   If above-normal returns persist for extended periods in a given industry or line of business, then elements of uniqueness are probably at work.

2.   The search for an economic advantage or a favorable competitive position in an industry or line of business is called competitive strategy.

a.   If a competitive firm can offer products that are faster, better or cheaper than the competition, then it will be able to earn economic rents, or profits due to uniquely productive inputs.

X.   **SUMMARY**

PROBLEMS & SOLUTIONS

P11.1   *Social Welfare Concepts.*   *Indicate whether each of the following statements is true or false, and explain why.*

> **A.**   The market demand curve indicates the maximum price buyers are willing to pay at each level of production.
>
> **B.**   The market supply curve indicates the maximum price required by sellers as a group to bring forth production.
>
> **C.**   Consumer surplus is the amount that consumers are willing to pay for a given good or service.
>
> **D.**   Producer surplus measures the amount of profit earned from production.
>
> **E.**   In competitive market equilibrium, the total benefits derived from consumption equal the total costs incurred in production.

P11.1   **SOLUTION**

> **A.**   True. The market supply demand curve indicates the maximum price buyers are willing to pay to bring forth each level of production. The height of the market demand curve measures the maximum value placed on production by buyers at each production level.
>
> **B.**   False. The market supply curve indicates the minimum price required by sellers as a group to bring forth production. The height of the market supply curve measures minimum production cost at each and every activity level.
>
> **C.**   False. Consumer surplus is the area under the demand curve that lies above the market price. It represents the amount that consumers are willing to pay for a given good or service minus the amount that they are required to pay. Consumer surplus represents value derived from consumption that consumers are able to enjoy at zero cost. It also describes the net benefit derived by consumers from consumption, where net benefit is measured in the eyes of the consumer. From the standpoint of society as a whole, consumer surplus is an attractive measure of the economic well-being of consumers.
>
> **D.**   False. Whereas consumer surplus is closely related to the demand curve for a product, producer surplus is closely related to the supply curve for a product. It measures the amount by which the total revenues exceeds the marginal costs of

production. Producer surplus makes a contribution to profits, but the amount of profit earned equals total revenue minus total costs, and total costs include fixed costs.

E.   False. In competitive market equilibrium, the marginal costs of production equal the marginal benefits derived from consumption. This maximizes the amount of social welfare derived by consumers and producers. Social welfare is the sum of consumer surplus and producer surplus.

P11.2   ***Labor Policy.*** *Supporters of minimum wage laws in the United States argue that the minimum wage has been an important part of the U.S. economy for 70 years. They contend that the minimum wage is a statement of how the nation values work, and a tangible measure of how Americans view employers' obligation to their workers. They also assert that it is an effective policy tool that helps low- and middle-income families with low-wage workers.*

A.   *Most low-wage workers in the United States are secondary wage earners that do not live in low-income families. Does this fact undermine the argument that minimum wage laws are an effective means for helping low- and middle-income families with low-wage workers?*

B.   *An important reason why many minimum-wage and low-wage workers earn low incomes is that they are seldom able to find work for a full 40 hours per week, and frequently endure periods of long unemployment. Explain how higher minimum wages can contribute to greater unemployment among the working poor.*

P11.2   **SOLUTION**

A.   In the United States, about one in seven workers can be described as low-wage workers earning between $5.15 and $7.99 an hour. Raising the minimum wage is apt to have a direct or indirect effect on the earnings and employment prospects of many of these workers. Perhaps surprisingly, more than 60% of low-wage workers are from families with incomes that exceed $29,000 per year, a level that cannot be described as low-income. (Low-income families earn less than twice the poverty level.)

        Opponents of minimum wage laws make much of the fact that many low-wage workers do not live in low-income families. Opponents contend that this fact undermines the argument that minimum wage laws are an effective policy tool that helps low- and middle-income families with low-wage workers. Supporters of minimum wage laws argue that, for the most part, earnings from low-wage jobs are an important component of family income, even if the families are not technically "poor." Proponents of minimum wage laws contend that the fact that a higher minimum wage helps middle- and upper income families is hardly a mark against it.

B. Studies show that an important reason why many minimum-wage and low-wage workers earn low incomes is that they are seldom able to find work for a full 40 hours per week, and frequently endure periods of long unemployment. Higher minimum wage laws can contribute to greater unemployment among the working poor because they mandate higher pay for workers that are often unable to justify higher pay because of low worker productivity. In competitive labor markets, the wage rate closely reflects each worker's marginal productivity. If productivity increases due to better worker training or education, employers can afford to pay higher wages. Without such increases in worker productivity, however, higher minimum wages effectively price low-skill workers out of a job.

In the United States, many low-skill workers have lost their jobs following recent increases in minimum wages. The best substitute for unskilled labor is often self-service, or "do-it-yourself" labor. Rather than pay high costs for unskilled labor, many consumers choose self-service gas stations, do-it-yourself car washes, and fast-food restaurants that minimize customer service. Many proponents of higher minimum wages blame greedy employers for not paying higher wages. In fact, it's cost-conscious consumers that are to blame, if any blame is to be assigned, for the lack of demand for high-priced unskilled labor.

P11.3   ***Marginal Analysis.*** *Terri Jones is a barber at Calvin's Barbershop on the near south side in Chicago, Illinois. Calvin's is presently open 8 hours per day, Tuesday through Saturday. Given the growing popularity of Sunday shopping, Jones is considering making a proposal to keep the shop open for limited hours on Sundays. Prices are stable in this competitive market at $15 per haircut, and Jones must pay chair rent and other variable costs of $9 per haircut. The following table shows Jones expectations for Sunday business.*

Hours	Haircuts
0	10
1	9
2	8
3	7
4	6
5	5
6	4
7	3
8	2
9	1

A. *Complete a table that shows Jones' anticipated marginal revenue per hour of Sunday operation.*

B. *Calculate the optimal number of hours of Sunday operation if Jones places as $30 per hour value on her time.*

P11.3 SOLUTION

A.

Hours	Haircuts	Marginal Revenue
0	10	$60
1	9	54
2	8	48
3	7	42
4	6	36
5	5	30
6	4	24
7	3	18
8	2	12
9	1	6

B. Notice that with 5 hours of operation on Sundays, Jones anticipates giving 5 haircuts per hour. At that point, the marginal revenue earned per hour is just sufficient to cover her $30 per hour marginal value of time. Jones should seek to open the Downtown Barbershop for business 5 hours on Sundays.

P11.4 ***Profit Maximization.*** *Mike Delfino is a self-employed owner-operator of an over-the-road tractor trailer. Delfino receives a fixed rate of $3 per mile on long-haul trips between Delfino's home in Los Angeles, California, and Dallas, Texas. Fixed costs for insurance, truck financing, and depreciation average $20,000 per year. Delfino's total cost and marginal cost relations are*

$$TC = \$20 + \$0.75Q + \$0.01125Q^2, \qquad \textit{(Total Cost)}$$

$$MC = \partial TC/\partial Q = \$0.75 + \$0.0225Q, \qquad \textit{(Marginal Cost)}$$

where costs are measured in thousands of dollars, and Q represents the number of miles driven per year (in thousands).

A. *Set P = MR = MC to determine Delfino's profit-maximizing number of miles to drive per year.*

> **B.**   *Calculate Delfino's revenues and profit at this activity level.*

P11.4   **SOLUTION**

> **A.**   To maximize profits, set

$$P = MC$$

$$\$3 = \$0.75 + \$0.0225Q$$

$$0.0225Q = 2.25$$

$$Q = 100 \ (000) \text{ miles per year}$$

> **B.**   At $Q = 100 \ (000)$,

$$TR = P \times Q$$

$$= \$3 \times 100$$

$$= \$300 \ (000) \text{ or } \$300,000 \text{ per year}$$

$$\pi = TR - TC$$

$$= \$300 - \$20 - \$0.75Q - \$0.01125Q^2$$

$$= \$300 - \$20 - \$0.75(100) - \$0.01125(100)^2$$

$$= \$92.5 \ (000) \text{ or } \$92,500 \text{ per year}$$

P11.5   **Minimum Wage Effects.** *Rex Van De Camp is the owner-manager of the University Car Wash, a major employer of unskilled labor in Athens, Ohio. The price for a standard wash and hand dry is well established at $8. Total cost and marginal cost relations are*

$$TC = \$25,000 + \$2Q + \$0.0001Q^2, \qquad \textit{(Total Cost)}$$

$$MC = \partial TC/\partial Q = \$2 + \$0.0002Q, \qquad \textit{(Marginal Cost)}$$

where costs are measured in dollars, and Q represents the number of car washes given per year.

A. *Set P = MR = MC to determine the profit-maximizing number of car washes per year. Calculate revenues and profits at this activity level.*

B. *Now assume that an increase in the minimum wage causes marginal costs to rise by 25%. Figure the company's new profit-maximizing number of car washes, as well as revenues and profits at this activity level.*

C. *Describe the long-run impact on employment of this increase in the minimum wage if the owner of the University Car Wash has a minimum required return of $50,000 per year .*

P11.5   SOLUTION

A.   To maximize profits, set

$$P \ = \ MC$$

$$\$8 \ = \ \$2 + \$0.0002Q$$

$$0.0002Q \ = \ 6$$

$$Q \ = \ 30,000$$

$$TR \ = \ P \times Q$$

$$= \ \$8 \times 30,000$$

$$= \ \$240,000 \text{ per year}$$

$$\pi \ = \ TR - TC$$

$$= \ \$240,000 - \$25,000 - \$2Q - \$0.0001Q^2$$

$$= \ \$240,000 - \$25,000 - \$2(30,000) - \$0.0001(30,000)^2$$

$$= \ \$65,000 \text{ per year}$$

B.   After the 25% increase in marginal costs, to maximize profits set

$$P \ = \ MC'$$

$$\$8 \ = \ 1.25(\$2 + \$0.0002Q)$$

$$8 = 2.5 + \$0.00025Q$$

$$0.00025Q = 5.5$$

$$Q = 22,000$$

$$TR = P \times Q$$

$$= \$8 \times 22,000$$

$$= \$176,000 \text{ per year}$$

$$\pi = TR - TC$$

$$= \$176,000 - \$25,000 - \$2.5Q - \$0.000125Q^2$$

$$= \$176,000 - \$25,000 - \$2(22,000) - \$0.000125(22,000)^2$$

$$= \$46,500 \text{ per year}$$

C. If the owner of the University Car Wash has a minimum required return on investment of $50,000 per year, an increase in the minimum wage will create economic losses for the firm. In that case, the owner would cease operation and commit the capital employed in the University Car Wash operation to other more highly valued use. In that case, the University Car Wash would cease operations and lay off all of its unskilled workers.

P11.6 **Consumer Surplus.** *Computer service technicians perform hands-on repair, maintenance, and installation of computers and related equipment. Workers who provide technical assistance, in person or by telephone, to computer system users are known as computer support specialists. When equipment breaks down, many computer service technicians travel to the customers' workplace to make necessary repairs. These field technicians often have assigned areas in which they perform preventive maintenance on a regular basis. Bench technicians work in repair shops located in stores, factories, or service centers. In the case of many small computer service providers, computer service technicians may work both in repair shops and at customer locations.*

Suppose computer technical service is supplied to consumers and small businesses in the greater San Francisco area at a competitive market price of $75 per hour. Also assume that the market demand curve can be described as follows:

$$P = \$250 - \$1.25Q_D \qquad \textit{(Market Demand)}$$

where Q is output in thousands of hours of service provided per year and P is price per hour of service provided.

A.   *Calculate and graph the equilibrium price/output solution.*

B.   *Use this graph to help you algebraically determine the amount of consumer surplus generated in this market.*

P11.6   **SOLUTION**

A.   The market demand curve is given by the equation

$$P = \$250 - \$1.25 Q_D$$

To find the market equilibrium quantity when $P = \$75$, set equal the market supply and market demand curves where price is expressed as a function of quantity, and $Q_S = Q_D$:

$$\text{Supply} = \text{Demand}$$

$$\$75 = \$250 - \$1.25 Q_D$$

$$1.25 Q_D = 175$$

$$Q_D = 140 \ (000)$$

Therefore, the equilibrium price/output combination is a market price of $75 with an equilibrium output of 140 (000) hours of service being provided.

B.   The value of consumer surplus is equal to the area of the region under the market demand curve that lies above the market equilibrium price of $75. Because the area of such a triangle is one-half the value of the base times the height, the value of consumer surplus equals:

$$\text{Consumer Surplus} = \frac{1}{2} [140 \times (\$250 - \$75)]$$

$$= \$12,250 \ (000)$$

In words, this means that at a price of $75 per hour, the quantity demanded is 140 (000) hours of service, resulting in total revenues of $10.5 million. The fact that consumer surplus equals $12.25 million means that customers as a group would have been willing to pay an additional $12.25 million for this level of market output. This is an amount above and beyond the $10.5 million paid. Customers received a real bargain.

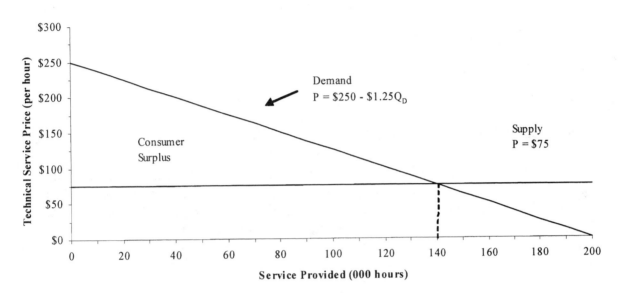

Computer Technical Service

P11.7   ***Producer Surplus.*** *Obtaining affordable, quality child daycare, especially for children under age 5, is a major concern for many parents. Formal child daycare centers include nursery schools, preschool centers, Head Start centers, and group daycare centers. Self-employed workers in this industry often provide care in their home for a fee. Others provide care for children in the child's home. The for-profit sector of the industry includes centers that operate independently or as part of a local or national chain. Nonprofit child daycare organizations may provide services in religious institutions, YMCAs and other social and recreation centers, colleges, public schools, social service agencies, and worksites ranging from factories to office complexes. Many employers offer child daycare benefits to their employees. They recognize that the lack of child daycare benefits is a barrier to the employment of many parents, especially qualified women, and that the cost of the benefits is offset by increased employee morale and reduced absenteeism. Some employers sponsor child daycare centers in or near the workplace; others offer direct financial assistance, vouchers, or discounts for child daycare, after-school or sick-child daycare services, or a dependent care option in a flexible benefits plan.*

    In most local markets, the market for child daycare services is highly competitive. Imagine that market demand in Madison, Wisconsin, is stable at $350 per week, and that the market supply function can be written

$$P = \$50 + \$0.05Q_S \qquad \textit{(Market Supply)}$$

where *Q* is output in weeks of quality child daycare service provided and *P* is price per week of service provided.

A.   Calculate and graph the equilibrium price/output solution.

B.   Use this graph to help you algebraically determine the amount of producer surplus generated in this market.

P11.7   SOLUTION

A.   The market supply curve is given by the equation

$$P = \$50 + \$0.05Q_S$$

To find the market equilibrium quantity, set equal the market supply and market demand curves where price is expressed as a function of quantity, and $Q_S = Q_D$:

$$\text{Supply} = \text{Demand}$$

$$\$50 + \$0.05Q = \$350$$

$$0.05Q = 300$$

$$Q = 6,000$$

Therefore, the equilibrium price/output combination is a market price of $350 with an equilibrium output of 6,000 weeks of service provided.

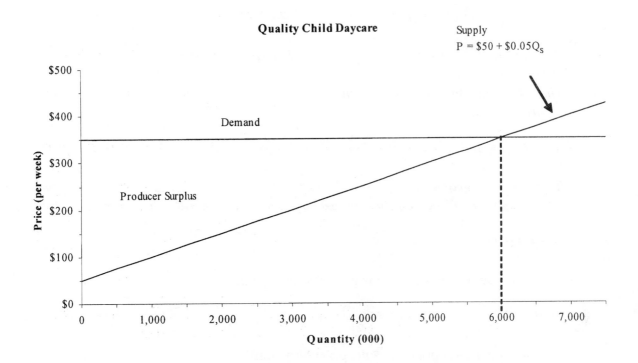

Quality Child Daycare

Supply
P = $50 + $0.05Q_s

B. The value of producer surplus is equal to the region above the market supply curve at the market equilibrium price of $350. Because the area of such a triangle is one-half the value of the base times the height, the value of producer surplus equals:

$$\text{Producer Surplus} = \frac{1}{2}\,[6{,}000 \times (\$350 - \$50)]$$

$$= \$900{,}000 \text{ per week}$$

At a unit price of $350, producer surplus equals $900,000 per week. Producers as a group received $900,000 more than the absolute minimum required for them to produce the market equilibrium output of 6,000 units per week. Producers received a real bargain.

P11.8   ***Social Welfare.*** *Banks and other financial institutions have come to rely heavily upon income from retail services and user fees. At the same time, consumers have become extremely price conscious for standard services such as checking accounts, debit cards, and ATM (automatic teller machine) withdrawal charges. In most major cities, ATMs are everywhere, and user fee price competition is brutal. To illustrate the net amount of social welfare generated in this highly competitive service market, assume that market supply and demand conditions for withdrawals from an institution's own ATMs can be described as:*

$$Q_S \quad = \ -7 + 0.8P \qquad\qquad \textit{(Market Supply)}$$

$$Q_D \quad = \ 115 - P \qquad\qquad \textit{(Market Demand)}$$

where Q is the number of ATM transactions per week in thousands, and P is in cents per transaction.

A. *Graph and calculate the equilibrium price/output solution.*

B. *Use this graph to help you algebraically determine the amount of consumer surplus, producer surplus and net social welfare generated in this market.*

P11.8 **SOLUTION**

A. The market supply curve is given by the equation

$$Q_S = -7 + 0.8P$$

or, solving for price (in cents per transaction),

$$0.8P \ = \ 7 + Q_S$$

$$P \ = \ 8.75 + 1.25Q_S$$

The market demand curve is given by the equation

$$Q_D = 115 - P$$

or, solving for price (in cents per transaction),

$$P \ = \ 115 - Q_D$$

Graphically, demand and supply curves appear as follows:

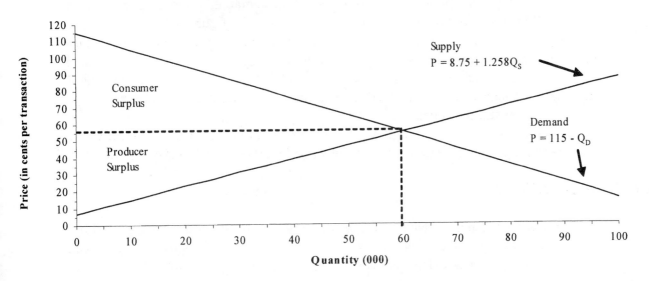

ATM User Fee Equilibrium

Algebraically, to find the market equilibrium levels for price and quantity, simply set the market supply and market demand curves equal to one another so that $Q_S = Q_D$. To find the market equilibrium price, equate the market demand and market supply curves where quantity is expressed as a function of price:

$$\text{Supply} = \text{Demand}$$

$$-8.75 + 1.25P = 115 - P$$

$$2.25P = 123.75$$

$$P = 55 \text{ cents per transaction}$$

To find the market equilibrium quantity, set equal the market supply and market demand curves where price is expressed as a function of quantity, and $Q_S = Q_D$:

$$\text{Supply} = \text{Demand}$$

$$7 + 0.8Q = 115 - Q$$

$$1.8Q = 108$$

$$Q = 60 \, (000)$$

The equilibrium price/output combination is a market price of 55¢ with an equilibrium output of 60 (000) units, as shown in the figure.

B.   The value of consumer surplus is equal to the region under the market demand curve that lies above the market equilibrium price of 55¢. Because the area of such a triangle is one-half the value of the base times the height, the value of consumer surplus equals:

$$\text{Consumer Surplus} = \tfrac{1}{2}\,[60 \times (115 - 55)]$$

$$= 1{,}800 \, (000) \text{ cents per week}$$

In words, this means that at a unit price of 55¢, the quantity demanded is 60 (000) transactions per week, resulting in total revenues of 1,800 (000) cents per week ($18,000 per week). The fact that consumer surplus equals 1,800 (000) cents per week means that customers as a group would have been willing to pay an additional 1,800 (000) cents per week for this level of market output. This is an amount above and beyond the 3,300 (000) cents per week ($= 55 \times 60$) already paid. Customers received a real bargain.

The value of producer surplus is equal to the region above the market supply curve at the market equilibrium price of 55¢. Because the area of such a triangle is one-half the value of the base times the height, the value of producer surplus equals:

$$\text{Producer Surplus} = \tfrac{1}{2}\,[60 \times (55 - 7)]$$

$$= 1{,}440 \, (000) \text{ cents per week}$$

At a unit price of 55¢, producer surplus equals 1,440 (000) cents per week. Producers as a group received 1,440 (000) cents per week (or $14,400 per week) more than the absolute minimum required for them to produce the market equilibrium output of 60 (000) transactions per week. Producers received a real bargain.

In competitive market equilibrium, social welfare is measured by the sum of net benefits derived by consumers and producers. Social welfare is the sum of consumer surplus and producer surplus:

$$\text{Social Welfare} = \text{Consumer Surplus} + \text{Producer Surplus}$$

$$= 1{,}800 + 1{,}440$$

$$= \quad 3,240 \; (000) \text{ cents per week (or \$32,400)}$$

P11.9 ***Deadweight Loss of Taxation.*** *To stem the rising costs of writing new software code, several U.S. software companies have turned to low-cost but highly-skilled labor markets in India and other Asian countries. At the wholesale level, the market for basic software code writing and validation services is fiercely price competitive. Literally hundreds of large and small foreign companies compete vigorously for business from Microsoft and other large software providers. Suppose that market supply and demand conditions for software quality assurance can be written*

$$Q_S \quad = \; -35 + 2P \qquad\qquad \text{(Market Supply)}$$

$$Q_D \quad = \; 350 - 5P \qquad\qquad \text{(Market Demand)}$$

where Q is output in units of software code (000), and P is the market price per unit.

A. *Calculate and graph the equilibrium price/output solution before and after imposition of a $17.50 per unit tax.*

B. *Calculate the deadweight loss to taxation caused by imposition of the $17.50 per unit tax. How much of this deadweight loss was suffered by consumers versus producers? Explain.*

P11.9 **SOLUTION**

A. The market supply curve is given by the equation

$$Q_S = -35 + 2P$$

or, solving for price,

$$2P = 35 + Q_S$$

$$P = \$17.50 + \$0.5Q_S$$

The market demand curve is given by the equation

$$Q_D = 350 - 5P$$

or, solving for price,

$$5P = 350 - Q_D$$

$$P = \$70 - \$0.2Q_D$$

To find the market equilibrium levels for price and quantity, simply set the market supply and market demand curves equal to one another so that $Q_S = Q_D$. For example, to find the market equilibrium price, equate the market demand and market supply curves where quantity is expressed as a function of price:

$$Supply = Demand$$

$$-35 + 2P = 350 - 5P$$

$$7P = 385$$

$$P = \$55$$

To find the market equilibrium quantity, set equal the market supply and market demand curves where price is expressed as a function of quantity, and $Q_S = Q_D$:

$$Supply = Demand$$

$$\$17.5 + \$0.5Q = \$70 - \$0.2Q$$

$$0.7Q = 52.5$$

$$Q = 75 \ (000)$$

Therefore, the equilibrium price/output combination is a market price of $55 with an equilibrium output of 75 (000) units. Following imposition of a $17.50 per unit tax, the new market supply curve is given by the equation

$$P = \$17.50 + \$0.5Q_S + tax$$

$$= \$17.50 + \$0.5Q_S + \$17.50$$

$$= \$35 + \$0.5Q_S$$

or, solving for quantity,

$$P = \$35 + \$0.5Q_S$$

$$0.5Q_S = -35 + P$$

$$Q_s = -70 + 2P$$

To find the market equilibrium price, equate the market demand and new market supply curves where quantity is expressed as a function of price:

$$\text{Supply} = \text{Demand}$$

$$-70 + 2P = 350 - 5P$$

$$7P = 420$$

$$P = \$60$$

To find the market equilibrium quantity, set equal the new market supply and market demand curves where price is expressed as a function of quantity, and $Q_S = Q_D$:

$$\text{Supply} = \text{Demand}$$

$$\$35 + \$0.5Q = \$70 - \$0.2Q$$

$$0.7Q = 35$$

$$Q = 50 \ (000)$$

Therefore, the equilibrium price/output combination with a \$17.50 per unit tax is a market price of \$60 with an equilibrium output of 50 (000) units. Graphically,

Software Code Writing and Validation

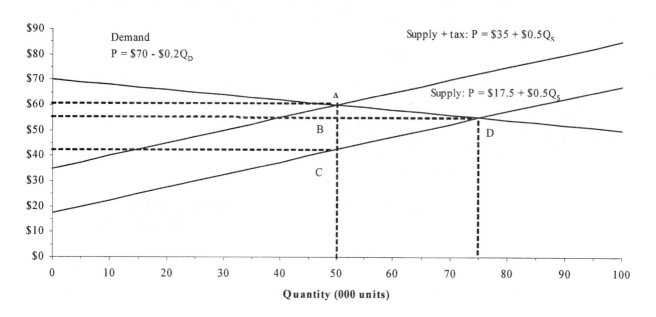

B.   The amount of deadweight loss due to taxation suffered by consumers is given by the triangle bounded by ABD. Because the area of a such a triangle is one-half the value of the base times the height, the value of lost consumer surplus equals:

$$\text{Consumer Deadweight Loss} \;=\; \tfrac{1}{2}\,[(75 - 50) \times (\$60 - \$55)]$$

$$=\; \$62.5 \,(000)$$

In the absence of a tax, a supply price of $42.50 [= $17.50 + $0.5(50)] would be associated with a quantity supplied of 50 (000) units. Therefore, amount of deadweight loss due to taxation suffered by producers is given by the triangle bounded by BCD. Because the area of a such a triangle is one-half the value of the base times the height, the value of lost producer surplus equals:

$$\text{Producer Deadweight Loss} \;=\; \tfrac{1}{2}\,[(75 - 50) \times (\$55 - \$42.50)]$$

$$=\; \$156.25 \,(000)$$

The total amount of deadweight loss due to taxation suffered by consumers and producers is given by the triangle bounded by ACD. The area of a such a triangle is simply the amount of consumer deadweight loss plus producer deadweight loss:

$$\text{Total Deadweight Loss} = \text{Consumer Loss} + \text{Producer Loss}$$

$$= \$62.5 \,(000) + \$156.25 \,(000)$$

$$= \$218.75 \,(000)$$

P11.10 **Competitive Market Equilibrium.** *Standardized Testing Services, Inc., based in Tempe, Arizona, provides practice exams and short courses for high school students studying to prepare for standardized college entrance exams. Relevant demand and cost relations for STS short courses are*

$$P = \$100 - \$0.0077Q, \qquad\qquad \text{(Demand)}$$

$$MR = \partial TR/\partial Q = \$100 - \$0.0154Q, \qquad \text{(Marginal Revenue)}$$

$$TC = \$28,125 + \$18Q + \$0.0005Q^2, \qquad \text{(Total Cost)}$$

$$MC = \partial TC/\partial Q = \$18 + \$0.001Q, \qquad \text{(Marginal Cost)}$$

where Q is the number of students attending a STS short course per year, and total costs include a risk-adjusted normal rate of return on investment.

A. *Calculate the company's short-run profit-maximizing price/output combination and profit level.*

B. *Calculate the long-run price/output equilibrium in this competitive market if entry forces STS to operate at the average cost-minimizing price/output combination.*

C. *Calculate economic profits at the average cost-minimizing price/output combination.*

P11.10 **SOLUTION**

A. To find the profit-maximizing activity level, set $M\pi = MR - MC = 0$:

$$M\pi = MR - MC$$

$$0 = \$100 - \$0.0154Q - \$18 - \$0.001Q$$

$$0.0164Q = 82$$

$$Q = 5,000.$$

$$P = \$100 - \$0.0077(5{,}000)$$

$$= \$61.50$$

$$\pi = TR\text{-}TC$$

$$= \$100Q - \$0.0077Q^2 - \$28{,}125 - \$18Q - \$0.0005Q^2$$

$$= -\$28{,}125 + \$82Q - \$0.0082Q^2$$

$$= -\$28{,}125 + \$82(5{,}000) - \$0.0082(5{,}000^2)$$

$$= \$176{,}875$$

Because total profit is declining for Q > 5,000, Q = 5,000 is a point of maximum profits per month. The company is earning economic profits of $176,875 per year.

B.   To find the average cost-minimizing activity level, set MC = AC and solve for Q.

$$MC = AC = TC/Q$$

$$\$18 + \$0.001Q = (\$28{,}125 + \$18Q + \$0.0005Q^2)/Q$$

$$\$18 + \$0.001Q = \$28{,}125/Q + \$18 + \$0.0005Q$$

$$0.0005Q = 28{,}125/Q$$

$$Q^2 = 56{,}250{,}000$$

$$Q = 7{,}500$$

$$P = AC$$

$$= \$28{,}125/Q + \$18 + \$0.0005Q$$

$$= \$28{,}125/7{,}500 + \$18 + \$0.0005(7{,}500)$$

$$= \$25.50$$

Because average cost is rising for Q > 7,500, Q = 7,500 is a point of minimum average costs per year.

C.   In competitive market long-run equilibrium, $P = MR = MC = AC$ and economic profits equal zero. Each competitive firm in long-run equilibrium is able to earn just a risk-adjusted normal rate of return on investment.

$$
\begin{aligned}
\pi &= \text{TR-TC} \\[6pt]
&= \$25.50Q - \$28,125 - \$18Q - \$0.0005Q^2 \\[6pt]
&= -\$28,125 + \$7.50(7,500) - \$0.0005(7,500)^2 \\[6pt]
&= -\$28,125 + \$7.50(7,500) - \$0.0082(7,500^2) \\[6pt]
&= \$0
\end{aligned}
$$

Chapter 12

MONOPOLY AND MONOPSONY

Monopoly is a market structure characterized by a single seller of a unique product with no close substitutes. As a single seller, monopoly firm demand is also market demand. This gives monopoly firms the ability to set prices and/or the quantity sold. Monopoly firms are often described as price makers because they have the ability to set prices, but no firm can ever charge more than buyers are willing to pay. Like any market demand curve, the monopoly demand curve is downward sloping. Monopoly is the polar opposite of perfect competition where numerous sellers of homogenous products are price takers with the potential to earn only a risk-adjusted normal rate of return in long-run equilibrium. Monopoly sellers are able to earn above-normal profits even in long-run equilibrium. True monopoly requires a complete lack of close substitutes, and is rarely observed. Microsoft Corp. dominates the market for desktop computer operating systems and applications software, but incipient competition from Apple, Linux and other operating systems constrains Microsoft's price-setting ability. Individuals with unique skills or customer appeal have the potential for monopoly profits in the labor market. For example, an actor who has starred as the central character in a highly successful motion picture would have near-monopoly status in competing for the right to star as the same character in the inevitable sequel.

Monopsony is a market characterized by a single buyer; monopsony is the buy-side equivalent of a sell-side monopoly. Monopsony is found in some labor markets, and in defense procurement. However, like monopoly, monopsony is quite rare.

CHAPTER OUTLINE

I.   MONOPOLY MARKET CHARACTERISTICS

   A.   Basic Features: Monopoly exists when a firm is the sole producer of a distinctive good or service that has no close substitutes. In other words, under monopoly the firm is the industry.

   1.   Monopoly firms are price makers as opposed to firms in competitive markets who are price takers.

   2.   Monopoly firms enjoy the ability to earn above-normal profits in long-run equilibrium.

   3.   Monopoly markets share the following common characteristics:

      a.   A single seller.

b. Unique product.

c. Blockaded entry and/or exit.

d. Imperfect dissemination of information.

e. Opportunity for economic profits in long-run equilibrium.

B. **Examples of Monopoly:** Classic examples of monopoly have been the public utilities, including: electricity, gas and sanitary services.

1. The erosion of actual or perceived monopoly power in the telecommunications market is repeated in numerous other instances.

2. On an international level, the Organization of the Petroleum Exporting Countries (OPEC) has long been criticized for its aggressive use of monopoly power to restrict output, create soaring oil prices, and wreck economic havoc.

II. PROFIT MAXIMIZATION UNDER MONOPOLY

A. **Price/Output Decisions:** Profit maximization always requires that firms operate at the output level at which marginal revenue and marginal cost are equal

1. In a competitive market, $P = MR = MC = AC$ in long-run equilibrium.

2. In monopoly markets, profit maximization also requires $MR = MC$, but barriers to entry make above-normal profits possible, and $P > AC$ in long-run equilibrium.

B. **Role of Marginal Analysis:** As in the case of competitive markets, discovering the point of optimal production for a monopoly firm is made easier with marginal analysis.

1. As in the case of competitive markets, monopoly profits are maximized when $M\pi = MR - MC = 0$.

a. An added condition for profit maximization by monopoly firms, sometimes referred to as a second-order condition, is that total profits must always be decreasing beyond the point where $MR = MC$.

2.   Because the monopoly firm serves the entire market, the monopoly firm demand curve is downward sloping.

    a.   The monopoly demand curve is always above the marginal revenue curve in monopoly markets, P = AR > MR.

    b.   Because profit maximization requires MR = MC, price will always exceed marginal cost at the profit-maximizing point in monopoly markets.

3.   Barriers to entry or exit limit competition, and economic profits can persist for monopolists in long-run equilibrium.

III.   SOCIAL COSTS OF MONOPOLY

A.   Monopoly Underproduction: Monopoly sells less output at higher prices than would be the case if the same market were perfectly competitive.

1.   Monopoly underproduction results because monopoly firms curtail output to a level at which the marginal value of resources employed, as measured by the marginal cost of production, is less than the marginal social benefit derived, where marginal social benefit is measured by the price that customers are willing to pay for additional output.

    a.   Under monopoly, marginal cost is less than the price charged at the profit-maximizing output level.

B.   Deadweight Loss from Monopoly: The tendency for monopoly firms to restrict output to increase prices and earn economic profits gives rise to a deadweight loss from monopoly problem.

1.   Like any restriction on supply, the reduced levels of economic activity typical of monopoly markets creates a loss in social welfare due to the decline in mutually beneficial trade activity.

2.   In addition to the deadweight loss from monopoly problem, there is a wealth transfer problem associated with monopoly.

3.   Under monopoly, consumer surplus is transferred to producer surplus.

IV.   SOCIAL BENEFITS OF MONOPOLY

A. **Economies of Scale:** Monopoly is sometimes the natural result of vigorous competitive forces.

1. A natural monopoly evolves in markets subject to overwhelming economies of scale in production created by extremely large capital requirements, scarce inputs, insufficient natural resources, and so on.

   a. In natural monopoly, the market-clearing price, where $P = MC$, occurs at a point at which long-run average total costs are still declining.

   b. A single monopolist can produce the total market supply at a lower total cost than could any number of smaller firms, and vigorous competition naturally eliminates inefficient competitors until only a single monopoly supplier remains.

   c. From a social standpoint, natural monopoly presents something of a dilemma.

      (1) Economic efficiency can sometimes be enhanced by allowing a single firm to dominate an industry.

      (2) Monopolies have an incentive to under-produce and can generate unwarranted economic profits.

2. Most real-world examples of monopoly do not naturally result from economies of scale in production.

3. Many real-world monopolists owe their existence to government-created or government-maintained barriers to entry.

B. **Invention and Innovation:** To achieve the benefits flowing from innovative leading firms, public policy sometimes confers explicit monopoly rights.

1. Patents grant an exclusive right to produce, use, or sell an invention or innovation for 20 years from the date of the patent application.

2. Monopoly profits are sometimes the just rewards flowing from truly important contributions of unique firms and individuals.

3. Monopoly profits are often fleeting.

V. **MONOPOLY REGULATION**

A.   **Dilemma of Natural Monopoly:** Natural monopoly poses a dilemma because monopoly has the potential for greatest efficiency, but unregulated monopoly can lead to economic profits and underproduction.

1.   One possible solution is to allow natural monopoly to persist but to impose price and profit regulations.

B.   **Utility Price and Profit Regulation:** The most common method of monopoly regulation is price and profit control.

1.   Such regulations result in larger output quantities and lower profits than would be the case with unrestricted monopoly.

2.   The profit that the regulator allows is business profit, not economic profit.

C.   **Utility Price and Profit Regulation Example:** To find the profit-maximizing level of output, demand and marginal revenue curves for annual service must be derived.

1.   The profit-maximizing level of output is found by setting MC = MR (where Mπ = 0) and solving for Q.

2.   The appropriate regulated price provides service to the broadest customer base possible, given the need for the regulated utility to earn a risk-adjusted normal return on investment.

D.   **Problems with Utility Price and Profit Regulation:** Although the concept of utility price and profit regulation is simple, several practical problems arise in public utility regulation.

1.   In practice, it is impossible to exactly determine cost and demand schedules, or the minimum investment required to support a given level of output.

2.   If profits for the local electric power company are too low, should rates be raised for summer (peak) or for winter (off-peak) users? Should industrial, commercial, or residential customers bear the burden of higher rates?

3.   Rapid changes in technology and competitive conditions have rendered obsolete many traditional forms of regulation in the electricity and telecommunications industries.

        a.   When regulators are slow to react to such changes, both consumers and the industry suffer.

VI.   MONOPSONY

A.   **Buyer Power:** If only a few buyers exist in a given market, there will tend to be less competition than if there are many buyers.

    1.   Oligopsony exists when there are only a handful of buyers present in a market.

    2.   Monopsony exists when a market features a single buyer of a desired product or input.

        a.   When a single buyer is confronted in a market with many sellers, monopsony power enables the buyer to obtain lower prices than those that would prevail in competitive market.

            (1)   The federal government is a monopsony buyer of military weapons and equipment.

            (2)   Major retailers such as Wal-Mart, Target, and Sears all enjoy monopsony power in the purchase of apparel, appliances, auto parts, and other consumer products.

    3.   Monopsony is least harmful, and is sometimes beneficial, in those markets in which a monopsony buyer faces a monopoly seller, a situation called bilateral monopoly.

B.   **Bilateral Monopoly Illustration:** Competitive market price/output solutions reflect perfect balance in buyer and seller power.

    1.   In markets with varying amounts of seller power and buyer power, some divergence from the competitive market equilibrium is to be expected.

        a.   In markets with unrestrained monopoly, higher than competitive market prices are observed.

        b.   In markets with unrestrained monopsony, lower than competitive market prices are observed.

2.   Bilateral monopoly moderates the price/output outcomes observed in unrestrained monopoly and unrestrained monopsony markets.

    a.   Compromise achieved through bilateral monopoly has the beneficial effect of moving markets away from the inefficient unrestrained monopoly or monopsony solutions toward a more efficient competitive market equilibrium.

    b.   Depending on the relative power of the seller and the buyer, either an above-market or a below competitive-market price will result.

    c.   When a monopoly seller has the upper hand, higher than competitive market prices will prevail.

    d.   If a monopsony buyer has the upper hand, lower than competitive market prices will prevail.

VII.   ANTITRUST POLICY

A.   **Overview of Antitrust Law:** Antitrust laws are designed to promote competition and prevent unwarranted monopoly.

1.   By itself, large firm size or market dominance is no offense; it is any unfairly gained competitive advantage that is against the law.

    a.   The primary objection to monopolies, cartels, and other restraints of trade is that they injure consumers by increasing prices.

    b.   High monopoly prices also curtail consumption and thereby reduce consumer welfare.

2.   There is no single antitrust statute in the United States. Federal antitrust law is based on two important statutes -- the Sherman Act and the Clayton Act -- and their amendments.

    a.   Principles in antitrust law rest on judicial interpretation.

    b.   Individual court decisions, called case law, and statutory standards, called statutory law, must be consulted to assess the legality of business behavior.

B.   Sherman and Clayton Acts: The Sherman Act of 1890 was the first federal antitrust legislation.

1.   The Sherman Act is often criticized as being too vague.

    a.   Section 1 forbids contracts, combinations, or conspiracies in restraint of trade.

    b.   Section 2 forbids monopolizing behavior.

2.   The Clayton Act, addresses problems of mergers, interlocking directorates, price discrimination, and tying contracts.

    a.   Section 2 of the Clayton Act prohibits sellers from discriminating in price among business customers, unless cost differentials or competitive pressure justifies the price differentials.

    b.   The Robinson-Patman Act (1936) declares specific forms of price discrimination illegal, especially those related to chain-store purchasing practices.

    c.   Section 3 of the Clayton Act forbids tying contracts that reduce competition.

    d.   Section 7 of the Clayton Act prohibits stock mergers that reduce competition.

        (1)   The Celler-Kefauver Act closed asset an acquisition loophole, making asset acquisitions illegal when the effect of such purchases is to reduce competition.

3.   The Federal Trade Commission Act outlaws unfair methods of competition in commerce and establishes the FTC, an agency intended to enforce the Clayton Act.

C.   Antitrust Enforcement: The Justice Department may bring actions under the Sherman Act, and the FTC may initiate actions under the Federal Trade Commission Act. Both may initiate proceedings under the Clayton Act.

1.   The Sherman Act is brought to bear -- with both criminal and civil penalties -- in cases involving monopolization, price-fixing agreements, and other unreasonable restraints on trade.

2.   Civil proceedings under the Clayton Act address problems created by mergers and certain forms of price discrimination, exclusive dealing agreements, and tie-in sales conditioned on the purchase of related products.

    a.   Civil proceedings are typically the responsibility of the FTC.

    b.   The FTC holds hearings about suspected violations of the law and issues cease and desist orders if violations are found.

3.   The Justice Department focuses on flagrant offenses under the Sherman Act, as well as with mergers for monopoly covered by Section 7 of the Clayton Act.

    a.   The Justice Department usually brings charges under the Clayton Act only when broader Sherman Act violations are also involved.

    b.   Injunctive relief in the form of dissolution or divestiture decrees is a much more typical outcome of Justice Department suits than are criminal penalties.

VIII.   COMPETITIVE STRATEGY IN MONOPOLY MARKETS

A.   **Market Niches:** Above-normal returns tend to be fleeting in perfectly competitive industries but can be durable for efficient firms that benefit from meaningful monopoly advantages.

1.   Monopolists can benefit from temporary affluence due to unexpected changes in industry demand or cost conditions or uniquely productive inputs.

2.   What is unique about monopoly is the potential for long-lasting above-normal rates of return.

3.   Only new and unique products or services have the potential to create durable monopoly profits.

    a.   A market niche is a segment of a market that can be successfully exploited through the special capabilities of a given firm or individual.

    b.   To be durable, above-normal profits derived from a market niche must not be vulnerable to imitation by competitors.

B. **Information Barriers to Competitive Strategy:** Published data sometimes measure economic profits only imperfectly.

1. Reported business profit rates, such as ROE, can substantially misstate economic profits.

2. Depending on the true rate of economic amortization for intangible assets like advertising and R&D, business profit rates can be either understated or overstated.

3. Beyond the obvious limitations of accounting data, business practices are often expressly intended to limit the loss of valuable trade secret information.

IX. SUMMARY

PROBLEMS & SOLUTIONS

P12.1   ***Monopoly v. Competitive Markets.*** *Identify each of the following statements as true or false, and explain why.*

   A.   *In perfectly competitive markets P = MR, but P > MR in monopoly markets.*

   B.   *Profit maximization in perfectly competitive and monopoly markets requires setting MR = MC.*

   C.   *In long-run equilibrium, monopoly results in lower prices than would be typical of a perfectly competitive industry.*

   D.   *In monopoly markets, firm and market demand curves always have identical slope.*

   E.   *In long-run equilibrium, P > AC in perfectly competitive and monopoly markets.*

P12.1   *SOLUTION*

   A.   True. In perfectly competitive markets, firms are price takers and P = MR. In monopoly markets, firms are price makers. This means that monopoly firms set prices and/or output, and P > MR in monopoly market equilibrium

   B.   True. Profit maximization always requires that MR = MC. In monopoly and competitive markets, profit maximization requires setting MR = MC. Because P > MR in monopoly markets, profit maximization does not imply setting P = MC, as is the case in perfectly competitive markets.

   C.   False. In long-run equilibrium, monopoly results in higher prices and lower levels of output than would be typical of a perfectly competitive industry.

   D.   True. In monopoly markets, the firm is the industry. Therefore, monopoly firm and monopoly market demand curves always have identical slopes.

   E.   False. In long-run equilibrium, P = AC in perfectly competitive markets and zero excess profits are earned. In monopoly market equilibrium, P > MR = MC. This means that above-normal profits are possible in long-run monopoly equilibrium, and P > AC.

P12.2   ***Monopoly Concepts.*** *Distinguish each of the following characteristics as typical of competitive markets and/or monopoly markets, and illustrate why.*

A.   *Downward sloping industry demand curves.*

B.   *Horizontal firm demand curves.*

C.   *Differentiated output.*

D.   *High barriers to entry.*

E.   *Excess profits in short-run disequilibrium.*

P12.2   **SOLUTION**

A.   Both perfect competition and monopoly. Both perfectly competitive and monopoly market structures are characterized by downward sloping industry demand curves. Downward sloping industry demand curves result from the law of diminishing marginal utility discussed earlier in the book.

B.   Perfect competition. Horizontal firm demand curves in perfectly competitive markets reflect the fact that such firms are price takers, and imply that $P = MR$ in these markets.

C.   Monopoly. Monopoly is characterized by a lack of competition from close substitutes. Thus, highly differentiated output is a key characteristic of monopoly markets.

D.   Monopoly. High barriers to entry limit competition from rivals able to offer close substitutes. Thus, high barriers to entry are a key characteristic of monopoly markets.

E.   Both perfect competition and monopoly. Excess profits in short-run disequilibrium reflect the effects of unexpected changes in industry demand and supply relations. They are observed in all types of market structures, including perfect competition and monopoly.

P12.3   **Equilibrium.** *Demand conditions for household chemical spray treatments to control insects and other pests in the St. Louis, Missouri market area are described as follows:*

Spray Treatments per year	Price
0	$25
1	24

2	23
3	22
4	21
5	20
6	19
7	18

The marginal cost of service is stable at $20 per spray treatment.

A. Use the indicated price and output data to complete the following table.

Spray Treatments per year	Price	Total Revenue	Marginal Revenue
0	$25		
1	24		
2	23		
3	22		
4	21		
5	20		
6	19		
7	18		

B. Determine price and the level of service per customer if a perfectly competitive market structure is present.

C. Determine price and the level of service if the city grants a monopoly franchise.

P12.3 **SOLUTION**

A.

Spray Treatments per year	Price	Total Revenue	Marginal Revenue
0	$25	$0	--
1	24	24	$24
2	23	46	22

3	22	66	20
4	21	84	18
5	20	100	16
6	19	114	14
7	18	126	12

B. In a perfectly competitive industry, P = MR, so the optimal activity level occurs where P = MC. Here, P = MC = $20 at Q = 5 treatments per year.

C. A monopoly will maximize profits by setting MR = MC. Here, MR = MC = $20 at Q = 3 treatments and P = $22.

P12.4 *Capture Problem.* On May 9, 2005, *The Wall Street Journal* carried a front-page article titled "U.S. Plans Antitrust Suit Over Real-Estate Listings." The article described how government antitrust enforcers were preparing to sue the National Association of Realtors, alleging that its policies illegally restrict the discounting of real estate sales commissions and put online competitors at a disadvantage. Real estate brokers and sales agents typically charge 5-6% commissions on the sale of new and previously occupied homes. It's a huge business. In 2004, home sales totaled nearly eight million units, and real estate commissions amounted to $61 billion. The Justice Department is concerned by the fact that NAR bylaws encourage its 1.2 million members to withhold their property listings from online brokers. When barred from the multiple listing service, online brokers fid it difficult to get the attention of real estate buyers and sellers. The Justice Department is also targeting industry-backed efforts to get state legislatures and real-estate boards, which set licensing standards, to enact regulations that protect full-service real-estate agents and their commissions. The Justice Department and the FTC have warned several states that such laws hamper innovation and competition, and have formally objected to industry-supported proposals in Oklahoma and Texas. The Justice Department also sued a Kentucky state agency that sought to fix commissions and deprive consumers of the benefits of price competition among brokers.

Briefly explain the following:

A. The causes and consequences of regulation according to the public interest theory of regulation.

B. The causes and consequences of regulation according to the capture theory of regulation.

C. How the preceding article supports and/or contradicts each theory of regulation.

P12.4   ***SOLUTION***

A.   According to the "public interest" theory of regulation, regulation is imposed on industry to protect larger social interests.

B.   According to the "capture" theory of regulation, regulation is imposed by industry, or other politically effective groups, in order to further the narrow self-interest of the regulated.

C.   In an era when competition from online brokers has collapsed stock brokerage commission rates, it is an anomaly that real estate commission rates remain stubbornly stuck at 5-6%. In mid-2005, for example, online investors could buy 1,000 shares of common stock in the Washington Post Co. for $840 per share and pay an online brokerage fee of as little as $5 to $10. At the same time, the sale of a new or previously lived in $500,000 home would involve a typical real estate commission of $25,000 to $30,000.

   According to the Justice Department, price fixing by real estate agents is to blame for the high level of real estate commission costs. In support of the public interest theory of regulation, the *Wall Street Journal* article describes how government antitrust enforcers were moving against the National Association of Realtors for pursuing policies that illegally restrict the discounting of real estate sales commissions and put online competitors at a disadvantage. The public interest theory is also supported by the fact that the Justice Department is opposing industry-backed efforts to get state legislatures and real-estate boards, which set licensing standards, to enact regulations that protect full-service real-estate agents and their commissions.

   In support of the capture theory of regulation, it is worth noting that it is necessary for the Justice Department and the FTC to warn several states that they have enacted laws that hamper innovation and competition in the real estate market. In several states, it appears that regulators have been "captured" by the real estate agent lobbying group. When state laws and regulatory agencies help any industry by stifling competition and restricting price competition, they are working for the industry and against consumer interests.

P12.5   ***Antitrust Law****. Indicate whether or not each of the following examples of business behavior are legal or illegal under current antitrust law, and mention whether violations under the Sherman Act, Clayton Act, and/or Federal Trade Commission Act are involved. Explain your answer.*

A.   *Charging higher markups for younger versus older consumers.*

B.   *False and misleading advertising.*

C. *Mergers for monopoly.*

D. *Charging different markups to various business customers.*

E. *A business strategy of using patents to limit competition.*

P12.5 **SOLUTION**

A. Legal. The Clayton Act, as amended by the Robinson-Patman Act, explicitly prohibits price discrimination among business customers unless lower markups are required to meet the competition. However, price discrimination among final consumers is legal and widely practiced by business and government entities.

B. Illegal under the Federal Trade Commission Act. False and misleading advertising is a prime example of the type of unfair competition made illegal by the FTC Act.

C. Illegal under the Sherman and Clayton Acts. The Sherman Act explicitly forbade contracts, combinations, and conspiracies in restraint of trade. Similarly, the Clayton Act forbade mergers and asset acquisitions intended to create monopoly power.

D. Illegal under the Clayton Act. The Clayton Act, as amended by the Robinson Patman Act, explicitly prohibits price discrimination among business customers unless lower markups are required to meet the competition. Charging different markups to business customers is only legal in the unlikely event that no harm to competition would result.

E. Illegal under the Sherman and Federal Trade Commission Acts. A business strategy of using patents to limit competition is an example of monopolizing behavior and an unfair method of competition.

P12.6 ***Social Costs of Monopoly.*** *In what is an industry-wide labor agreement, the U.S. auto industry has agreed to pay generous health care benefits to employed and retired autoworkers. Following rapid unanticipated growth in health care costs over the past decade, the resulting health care liability to the auto industry has grown into the billions of dollars. To alleviate this burden, the auto industry sponsors a vigorous lobbying effort in Washington, D.C. to press for passage of an expensive government-guaranteed health care plan for all Americans. Under these circumstances, explain why passage of a government-guaranteed health care plan would increase, decrease or have no effect on:*

A. *Auto industry health care costs.*

B.   *Auto industry profits.*

C.   *Car prices.*

D.   *National demand for health care.*

E.   *National health care costs.*

P12.6   **SOLUTION**

A.   Decrease. Passage of a government-guaranteed health care plan would decrease auto industry health care costs because these expenses would be paid out of general tax revenues.

B.   Increase. Auto industry profits would rise following passage of a government-guaranteed health care plan because industry costs would fall (see Part A.)

C.   Decrease. Passage of a government-guaranteed health care plan has the potential to result in some decrease in car prices. Because auto industry labor costs are at least somewhat variable, a decrease in health care costs could translate into lower marginal costs and somewhat lower car prices. However, the car price effect of a national health care plan is likely to be quite small.

D.   Increase. Passage of a government-guaranteed health care plan would increase the national demand for health care. Unlike most goods and services that must be directly paid for by consumers, "free" health care is indirectly paid for through tax revenues.

E.   Increase. Passage of a government-guaranteed health care plan would increase national health care costs given the burst in demand that can be anticipated.

P12.7   ***Import Competition.*** *ControlSoft, Inc. is a Minneapolis-based supplier of inventory management and control software that is popular with car dealers in the United States. The company has retained an independent management consulting firm to provide advice concerning supply and demand conditions in the industry. Using Department of Commerce data, the consultant estimates market supply and demand conditions for the domestic market as*

$$Q_S = 4,000P \qquad \text{(Supply)}$$

$$Q_D = 1,500,000 - 2,000P \qquad \text{(Demand)}$$

A.   *Assuming the industry is perfectly competitive, calculate the domestic industry equilibrium price/output combination.*

B.   *Now assume that import restrictions eliminate ControlSoft's leading competitors, thereby giving the company a monopoly position in its home market. Based on the same supply and demand conditions stated above, calculate the new monopoly equilibrium price/output combination for the domestic industry.*

P12.7   SOLUTION

A.   The perfectly competitive industry equilibrium price is:

$$Q_S = Q_D$$

$$4{,}000P = 1{,}500{,}000 - 2{,}000P$$

$$6{,}000P = 1{,}500{,}000$$

$$P = \$250$$

At P = \$250, industry equilibrium output is:

$$Q_S = 4{,}000(\$250)$$

$$= 1{,}000{,}000$$

B.   The new monopoly equilibrium price/output combination is found at the profit-maximizing activity level where MC = MR. It is important to recognize that the industry supply curve represents the horizontal sum of the marginal cost curves for individual producers. When the industry is transformed into a monopoly, the industry supply curve represents the relevant marginal cost curve:

$$Q_S = 4{,}000P \qquad\qquad \text{(Supply)}$$

$$MC = P = \$0.00025Q$$

And the profit maximizing activity level is where:

$$MC = MR$$

$$\partial TC/\partial Q = \partial TR/\partial Q$$

$$\$0.00025Q \quad = \quad \$750 - \$0.001Q$$

$$0.00125Q \quad = \quad 750$$

$$Q \quad = \quad 600,000$$

$$P \quad = \quad \$750 - \$0.0005(600,000)$$

$$= \quad \$450$$

From parts A and B, it is clear that import restrictions reduce the level of industry output from 1,000,000 to 600,000 units, and increase prices from \$250 to \$450 per unit. Generally, speaking, monopolists offer consumers too little output at too high a price. (*Note:* If P = \$750 - \$0.0005Q, then TR = \$750Q - \$0.0005Q^2).

P12.8   ***Monopoly Franchises.*** *Internet Voice, also known as Voice over Internet Protocol (VoIP), is a technology that allows consumers to make telephone calls using a broadband Internet connection instead of a traditional analog phone line. Some services using VoIP only allow users to call other people using the same service, but many allow users to call anyone who has a telephone number - including local, long distance, mobile, and international numbers. While early VoIP services only worked over a computer or a special VoIP phone, newer services allow users to operate a traditional phone through an adaptor.*

To speed the adoption of VoIP technology and provide much needed competition for the local phone company, many towns and municipalities offer short-term monopoly franchises to cable TV operators who offer VoIP to their customers. Suppose one such government body offered the local cable company a monopoly franchise on the offering of VoIP service when market demand conditions are as follows:

$$TR \quad = \quad \$100Q - \$0.0002Q^2 \qquad \qquad \text{\textit{(Total Revenue)}}$$

$$MR \quad = \quad \partial TR/\partial Q = \$100 - \$0.0004Q \qquad \text{\textit{(Marginal Revenue)}}$$

Q is the number of VoIP service customers, and both revenues and costs are expressed in dollars per month. Assume marginal costs are stable at \$20 per customer, and that no fixed costs are relevant.

A.   *As a monopoly, calculate the local cable TV company's VoIP output, price, and profits at the profit maximizing activity level.*

B.   *What output, price and profit levels would prevail following expiration of the local monopoly franchise based on the assumption that vigorous competition evolves*

between the local cable TV company and the local phone company, and that a
competitive market solution results?

P12.8   SOLUTION

    A.   Set MR = MC to find the monopoly profit-maximizing activity level:

$$MR = MC$$

$$\$100 - \$0.0004Q = \$20$$

$$0.0004Q = 80$$

$$Q = 200,000$$

$$P = TR/Q$$

$$= (\$100Q - \$0.0002Q^2)/Q$$

$$= 100 - 0.0002Q$$

$$= 100 - 0.0002(200,000)$$

$$= \$60$$

$$\pi = TR - TC$$

$$= \$60(200,000) - \$20(200,000)$$

$$= \$8,000,000$$

    B.   In a perfectly competitive industry, P = MR = MC in equilibrium. Thus, after
expiration of the local cable TV company's monopoly franchise, P = MC = \$20
would result. Because MC = AC, P = MC implies that $\pi = 0$. To find the amount
of market demand at a price of \$20 per month,

$$P = TR/Q$$

$$20 = (\$100Q - \$0.0002Q^2)/Q$$

$$20 = 100 - 0.0002Q$$

$$0.0002Q = 80$$

$$= 400,000$$

$$\pi = TR - TC$$

$$= \$20(400,000) - \$20(400,000)$$

$$= 0$$

P12.9   ***Monopoly Versus Perfectly Competitive Equilibrium.*** *The Hotpoint Inspection &
Insurance Company is the leading underwriter of boiler and machinery insurance.
Market demand for the company's insurance given by the relation:*

$$P = \$7,500 - \$1.1Q$$

$$MR = \partial TR/\partial Q = \$7,500 - \$2.2Q$$

All costs are variable, and are constant at $2,000 per policy (Q).

A.   *Calculate the profit-maximizing price/output combination and economic profits
if the company enjoys a monopoly due to state licensing requirements.*

B.   *Calculate the profit-maximizing price/output combination if a relaxation of entry
restrictions transforms the industry into one that is perfectly competitive.*

P12.9   **SOLUTION**

A.   The profit-maximizing price/output combination is found by setting MR = MC.
Because AVC is constant, MC = AVC = $2,000. Therefore:

$$MR = \partial TR/\partial Q = MC$$

$$\$7,500 - \$2.2Q = \$2,000$$

$$2.2Q = 5,500$$

$$Q = 2,500$$

$$P = \$7,500 - \$1.1(2,500)$$

$$= \$4,750$$

$$\text{Economic Profits} = P \times Q - AVC \times Q$$

$$= \$4,750(2,500) - \$2,000(2,500)$$

$$= \$6,875,000$$

(*Note*: As a monopolist, Hotpoint is the industry. Also remember that the marginal revenue curve has the same intercept but twice the slope as the demand curve.)

B. In a perfectly competitive market, P = MC. In this instance where AVC is constant and, therefore, MC = AVC, perfectly competitive equilibrium will occur when:

$$P = MC = AVC$$

$$\$7,500 - \$1.1Q = \$2,000$$

$$1.1Q = 5,500$$

$$Q = 5,000$$

$$P = \$7,500 - \$1.1(5,000)$$

$$= \$2,000$$

$$\text{Economic Profits} = P \times Q - AVC \times Q$$

$$= \$2,000(5,000) - \$2,000(5,000)$$

$$= \$0$$

In words, the transformation of the industry from monopoly to perfect competition has brought a \$2,750 reduction in price and a 2,500-unit expansion in output. At the same time, economic profits have been eliminated.

P12.10 ***Utility Regulation.*** *The Electric Company is under review by a state regulatory commission. Relevant revenue and cost curves including a "fair" rate of return agreed upon by both the firm and the commission are as follows:*

$$P = \$85Q - \$0.2Q^2 \qquad\qquad \text{(Demand)}$$

$$MR = \partial TR/\partial Q = \$85 - \$0.4Q \qquad \textit{(Marginal Revenue)}$$

$$TC = \$900 + \$20Q + \$0.8Q^2 \qquad \textit{(Total Cost)}$$

$$MC = \partial TC/\partial Q = \$20 + \$1.6Q \qquad \textit{(Marginal Cost)}$$

where P is price (in dollars), Q is output (in thousands of megawatt hours) and TC is total cost (in thousands of dollars).

A. *If the firm were operating as a pure monopoly, what would be its optimal price/ output solution and level of economic profits?*

B. *What price should be set if the commission wishes to eliminate economic profits?*

P12.10 SOLUTION

A. Set $M\pi = MR - MC = 0$ to find the profit-maximizing output level where:

$$M\pi = MR - MC$$

$$0 = \$85 - \$0.4Q - \$20 - \$1.6Q$$

$$2Q = 65$$

$$Q = 32.5 \ (000) \text{ or } 32,500 \text{ megawatt hours}$$

$$P = \$85 - \$0.2(32.5)$$

$$= \$78.50$$

$$\pi = TR - TC$$

$$= \$85Q - \$0.2Q^2 - \$900 - \$20Q - \$0.8Q^2$$

$$= -\$1Q^2 + \$65Q - \$900$$

$$= -\$1(32.5^2) + \$65(32.5) - \$900$$

$$= \$156.25 \ (000) \text{ or } \$156,250$$

(*Note*: Profit is falling for $Q > 32.5$, so $Q = 32.5$ is a point of maximum profits).

B.   To preclude monopoly profits, the commission must set:

$$P = AR = AC \;=\; TC/Q$$

$$\$85 - \$0.2Q \;=\; (\$900 + \$20Q + \$0.8Q^2)/Q$$

$$85Q - 0.2Q^2 \;=\; 900 + 20Q + 0.8Q^2$$

$$-1Q^2 + 65Q - 900 \;=\; 0$$

This is a quadratic equation of the form:

$$aQ^2 + bQ + c = 0$$

where a = -1, b = 65 and c = -900. Its two roots can be obtained using the quadratic formula where:

$$Q \;=\; \frac{-b \pm \sqrt{b^2 - 4ac}}{2a}$$

$$=\; \frac{-65 \pm \sqrt{(65^2) - 4(-1)(-900)}}{2(-1)}$$

$$=\; \frac{-65 \pm \sqrt{4{,}225 - 3{,}600}}{-2}$$

$$=\; \frac{-65 \pm 25}{-2}$$

$$=\; 20\,(000) \text{ or } 45\,(000) \text{ megawatt hours}$$

The "upper" Q is the relevant solution because regulatory commissions generally seek the "largest quantity of service consistent with the public interest." Therefore,

$$P \;=\; \$85 - \$0.2Q$$

$$=\; \$85 - \$0.2(45)$$

$$=\; \$76$$

$$\pi = -\$1(45^2) + \$65(45) - \$900$$

$$= \$0$$

Chapter 13

MONOPOLISTIC COMPETITION AND OLIGOPOLY

Perfect competition and monopoly are relatively rare. Intel and Microsoft dominate their respective markets, for example, but both are subject to intense rivalry from a swarm of nonleading firms. Most firms compete with a large number of rivals that offer highly similar products, but many retain some control over the prices of their products. They cannot sell all that they want at a fixed price, nor would they lose all their sales if they raised prices slightly. In other words, most firms face downward-sloping demand curves. This means that above-normal returns are possible, at least during the short-run time frame. For this reason, study of the partly-competitive, partly-monopolistic market structures of monopolistic competition and oligopoly is integral to managerial economics.

When vigorous price and product competition from firms offering close substitutes eliminates the potential for above-normal or economic profits in long-run equilibrium, a market is called monopolistically competitive. Oligopoly markets involve competition among only a handful of competitors. Products offered could be homogeneous, as in aluminum and steel, or differentiated, as in soft drinks and cigarettes. In both instances, limits on the number of competitors stem from meaningful impediments to new entry or nonleading firm growth. Competition among the few has the potential to result in excess profits if so-called "competitors" make implicit or explicit agreements not to compete. This chapter illustrates the nature of competition in imperfectly competitive markets, and shows how the principles of managerial economics can be used to develop an effective competitive strategy.

CHAPTER OUTLINE

I. **CONTRAST BETWEEN MONOPOLISTIC COMPETITION AND OLIGOPOLY**

    A. **Monopolistic Competition:** This market structure is characterized by a large number of sellers that offer differentiated products.

        1. Only a risk-adjusted normal rate of return is possible in monopolistically competitive long-run equilibrium.

    B. **Oligopoly:** Oligopoly is a market structure characterized by few sellers.

        1. Economic profits are possible in oligopoly markets, even in long-run equilibrium.

C.   Dynamic Nature of Competition: In many formerly oligopolistic markets, the market discipline provided by a competitive fringe of smaller domestic and foreign rivals is sufficient to limit the potential abuse of a few large competitors.

    1.   Timely and accurate market structure information is required to form the basis for managerial investment decisions that relate to entry or exit from specific lines of business.

II.   MONOPOLISTIC COMPETITION

A.   Monopolistic Competition Characteristics: Monopolistic competition exists when a large number of firms offer close but not identical substitutes. Elements of perfect competition and monopoly are involved because monopolistically competitive markets feature:

    1.   Large numbers of buyers and sellers.

    2.   Product heterogeneity.

    3.   Free entry and exit.

    4.   Perfect dissemination of information.

    5.   Opportunity for normal profits in long-run equilibrium.

B.   Monopolistic Competition Price/Output Decisions: Profit maximization requires that firms operate at a point where marginal revenue equals marginal cost.

    1.   Monopolistic competition causes zero economic profits in the long-run because $P = AR = AC$.

    2.   Equilibrium prices are found within a range.

        a.   The high-price/low-output solution is the point of tangency between the LRAC curve and a new firm demand curve created through a parallel leftward shift in the original (monopoly) demand curve.

        b.   The low-price/high-output solution is the point of tangency between the minimum LRAC point and a new horizontal firm demand curve.

            (1)   This is also the perfectly competitive solution.

3.   Average cost is higher with monopolistic competition than in the case of pure competition.

a.   These higher costs can be viewed as the value of product diversity.

III.   MONOPOLISTIC COMPETITION PROCESS

A.   **Short-run Monopoly Equilibrium:** In the short run, monopolistically competitive industries begin from a point of monopoly equilibrium.

1.   In the short run, monopolistically competitive firms take full advantage of their monopoly position and maximize short-run profits

B.   **Long Run High-price/low output Equilibrium:** In the long run, if competition from distinctive products produced by competitors eliminates any potential for economic profits, $P = AC$ at a point above minimum long-run average costs.

1.   This is a monopolistically competitive market equilibrium with differentiated production.

C.   **Long Run Low-price/high output Equilibrium:** In the long run, if competition from homogenous products produced by competitors eliminates any potential for economic profits, $P = AC$ at minimum long-run average costs.

1.   This is a competitive market equilibrium with homogeneous production..

IV.   OLIGOPOLY

A.   **Oligopoly Markets Characteristics:** Oligopoly is a market structure with few competitors; individual price/output decisions often produce reactions from rivals. Oligopoly markets feature:

1.   Few sellers.

2.   Homogenous or unique products.

3.   Blockaded entry and exit.

4.   Imperfect dissemination of information.

5.   Opportunity for above-normal (economic) profits in long-run equilibrium.

B. **Examples of Oligopoly:** In the United States, aluminum, cigarettes, electrical equipment, filmed entertainment production and distribution, glass, long-distance telecommunications, and ready-to-eat cereals are all produced and sold under conditions of oligopoly.

1. Oligopoly also is present in a number of local markets. In many retail markets for gasoline and food, for example, only a few service stations and grocery stores compete within a small geographic area.

V. CARTELS AND COLLUSION

A. **Overt and Covert Agreements:** All firms in an oligopoly market could benefit if they formally or informally got together and set prices to maximize industry profits.

1. A group of competitors operating under a formal overt agreement is called a cartel.

   a. A cartel that has absolute control over all firms in an industry can function as a monopoly.

2. If an informal covert agreement is reached, the firms are said to be operating in collusion.

B. **Enforcement Problems:** Cartels are typically rather short-lived because coordination problems often lead to cheating.

1. Cartel subversion can be extremely profitable.

2. At the same time, detecting the source of secret price concessions can be extremely difficult.

VI. OLIGOPOLY OUTPUT-SETTING MODELS

A. **Cournot Oligopoly:** The Cournot model posits that firms in oligopoly markets make simultaneous and independent output decisions.

1. The relationship between an oligopoly firm's profit-maximizing output level and competitor output is called the oligopoly output-reaction curve because it shows how oligopoly firms react to competitor production decisions.

2. The Cournot market equilibrium level of output is found by simultaneously solving the output-reaction curves for both competitors.

3. Cournot equilibrium output exceeds the amount produced under monopoly, but is less that the amount produced in a competitive market.

B. **Stackelberg Oligopoly:** The noncooperative Stackelberg model posits a first-mover advantage for the oligopoly firm that initiates the process of determining market output.

1. If leading firms cannot agree on which firm is the leader and which firm is the follower, a price war can break out with the potential to severely undermine the profitability of both leading and following firms.

2. An informal but sometimes effective means for reducing uncertainty in oligopoly markets is through price signaling.

3. Price leadership occurs when one firm establishes itself as the industry leader and other firms follow its pricing policy.

4. With barometric price leadership, the price leader is not necessarily the largest or the dominant firm in the industry.

VII. OLIGOPOLY PRICE-SETTING MODELS

A. **Bertrand Oligopoly: Identical Products** The Bertrand model focuses upon the price reactions, rather than the output reactions, of oligopoly firms.

1. Bertrand equilibrium is reached when no firm can achieve higher profits by charging a different price.

   a. The Bertrand model predicts cutthroat price competition and a competitive market price/output solution in oligopoly markets with identical products.

2. According to contestable markets theory, there is no necessary link between the number of actual competitors and the vigor of competition.

   a. As predicted by Bertand, contestable markets theory suggests that oligopoly firms producing identical products will behave much like firms in perfectly competitive markets.

B.   Bertrand Oligopoly: Differentiated Products Many economists believe that price-setting models, including the Bertrand model, are more plausible than quantity-setting models, like the Cournot model, when products are differentiated.

1.   The Bertrand model demonstrates how price-setting oligopoly firms can profit by selling differentiated products.

2.   In the Bertrand model, the relationship between the profit-maximizing price level and competitor price is called the oligopoly price-reaction curve because it shows how the oligopoly firm reacts to competitor pricing decisions.

C.   Sweezy Oligopoly: The Sweezy model hypothesizes that when making price decisions, oligopoly firms have a tendency to follow rival price decreases but ignore rival price increases.

1.   Such rigid prices are explained as reflecting a kinked demand curve.

   a.   A kinked demand curve is a firm demand curve that has different slopes for price increases as compared with price decreases.

   b.   The kinked demand curve describes a behavior pattern in which rival firms follow any decrease in price to maintain their respective market shares but refrain from following price increases, allowing their market shares to grow at the expense of the competitor increasing its price.

   c.   The demand curve facing individual firms is kinked (and prices are "stuck") at the established price/output combination.

D.   Oligopoly Model Comparison: Oligopoly theory is comprised of a rich series of models that together help explain competition among the few.

1.   Modeling the behavior of firms in oligopoly markets is made difficult by the fact that assumptions made about rival behavior are an important determinant of the firm's own decision making process.

VIII.   MARKET STRUCTURE MEASUREMENT

A.   Economic Markets: An economic market consists of all individuals and firms willing and able to buy or sell competing products during a given period.

1. The key criterion in identifying competing products is similarity in use.

    a. When cross-price elasticities are large and positive, goods are substitutes for each other and can be thought of as competing products in a single market.

    b. Large negative cross-price elasticities indicate complementary products.

B. Economic Census: To identify relevant economic markets, firms in the United States make extensive use of economic data collected by the Bureau of the Census of the U.S. Department of Commerce.

1. The economic census provides a comprehensive statistical profile of the economy, from the national, to the state, to the local level.

2. Industry statistics contained in the economic census are largely classified using the North American Industry Classification System (NAICS).

3. Up to date census information can be obtained on the Internet (http://www.census.gov).

IX. CENSUS MEASURES OF MARKET CONCENTRATION

A. Concentration Ratios: A small number of competitors can sometimes have direct implications for regulation and antitrust policy.

1. Questions about the intensity of competition sometimes arise when only a limited number of competitors are present, or when only a handful of large firms dominate the industry.

2. Group market share data are called concentration ratios because they measure the percentage market share concentrated in (or held by) an industry's top four (CR_4), eight (CR_8), twenty (CR_{20}), or fifty (CR_{50}) firms.

3. By definition:

$$CR_i = \sum_{i=1}^{n} X_i,$$

here CR is a concentration ratio for the ith number of firms and X_i is a relative percentage measure of firm input or output (employment, sales, etc.).

    a.   CR = 100 for a monopoly.

    b.   CR → 0 for a perfectly competitive industry.

B.   **Herfindahl-Hirschmann Index:** The Herfindahl-Hirschmann Index (HHI) is a popular measure of competitor size inequality that reflects size differences among large and small firms.

    1.   Calculated in percentage terms, the HHI is the sum of the squared market shares for all n industry competitors:

$$HHI = \sum_{i=1}^{n} \left(\frac{Firm\ Sales_i}{Industry\ Sales} \times 100 \right)^2$$

    a.   HHI = 10,000 for a monopoly.

    b.   HHI → 0 for a perfectly competitive industry.

C.   **Limitations of Census Information:** Despite obvious value, concentration ratios and HHI data suffer from important limitations.

    1.   They take a long time to collect and publish.

    2.   Concentration ratio and HHI information ignore domestic sales by foreign competitors (imports) as well as exports by domestic firms.

    3.   If high transportation costs or other product characteristics keep markets regional or local rather than national in scope, national concentration ratios and HHI data can significantly understate the relative importance of leading firms.

X.   **SUMMARY**

PROBLEMS & SOLUTIONS

P13.1 **Market Structure Concepts**. *Identify each of the following characteristics as typical of monopolistic competition and/or oligopoly market structures, and explain why.*

    A. *Downward sloping industry demand curves.*

    B. *Kinked firm demand curves.*

    C. *Differentiated output.*

    D. *High barriers to entry.*

    E. *Excess profits in long-run equilibrium.*

P13.1 **Solution**

    A. Both monopolistic competition and oligopoly. Both monopolistically competitive and oligopoly market structures are characterized by downward sloping industry demand curves. Downward sloping industry demand curves result from the law of diminishing marginal utility discussed earlier in the book.

    B. Oligopoly. Kinked firm demand curves in oligopoly markets reflect competitor matching of price cuts, but a failure by competitors to match price increases. This stems from the oligopoly firm's desire to maintain market share, and results in somewhat sticky market prices.

    C. Both monopolistic competition and oligopoly. Monopolistic competition and oligopoly markets are characterized by a lack of competition from identical substitutes. Differentiated output is a key characteristic of both types of market structure.

    D. Oligopoly. High barriers to entry limit rivals' ability to offer close substitutes. High barriers to entry are a key characteristic of oligopoly markets.

    E. Oligopoly. Excess profits in long-run equilibrium reflect the effects of high barriers to entry. They are observed in oligopoly market structures, but not in those markets characterized as monopolistically competitive.

P13.2 **Equilibrium**. *Indicate whether each of the following statements is true or false and why.*

A. *Equilibrium in oligopoly markets requires that firms be operating at the point where marginal revenue equals marginal cost.*

B. *A high ratio of distribution cost to total cost tends to increase competition by widening the geographic area over which any individual producer can compete.*

C. *The price elasticity of demand tends to fall as new competitors introduce substitute products.*

D. *An efficiently functioning cartel achieves the monopoly price/output combination.*

E. *An increase in price advertising tends to increase the slope of firm demand curves.*

P13.2 **SOLUTION**

A. True. Stable equilibrium in all market structures requires that firms operate at the point where marginal revenue equals marginal cost.

B. False. A low ratio of distribution cost to total cost tends to increase competition by widening the geographic area over which any individual producer can compete.

C. False. The price elasticity of demand rises as new competitors introduce substitute products.

D. True. A perfectly functioning cartel achieves the monopoly price-output combination.

E. False. An increase in price advertising decreases the slope of individual firm demand curves.

P13.3 **Monopolistically Competitive Equilibrium.** *Information Systems, Inc., is a small supplier of computer software information systems to hospitals.*

A. *Use ISI's price, output, and weekly total cost data to complete the following table:*

Price	Output	Total Revenue	Marginal Revenue	Total Cost	Marginal Cost	Average Cost
$7,500	0	$0	--	$2,500	--	--
5,000	1			5,000		
3,500	2			7,000		
2,800	3			8,100		

Price	Output	Total Revenue	Marginal Revenue	Total Cost	Marginal Cost	Average Cost
2,400	4			9,600		
2,000	5			12,500		
1,700	6			16,500		

B. What is the monopolistically competitive high-price/low-output equilibrium?

C. What is the monopolistically competitive low-price/high-output equilibrium?

P13.3   **SOLUTION**

   A.

Price	Output	Total Revenue	Marginal Revenue	Total Cost	Marginal Cost	Average Cost
$7,500	0	$0	--	$2,500	--	--
5,000	1	5,000	$5,000	5,000	$2,500	$5000
3,500	2	7,000	2,000	7,000	2,000	3,500
2,800	3	8,400	1,400	8,100	1,100	2,700
2,400	4	9,600	1,200	9,600	1,500	2,400
2,000	5	10,000	400	12,500	2,900	2,500
1,700	6	10,200	200	16,500	4,000	2,750

   B. The monopolistically competitive high-price/low-output equilibrium is at P = AC = $3,500, Q = 2 and π = TR - TC = 0. No excess profits are being earned, and there would be no incentive for either expansion or contraction because MR = MC = $2,000. Such an equilibrium is typical of monopolistically competitive industries where each individual firm retains some pricing discretion in the long-run.

   C. The monopolistically competitive low-price/high-output equilibrium is at P = AC = $2,400, Q = 4 and π = TR - TC = 0. No excess profits are being earned, and there would be no incentive for either expansion or contraction. This is similar to the perfectly competitive equilibrium. (Note that MR < MC and average cost is rising for Q > 4.)

P13.4   ***Short-run Equilibrium.*** *CATV, Inc., has been granted a limited-term exclusive license to operate a cable television system in Jackson, Wyoming. Recent operating experience* *in similar locations suggests a close relation between the monthly price for basic service and the number of residential subscribers.*

A.   Complete the following table based on CATV's projected price, output, and monthly total cost data:

Price	Output (000)	Total Revenue	Marginal Revenue ($000)	Total Cost ($000)	Marginal Cost ($000)
$50	0			$0	
40	1			20	
30	2			40	
25	3			60	
20	4			80	
15	5			100	

B.   Calculate the short-run equilibrium monopoly price/output combination and profit level.

C.   Calculate the long-run equilibrium price/output combination and profit level if competitive bidding for the franchise resulted in a perfectly competitive market outcome.

P13.4   **SOLUTION**

A.

Price	Output (000)	Total Revenue	Marginal Revenue ($000)	Total Cost ($000)	Marginal Cost ($000)
$50	0	$0	--	$0	--
40	1	40	$40	20	$20
30	2	60	20	40	20
25	3	75	15	60	20
20	4	80	5	80	20
15	5	75	-5	100	20

B. The profit maximizing activity level is found where MR = MC. As a monopoly, MR = MC = $20,000 at the Q = 2(000) activity level. This implies P = $30 and π = TR = TC = $60 - $40 = $20,000 per month.

C. The perfectly competitive equilibrium occurs where P = MC = AC and zero excess profits are earned, and TR = TC. Here, MR = MC = $20(000) and TR = TC = $80(000) at Q = 4(000) units per month, with P = $20 and π = TR - TC = $0 per month.

P13.5   ***Market Share Analysis.*** *No-reservation (shuttle) airline passenger service is currently provided in the Washington, D.C. to New York city-pair market by only three firms. Weekly output measured in passengers flown and the marginal cost per passenger are as follows:*

Weekly Output (000,000)	*Marginal Cost of Service:*		
	Apple Airlines, Inc. *(A)*	*Big Bird, Inc.* *(B)*	*Continuity Airlines, Ltd.* *(C)*
1	$40	$20	$50
2	30	25	40
3	25	30	45
4	35	35	55
5	50	40	65
6	60	50	75

The current fare (market price) of $45 cannot be raised given the threat of competitor entry. Nevertheless, each airline is able to greatly expand service without lowering prices. Thus, P = MR = $45.

A. *Calculate current industry output and the market share of each airline.*

B. *Calculate industry output if the introduction of a high-speed passenger train forces airline industry prices down to $35.*

P13.5   **SOLUTION**

A. Each industry participant will produce to the point where MR = MC, but never where MR < MC. Given P = MR = $45, each firm will produce such that MC = MR = $45. A total Q = 12 units will be produced as follows:

Firm	Output	Market Share
Apple Airlines (A)	4	33%
Big Bird, Inc. (B)	5	42%
Continuity Airlines, Ltd. (C)	3	25%
Total	12	100%

B. Following a decrease in industry prices to P = MR = $35, industry output will fall to Q = 8 distributed as follows:

Firm	Output	Market Share
Apple Airlines (A)	4	50%
Big Bird, Inc. (B)	4	50%
Continuity Airlines, Ltd. (C)	0	0%
Total	8	100%

Note that a fare reduction has the most severe effect on Continuity, the high-cost carrier.

P13.6 ***Monopolistically Competitive Equilibrium.*** *401k Specialists, Ltd., offers pension planning advice to individuals and small businesses. Demand and cost information for 401k's standard pension plan assessment service is*

$$P = \$4,500 - Q \qquad\qquad \text{(Demand)}$$

$$MR = \partial TR/\partial Q = \$4,500 - \$2Q \qquad\qquad \text{(Marginal Revenue)}$$

$$TC = \$150,000 + \$400Q \qquad\qquad \text{(Total Cost)}$$

$$MC = \partial TC/\partial Q = \$400 \qquad\qquad \text{(Marginal Cost)}$$

where Q is output, P is price, MR is marginal revenue, TC is total costs and MC is marginal cost. Both cost functions include a normal return of 12% on capital investment.

A. *Determine the profit-maximizing price/output combination and profit level.*

B. *Compute price, output and profits under the assumption that 401k seeks to maximize revenue. If 401k operates in a monopolistically competitive industry, is the industry in equilibrium?*

C. *What price/output combination and economic profits will occur in equilibrium? Assume equilibrium occurs through a parallel leftward shift in the firm demand curve to calculate the firm's new equilibrium demand curve. (Hint: The slope of the average cost curve $\partial AC/\partial Q = -\$150,000/Q^2$.)*

P13.6 SOLUTION

A. Set MR = MC to determine the profit-maximizing level of output:

$$MR = MC$$

$$\$4,500 - \$2Q = \$400$$

$$2Q = 4,100$$

$$Q = 2,050 \text{ units}$$

$$P = \$4,500 - Q$$

$$= 4,500 - 2,050$$

$$= \$2,450$$

$$\pi = TR - TC$$

$$= \$4,500Q - Q^2 - \$150,000 - \$400Q$$

$$= -\$150,000 + \$4,100Q - Q^2$$

$$= -150,000 + 4,100(2,050) - 2,050^2$$

$$= \$4,052,500$$

(*Note*: Profits are decreasing for Q > 2,050, thus Q = 2,050 is a profit maximum).

B. Set MR = 0 to determine the revenue-maximizing level of output:

$$MR = \$0$$

$$4,500 - 2Q = 0$$

$$2Q = 4,500$$

$$Q = 2,250$$

$$P = \$4,500 - Q$$

$$= 4,500 - 2,250$$

$$= \$2,250$$

$$\pi = -\$150,000 + \$4,100Q - Q^2$$

$$= -150,000 + 4,100(2,250) - 2,250^2$$

$$= \$4,012,500$$

The industry is not in equilibrium because the firm is earning substantial economic profits. Under monopolistic competition, only normal profits can be earned in equilibrium. (*Note*: Total revenue is falling for Q > 2,250, thus Q = 2,250 is a revenue maximum.)

C.   Economic profits will attract new competitors. These new firms will attract business away from 401k with the result being that the firm demand curve will shift in a leftward direction until P = AC and economic profits are eliminated. This process is described graphically below. (*Note*: Here there is no low-price/high-output equilibrium point because the AC curve declines continuously, i.e., there is no minimum AC point.)

Algebraically, one can determine equilibrium output, price and profit by following a few simple steps:

<u>Step 1</u>: The problem specifies that the demand curve shifts in a parallel fashion, so the demand curve intercept changes but the slope remains constant and equal to -1, so the new demand curve is Q = a - P. It is not necessary to determine the intercept a at this point because one is only interested in the slope of the new demand curve.

<u>Step 2</u>: Find the point of tangency between the AC curve and the demand or AR curve. This occurs where the slope of the AC curve (given as $\partial AC/\partial Q = -150,000/Q^2$) equals the slope of the new demand curve:

$$\begin{array}{c} \text{Average cost} \\ \text{curve slope} \end{array} = \begin{array}{c} \text{New demand} \\ \text{curve slope} \end{array}$$

$$\frac{-150,000}{Q^2} = -1$$

$$Q^2 = 150,000$$

$$Q = \sqrt{150,000}$$

$$Q = 387.3 \text{ units}$$

Step 3: In equilibrium,

$$P = AC$$

$$= \frac{\$150,000 + \$400Q}{Q}$$

$$= \frac{150,000 + 400(387.3)}{387.3}$$

$$= \$787.30$$

Step 4: Because $P = AR = AC$, excess profits in equilibrium are zero.

Because $Q = 387.3$, $P = \$787.30$ and $\pi = 0$. Another point on the linear demand curve is $P = \$787.30$ and $Q = 387.3$, is where $Q = a - P$ (and $b = -1$). Thus,

$$387.3 = a - 787.3$$

$$a = 1,174.6$$

Therefore, $Q = 1,174.6 - P$ represents the firm's new equilibrium demand curve.

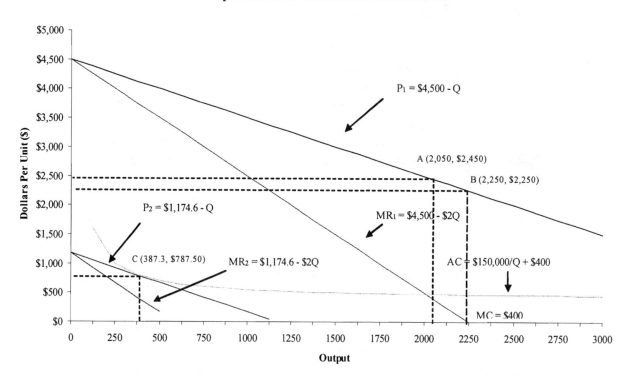

401k Specialists Demand and Cost Relations

P13.7   ***Kinked Demand Curve***. *Dewey, Cheetum & Howe, Ltd., is a securities litigation law firm located in Detroit, Michigan. Dewey, Cheetum & Howe faces the following segmented demand curve for its services*

<u>*Over the range 0 - 50(000) hours*</u>:

$$P_1 \ = \ \$500 - \$1Q$$

$$MR_1 \ = \ \partial TR_1 / \partial Q = \$500 - \$2Q$$

<u>*When output exceeds 50(000) units*</u>:

$$P_2 \ = \ \$650 - \$4Q$$

$$MR_2 \ = \ \partial TR_2 / \partial Q = \$650 - \$8Q$$

The law firm's cost functions are:

$$TC = \$250 + \$50Q + \$2.5Q^2$$

$$MC = \partial TC / \partial Q = \$50 + \$5Q$$

where P is price (in dollars), Q is hours of service billed to clients (in thousands) and TC is total cost (in thousands of dollars).

A. *Graph the company's demand, marginal revenue and marginal cost curves.*

B. *How would you describe the market structure of the securities litigation industry? Explain your answer in some detail, including an explanation of why the demand curve takes the shape given above.*

C. *What is the firm's optimal price and quantity, and what profits or losses will be earned at this output level?*

D. *How much could marginal costs rise before the optimal price would increase? How much could they fall before the optimal price would decrease?*

P13.7   SOLUTION

A.   A graph of revenue and cost relations for Dewey, Cheetum & Howe, Inc. is as follows:

Dewey, Cheetum & Howe

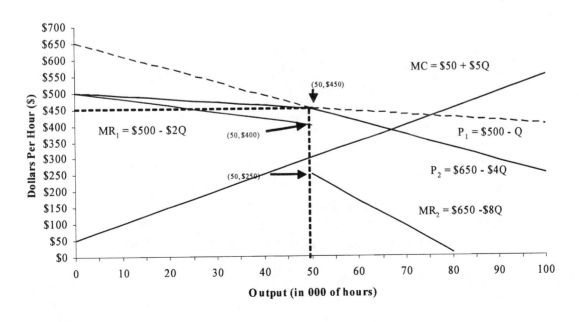

B.   The firm is in an oligopolistic industry. It faces a kinked demand curve meaning that competitors react to price reductions by cutting their own prices, thereby causing the segment of the demand curve below the kink to be relatively inelastic. Price increases are not followed, causing the portion of the demand curve above the kink to be relatively elastic.

C.   An examination of the graph indicates that the marginal cost curve passes through the gap in the marginal revenue curve. Graphically, this indicates that optimal P = $450 and Q = 50(000). Analytically,

$$MR_1 \ = \ \$500 - \$2Q \qquad\qquad Q \ \leq \ 50(000)$$

$$MR_2 \ = \ \$650 - \$8Q \qquad\qquad Q \ > \ 50(000)$$

$$MC = \$50 + \$5Q$$

If one solves for the output levels where MR = MC, it becomes obvious that MR_1 > MC over the range Q ≤ 50(000), and MR_2 < MC for the range Q ≥ 50(000). Therefore, the firm will produce 50(000) units of output and market them at P = $450 per hour. And finally,

$$\pi \ = \ P \times Q - TC$$

$$= \ \$450(50) - \$250 - \$50(50) - \$5(50^2)$$

$$= \ \$7,250(000) \text{ or } \$7,250,000$$

D.   At Q = 50(000),

MR_1	= $500 - $2Q	MR_2	= $650 - $8Q
	= $500 - $2(50)		= $650 - $8(50)
	= $400		= $250

This implies that if marginal costs at Q = 50(000) exceed $400, the optimal price would increase. Conversely, if marginal costs at Q = 50(000) fall below $250, the optimal price would decrease. So long as marginal cost at Q = 50(000) is in the range of $250 to $400, the firm will have no incentive to change its price.

P13.8   ***Supply Reactions****. Computer Management Corporation specializes in the development of management information and decision assistance software programs. CMC has just* finished development of a new software package that will permit small retail firms to computerize their inventory management at a lower cost than has previously been possible. On the basis of sales data for similar software packages, management believes that demand for the product will be greatly influenced by the reactions of other computer software companies to the introduction of CMC's new product. No reaction will result in the monthly demand and marginal revenue functions:

$$P = \$150 - \$0.1Q$$

$$MR = \partial TR/\partial Q = \$150 - \$0.2Q$$

A major reaction will lead to the more elastic curves:

$$P = \$130 - \$0.4Q$$

$$MR = \partial TR/\partial Q = \$130 - \$0.8Q$$

CMC's total monthly cost for marketing this product is composed of $3,000 additional administrative expenses and $50 per unit for production and distribution costs. That is, the relevant total cost and marginal cost functions are given by the expression:

$$TC = \$3,000 + \$50Q$$

$$MC = \partial TC/\partial Q = \$50$$

A. What is the profit-maximizing price for CMC's product, assuming no competitor reaction?

B. Calculate this price based on the assumption competitors will react.

C. In light of CMC's cost conditions, and absent any substantial barriers to entry, which scenario is more likely?

P13.8   SOLUTION

A. With no competitor reaction, set:

$$MR = MC$$

$$\$150 - \$0.2Q = \$50$$

$$0.2Q = 100$$

$$Q = 500$$

$$P = \$150 - \$0.1(500)$$

$$= \$100$$

B.   With a major competitor reaction, set:

$$MR = MC$$

$$\$130 - \$0.8Q = \$50$$

$$0.8Q = 80$$

$$Q = 100$$

$$P = \$130 - \$0.4(100)$$

$$= \$90$$

C.   In this situation, a reaction is probable. Note that:

$$MC = \$50$$

Therefore, CMC prices of P = \$100 (in part A) or P = \$90 (in part B) are both substantially above marginal costs, and likely to attract substantial entry. Still, the industry does not have the potential to achieve a stable perfectly competitive long-run equilibrium because average costs will decline continuously as output expands. Therefore, a monopolistically competitive long-run equilibrium where P = AC > MC and no excess profits seems likely.

In real world markets where software packages enjoy copyright protection, software publishing companies may have at least a short-run opportunity to earn above-normal profits. This assumes, of course, that copyright laws are effectively enforced,

P13.9   ***Cournot Equilibrium.*** *Weekly residential trash hauling is subject to enormous economies of density. Once a single firm is in the neighborhood picking up garbage, it costs very little to pick up refuse from another customer. As a result, collusion among private companies often seeks to divide market areas to maximize monopoly profits. To illustrate the competitive process in markets dominated by few firms, assume that a two-firm duopoly dominates the market for weekly residential trash hauling in Akron, Ohio and that the firms face a linear market demand curve*

$$P = \$1,000 - Q$$

where P is price and Q is the number of customers served per year (in thousands). Thus $Q = Q_A + Q_B$. For simplicity, also assume that both firms offer an identical service, have no fixed costs and marginal cost $MC_A = MC_B = \$100$. In this circumstance, total revenue for Firm A is

$$TR_A = \$1,000Q_A - Q_A^2 - Q_AQ_B$$

Marginal revenue for Firm A is

$$MR_A = \partial TR_A/\partial Q_A = \$1,000 - \$2Q_A - Q_B$$

Similar total revenue and marginal revenue curves hold for Firm B.

A.   *Derive the output reaction curves for Firms A and B.*

B.   *Calculate the Cournot market equilibrium price-output solutions.*

P13.9   SOLUTION

A.   Because $MC_A = \$100$, Firm A's profit-maximizing output level is found by setting $MR_A = MC_A = 0$:

$$MR_A = MC_A$$

$$\$1,000 - \$2Q_A - Q_B = 100$$

$$\$2Q_A = \$900 - Q_B$$

$$Q_A = 450 - 0.5Q_B$$

Notice that the profit-maximizing level of output for Firm A depends upon the level of output produced by itself and Firm B. Similarly, the profit-maximizing level of output for Firm B depends upon the level of output produced by itself and Firm A. These relationships are each competitor's output-reaction curve

Firm A output-reaction curve: $Q_A = 450 - 0.5Q_B$

Firm B output-reaction curve: $Q_B = 450 - 0.5Q_A$

B. The Cournot market equilibrium level of output is found by simultaneously solving the output-reaction curves for both competitors. To find the amount of output produced by Firm A, simply insert the amount of output produced by competitor Firm B into Firm A's output-reaction curve and solve for Q_A. To find the amount of output produced by Firm B, simply insert the amount of output produced by competitor Firm A into Firm B's output-reaction curve and solve for Q_B. For example, from the Firm A output-reaction curve

$$Q_A = 450 - 0.5Q_B$$

$$Q_A = 450 - 0.5(450 - 0.5Q_A)$$

$$Q_A = 450 - 225 + 0.25Q_A$$

$$0.75Q_A = 225$$

$$Q_A = 300 \ (000) \ units$$

Similarly, from the Firm B output-reaction curve, the profit-maximizing level of output for Firm B is $Q_B = 300$. With just two competitors, the market equilibrium price/output combination is

$$\text{Cournot equilibrium output} = Q_A + Q_B$$

$$= 300 + 300$$

$$= 600 \ (000) \ units$$

$$\text{Cournot equilibrium price} = \$1,000 - Q$$

$$= \$1,000 - \$1(600)$$

$$= \$400 \ per \ year$$

P13.10 ***Stackelberg Model.*** *The Stackelberg model allows for strategic behavior by leading firms, and can be used to illustrate how leading firms maintain dominance of important industries. To illustrate the concept of Stackelberg first-mover advantages, again imagine that a two-firm duopoly dominates the market for residential trash hauling in the Akron, Ohio market. Also assume that the firms face a linear market demand curve*

$$P = \$1,000 - Q$$

where P is price and Q is total output in the market (in thousands). Thus $Q = Q_A + Q_B$. For simplicity, also assume that both firms produce an identical product, have no fixed costs and marginal cost $MC_A = MC_B = \$100$. In this circumstance, total revenue for Firm A is

$$TR_A = \$1,000Q_A - Q_A^2 - Q_AQ_B$$

Marginal revenue for Firm A is

$$MR_A = \partial TR_A/\partial Q_A = \$1,000 - \$2Q_A - Q_B$$

Similar total revenue and marginal revenue curves hold for Firm B.

A. *Calculate the Stackelberg market equilibrium price-output solutions.*

B. *How do the Stackelberg equilibrium price-output solutions differ from those suggested by the Cournot model? Why?*

P13.10 SOLUTION

A. To illustrate Stackelberg first-mover advantages, reconsider the Cournot model but now assume that Firm A, as a leading firm, correctly anticipates the output reaction of Firm B, the following firm. With prior knowledge of Firm B's output-reaction curve, $Q_B = 450 - 0.5Q_A$, Firm A's total revenue curve becomes

$$\begin{aligned} TR_A &= \$1,000Q_A - Q_A^2 - Q_AQ_B \\ &= \$1,000Q_A - Q_A^2 - Q_A(450 - 0.5Q_A) \\ &= \$550Q_A - 0.5Q_A^2 \end{aligned}$$

With prior knowledge of Firm B's output-reaction curve, marginal revenue for Firm A is

$$MR_A = \partial TR_A/\partial Q_A = \$550 - \$1Q_A$$

Because $MC_A = \$100$, Firm A's profit-maximizing output level with prior knowledge of Firm B's output-reaction curve is found by setting $MR_A = MC_A = \$100$:

$$MR_A = MC_A$$

$$\$550 - \$1Q_A = \$100$$

$$Q_A = 450$$

After Firm A has determined its level of output, the amount produced by Firm B is calculated from Firm B's output-reaction curve

$$Q_B = 450 - 0.5Q_A$$

$$= 450 - 0.5(450)$$

$$= 225$$

With just two competitors, the Stackelberg market equilibrium level of output is

$$\text{Stackelberg equilibrium output} = Q_A + Q_B$$

$$= 450 + 225$$

$$= 675 \ (000) \ \text{units}$$

The Stackelberg market equilibrium price is

$$\text{Stackelberg equilibrium price} = \$1,000 - Q$$

$$= \$1,000 - \$1(675)$$

$$= \$325 \ \text{per year}$$

B.   Notice that market output is greater in Stackelberg equilibrium than in Cournot equilibrium because the first mover, Firm A, produces more output while the follower, Firm B, produces less output. Stackelberg equilibrium also results in a lower market price than that observed in Cournot equilibrium. In this example, Firm A enjoys a significant first-mover advantage. Firm A will produce twice as much output and earn twice as much profit as Firm B so long as Firm B accepts the output decisions of Firm A as given and does not initiate a price war. If Firm A and Firm B cannot agree on which firm is the leader and which firm is the follower, a price war can break out with the potential to severely undermine the profitability of both leading and following firms. If neither duopoly firm is willing to allow its competitor to exercise a market leadership position, vigorous price competition and a competitive market price/output solution can result.

Obviously, participants in oligopoly markets have strong incentives to resolve the uncertainty surrounding the likely competitor response to leading-firm output decisions.

Chapter 14

GAME THEORY AND COMPETITIVE STRATEGY

Game theory had its start as a branch of mathematics that uses models to study interactions with formalized incentive structures, so-called "games." Game theorists study the predicted and actual behavior of individuals, and use game theory techniques to devise optimal competitive strategies. Because seemingly different types of interactions among players can exhibit similar incentive structures, game theory concepts can be used as a unifying method of analysis in a wide variety of applications. Game theory has been successfully applied in a wide variety of fields, including economics, international relations, evolutionary biology, political science, and military strategy. Game theory techniques have also been implemented in the design of regulatory and bidding policies for public oil deposits, radio spectrum, and so on.

In general, simple mathematical games like puzzles can be played by a single player. Games become much more interesting when they involve multiple players, and each player realizes that they are in conflict with other players. In a competitive game, players choose strategies that have the potential to maximize their personal payoff. When a game involves exactly two players and one player's loss is the other's gain, the game is called a zero sum game. In the case of a zero-sum game, the payoff matrix describes the reward earned by each player at the expense of the other player. In practical applications, game theory is used to illustrate strategic interactions among multiple players like firms, government agencies, and customers where each player has a perceptible and recognized influence on other players.

CHAPTER OUTLINE

I.   **GAME THEORY BASICS**

      A.   **Types of Games:** Game theory is applied during situations in which decision makers must take into account the reasoning of other decision makers.

            1.   In a zero-sum game, one player's gain is another player's loss.

            2.   If parties are engaged in a game that holds the potential for mutual gain, it is called a positive-sum game.

            3.   When conflict holds the potential for mutual loss, it is called a negative-sum game.

            4.   In cooperative games, joint action is favored.

B.   Role of Interdependence: The essence of a game is the interdependence of player strategies.

1.   In a sequential game, each player moves in succession, and each player is aware of all prior moves.

a.   The general principle for players in a sequential game is to look ahead and extrapolate back.

2.   In a simultaneous-move game, players act at the same point in time and must make their initial moves in isolation without any direct knowledge of moves made by other players.

3.   A given allocation of payoffs is called an equilibrium outcome if the payoff to no player can be improved by unilateral action.

C.   Strategic Considerations: In some sequential conflict situations, systematic action becomes predictable and can be exploited by rivals.

1.   Firms often use threats and promises to alter the expectations and actions of other firms.

a.   To succeed, threats and promises must be credible.

2.   To successfully implement game theory concepts, decision makers must understand the benefits to be obtained from concealing or revealing useful information.

II.   PRISONER'S DILEMMA

A.   Classic Riddle: A simple introduction to game theory strategy is provided by the Prisoner's Dilemma.

1.   Two suspects held in isolation face a classic conflict-of-interest situation.

a.   If only one suspect confesses and implicates the other, then the one confessing will get a relatively light penalty.

b.   If both suspects confess, then each will receive a stiff penalty.

2.   In this situation, there is no dominant strategy that creates the best result for either suspect regardless of the action taken by the other.

a.   Both would be better off if they could be assured that the other would not confess, since if neither confesses both are set free.

b.   In failing to confess, each is exposed to the risk that the other will confess. By not confessing they would then receive a harsh penalty.

3.   A secure strategy, sometimes called the maximin strategy, guarantees the best possible outcome given the worst possible scenario.

a.   For each suspect, the secure strategy is to confess, thereby becoming a prisoner.

B.   Business Application: Though the prisoner's dilemma is posed within the scope of a bargaining problem between two suspects, it has obvious practical applications in business.

C.   Broad Implications: The Prisoner's Dilemma game fascinates game theorists for a variety of reasons.

1.   The Prisoner's Dilemma game is often used to describe decision problems involving positive and negative externalities.

2.   The Prisoner's Dilemma game describes a wide variety of business decisions made where the resulting payoff depends upon competitor responses.

a.   Theory shows that when games are repeated, the potential for cooperation or collusion increases.

III.   NASH EQUILIBRIUM

A.   Nash Equilibrium Concept: A Nash equilibrium is reached when neither player can improve its own payoff by unilaterally changing its own strategy given the strategy of its competitor.

1.   In some instances, even two-party games have no stable Nash equilibrium.

B.   Nash Bargaining: A Nash bargaining game is another application of the simultaneous-move, one-shot game.

1.   In Nash bargaining, two competitors or players "bargain" over some item of value.

2. In a simultaneous-move, one-shot game, the players have only one chance to reach an agreement.

IV. INFINITELY REPEATED GAMES

A. **Role of Reputation:** An infinitely repeated game is a competitive game that is repeated over and over again without boundary or limit.

1. In an infinitely repeated game, firms receive sequential payoffs that shape current and future strategies.

2. The repeat nature of competitor interactions can sometimes harm consumers, but repetitive interactions in the marketplace can also be helpful to consumers.

     a. The ongoing interaction between firms and their customers provides incentives for firms to maintain product consistency.

B. **Product Quality Games:** Consistency and reliability are cherished commodities that stem from the fact that firms are involved in long-term relationships with customers, suppliers and competitors.

1. The theory of infinitely repeated games can by used to show the desirability of maintaining a reputation for selling high-quality goods.

V. FINITELY REPEATED GAMES

A. **Uncertain Final Period:** A finitely repeated game is one that occurs only a limited number of times, or has limited duration in time.

1. If there is uncertainty about when a game will end, the conduct of a finitely repeated game mirrors an infinitely repeated game.

2. A trigger strategy is a system of behavior that remains the same until another player takes some course of action that precipitates a different response.

     a. Trigger strategies can be used to ensure that the costs of breaking agreements exceed any resulting benefits, where both costs and benefits are measured in present value terms.

B.   End-of-Game Problem: The end-of-game problem stems from the fact that it becomes difficult to properly motivate managers and workers at the ends of their career.

1.   Savvy employers solve the end-of-game problem by using rewards or punishments that extend beyond the employment period.

C.   First-mover Advantages: A first-mover advantage is a benefit earned by the player able to make the initial move in a sequential move or multistage game.

1.   Multistage games and the assertion of first-mover advantages are complicated by the difficulty of making credible threats, especially between strangers.

VI.   COMPETITIVE STRATEGY

A.   Basic Concepts: Developing and implementing an effective competitive strategy in imperfectly competitive markets involves a never-ending search for uniquely attractive products.

1.   It is always helpful to consider the number and size distribution of competitors, degree of product differentiation, level of information available in the marketplace, and conditions of entry when assessing the profit potential of current products or prospective lines of business.

B.   Competitive Advantage: A competitive advantage is a unique or rare ability to create, distribute, or service products valued by customers.

1.   It is the business-world analog to what economists call comparative advantage, or when one nation or region of the country is better suited to the production of one product than to the production of some other product.

2.   Long-lasting above-normal rates of return require a sustainable competitive advantage that, by definition, cannot be easily duplicated.

C.   When Large Size Is a *Disadvantage:* When diseconomies of scale are operative, larger firms suffer a cost disadvantage when compared to smaller rivals.

1.   Smaller and more nimble firms are sometimes able to translate the benefits of small size into a distinct competitive advantage.

VII.   PRICING STRATEGIES

A. **Limit Pricing:** Limit pricing is a competitive strategy to set less than monopoly prices in an effort to deter market entry by new and viable competitors.

1. Limit pricing strategies are widely adopted by monopoly firms and other firms with pricing power as means for maintaining lead market positions, albeit with less than maximum short-term profits.

2. Predatory pricing is pricing below marginal cost in the hope of knocking out rival producers and subsequently raising prices to obtain monopoly profits.

B. **Market Penetration Pricing:** Many successful firms are sometimes able to create a customer lock-in effect that yield important long-term benefits.

1. Customer lock-in effects are often tied to network externalities that lead to significant first-mover advantages.

   a. A network is a series of valuable links among producers or customers that can be physical or economic in nature.

   b. Ebay benefits from a community of buyers and sellers with significant network externalities.

2. Market penetration pricing is a pricing strategy of charging very low initial prices to create a new market or grab market share in an established market.

   a. The objective is to gain a critical mass of customers, create strong network effects, and eventually establish a viable business.

   b. Once a large customer base is established, Microsoft and others then increase prices and profit margins to take advantage of the fact that switching computer software becomes more difficult once use has become widespread throughout an organization or profession.

VIII. **NON-PRICE COMPETITION**

A. **Advantages of Non-price Competition:** Many successful entrants find non-price methods of competition to be an effective means for growing market share and profitability in the face of entrenched rival

1. Non-price competition takes a variety of forms: affinity and frequent user programs, home delivery systems, innovative use of technology, Internet

shopping, media advertising, price incentives to shop at off-peak times, 24/7 shopping or service hours, and so on.

B.   Optimal Level of Advertising: Advertising is one of the most common methods of non-price competition

1.   The profit-maximizing amount of non-price competition is found by setting the marginal cost of the activity involved equal to the marginal revenue or marginal benefit derived from it.

C.   Optimal Advertising Example: The optimal level of advertising is achieved when $MR_A = MC_A$, and $M\pi_A = 0$.

1.   The profit implications of other types of non-price competition can be measured in a similar fashion.

IX.   SUMMARY

PROBLEMS & SOLUTIONS

P14.1 **Game Types.** *Characterize each of the following circumstances as a zero-sum game, a positive-sum game, or a negative-sum game. Explain.*

 A. *A work rules mediation between labor and management.*

 B. *A supplier-customer relationship.*

 C. *The relationship between two competitors.*

 D. *The negotiation between a company and its insurer concerning the allocation of payment responsibility for a legal settlement.*

 E. *The bargaining that occurs among departments of an organization that is downsizing employment.*

P14.1 **SOLUTION**

 A. Positive-sum game. In many game theory situations, there is the potential for mutual gain or mutual harm. If parties are engaged in a game that holds the potential for mutual gain, it is called a positive-sum game. A work rules mediation between labor and management is a positive-sum game because both parties stand to gain from a favorable mediation. With a mutually agreeable resolution, workers get more pay and employers get better motivated employees.

 B. Positive-sum game. Every supplier-customer relationship can be described as a positive-sum game because the potential for mutually beneficial exchange is the basic motivation for such interactions.

 C. Zero-sum game. In a zero-sum game, one competitor's gain is another competitor's loss. In a competitive interaction, for example, any profit recorded by one competitor on a business deal is exactly matched by the profit opportunity loss suffered by the unlucky competitor that got shut out. The only way for a firm to win in the competitive game is for the unlucky competitor to lose.

 D. Negative-sum game. When conflict holds the potential for mutual loss, it is called a negative-sum game. The negotiation between a company and its insurer concerning the allocation of payment responsibility for a legal settlement is an example of a negative-sum game because both parties come out of such negotiations with the responsibility for paying some of the costs of the legal settlement. They are sharing in a bad result.

E. Negative-sum game. The bargaining that occurs among departments of an organization that is downsizing employment is a classic example of a negative-sum game because all such parties share, in greater or lesser degree, the pain associated with corporate layoffs.

P14.2 *Classic Prisoner's Dilemma. In the classic characterization of the prisoner's dilemma, two suspects are arrested by the police. The police have insufficient evidence for a conviction, and having separated both prisoners, visit each of them and offer the same deal: if one confesses and the other remains silent, the silent accomplice receives the full 10-year sentence and the confessor goes free. If both stay silent, the police can only gain a conviction on a lesser charge for which both prisoners will spend 6 months in prison. If both confess, they will each receive a 2-year sentence. Each prisoner has two options: to stay quiet, or to betray the accomplice and confess. The outcome of each choice depends on the choice of the accomplice. However, neither prisoner knows the choice of the accomplice. Assume both prisoners are completely selfish and their only goal is to minimize their own jail terms.*

		Prisoner #1	
	Confession Strategy	*Deny Guilt*	*Confess Guilt*
Prisoner #2	*Deny Guilt*	*Both serve 6 months*	*Prisoner #2 gets 10 years; Prisoner #1 goes free*
	Confess Guilt	*Prisoner #1 gets 10 years; Prisoner #2 goes free*	*Both serve 2 years*

A. *Is there a dominant strategy in the classic prisoner's dilemma problem?*

B. *Illustrate how the classic prisoner's dilemma problem shows that independent rational behavior can sometimes lead to a suboptimal outcome for everybody.*

P14.2 **SOLUTION**

A. Yes. In the classic prisoner's dilemma game, confessing is a dominant strategy for both players. If either prisoner expects their accomplice to deny their guilt (stay quiet), the optimal personal strategy choice is to confess, as this means going free immediately while the accomplice lingers in jail for 10 years. If either prisoner expects their accomplice to confess, the best personal strategy choice is to confess as well because that allows them to avoid having to spend 10 years in prison. In the event that both confess, both will spend 2 years in prison. If, however, both prisoners deny their guilt (stay quiet), both would be able to get out in 6 months.

Therefore, in the classic prisoner's dilemma game, confessing is a dominant strategy for both players. No matter the decision choice of the other player, each player can always reduce their expected sentence by confessing. Unfortunately for the prisoners involved, this leads to a poor outcome where both confess and both get heavy jail sentences. This is the core of the classic prisoner's dilemma. Independent rational behavior leads to a suboptimal outcome for all.

B. If reasoned from the perspective of the optimal interest for the group, the best outcome would be for both prisoners to implicitly cooperate with each other, continue to deny their guilt (stay quiet), and thereby reduce the total jail time served by the group to one year total. Considered from a group perspective, any other decision would be worse for the two prisoners considered together. However by each following their selfish interests, the two prisoners each receive a lengthy sentence and suffer from their lack of cooperation.

P14.3 *Dominant Strategies. Suppose two competitors each face important strategic decisions where the payoff to each decision depends upon the reactions of the competitor. Firm A can choose either row in the payoff matrix defined below, whereas firm B can choose either column. For firm A the choice is either "up" or "down;" for firm B the choice is either "left" or "right." Notice that neither firm can unilaterally choose a given cell in the profit payoff matrix. The ultimate result of this one-shot, simultaneous-move game depends upon the choices made by both competitors. In this payoff matrix, strategic decisions made by firm A or firm B could signify decisions to offer a money-back guarantee, lower prices, offer free shipping, and so on. The first number in each cell is the profit payoff to firm A; the second number is the profit payoff to firm B.*

		Firm B	
	Competitive Strategy	Left	Right
Firm A	Up	$750,000, $100,000	$500,000, $400,000
	Down	$250,000, $250,000	$800,000, $300,000

A. *Is there a dominant strategy for firm A? If so, what is it?*

B. *Is there a dominant strategy for firm B? If so, what is it?*

P14.3   SOLUTION

A.   No, there is no dominant strategy for firm A. Notice that if firm B chooses "left," the highest payoff of $750,000 can be achieved if Firm A chooses "up." On the other hand, if firm B chooses "right," the highest payoff of $800,000 can be achieved if firm A chooses "down." Therefore, there is no dominant strategy for firm A. The profit-maximizing choice by firm A depends upon the choice made by firm B.

B.   Yes, "right" is a dominant strategy for firm B. If firm A chooses "up," the highest payoff of $400,000 can be achieved if firm B chooses "right." On the other hand, if firm A chooses "down" the highest payoff of $300,000 can be achieved if firm B again chooses "right." No matter what firm A chooses, the highest payoff for firm B results if B chooses "right." Therefore, "right" is a dominant strategy for firm A.

P14.4   *Game Theory Concepts.* *In 2005, Verizon Communications Inc. and Qwest Communications International Inc. were locked in a bitter struggle to acquire telecommunications giant MCI Inc. In a series of moves, Verizon made an offer to buy MCI, only to be topped by a later and higher bid by Qwest. This process continued until the ultimate victor was determined.*

A.   *Examine how the bidding war between Verizon and Qwest over MCI could be described as a noncooperative game.*

B.   *Discuss how the the bidding war between Verizon and Qwest over MCI also could be described as a sequential game.*

P14.4   SOLUTION

A.   If Verizon independently entered its bid amounts for MCI, and these bid amounts were quickly matched by Qwest, and *vice versa*, these actions could be described as reflective of a noncooperative game. Cooperative games favor collaboration in decision making, and the decision to change bid amounts in this case was made without consultation among competitors.

B.   The bidding war between Verizon and Qwest over MCI could be described as a sequential game. In a sequential game, each player moves in succession, and each player is aware of all prior moves. The general principle for players in a sequential game is to look ahead and extrapolate back. A simultaneous game is one in which all players make decisions (or select a strategy) without knowledge of the strategies that are being chosen by other players. Even though the decisions may be made at different points in time, the game is synchronous because each player has no information about the decisions of others; it is as if the decisions are made simultaneously. Simultaneous games are solved using the concept of a Nash equilibrium.

P14.5   ***Randomized Strategies.*** *Employers often meticulously recount cash receipts that are collected and turned in by key employees. However, recounting cash receipts is a time-consuming, laborious, and costly process. Furthermore, if key employees are both diligent and honest in their handling of company cash receipts, there is no need for a meticulous recount every time a key employee turns in cash receipts.*

     A.   *Explain how this problem of motivating prudence and honesty among key employees resembles a game theory problem.*

     B.   *What does game theory prescribe for employers facing the problem of needing to motivate prudence and honesty among key employees?*

P14.5   **SOLUTION**

     A.   The on-going battle between employers and their employees concerning diligence and honesty is a classic game theory problem. Employers typically use audits to motivate employees to be meticulous and honest in their handling of company cash. However, routine audits can be time-consuming and tedious. Moreover, if employees are routinely meticulous and honest in their dealings, there is no need for routine audits. This is a classic game theory problem with no stable Nash equilibrium. If employees are meticulous and honest, there is no need for audits. However, if there are no audits, there is no need for employees to be meticulous and honest.

     B.   Game theory has a simple randomized strategy prescription for such situations: random audits. In a two-party game with no stable Nash equilibrium, a player's preferred strategy changes once its rival has adopted its strategy. The classic case is where managers monitor worker performance. If a manager chooses to monitor worker performance, the worker will choose to perform as expected. However, given that a worker has chosen to perform as expected, there is no need for managerial monitoring. In such instances, both workers and managers have strong incentives to keep their planned moves secret. The lack of a Nash equilibrium also provides incentives for randomized strategies whereby players flip a coin or otherwise randomly choose among available strategies in order to keep rivals from being able to predict strategic moves.

P14.6   ***Secure Strategies.*** *In 1979, cable-television sports broadcasting juggernaut ESPN was called the Entertainment and Sports Programming Network. That name was dropped in February 1985 when the company adopted the ESPN acronym as its corporate name. Today, ESPN, Inc., is 80 percent owned by ABC, Inc., a subsidiary of The Walt Disney Company; the Hearst Corporation holds the remaining 20 percent interest. ESPN finds itself in an ongoing battle with FOX Sports for distinctive sports programming, such as the rights to broadcast a NCAA Division I football tournament and championship game. Assume that ESPN can choose either row in the bid cost matrix defined below, whereas FOX Sports can choose either column. Neither firm can unilaterally choose a specific cell in the bid cost matrix; both companies would like to minimize the bid (cost) amount. The ultimate result of this one-shot, simultaneous-move game depends upon the choices made by both competitors. The first number in each cell is the bid cost to ESPN; the second number is the bid cost to FOX Sports.*

		FOX Sports	
	Bid Strategy	*Exclusive Bid*	*Nonexclusive Bid*
ESPN	*Exclusive Bid*	*$10 billion, $10 billion*	*$4 billion, $2 billion*
	Nonexclusive Bid	*$5 billion, $8 billion*	*$3 billion, $3 billion*

A.   *Is there a secure strategy for ESPN? If so, what is it?*

B.   *Is there a secure strategy for FOX Sports? If so, what is it?*

P14.6   **SOLUTION**

A.   Yes, the secure strategy for ESPN is to make a nonexclusive bid. Irrespective of the choice made by FOX Sports, with its nonexclusive bid secure strategy ESPN can insure that it avoids the worst-possible outcome of having to pay $10 billion for broadcast rights.

B.   Yes, the secure strategy for FOX Sports is also to make a nonexclusive bid. Irrespective of the choice made by ESPN, with its nonexclusive bid secure strategy FOX Sports can insure that it avoids the worst-possible outcome of having to pay $10 billion for broadcast rights.

P14.7   ***Nash Equilibrium.*** *Mars and Hershey's dominate the domestic chocolate candy bar business. In this mature market, advertising by individual firms does little to convince more people to eat candy. Effective advertising simply steals sales from rivals. Big profit gains could be had if these rivals could simply agree to stop advertising. Assume Mars and Hershey's are trying to set optimal advertising strategies. Mars can choose* *either row in the payoff matrix defined below, whereas Hershey's can choose either column. The first number in each cell is Mars' payoff; the second number is the payoff to Hershey's. This is a one-shot, simultaneous-move game and the first number in each cell is the profit payoff to Mars. The second number is the profit payoff to Hershey's.*

		Hershey's	
	Competitive Strategy	Advertise	Don't Advertise
Mars	Advertise	$500 million, $500 million	$1 billion, $300 million
	Don't Advertise	$300 million, $1 billion	$800 million, $800 million

A. *Briefly describe the Nash equilibrium concept.*

B. *Is there a Nash equilibrium strategy for each firm? If so, what is it?*

P14.7 **SOLUTION**

A. A set of strategies constitutes a Nash equilibrium if no player can improve their payoff through a unilateral change in strategy. The concept of Nash equilibrium is important because it represents a stable situation in which no player can improve their situation given the strategies adopted by other players.

B. Yes. The Nash equilibrium strategy is for both Mars and Hershey's to advertise. Given that Mars chooses to advertise, Hershey's makes the most profit by also choosing to advertise. Similarly, given that Hershey's has chosen to advertise, the best Mars can do is to advertise as well. Given the dual decision to advertise, neither competitor can improve profits by changing its advertising decision.

P14.8 **Collusion.** *In the United States any contract, combination or conspiracy in restraint of trade is illegal. In practice, this means it is against the law to control or attempt to control the quantity, price or exchange of goods and services. In addition to this legal prohibition, potential conspirators face practical problems in any overt or tacit attempt at collusion. To illustrate the problems encountered, consider the following profit payoff matrix faced by two potential conspirators in a one-shot, simultaneous-move game. The first number in each cell is firm A's profit payoff; the second number is the profit payoff to firm B.*

	Firm B		
Firm A	*Pricing Strategy*	*Low Price*	*High Price*
	Low Price	$10 million, $10 million	$35 million, -$5 million
	High Price	-$5 million, $35 million	$30 million, $30 million

A.   *Is there a dominant strategy and a Nash equilibrium strategy for each firm? If so, what are they?*

B.   *If the firms agreed to collude and charge high prices, both would earn $30 million and joint profits of $60 million would be maximized. However, the joint high-price strategy is not a stable equilibrium. Explain.*

P14.8   SOLUTION

A.   In this problem, the low-price strategy is a dominant strategy for both firms. If firm B charged low prices, firm A will also choose to charge low prices because the $10 million profit then earned is more than the $5 million loss that would be suffered by firm A if it pursued a high-price strategy. If firm B charged high prices, firm A would still choose to charge low prices because the $35 million profit then earned is more than the $30 million profit that would be earned if firm A pursued a high-price strategy. If firm A charged low prices, firm B will also choose to charge low prices because the $10 million profit then earned is more than the $5 million loss that would be suffered by firm B if it pursued a high-price strategy. If firm A charged high prices, firm B would still choose to charge low prices because the $35 million profit then earned is more than the $30 million profit that would be earned if firm B pursued a high-price strategy.

In this case, if both firms pursue a low-price strategy a Nash equilibrium also results. A set of strategies constitutes a Nash equilibrium if no player can improve their payoff through a unilateral change in strategy. The concept of Nash equilibrium is important because it represents a stable situation in which no player can improve their situation given the strategies adopted by other players.

B.   If the firms agreed to collude and charge high prices, both would earn $30 million and joint profits of $60 million would be maximized. However, the joint high-price strategy is not a stable equilibrium. To see the instability of having both firms choose high-price strategies, see how each firm has strong incentives to cheat on any covert or overt agreement to collude. If firm B chose a high-price strategy, firm A could see profits jump from $30 million to $35 million by switching from a high-price to a low-price strategy. Similarly, if firm A chose a high-price strategy, firm B could see profits jump from $30 million to $35 million by switching from a high-price to a low-price strategy. Both firms have strong incentives to cheat on any covert or overt agreement for both of them to charge high prices. Such situations are common and help explain the difficulty of maintaining cartel-like agreements.

P14.9   ***Limit Pricing.*** *Google, Inc., maintains an online index of Websites and other content, that the Company makes freely available to anyone with an Internet connection. Google's automated search technology helps people obtain nearly instant access to relevant information from its vast online index. The Company generates revenue by delivering relevant, cost-effective online advertising. Businesses use the Company's AdWords program to promote their products and services with targeted advertising. In addition, the thousands of third-party Websites that comprise the Google Network use the Google AdSense program to deliver relevant ads that generate revenue.*

    A.   *Describe Google's policy of offering free Internet search within the context of the limit pricing concept.*

    B.   *Is Google's policy of offering free Internet search a good example of limit pricing, predatory pricing, or market penetration?*

P14.9   **SOLUTION**

    A.   Google's policy of offering free Internet search can be best understood within the context of the limit pricing concept. A limit pricing strategy is one where the incumbent charges such a low price that the entrant is discouraged by the potential for even a normal rate of return and decides not to enter the market. Limit pricing strategy is generally aimed at potential entrants.

    B.   Google's policy of offering free Internet search is a good example of limit pricing and market penetration pricing. Limit pricing and predatory pricing strategies have significant similarities, but important differences as well. Both pricing strategies have the potential to be used as means for making competition from smaller competitors unpalatable. However, limit pricing and predatory pricing strategies differ in terms of when they are instituted and in terms of the target. Before entry by a new and credible competitor, a limit pricing strategy is one where the incumbent charges such a low price that the entrant is discouraged by the potential for even a normal rate of return and decides not to enter the market. Limit pricing strategy is generally aimed at potential entrants. After entry by a new and viable competitor, a predatory pricing strategy is one where the incumbent lowers prices below marginal cost so that the entrant incurs losses and ultimately exits the market. Predatory pricing strategy is generally aimed at established competitors. Moreover, in the case of Internet search, Google might reasonably maintain that the marginal cost of service is zero.

Market penetration pricing is a pricing strategy of charging very low initial prices to create a new market or grab market share in an established market. The objective is to gain a critical mass of customers, create strong network effects, and eventually establish a viable business. In the computer software business, Microsoft and other vendors are known to have sold initial versions of PC-based software programs at promotional prices in order to create a large base of enthusiastic customers. Once a large customer base is established, Microsoft and others then increase prices and profit margins to take advantage of the fact that switching computer software becomes more difficult once use has become widespread throughout an organization or profession. On the Internet, Google and several other software companies have taken the market penetration pricing concept to its logical extreme by actually giving away their services.

P14.10   ***End-of-game problem.*** *During recent years, critics of option-based compensation plans argue that such plans link CEO pay to stock market volatility in a way that can reward or penalize managers for events they don't control. In addition, top management focused on options-based compensation sometimes appears to have made decisions based upon short-term considerations that are contrary to the long-term interests of the firm, its employees and customers.*

A.   *Explain how incentive problems caused by poorly designed options-based compensation plans can be a manifestation of the end-of-game problem.*

B.   *What methods do you suggest for remedying such problems?*

P14.10   SOLUTION

A.   Boards of directors and stockholders face a classic end-of-game problem when it comes to the employment of top executives. To guard against shirking or malfeasance in the period just prior to retirement, savvy employers solve the end-of-game problem by using rewards or punishments that extend beyond the employment period. In the case of top executives, corporate governance experts insist that CEOs invest 7-10 years pay in company common stock as a means for insuring that managerial motivation coincides with stockholder incentives. In the case of managers and lower-level workers, employers are often asked to provide letters of recommendation to subsequent employers and can thereby punish workers who take advantage of the end-of-game problem. Policemen and policewomen are modestly paid and often face strong temptation to accept bribes or give favors, especially late in their careers. To fight corruption, many cities require those convicted of corrupt behavior to forfeit all retirement pay and benefits.

B. On Wall Street, investment bankers typically require traders and top managers to take a significant portion of total compensation in the form of pay tied to long-term stock-price appreciation. In some cases, managers cannot liquidate stock or employee stock options until several years after retirement. In these and other cases, employers have settled on simple means for solving the end-of-game problem: simply extend the game!

Chapter 15

PRICING PRACTICES

The fundamental prescription of managerial economics is that managers set marginal revenue equal to marginal cost for each product or product line to achieve maximum profits. If the value-maximizing theory of the firm is descriptive of actual business practice, then the pricing practices of success firms must be consistent with profit-maximizing behavior. It is therefore worth asking if the pricing practices of successful firms are consistent with profit maximization. If so, then the value maximization theory of the firm can be taken as relevant. If not, then the value maximization theory of the firm would have to be rejected as a practical guide to managerial practice.

This chapter begins with the observation that markup pricing is the most commonly employed pricing method. When the underlying basis for markup pricing methods is fully understood, these methods can be seen as a practical means for deriving profit-maximizing prices. The optimal markup is large when the underlying price elasticity of demand is low; the optimal markup is small when the underlying price elasticity of demand is high. With multiple markets or customer groups, the potential can exist to enhance profits by charging different prices and different price markups to each relevant market segment. This practice, called price discrimination, is profitable because it allows the firm to enhance revenues without increasing costs. In all instances, profit-maximizing prices are found by setting marginal revenue equal to marginal cost.

CHAPTER OUTLINE

I.   **PRICING RULES OF THUMB**

      A.   **Competitive Markets:** Profit maximization always requires finding the firm's price/output combination that will set MR = MC.

            1.   In competitive markets, firms are price takers and P = MR.

            2.   The competitive market pricing rule-of-thumb for profit maximization is to set P = MR = MC.

      B.   **Imperfectly Competitive Markets:** When the firm demand curve is downward sloping, P > MR and the competitive market pricing rule-of-thumb for profit maximization does not apply.

            1.   Like firms in competitive markets, firms active in monopolistic competition, oligopoly, and monopoly markets must find the price/output combination that will set MR = MC.

2.   When the firm demand curve is downward sloping, two effects on revenue follow a price reduction.

   a.   By selling an additional unit, total revenue goes up by P.

   b.   However, by charging a lower price, some revenue is lost on units sold previously at the higher price.

   c.   When price is a function of output, the change in total revenue following a change in output (marginal revenue) is given by the expression MR = P + Q × ∂P/∂Q

   d.   A simple relation exists between marginal revenue and the point price elasticity of demand in markets with downward-sloping demand curves: MR = P[1 + (1/ε_p)]

3.   When price is a function of output in imperfectly competitive markets, imperfectly competitive market pricing rule-of-thumb for profit maximization is to set

$$P = MC/[1 + (1/\varepsilon_p)]$$

   a.   Flexible pricing practices that reflect differences in marginal costs and demand elasticities constitute an efficient method for ensuring that MR = MC for each product sold.

II.   MARKUP PRICING AND PROFIT MAXIMIZATION

A.   **Optimal Markup on Cost:** Markup pricing is an efficient means for achieving the profit maximization objective. The profit-maximizing markup on cost is:

$$\frac{\text{Optimal markup}}{\text{on cost}} = \frac{-1}{\varepsilon_p + 1}$$

here ε_p is the price elasticity of demand.

B.   **Optimal Markup on Price:** The profit-maximizing markup on price is:

$$\frac{\text{Optimal markup}}{\text{on price}} = \frac{-1}{\varepsilon_p}$$

1.   Empirical evidence strongly suggests that firms employ markup pricing strategies in a manner that is consistent with profit maximization.

2.   Both cost definitions and markup percentages must be studied to determine optimal pricing practices.

III.   **PRICE DISCRIMINATION**

A.   **Requirements for Profitable Price Discrimination:** Price discrimination exists whenever different classes of customers are charged different markups for the same product.

1.   Price discrimination exists whenever:

$$\frac{P_1}{P_2} \neq \frac{MC_1}{MC_2}.$$

2.   Requirements for profitable price discrimination are:

a.   The firm must be able to segment the market for a product.

b.   Multiple markets must exist and reselling from one market to another must be prevented.

c.   Different price elasticities of demand for the product must exist in the various submarkets.

B.   **Degrees of Price Discrimination:** Price discrimination can be encountered in three different orders of magnitude.

1.   First degree: Separate prices for each consumer. This creates maximum profits for sellers.

2.   Second degree: Block-rates or quantity discounts based on usage.

3.   Third degree: Different prices for each customer class defined on the basis of age, sex, income, etc.

a.   Third degree is the most common type of price discrimination.

IV.   PRICE DISCRIMINATION EXAMPLE

A.   Price/Output Determination: A firm that can segment its market maximizes profits by operating in such a way that marginal revenue equals marginal cost in each market segment.

B.   One-Price Alternative: Price discrimination increases revenues without affecting cost, thereby increasing profits.

1.   Without price discrimination, MR = MC for all customers as a group.

2.   With price discrimination, MR = MC for each customer or customer segment.

3.   Profitable price discrimination *always* benefits sellers at the expense of at least some customers.

C.   Graphic Illustration: Demand and marginal revenue curves for the combined market are drawn as the horizontal sum of submarket demand and marginal revenue curves.

1.   The optimal single price/output combination is indicated where MR = MC for the combined market.

2.   The optimal price/output combination for each market is indicated where MR = MC for each submarket.

3.   Profitable price discrimination allows the firm to better match marginal revenues and marginal costs.

V.   MULTIPLE-PRODUCT PRICING

A.   Demand Interrelations: Multiple product pricing analysis can be complicated by elaborate relationships between output demand and production costs.

1.   Cross-marginal revenue terms indicate how revenues generated by one product are affected by a change in sales for other products.

B.   Production Interrelations: Products may be produced in a fixed or variable ratio.

1.   Joint products may compete for the resources of the firm or be complementary.

2.   A by-product is any output that is customarily produced as a direct result of an increase in the production of some other output.

VI.   JOINT PRODUCTS

A.   **Joint Products in Variable Proportions:** If two or more products can be produced in variable proportions, they can be considered as individually distinct products.

1.   For joint products produced in variable proportion, profit maximization requires $MR_A = MC_A$ and $MR_B = MC_B$.

2.   Common costs are expenses necessary for manufacture of a joint product.

a.   Any allocation of common costs is wrong and arbitrary.

B.   **Joint Products in Fixed Proportions:** If two or more products must be produced in a fixed ratio, they are joint products and must be considered as a package of output.

1.   For joint products A and B where $Q = A = B$, profit maximization requires setting:

$$MR_A + MR_B = MC_Q$$

VII.   JOINT PRODUCT PRICING EXAMPLE

A.   **Joint Products Without Excess Byproduct:** In this instance, profit-maximization requires setting $MR_A + MR_B = MC_Q$.

1.   Marginal revenue from each byproduct makes a contribution toward covering MC_Q.

B.   **Joint Production With Excess By-product (Dumping):** As previously, profit-maximization requires setting $MR_A + MR_B = MC_Q$. With excess byproduct, dumping occurs because there is insufficient byproduct demand at a price that yields a positive marginal revenue.

1.   Marginal revenue from the primary product covers the marginal cost of production.

2.   Marginal revenue from the byproduct is set equal to zero, the byproduct's marginal cost.

VIII. **TRANSFER PRICING**

    A.   **Transfer Pricing Problem:** Setting an appropriate price for the transfer of goods and services among divisions of a single firm can become complicated.

        1.   A vertical relation is one where the output of one division or company is the input to another.

        2.   Vertical integration occurs when a single company controls various links in the production chain from basic inputs to final output.

    B.   **Products Without External Markets:** When transferred products cannot be sold in external markets, the marginal cost of the transferring division is the optimal transfer price.

        1.   Without external markets, marginal cost represents the relevant opportunity cost and appropriate transfer price.

    C.   **Products With Competitive External Markets:** When transferred products can be sold in perfectly competitive external markets, the external market price is the optimal transfer price.

        1.   With perfectly competitive external markets, the external market price represents the relevant opportunity cost for within company use of a product.

    D.   **Products with Imperfectly Competitive External Markets:** When transferred products can be sold in imperfectly competitive external markets, the optimal transfer price is the marginal revenue derived from the combined internal and external markets.

        1.   With imperfectly competitive external markets, marginal revenue represents the relevant opportunity cost for within company use of a product.

IX. **GLOBAL TRANSFER PRICING EXAMPLE**

    A.   **Profit Maximization for an Integrated Firm:** The optimal transfer price ensures operation at the profit-maximizing activity level.

    B.   **Transfer Pricing With No External Market:** The optimal transfer price ensures a perfect balance of within-firm supply and demand at the profit-maximizing activity level.

C.   **Competitive External Market With Excess Internal Demand:** In the case of excess internal demand, the firm will employ inputs produced internally and by external suppliers.

D.   **Competitive External Market With Excess Internal Supply:** In the case of excess internal supply, the firm will supply inputs to both the internal and external market.

X.   **SUMMARY**

PROBLEMS & SOLUTIONS

P15.1 **Optimal Markup.** *Marketing consultant John Blutarsky as been retained to assess the pricing practices of Animal House Furniture, Inc. As Blutarsky's assistant, use the following demand elasticity estimates to calculate the profit-maximizing markup on cost and markup on price for a variety of sofa and easy chair products.*

Furniture Item	Price Elasticity	Optimal Markup on Cost	Optimal Markup on Price
A.	-1		
B.	-4		
C.	-8		
D.	-20		
E.	-50		

P15.1 SOLUTION

Furniture Item	Price Elasticity	Optimal Markup on Cost	Optimal Markup on Price
A.	-1	----%	100.0%
B.	-4	33.3%	25.0%
C.	-8	14.3%	12.5%
D.	-20	5.3%	5.0%
E.	-50	2.0%	2.0%

P15.2 **Optimal Markup on Cost.** *Air California is a regional airline serving a large number of west coast markets. Using recent operating data, the company wants to determine a profit maximizing price for service provided between the Orange County, CA, and Sacramento, CA, airports. During recent weeks, the company found that a one-way fare reduction from $75 to $69 had increased route traffic from 50 to 60 passengers per flight. On average, the company projects a cost per departure of $2,484.*

A. *Using the $75 price as a base, calculate the point price elasticity of demand for the airline service. (Assume a linear demand curve.)*

B. *In light of operating costs, will the new $69 fare result in an optimal markup on cost? If so, why? If not, why not?*

P15.2   SOLUTION

A.
$$\varepsilon_P = \partial Q/\partial P \times P/Q$$

$$= \frac{(60 - 50)}{(\$69 - \$75)} \times \frac{\$75}{50}$$

$$= -2.5$$

B.   Yes, the marginal cost per passenger is $41.40 (= 2,484/60). Given P = $69, the implied markup on cost is:

$$\text{Markup on cost} = \frac{\text{Price} - \text{Cost}}{\text{Cost}}$$

$$= \frac{\$69 - \$41.40}{\$41.40}$$

$$= 0.67 \text{ or } 67\%$$

Given MC = $41.40, the optimal price is:

$$P = MC\left(\frac{1}{1 + \dfrac{1}{\varepsilon_p}}\right)$$

$$= \$41.40\left(\frac{1}{1 + \dfrac{1}{-2.5}}\right)$$

$$= \$69$$

Alternatively, using the optimal markup-on-cost formula:

$$\text{Optimal markup on cost} = \frac{-1}{\varepsilon_p + 1}$$

$$= \frac{-1}{-2.5 + 1}$$

$$= 0.67 \text{ or } 67\%$$

P15.3   ***Optimal Markup on Price.*** *Quick Lube, Inc., provides while-you-wait oil lubrication services to customers throughout the Cleveland, Ohio market. In an effort to expand its customer base, Quick Lube recently offered $5 off its regular $25 price. Customer response was enthusiastic, with sales rising to 1,100 units from 700 units per week.*

   A.   *Calculate the arc price elasticity of demand for Quick Lube service.*

   B.   *Assume that the arc price elasticity (from part A) is the best available estimate of the point price elasticity of demand. Calculate Quick Lube's optimal markup on price.*

P15.3   **SOLUTION**

   A. $E_P = \dfrac{\Delta Q}{\Delta P} \times \dfrac{P_2 + P_1}{Q_2 + Q_1}$

   $$= \frac{1,100 - 700}{\$20 - \$25} \times \frac{\$20 + \$25}{1,100 + 700}$$

   $$= -2$$

   B.   Given $\varepsilon_p = E_p = -2$, the optimal markup on price is:

   $$\text{Optimal Markup on Price} = \frac{-1}{\varepsilon_p}$$

   $$= \frac{-1}{-2}$$

   $$= 0.5 \text{ or } 50\%$$

P15.4   ***Optimal Price.*** *Last week, Paul Young's Superette offered a 25¢ coupon on 12-packs of Diet Cola, regularly priced at $4. Coupons were used on 40% of all purchases, and resulted in an increase from 400 to 490 cases sold per week.*

    A.   *Using the regular $4 price as a base, calculate the point price elasticity of demand for Diet Cola.*

    B.   *Calculate the optimal markup on cost for Diet Cola.*

    C.   *If the marginal cost per unit is $3 plus 20¢ in handling costs, calculate the profit-maximizing price on Diet Cola.*

    D.   *Using P = $4 and Q = 400 as a base and the point price elasticity of demand formula, calculate expected unit sales, revenues and profits at the profit-maximizing activity level. (Note: For simplicity, assume MC = AVC).*

P15.4   **SOLUTION**

    A.   Because coupons were used on 40% of all purchases, the average price reduction was 10¢ (=0.4 × 25¢). Thus,

$$\varepsilon_p = \partial Q/\partial P \times P/Q$$

$$= \frac{(490 - 400)}{(\$3.90 - \$4)} \times \frac{\$4}{400}$$

$$= \text{-}9$$

    B.   Given $\varepsilon_p = \text{-}9$, the optimal markup on cost is:

$$\text{Optimal markup on cost} = \frac{-1}{\varepsilon_p + 1}$$

$$= \frac{-1}{-9 + 1}$$

$$= 0.125 \text{ or } 12.5\%$$

    C.   With an optimal markup of 12.5%, the profit-maximizing price on *Diet Cola* is:

$$\text{Markup} = \frac{\text{Price} - \text{Cost}}{\text{Cost}}$$

$$0.125 = \frac{\text{Price} - \$3.20}{\$3.20}$$

$$0.40 = \text{Price} - 3.20$$

$$\text{Price} = \$3.60$$

D. Expected unit sales at the profit maximizing activity level can be calculated using the point price elasticity formula:

$$\varepsilon_p = \partial Q/\partial P \times P/Q$$

$$-9 = \frac{(Q_2 - 400)}{(\$3.60 - \$4)} \times \frac{\$4}{400}$$

$$3.60 = 0.01(Q_2 - 400)$$

$$360 = Q_2 - 400$$

$$Q_2 = 760 \text{ cases per week}$$

$$TR = P \times Q$$

$$= \$3.60(760)$$

$$= \$2,736 \text{ per week}$$

$$\pi = TR - TC$$

$$= (P - AVC)Q$$

$$= (\$3.60 - \$3.20)760$$

$$= \$304 \text{ per week}$$

P15.5 **_Peak Load Pricing._** *Midwestern Digital, Inc., manufactures 500-gigabyte external USB hard drives. Due to growing demand, MDI has increased plant capacity to 300,000 units. The firm's expected output for next year was 250,000 units, but it has received a special order for 100,000 units from a firm outside its normal market. The standard*

selling price is $50 per unit, but this firm has offered $40 per unit for the special order.
Relevant cost data for the saw are as follows:

Cost Per Unit	
Raw materials	$20
Direct labor	10
Variable overhead	3
Fixed overhead	2

Using the incremental profit framework, should MDI accept the special order?

P15.5   **SOLUTION**

Incremental Revenue calculation:

Price per unit	$ 40
Units	× 100,000
Incremental revenue	$4,000,000

Incremental Cost Calculation:

Raw materials		$2,000,000
Direct labor		1,000,000
Variable overhead		300,000
Opportunity cost:		
Capacity is 300,000 units; 50,000 units of next year's expected demand will have to be foregone if the order is accepted:		
Sales revenue	2,500,000	
Variable costs	1,650,000	
Profit lost on foregone orders		850,000
Incremental Cost		$4,150,000
Incremental Profit		-$150,000

The firm should not accept the special order, because the incremental profit from the special order is negative.

P15.6   ***Peak Load Pricing.*** *The Modern Appliance Company manufactures an electric mixer-juicer. Sales of the appliance have increased steadily during the previous five years and, because of a recently completed expansion program, annual capacity is now 500,000 units. Production and sales for next year are forecast at 400,000 units, and production costs are estimated as:*

Cost Category	Amount
Materials	$3.00
Direct labor	2.00
Variable indirect labor	1.00
Overhead	1.50
Standard costs per unit	$7.50

In addition to production costs, Modern projects fixed selling expenses and variable warranty repair expenses of 75¢ and 60¢ per unit, respectively. Modern is currently receiving $10 per unit from its wholesale customers (primarily retail appliance stores), and expects this price to hold during the coming year.

After making these projections, Modern received an inquiry about the purchase of a large quantity of mixers-juicers from a discount department store chain. The discount chain's inquiry contained two purchase offers:

Offer 1.   *The chain would purchase 80,000 units at $7.30 per unit. These units would bear the Modern label and the Modern warranty would be provided.*

Offer 2.   *The chain would purchase 120,000 units at $7 per unit. These units would be sold under the buyer's private label and Modern would not provide warranty service.*

A.   *Evaluate the effect of each offer on pretax net income for next year.*

B.   *Should other factors be considered in deciding whether to accept one of these offers?*

C.   *Which offer, if either, should Modern accept? Why?*

P15.6 **SOLUTION**

A. The incremental net income from the offers can be determined as follows:

	Offer 1		Offer 2	
Unit price		$7.30		$7.00
Unit variable costs:				
Materials	$3.00		$3.00	
Direct labor	2.00		2.00	
Variable indirect labor	1.00		1.00	
Variable warranty expense	0.60		--	
Unit variable costs		$6.60		$6.00
Unit incremental profit		$0.70		$1.00
Units to be sold		× 80,000		× 120,000
Total variable profit on units sold at special price		$56,000		$120,000
Less variable profit lost on regular sales:				
Regular price			$10.00	
Regular variable cost			- 6.60	
Regular variable profit			$3.40	
Units which cannot be sold at regular price if offer 2 is accepted			× 20,000	
Opportunity cost of lost regular sales				$ 68,000
Incremental profit		$56,000		$ 52,000

B. Other factors to be considered by Modern include:

1. The image of Modern's quality may be affected by sales of the appliance in the discount chain with Modern's label.

2. Other buyers may demand the reduced price if Modern accepts Offer 1, and the discount chain undercuts them at the retail price.

3.   The sales lost if Modern accepts Offer 2 may affect future orders from regular customers.

C.   It depends upon how you evaluate the factors discussed in Part B above. The incremental profits of Offer 1 exceed those of Offer 2, but other factors might well dictate that Offer 1 not be accepted.

P15.7   ***Price Discrimination.*** *The Midcontinent Railroad Company runs a freight train daily between Indianapolis and Chicago. It has two major users of this service: Indiana Steel Companies and Midwestern Agriculture. The demand for freight cars and marginal revenue curves for each market are given by the equations:*

Indiana Steel Companies Demand

$$P_1 = \$550 - \$5Q_1$$

$$MR_1 = \partial TR_1/\partial Q_1 = \$550 - \$10Q_1$$

Midwestern Agriculture Demand

$$P_2 = \$300 - \$1.25Q_2$$

$$MR_2 = \partial TR_2/\partial Q_2 = \$300 - \$2.5Q_2$$

P_i *is the price charged by Midcontinent for hauling one freight car of materials between Indianapolis and Chicago, and* Q_i *represents the number of cars demanded by each user. Midcontinent's total and marginal cost functions for the daily train service is given by:*

$$TC = \$10,000 + \$50Q$$

$$MC = \partial TC/\partial Q = \$50$$

where Q is the number of freight cars hauled on a particular trip.

A.   *What conditions are necessary for profitable price discrimination by Midcontinent?*

B.   *What profit maximizing rule will Midcontinent employ to set prices as a price discriminator? Graphically determine the profit maximizing quantity of freight service Midcontinent will supply, show how it will divide this quantity between the steel and agricultural markets, and indicate the corresponding prices to be charged each company. Show that marginal revenue is equal in the two markets.*

C.   *Assume that Midcontinent is prevented by law from engaging in price discrimination. What is the profit maximizing rule for determining profit and output under these conditions? Graphically determine Midcontinent's profit maximizing output and price under these conditions.*

P15.7   SOLUTION

A.   For price discrimination to be profitable, Midcontinent must be able to segment the market and prevent resale from one segment to another. The elasticity of demand in one segment of the market must also be lower than in the other segment of the market if price discrimination is to be profitable.

B.   With price discrimination, the profit maximizing rule is to equate marginal revenue with marginal cost in each market. When MR = MC in each market, total output (150 freight cars) will be efficiently allocated between steel (50 freight cars) and agriculture. With price discrimination, $P_1 = \$300$ and $Q_1 = 50$ freight cars in the steel market, and $P_2 = \$175$ and $Q_2 = 100$ freight cars in the ag market. These are profit-maximizing prices charged each user. In each market, marginal revenue is $50 and equal to marginal cost.

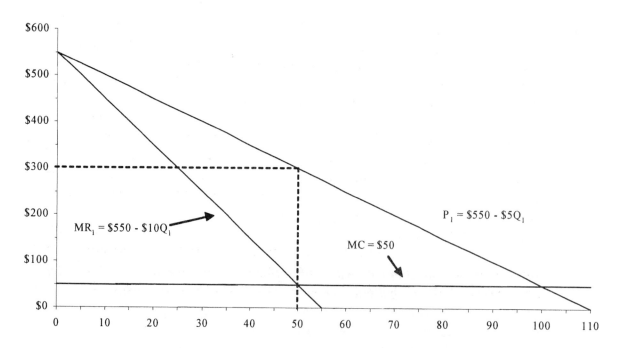

Midcontinent Railway Price Discrimination
Steel Pricing

Midcontinent Railway Price Discrimination
Ag Pricing

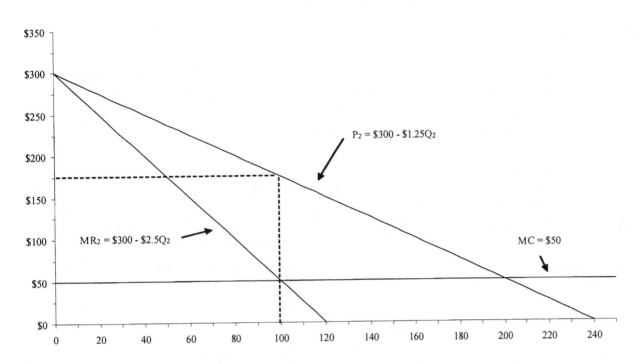

C. Without price discrimination, the profit maximizing rule is to equate marginal revenue with marginal cost in the combined market for steel and ag freight services (point Z on graph). Notice that the combined market is the market demand curve for steel freight services when the market price exceeds $300, and the combined market is the market demand curve for steel freight services plus ag freight services when the market price is less than $300. A vertical line from Z intersects the aggregate demand curve (point Y) determining the equal price ($200) to be charged in each market. A horizontal line at that price level will intersect the individual submarket demand curves (points W and X) and indicate the quantity of service (70 and 80 freight cars for steel and ag freight services, respectively) that will be sold in each market.

The important point to remember is that total output and total costs are identical with and without price discrimination. However, because price discrimination allows the seller to charge higher average prices by setting MR = MC in each market, price discrimination will always increase seller profits.

Midcontinent Railway No Price Discrimination
Steel Pricing

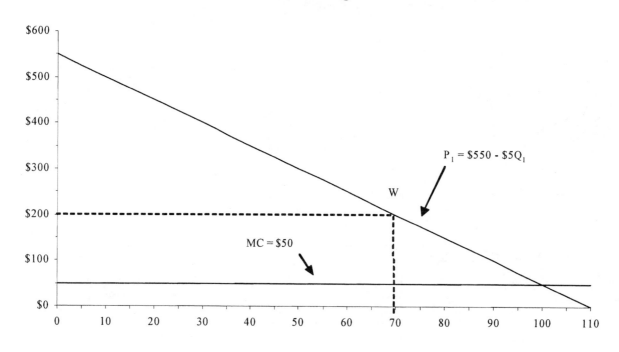

$P_1 = \$550 - \$5Q_1$

W

MC = \$50

Midcontinent Railway No Price Discrimination
Ag Pricing

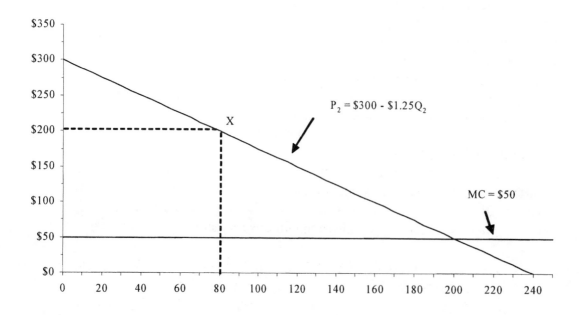

$P_2 = \$300 - \$1.25Q_2$

X

MC = \$50

Midcontinent Railway No Price Discrimination
Steel and Ag Pricing

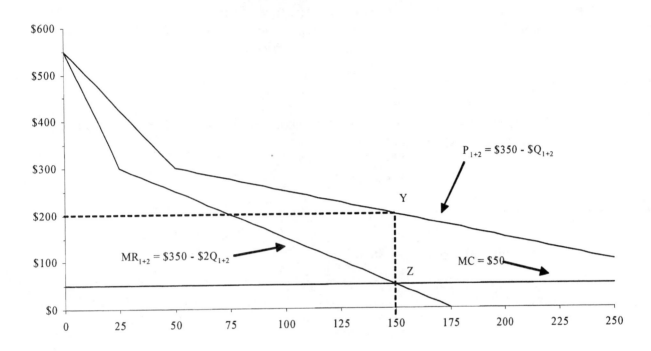

P15.8   ***Price Discrimination.*** *Ed Deline Insulation, Inc. is an insulation contractor serving both residential and commercial customers in Las Vegas, Nevada. Demand and marginal revenue relations for installing treated cellulose fiber insulation, a popular product, have been estimated as:*

<u>Residential Market</u>

$$P_R = \$1{,}000 - \$0.0025Q_R$$

$$MR_R = \partial TR_R / \partial Q_R = \$1{,}000 - \$0.005Q_R$$

<u>Commercial Market</u>

$$P_C = \$750 - \$0.000625Q_C$$

$$MR_C = \partial TR_C / \partial Q_C = \$750 - \$0.00125Q_C$$

where Q is tons of insulation installed and P is dollars. Each ton of installed insulation results in $600 of marginal labor and materials expenses.

A.   *Assuming the company can price discriminate between its two types of customers, calculate profit maximizing price, output and total profit contribution levels.*

B.   *Calculate point price elasticities for each type of customer at the activity levels identified in part A. Are the differences in these elasticities consistent or inconsistent with your recommended price differences in part A? Why or why not?*

P15.8   SOLUTION

A.   With price discrimination, profits are maximized by setting MR = MC in each market, where MC = $600.

<u>Residential</u>

$$MR_R = MC$$

$$\$1{,}000 - \$0.005Q_R = \$600$$

$$0.005Q_R = 400$$

$$Q_R = 80{,}000$$

and

$$P_R = \$1{,}000 - \$0.0025(80{,}000)$$

$$= \$800 \text{ per ton}$$

<u>Commercial</u>

$$MR_C = MC$$

$$\$750 - \$0.00125Q_C = \$600$$

$$0.00125Q_C = 150$$

$$Q_C = 120{,}000$$

and

$$P_C = \$750 - \$0.000625(120{,}000)$$

$$= \$675 \text{ per ton}$$

The profit contribution earned by the company is:

$$\pi = P_R Q_R + P_C Q_C - AVC(Q_R + Q_C)$$

$$= \$800(80{,}000) + \$675(120{,}000)$$

$$- \$600(80{,}000 + 120{,}000)$$

$$= \$25{,}000{,}000$$

B. Yes, a higher price for residential customers is consistent with the lower degree of price elasticity observed in that market.

<u>Residential</u>

$$\varepsilon_P = \partial Q_R/\partial P_R \times P_R/Q_R$$

$$= -400 \times (\$800/80{,}000)$$

$$= -4$$

<u>Commercial</u>

$$\varepsilon_P = \partial Q_C/\partial P_C \times P_C/Q_C$$

$$= -1{,}600 \times (\$675/120{,}000)$$

$$= -9$$

P15.9 ***Joint Product Pricing.*** *Soprano Enterprises produces two products in a joint production process. The products are produced in fixed proportions in a 1:1 ratio. Relevant cost functions are:*

$$TC = \$250{,}000 + \$200Q + \$0.25Q^2$$

$$MC = \partial TC/\partial Q = \$200 + \$0.5Q$$

where Q is a unit of output consisting of one unit of product A and one unit of product B.

A. *Assume the demand and marginal revenue curves for Soprano's two products are:*

$$P_A = \$950 - \$0.125Q_A$$

$$MR_A = \partial TR_A/\partial Q_A = \$950 - \$0.25Q_A$$

and

$$P_B = \$250 - \$0.625Q_B$$

$$MR_B = \partial TR_B/\partial Q_B = \$250 - \$1.25Q_B$$

What are the optimal sales quantities and prices for each of these products? (Assume unsold production can be costlessly dumped.)

B. *Assume now that Soprano incurs disposal cost of $75 for any excess production of product A or B manufactured but not sold. What are the optimal sales quantities and product prices under these conditions?*

P15.9   SOLUTION

A. If each unit of production generates revenues for both products A and B, the appropriate output level is found as:

$$MR_A + MR_B = MC$$

$$\$950 - \$0.25Q + \$250 - \$1.25Q = \$200 + \$0.5Q \text{ (Because } Q = Q_A = Q_B)$$

$$2Q = 1,000$$

$$Q = 500$$

Thus, profit maximization with equal sales of each product requires that the firm operate at the level $Q = 500$. Marginal revenues for the two products are:

$$MR_A = \$950 - \$0.25Q_A = \$950 - \$0.25(500) = \$825$$

$$MR_B = \$250 - \$1.25Q_B = \$250 - \$1.25(500) = -\$375$$

Despite the fact that $MR_A + MR_B = \$825 - \$375 = \$450$ and equals marginal production costs ($MC = \$200 + \$0.5(500) = \$450$), the negative marginal revenue for B invalidates this solution. With the negative marginal revenue for B, this solution is incorrect if Soprano can dispose of B, or otherwise hold it off the market, without incurring additional costs. Soprano would like to produce more output to sell additional product A which more than covers marginal production costs. The negative marginal revenue on product B is therefore "holding back" production and sales of product A. If B can be costlessly held off the market, Soprano would sell B only up to the point where its marginal revenue is zero because, given production of A, the relevant marginal cost of B is zero.

$$MR_B = MC_B$$

$$\$250 - \$1.25Q_B = 0$$

$$1.25Q_B = 250$$

$$Q_B = 200$$

and

$$P_B = \$250 - \$0.625(200)$$

$$= \$125$$

Determination of the optimal production and sales level for A is found by equating the marginal revenue from A, the only product being sold from the marginal production unit, with the marginal cost of production.

$$MR_A = MC_A = MC_Q$$

$$\$950 - \$0.25Q = \$200 + \$0.5Q \quad (\text{Because } Q_A = Q)$$

$$0.75Q = 750$$

$$Q_A = 1,000$$

and

$$P_A = \$950 - \$0.125(1,000)$$

$$= \$825$$

Here, note that $MR_A = \$950 - \$0.25(1,000) = \$700$, and $MR_B = \$250 = \$1.25(200) = \$0$. Thus, $MR_A + MR_B = MC$, because $MC = \$200 + \$0.5(1,000) = \$700$.

Unlike before, $MR_A = MC_A$ and $MR_B = MC_B$ as well. Thus, Soprano should produce 1,000 units of output, selling all 1,000 units of A at a price of $825. Only 200 units of B will be sold at a price of $125, with the remaining 800 units being destroyed or otherwise held off the market.

B.   The solution to part A assumes a cost-free disposal of excess B. Now, disposal of B will cost Soprano $75 per unit. In this situation, it will be more profitable for Soprano to continue selling B so long as its negative marginal revenue is less than the $75 per unit disposal cost. In other words, the marginal cost of selling as opposed to dumping B is -$75. Thus, the maximum sales quantity for B under these conditions is:

$$MR_B = MC_B \text{ - Disposal cost saving}$$

$$\$250 - \$1.25Q_B = \$0 - \$75$$

$$1.25Q_B = 325$$

$$Q_B = 260$$

$$P_B = \$250 - \$0.625(260)$$

$$= \$87.50$$

The optimal production level is found by setting MR_A equal to MC_Q plus the disposal cost on unsold B which is being produced and dumped at the margin.

$$MR_A = MC_Q + \text{Disposal cost} = MC_A$$

$$\$950 - \$0.25Q = \$200 + \$0.5Q + \$75 \text{ (Because } Q_A = Q)$$

$$0.75Q = 675$$

$$Q_A = 900$$

$$P_A = \$950 - \$0.125(900)$$

$$= \$837.50$$

Once again, $MR_A + MR_B = MC$, with $MR_A = MC_A$ and $MR_B = MC_B$. Soprano will produce 900 units of output selling all 900 units of A produced. Only 260 units of B will be sold, and 640 units of B will be dumped at a cost of $75 per unit.

When comparing the solutions to part A and part B, notice that imposition of a disposal cost (or pollution charge) reduces the amount of A and B produced, from 1,000 to 900, and disposal of B, from 800 to 640 units. Also note that P_A rises from $825 to $837.50, while P_B falls from $125 to $87.50.

P15.10 ***Joint Product Pricing****. Pee-Wee Petroleum, Inc., operates oil and gas producing wells in the Overthrust Belt region. On average, for each barrel of oil pumped to the surface, one thousand cubic feet of natural gas is also recovered. Therefore, the company views oil and gas as joint products where each unit of production involves 1 bbl: 1 mcf. Marginal costs are $15 per unit of production.*

Although each output is sold in perfectly competitive commodity markets; transport, handling and related costs have the effect of reducing the net price received by Pee-Wee. The net price/output and marginal revenue relations for oil is:

$$P_O = \$20 - \$0.000075Q_O$$

$$MR_O = \partial TR_O / \partial Q_O = \$20 - \$0.00015Q_O$$

and for gas is:

$$P_G = \$3 - 0.000025Q_G$$

$$MR_G = \partial TR_G / \partial Q_G = \$3 - \$0.00005Q_G$$

where Q_O is barrels of oil and Q_G is mcf of natural gas sold per month.

A. *Calculate the profit-maximizing price/output combination for oil and gas under current conditions.*

B. *Now assume that instability in the world oil market has caused the demand for domestic oil to double. Holding all else equal, calculate the new optimal price/ output combination for oil and gas.*

P15.10 **SOLUTION**

A. Begin analysis of this problem by examining the optimal activity level based on the assumption that all production of each byproduct will be sold. For profit maximization set,

$$MR = MR_O + MR_G = MC$$

$$\$20 - \$0.00015Q + \$3 - \$0.00005Q = \$15 \text{ (Because } Q = Q_O = Q_G)$$

$$0.0002Q = 8$$

$$Q = 40,000$$

Profit maximization with all production being sold requires that the firm produce 40,000 units of production involving 40,000 bbls of oil and 40,000 mcf of natural gas. Under this assumption, marginal revenues for each byproduct are:

$$MR_O = \$20 - \$0.00015(40,000) = \$14$$

$$MR_G = \$3 - \$0.00005(40,000) = \$1$$

Clearly, each byproduct is making a positive contribution to marginal costs. Because MR = \$14 + \$1 = \$15 = MC, Pee-Wee has no incentive to alter production from the $Q = Q_O = Q_G = 40,000$ optimal production and sales level.

Relevant prices are:

$$P_O = \$20 - \$0.000075(40,000) = \$17 \text{ per bbl}$$

$$P_G = \$3 - \$0.000025(40,000) = \$2 \text{ per mcf}$$

B.   A doubling (or 100% increase) in oil demand means that a given quantity could be sold at twice the original price. Alternatively, twice the original quantity demanded could be sold at a given price. Therefore the new oil demand and marginal revenue curves can be written:

$$P_O' = 2(\$20 - \$0.000075Q_O)$$

$$= \$40 - \$0.00015Q_O$$

$$MR_O' = 2(\$20 - \$0.00015Q_O)$$

$$= \$40 - \$0.0003Q_O$$

Now, assuming all output is sold,

$$MR' = MR_O' + MR_G = \$15$$

$$\$40 - \$0.0003Q + \$3 - \$0.00005Q = \$15 \text{ (Because } Q = Q_O = Q_G)$$

$$0.00035Q = 28$$

$$Q = 80,000$$

Profit maximization with sale of all production requires that the firm produce and sell $Q = Q_O = Q_G = 80,000$. Under this assumption, marginal revenues for the two products are

$$MR_O' = \$40 - \$0.0003(80,000) = \$16$$

$$MR_G = \$3 - \$0.00005(80,000) = -\$1$$

Although $MR' = MR_O' + MR_G = \$15 = MC$, the above $Q = 80,000$ solution is suboptimal. $MR_P' = \$16 > \$15 = MC$ implies that a \$1 profit contribution is earned on each unit of production when just considering oil sales. The company would like to expand production beyond $Q = 80,000$ just in order to sell more oil. The negative marginal revenue on gas is "holding down" oil production at the margin.

Pee-Wee will only sell gas up until the point where $MR_G = 0$ because, given expanded production to sell oil, the marginal cost of gas is zero. Set,

$$MR_G = MC_G$$

$$\$3 - \$0.00005Q_G = \$0$$

$$0.00005Q_G = 3$$

$$Q_G = 60,000$$

$$P_G = \$3 - \$0.000025(60,000)$$

$$= \$1.50 \text{ per mcf}$$

The optimal production and sales level for oil is found by setting $MR_O' = MC_O = MC$, because oil is the only product being sold from the marginal unit of production.

$$MR_O' = \$40 - \$0.0003Q_O = \$15$$

$$0.0003Q_O = 25$$

$$Q_O = 83,333$$

$$P_O = \$40 - \$0.00015(83,333) = \$27.50 \text{ per bbl}$$

Therefore, Pee-Wee will produce 83,333 units of production and sell all 83,333 bbls of oil produced at \$27.50 per bbl, but only 60,000 mcf of gas at \$1.50 per mcf. The remaining 23,333 mcf of gas produced will be flared off (burned or dumped) at the well head, or otherwise held off the market (stored for future sale). (*Note*: A doubling in oil demand doesn't have the effect of doubling oil prices because oil production increases.)

Chapter 16

MARKETS FOR LABOR AND OTHER INPUTS

The market for labor services is unlike any other economic market. In a typical economic market, buyers and sellers haggle over price, product quality, and terms of delivery. Once agreement is reached, goods and services and money are transferred from one party to another, and a final economic bargain is reached. In the real estate market, for example, home buyers and sellers study recent sales patterns for available properties, evaluate school districts and traffic flow patterns, carefully contemplate engineering reports of structural quality, and so on. Once all of this information has been digested, buyers and sellers can arrive at sensible judgements concerning an appropriate market price and a deal can be finalized.

Such one-time economic bargains are seldom possible in the labor market. When bargaining with employees, employers must deal with the fact that employee effort is continuously renegotiable in the labor market. If a given employee feels underpaid or otherwise poorly treated, that employee can reduce the amount and quality of work effort until such a point that the resulting wage rate per hour is deemed acceptable. Employers cannot unilaterally set labor costs because employees can adjust their work effort to achieve a desired wage rate. The same can be said for managers. If total compensation does not meet managerial expectations, managers can always adjust their lifestyle to fit lower expectations concerning total compensation. A well-functioning internal labor market does more than minimize unwanted attrition, it keeps the ROAD (retired on active duty) employee problem to a minimum.

CHAPTER OUTLINE

I.   EMPLOYMENT TRENDS

   A.   Overall Employment Statistics: Demand for productive inputs depends upon how much profit can be generated through their employment.

   1.   The number of persons employed in the United States is approaching 135 million.

   2.   Unemployment rates tend to fall in a broad range from lows near 4.5% to 5%, called "full employment," during economic booms, to recessionary highs that can approach 10% of the workforce, as was the case during the sharp recession of 1982-83.

   B.   Robust High-Wage Job Growth: Most job opportunities today are found in the services sector.

1.   Goods-producing industries account for less than 20% of all jobs.

2.   Service-providing industries account for more than 80% of all jobs.

II.   LABOR DEMAND CURVE

A.   Marginal Revenue Product of Labor: The economic productivity of an input is determined by the additional net revenue generated by the last unit employed

1.   The marginal revenue product of labor, MRP_L, equals the marginal product of labor (MP_L) multiplied by the marginal revenue of output (MR_Q):

$$MRP_L = MP_L \times MR_Q$$

B.   Value of Marginal Product: If the firm is marketing its goods and services in competitive output markets, the economic value of a marginal unit of an input factor x is referred to as its value of marginal product

$$VMP_x = MP_x \times P_Q$$

1.   In a competitive market, $P_Q = MR_Q$ and $VMP_x = MRP_x$.

2.   All profitable workers are employed at the optimal level of employment, but no unprofitable workers are employed.

III.   CHANGES IN LABOR DEMAND

A.   Labor Demand Curves Slope Downward: The downward sloping demand curve for labor (or any input) stems from the fact that as additional workers are added to a given set of complementary inputs, the marginal product of each additional worker eventually decreases.

1.   Diminishing marginal product is observed in every known production relationship.

2.   As wages fall, employers increase the quantity of labor demanded. Such changes are referred to as movements along the labor demand curve.

a.   Change in any demand-determining factor other than the price of labor causes a shift in the labor demand curve.

B. **Shifts in the Labor Demand Curve:** Input demand curve shifts rightward following any increase in the ability of workers to produce profits for their employer.

    1.   Any change that increases the ability of workers to generate revenues and profits causes a rightward shift in the labor demand curve.

    2.   Any change that decreases the ability of workers to generate revenues and profits causes a leftward shift in the labor demand curve.

    3.   Shifts in input demand stem from changes in output prices, technology (broadly defined), and the supply of other input factors.

IV. **CHANGES IN LABOR SUPPLY**

A. **Labor Supply Curves Slope Upward:** Input supply curves reflect the quantity of input that will be supplied at each input price.

    1.   As wages rise, workers increase the amount of work they are willing to expend.

        a.   High wages pull employees out of alternative jobs, or reduce worker preferences for leisure time.

    2.   A decline in wages is reflected in a downward movement along the labor supply curve.

        a.   As wages fall, employees decrease the quantity of labor supplied.

    3.   Such changes are referred to as movements along the labor supply curve.

    4.   Change in any supply-determining factor other than the price of labor causes a shift in the labor supply curve.

B. **Shifts in the Labor Supply Curve:** The labor supply curve shifts whenever workers change the amount of time they want to work at a given wage.

    1.   Shifts in labor supply occur whenever the supply of workers increases at every wage rate.

    2.   An increase in training and education can shift the labor supply curve rightward.

3.   Anything that reduces the pool of willing workers at every wage rate causes the supply of labor to decrease, and the labor supply curve to shift leftward.

V.   COMPETITIVE EQUILIBRIUM IN THE LABOR MARKET

A.   **Surplus and Shortage:** Surplus and shortage reflect disequilibrium in the labor market.

1.   When an above-market wage is offered, an excess supply of workers is created and unemployment results.

2.   When a below-market wage is offered, excess demand creates a shortage of workers.

B.   **Equilibrium:** When the labor market is in equilibrium, each employer hires as many workers as it finds profitable at the market wage rate.

1.   In equilibrium, there is exact balance between the marginal revenue product of labor and the wage rate, which represents the marginal cost of labor.

2.   No workers are employed that cost more than they bring in, and no worker is turned away that bring in at least enough revenue to pay the marginal cost of employment.

3.   In competitive equilibrium, there is perfect balance between the wage rate including all benefits, or marginal cost of employment, and the marginal revenue product of labor.

VI.   FIRM INPUT DEMAND

A.   **Input Demand Determination:** Input prices and data on the marginal revenue product of inputs give firms all the information that is necessary to determine an optimal level of input use.

1.   If $MRP_X > P_X$, it pays to expand usage of X.

2.   If $MRP_X < P_X$, it pays to cut back.

3.   When $MRP_X = P_X$, input use is optimal.

B.   **Input Demand Curve:** The process of determining an optimal level of employment involves a simple two-step process.

1. The firm must determine the optimal level of output.

2. Then, it becomes necessary to determine the amount of labor required to produce that level of output.

VII.   MINIMUM WAGE POLICY

A. **Policy Objectives:** In the United States, the Fair Labor Standards Act (FLSA) establishes a Federal minimum wage, overtime pay, record keeping, and child labor standards affecting full-time and part-time workers.

1. Child labor provisions of the FLSA are designed to protect the educational opportunities of youth, and prohibit their employment in jobs and under conditions detrimental to their health or safety.

2. Proponents of minimum wages and minimum wage hikes argue that minimum wage laws helps the working poor.

B. **Should the Minimum Wage be Increased?** The potential benefits of an increase in the minimum wage, namely higher incomes for teenagers and the working poor, are obvious.

1. What is less obvious is the cost in terms of lost employment opportunities.

VIII.   IMPERFECTLY COMPETITIVE INPUT MARKETS

A. **Unchecked Monoposony:** Unregulated monopsony (single) buyers of labor and other inputs can depress input prices and inefficiently restrict input use and output production.

1. In the labor market, the single company employer in a "one mill town" is the classic case of a monopsony buyer of labor.

2. Unchecked monopsony buyers of labor sometimes have the ability to depress wages and restrict employment opportunities.

B. **Unchecked Monopoly:** Unregulated monopoly (single) sellers of labor and other inputs can unfairly limit employment opportunities and inefficiently restrict input usage and output production.

1.   In the labor market, a powerful trade union confronting many small and powerless employers is the classic example of a monopoly seller of labor.

2.   Unchecked trade union monopoly power can restrict employment opportunities and exact economic rents, especially in the construction trades where employers tend to be relatively small and powerless.

C.   **Countervailing Power:** Countervailing power is an economic influence that creates a closer balance between previously unequal sellers and buyers.

1.   Wage/employment bargaining usually produces a compromise wage/employment outcome.

2.   Monopoly-monopsony confrontations can have the beneficial effect of improving economic efficiency by improving the situation faced under either unchecked monopoly or monopsony.

IX.   WAGES AND EMPLOYMENT WITH COUNTERVAILING POWER

A.   **Competitive Wage/Employment Solution:** In competitive market equilibrium, there exists perfect balance between buyer and seller power.

1.   Perfectly competitive labor markets, like those with exactly offsetting countervailing power, result in wage rates that exactly equal the marginal revenue product of labor.

2.   Because workers get the amount of economic value created by their efforts in competitive labor markets, many regard countervailing power as socially attractive and fair to workers.

B.   **Monopsony Wage/Employment Solution**: As the dominant employer of skilled labor, monopsony employers can exert some downward pressure on market wage rates.

1.   Unchecked monopsony in the labor market results in wage rates that are below the worker's marginal revenue product.

2.   Because workers get less than the amount of economic value created under monopsony, many regard unchecked monopsony as unfair to workers and the general public.

C. **Monopoly Wage/Employment Solution:** Whereas monopsony buyers in the labor market seek low wage costs, monopoly sellers of labor seek high wage income.

    1. Unchecked monopoly in the labor market results in wage rates that are above the worker's marginal revenue product.

    2. Because workers get more than the amount of economic value created under monopoly, many regard unchecked monopoly in the labor market as unfair to employers and the general public.

X. INTERNAL LABOR MARKETS

A. **Pay for Performance:** Pay for performance simply means to set compensation according to measurable indicators of worker productivity.

    1. Productivity that stems from the worker's natural dexterity, intelligence, or general education is derived from the worker's general human capital, where human capital is the capitalized value of future productivity derived from worker skills.

    2. Firm-specific human capital is any special aptitude, education, or skill that gives rise to added productivity in a unique work setting.

    3. The wage rate that could be obtained in any worker's next-best employment opportunity, sometimes called the reservation wage rate, is the opportunity cost of continuing to work for the worker's current employer.

B. **Matching Incentives with Objectives:** A well-designed incentive compensation plan is vital to the success of any organization.

C. **Managerial Labor Market:** Individual employees, including top managers, face both the opportunities and discipline of external and internal labor markets.

    1. Because firm performance is at least partly determined by the performance of the entire management "team," all managers have a stake in the performance of managers above and below them and will actively engage in two-way monitoring.

    2. As in the case of asymmetric information concerning managerial performance, the presence of firm-specific human capital can create a wedge within the market demand curve for managers.

3. The market for corporate control can be viewed as an economic mechanism for mitigating information problems in the managerial labor market.

XI. SUMMARY

PROBLEMS & SOLUTIONS

P16.1 **Demand for Labor**. *The demand for labor is determined by the marginal revenue product of labor, or the amount of net revenue generated by workers before considering labor costs. Illustrate how each of the following would increase, decrease or have no effect on the demand for labor.*

    A. *Falling worker productivity due to a decrease in business investment.*

    B. *Rising productivity due to better technical training.*

    C. *Falling employer sales due to economic recession.*

    D. *Rising prices for industry output due to growing product acceptance.*

    E. *Falling public support for worker training and education.*

P16.1 **SOLUTION**

    A. Decrease. Falling worker productivity due to a decrease in business investment means that workers have fewer tools and machines to work with and, as a result, are only able to produce lower profits for their employers. This decreases worker marginal revenue product and the demand for labor.

    B. Increase. Rising worker productivity due to better technical training means that workers become more capable and better able to produce profits for their employers. This increases worker marginal revenue product and the demand for labor.

    C. Decrease. As employer sales revenue fall during an economic recession, output demand and MR_Q would fall and decrease the pool of available funds for worker pay. This decreases worker marginal revenue product and the demand for labor.

    D. Increase. If employer sales revenue rise due to greater product acceptance, MR_Q would rise and increase the pool of available funds for worker pay. This increases worker marginal revenue product and the demand for labor.

    E. Decrease. Falling worker productivity due to declining public support for worker training and education means that workers will be less capable of working and, as a result, will be less able to produce profits for their employers. This decreases worker marginal revenue product and the demand for labor.

P16.2 **Minimum Wage Policy.** *Imagine that the minimum wage is above the equilibrium wage for unskilled workers. Demonstrate whether each of the following influences would increase, decrease or have no effect on the demand and/or supply of unskilled labor. Also point out whether a movement along the relevant curve(s) is involved, or if instead a shift from one curve to another is involved. Finally, suggest whether an increase, decrease, or no effect on unemployment among unskilled workers can be anticipated.*

    A.   *Mandated health care coverage for minimum wage workers.*

    B.   *Elimination of the Federal minimum wage.*

    C.   *Falling immigration.*

    D.   *A general decrease in welfare benefits.*

    E.   *Sagging popularity of self-service.*

P16.2 **SOLUTION**

    A.   Mandated health care coverage for minimum wage workers has the same effect as a real increase in the Federal minimum wage. Such a requirement will decrease the quantity demanded of unskilled labor and increase the quantity supplied of unskilled labor. An upward movement along both the labor demand and labor supply curves is indicated. With a decline in the quantity demanded, and a jump in the quantity supplied, an increase in unemployment can be anticipated for unskilled workers.

    B.   Elimination of a binding Federal minimum wage will increase the quantity demanded of unskilled labor and decrease the quantity supplied of unskilled labor. A downward movement along both the labor demand and labor supply curves is indicated. With an increase in the quantity demanded, and a decrease in the quantity supplied, an increase in unemployment can be anticipated for unskilled workers.

    C.   Falling immigration causes the supply curve for unskilled labor to fall (shift to the left). In a competitive market, this leftward shift in the unskilled labor supply curve would permit an upward movement along the unskilled labor demand curve.

    D.   A general decline in welfare benefits would cause the supply curve for unskilled labor to rise (shift to the right). In a competitive market, this rightward shift in the unskilled labor supply curve would allow an downward movement along the unskilled labor demand curve. If the new equilibrium wage is below the existing minimum wage, a rising supply of unskilled workers would cause an increase in employment and a downward movement along the labor demand curve. If the new equilibrium wage remains below the existing minimum wage, a rising supply of unskilled workers will simply cause an increase in unemployment among unskilled workers.

E. If self-service became less popular among consumers, the demand for unskilled labor would rise (shift rightward). If the minimum wage is above the equilibrium wage, the effect on employment would depend upon the magnitude of the rise in demand. In most cases, a simple rise in employment will be observed.

P16.3 ***Employment Costs.*** *According to the Bureau of Labor Statistics, private industry employer compensation costs averaged $23.90 per hour worked in December, 2004. Wages and salaries averaged $17.02 per hour (71.2 percent), while benefits averaged $6.88 (28.8 percent). Employer costs for paid leave averaged $1.53 per hour worked (6.4 percent), supplemental pay averaged 66 cents (2.7 percent), insurance benefits averaged $1.70 (7.1 percent), retirement and savings averaged 88 cents (3.7 percent), and legally required benefits $2.08 (8.7 percent) per hour worked.*

A. *Assume a full-time employee usually gets paid 40 hours per week for 52 weeks per year, or 2,080 hours per year. Calculate direct wage and salary expense per year for a typical employee. Also calculate the employer's total direct plus indirect wage and salary expenses per year for a typical employee.*

B. *To merit employment, explain how much profit margin before wage and salary expense the typical employee much generate for the average employer.*

P16.3 SOLUTION

A. The amount of direct wage expense per full-time employee is $17.02 per hour for 40 hours per week over 52 weeks. At $17.02 per hour for 2,080 (= 40 × 52) hours, the amount of direct wage expense per full-time worker is $35,401 (= $17.02 × 2,080). In addition to these direct wage expenses, an additional $6.88 per hour in indirect employer costs must be born for paid leave, supplemental pay, insurance, retirement, and legally-required payments, like social security (FICA) taxes and unemployment compensation. The total amount of direct plus indirect wage expense per full-time employee is $23.90 per hour for 2,080 hours per year, or $49,712 (= $23.90 × 2,080) per year.

B. The total amount of direct plus indirect wage expense per full-time employee of $23.90 per hour for 2,080 hours per year, or $49,712 (= $23.90 × 2,080) per year, is the relevant employer cost of hiring one additional full-time employee. Before wage expenses, a typical full-time worker must add $49,712 in additional profit margin in order to merit employment.

P16.4   ***Marginal Labor Costs.*** *The first summer camp opened its doors on an island in Squam Lake, New Hampshire in 1881. Five boys from rich American families were welcome at the camp that summer. They stayed in rustic log cabins and learned to fish and chop wood. Today, there are over 10,000 summer camps operating in North America with over four million kids attending them. A big challenge for camp operators is finding dedicated and dependable help. Suppose recruiters at a local college are offering students employment at a wage of $12 per hour for 40 hours per week over the 10-week season from mid-June through mid-August. Legally required benefits cost the employer $1.08 per hour for Social Security and Medicare, Federal and State unemployment insurance, and workers' compensation.*

   A.   *Calculate the amount of direct wage expense and total wage expense per part-time worker for the summer.*

   B.   *Which wage expense number is relevant for hiring purposes? In other words, how much added profit margin before wage expenses must a part-time worker add in order to justify part-time employment for the summer? Explain.*

P16.4   SOLUTION

   A.   The amount of direct wage expense per part-time employee is $12 per hour for 40 hours per week over 10 weeks. At $12 per hour for 400 hours, the amount of direct wage expense per part-time worker for the summer is $4,800 (= $12 × 400). In addition to these direct wage expenses, additional mandatory legal benefits of $1.08 per hour must be paid. The direct plus indirect wage expense per part-time employee is $13.08 per hour for 40 hours per week over 10 weeks. At $13.08 per hour for 400 hours, the amount of direct wage expense per part-time worker for the summer is $5,232 (= $13.08 × 400).

   B.   The total amount of direct plus indirect wage expense per part-time employee of $13.08 per hour for 40 hours per week over 10 weeks, or $5,232 (= $13.08 × 400), is the relevant employer cost of hiring one additional summertime employee. Before wage expenses, a part-time worker must add $5,232 in additional profit margin in order to justify employment for the summer

P16.5   ***Competitive Market Equilibrium.*** *Assume demand and supply conditions in the competitive market for unskilled labor are as follows:*

$$Q_D = 104 - 8P \qquad (Demand)$$

$$Q_S = 5P \qquad (Supply)$$

where Q is millions of hours of unskilled labor and P is the wage rate per hour.

A. *Illustrate the industry equilibrium price/output combination both graphically and algebraically.*

B. *Calculate the level of excess supply (unemployment) if the minimum wage is set at $10 per hour.*

P16.5 SOLUTION

A. From the graph, it is clear that $Q_D = Q_S = 40$ at a wage rate of $8 per hour. Thus, P = $8 and Q = 40 is the equilibrium price-output combination.

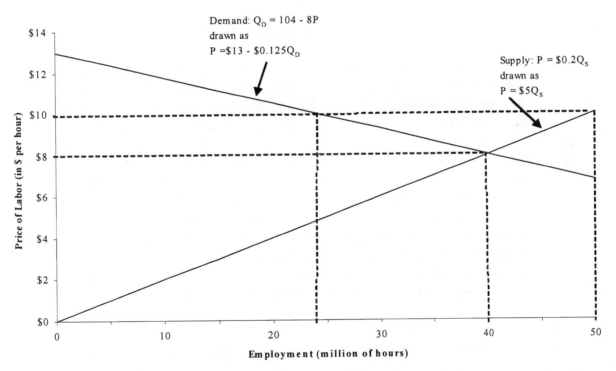

Unskilled Labor Demand and Supply Analysis

Demand: $Q_D = 104 - 8P$
drawn as
$P = \$13 - \$0.125Q_D$

Supply: $P = \$0.2Q_S$
drawn as
$P = \$5Q_S$

Price of Labor (in $ per hour)

Employment (million of hours)

Algebraically,

$$Q_D = Q_S$$

$$104 - 8P = 5P$$

$$13P = 104$$

$$P = \$8$$

Both demand and supply equal 40 because:

$$\text{Demand: } Q_D = 104 - 8(8) = 40$$

$$\text{Supply: } Q_S = 5(8) = 40$$

B. At a minimum wage of $10, excess supply of 26 units is created because:

$$\text{Supply: } Q_S = 5(10) = 50$$

$$\text{minus } \underline{\text{Demand: } Q_D = 104 - 8(10)} = \underline{24}$$

$$\text{Excess supply } = 26$$

Thus, an increase in the minimum wage will increase the quantity of labor supplied to the market by 10 million hours while decreasing the quantity demanded by 16 million hours. Excess supply (unemployment) of 26 million hours will result.

P16.6 ***Marginal Revenue Product.*** *Susan Mayer is a top-producing real estate agent with Suburban Realty, Ltd. Last year, Mayer sold or listed for sale 40 homes with a combined retail value of $10 million. When a house is sold, Suburban Realty collects a standard 6% commission. This amount is split on a 50/50 basis between the listing and selling broker. Thus, each agent generates gross revenue equal to 3% of the total value of homes that they are able to sell or list for selling.*

A. *Estimate Mayer's annual marginal revenue product before variable costs.*

B. *Now assume that Suburban Realty must incur variable advertising and office support costs of $85,000 per year to support Mayer's efforts. If Mayer was paid $175,000 in total compensation last year (including fringe benefits), was Mayer a profitable employee?*

P16.6 **SOLUTION**

A. In the long run, Mayer's marginal revenue product is the maximum amount Suburban Realty could pay in base salary plus all fringe benefits. It is the amount of added revenue after all other variable costs that Mayer's effort brings to the firm. Before variable costs, Mayer's marginal revenue product is determined by the dollar value of homes sold or listed for sale and the commission rate earned.

$$MRP_L = MP_L \times MR_Q$$

$$= \text{(Retail value sales and listings)} \times \text{(Commission rate)}$$

$$= \$10,000,000 \times 0.03$$

$$= \$300,000$$

Because Mayer is only engaged in the sales function, Mayer obviously does not produce real estate properties. What Mayer does produce are sales and listings, and the added value to the employer of Mayer' sales effort is what determines the amount the employer is willing and able to pay.

B. Mayer was a profitable employee last year. In addition to base salary plus fringes, employers must pay additional variable costs that are necessary make employees productive. If Mayer's employer must incur variable advertising expenses and office costs of $85,000 per year to support Mayer's efforts, then Mayer's marginal revenue product net of all variable costs was $215,000 last year. Because Mayer was paid total compensation (including fringes) of $175,000, Mayer generated a profit of $40,000 for Suburban Realty last year.

$$MRP_L = \$300,000 - \$85,000 < \$175,000 = P_L$$

In other words, Mayer brings in $215,000 per year in additional profit contribution, but costs Suburban Realty only $175,000. This means that Mayer brings in $40,000 per year more in net marginal revenues than the marginal cost of employment. At the margin, Mayer's employment represents a marginal profit to Suburban Realty. Mayer is a profitable employee.

P16.7 ***Unchecked Monopoly.*** *Construction workers are sometimes organized into powerful unions that act as monopoly sellers of skilled labor in the local labor market. In some local labor markets, powerful construction trade unions enter into master labor agreements with groups of small construction companies. In such instances, monopoly unions are sometimes able to exert their bargaining power to obtain wages and fringe benefits that greatly exceed amounts that would be earned in a competitive local labor* *market. Consider the following demand and supply curves for skilled labor in the construction trades:*

$$P_L = \$150 - \$0.5Q \quad \text{(Demand for Labor)}$$

$$P_L = 0.25Q \quad \text{(Supply of Labor)}$$

where P_L is the price of labor (including fringes) and Q_L is the amount of labor employed (in thousands of hours). In the local labor market, the employer demand for labor is equal to the MRP_L, and the supply of labor represents the marginal cost of employment in the eyes of the union seller.

A. *Set labor demand equal to labor supply to determine the wage/employment outcome that would be observed in competitive market equilibrium in the local labor market for construction workers.*

B. *Use the labor demand curve to find the union's marginal revenue curve derived from employment. Then, set the union's marginal revenue derived from employment equal to the labor supply curve to find the monopoly union's preferred employment level.*

C. *Compute the wage rate for the monopoly union's preferred employment level from the labor demand curve.*

P16.7   SOLUTION

A.   The wage/employment outcome that would be observed in competitive market equilibrium is found by setting the labor demand curve equal to the labor supply curve and solving for wages and employment:

Demand   =   Supply

$150 - \$0.5Q   =   \$0.25Q,

150   =   0.75Q

Q   =   200(000)

P_L =   \$150 - \$0.5(200) = \$50 per hour (Labor demand)

P_L =   \$0.25(200) = \$50 per hour (Labor supply)

B. The employment outcome that would be observed in unchecked monopoly equilibrium is found by setting the union's marginal revenue derived from employment equal to the labor supply curve, which represents the union worker's marginal cost of employment, and solving for employment. First, it is necessary to derive the union's marginal revenue derived from employment. This relationship is determined by using the labor demand curve to establish the total amount of revenue (income) derived from employment, and then taking the first derivative of this amount to find the union's marginal revenue derived from employment:

$$\text{Union's TR} = P_L \times Q \quad \text{(From the labor demand curve)}$$

$$= (\$150 - \$0.5Q)Q$$

$$= \$150Q - \$0.5Q^2$$

$$\text{Union's MR} = \partial TR/\partial Q$$

$$= \$150 - \$1Q$$

Once this relationship depicting the union's marginal revenue derived from employment has been determined, the employment outcome that would be observed in unchecked monopoly equilibrium is found by setting this relationship equal to the labor supply curve, which represents the union worker's marginal cost of employment, and solving for employment:

$$\text{Union's MR} = \text{Union's MC (Supply of labor)}$$

$$\$150 - \$1Q = \$0.25Q$$

$$150 = 1.25Q$$

$$Q = 120(000) \text{ hours}$$

P16.8   ***Countervailing Power.*** *Maytag Corporation is a leading producer of distinctive washers, dryers, dishwashers, and other home appliances that are distributed through retailers across the United States and Canada. Assume that Maytag has introduced a new energy-efficient washer/dryer combination unit with the following revenue and cost relations:*

$$TR = \$900Q - \$0.0016Q^2$$

$$MR = \partial TR/\partial Q = \$900 - \$0.0032Q$$

$$TC = \$9,000,000 + \$500Q + \$0.0004Q^2$$

$$MC = \partial TC/\partial Q = \$500 + \$0.0008Q$$

where TR is total revenue, Q is output measured in terms of the number of subscriptions in force, MR is marginal revenue, TC is total cost, including a risk-adjusted normal rate of return on investment, and MC is marginal cost.

A.   *If Maytag has a monopoly in this market, calculate the profit-maximizing price/output combination and optimal total profit. What is Maytag's profit margin on this product?*

B.   *Calculate Maytag's optimal price, output, and profits if large retail buyers like Best Buy and Home Depot effectively exert monopsony power and force a competitive equilibrium in this market.*

P16.8   SOLUTION

A.   The profit-maximizing monopoly price/output combination is found by setting MR = MC and solving for Q:

$$MR = MC$$

$$\$900 - \$0.0032Q = \$500 + \$0.0008Q$$

$$0.004Q = 400$$

$$Q = 100,000$$

$$P = TR/Q = \$900 - \$0.0016Q$$

$$= \$900 - \$0.0016(100,000)$$

$$= \$740$$

$$\pi = TR - TC$$

$$= \$900Q - \$0.0016Q^2 - [\$9,000,000 + \$500Q + \$0.0004Q^2]$$

$$= -\$0.002(100,000^2) + \$400(100,000) - \$9,000,000$$

$$= \$11,000,000$$

Profit Margin $= \pi / TR$

$$= \$11,000,000/[\$900Q - \$0.0016Q^2]$$

$$= \$11,000,000/[\$900(100,000) - \$0.0016(100,000^2)]$$

$$= 14.9\%$$

(*Note*: Profit is falling for Q > 100,000.)

B. If large appliance retailers effectively exert monopsony power and force a competitive market equilibrium, P = MR and, therefore, P = MC at the average cost minimizing output level. To find the output level where average cost is minimized, set MC = AC and solve for Q:

$$MC = AC$$

$$\$500 + \$0.0008Q = (\$9,000,000 + \$500Q + \$0.0004Q^2)/Q$$

$$\$500 + \$0.0008Q = \$9,000,000Q^{-1} + \$500 + \$0.0004Q$$

$$9,000,000Q^{-1} = 0.0004Q$$

$$9,000,000Q^{-2} = 0.0004$$

$$\frac{9,000,000}{Q^2} = 0.0004$$

$$Q = \sqrt{\frac{9,000,000}{0.0004}}$$

$$= 150,000$$

$$AC = \$9,000,000/150,000 + \$500 + \$0.0004(150,000)$$

$$= \$620$$

At the average-cost minimizing output level, MC = AC = \$620. Because P = MR in a competitive market at the profit-maximizing output level:

$$P = MR = MC = AC = \$620$$

$$\pi = P \times Q - TC$$

$$= \$620(150,000) - \$9,000,000 - \$500(150,000) - \$0.0004(150,000^2)$$

$$= \$0$$

(*Note*: Average cost is rising for Q > 150,000.)

P16.9   ***Optimal Employment***. *Young & Restless Design, Inc., is a manufacturer of fashionable dresses and evening gowns in New York City's garment district. The Y&R demand and marginal revenue relations are:*

$$P = \$1,000 - \$0.02Q,$$

$$MR = \partial TR/\partial Q = \$1,000 - \$0.04Q,$$

where Q is the quantity of dresses demanded per year (in hundred). Production of each unit of Q requires 100 hours of labor, 20 hours of capital-equipment time (sewing machines, etc.), and $50 of raw materials. Y&R has a total of 400,000 hours of capital equipment time available in its production facility each year and can purchase all the labor and materials it desires. The capital equipment investment by Y&R totals $6 million, and the firm requires a 12.5% return on capital. Assume that these are the only costs incurred and that Y&R has a profit maximization objective.

A.   *You have been employed by the State Unemployment Service to evaluate the effect on employment of an increase in the minimum wage. As a first step in the analysis, develop Y&R's short-run demand curve for labor.*

B.   *If Y&R currently pays a wage rate of $7 (including benefits) per hour for labor, calculate the short-run impact on employment of an increase to a $8 minimum wage (including benefits).*

C.   *Calculate Y&R profits at the $7 and $8 wage levels. What are the long-run employment implications of the higher minimum wage?*

P16.9   **SOLUTION**

A.   Y & R's operating rule for profit maximization is to set:

$$MC = MR.$$

To determine the firm's marginal cost function note that:

$$MC = \text{Per Unit Material Cost} + \text{Per Unit Labor Cost}$$

$$= \$50 + 100P_L$$

where P_L is the unskilled labor wage rate. Then,

$$MC = MR$$

$$\$50 + 100P_L = \$1,000 - \$0.04Q$$

$$100P_L = \$950 - \$0.04Q$$

$$P_L = \$9.5 - \$0.0004Q$$

Because 100 labor hours are required for each unit of Q,

$$L = 100Q \text{ or } Q = L/100$$

and the short-run demand for labor equation is:

$$P_L = \$9.5 - \$0.0004Q$$

$$= \$9.5 - \$0.0004(L/100)$$

$$= \$9.5 - \$0.000004L$$

or

$$L = 2,375,000 - 250,000P_L$$

B. Employment levels at \$7 and \$8 per hour are calculated using the demand for labor function derived in Part A:

$$L_1 = 2,375,000 - 250,000P_L$$

$$= 2,375,000 - 250,000(\$7)$$

$$= 625,000 \text{ worker hours}$$

$$L_2 = 2,375,000 - 250,000P_L$$

$$= 2,375,000 - 250,000(\$8)$$

$$= 375,000 \text{ worker hours}$$

Thus, a \$8 minimum wage would reduce the quantity of labor demanded and employment by:

$$\text{Employment Loss} = L_1 - L_2$$

$$= 625,000 - 375,000$$

$$= 250,000 \text{ worker hours.}$$

Assuming 2,000 worker hours per year for each employee, this is a reduction of 125 (= 250,000/2,000) jobs.

C. The long-run job loss question is addressed by analyzing Y&R's profits at optimal output levels with a \$7 and \$8 wage rate, respectively. With $P_L = \$7$, output equals Q = L/(L/Q) = 625,000/100 = 6,250. With $P_L = \$8$, output equals Q = L/(L/Q) = 375,000/100 = 3,750. Y&R's total revenue function is:

$$\text{TR} = P \times Q$$

$$= (\$1,000 - \$0.02Q)Q$$

$$= \$1,000Q - \$0.02Q^2$$

The total cost function is constructed as follows:

$$\text{TC} = \text{Fixed Cost} + (\text{Per Unit Material Cost}) \times Q$$

$$+ (\text{Per Unit Labor Cost}) \times Q$$

$$\text{Fixed Cost} = 0.125(\$6,000,000)$$

$$= \$750,000$$

$$\text{Per Unit Material Cost} = \$50$$

$$\text{Per Unit Labor Cost} = 100P_L, \text{ where } P_L \text{ is the labor wage rate}$$

Therefore,

$$TC = \$750,000 + \$50Q + 100P_LQ$$

$$\pi = TR - TC$$

$$= \$1,000Q - \$0.02Q^2 - \$750,000 - \$50Q - 100P_LQ$$

$$= -\$0.02Q^2 + \$950Q - 100P_LQ - \$750,000$$

With $P_L = \$7$ and $Q = 6,250$, total profit is:

$$\pi = -\$0.02(6,250^2) + \$950(6,250) - 100(\$7)(6,250) - \$750,000$$

$$= \$31,250$$

With $P_L = \$8$ and $Q = 3,750$, total profit is:

$$\pi = -\$0.02(3,750^2) + \$950(3,750) - 100(\$8)(3,750) - \$750,000$$

$$= -\$468,750 \ (A \ loss)$$

At the \$7 wage rate, economic profits are positive (recall that the \$750,000 fixed cost includes the required return on capital), the firm will operate and have an incentive to expand in the long run. At $P_L = \$8$, economic profits are negative, indicating that the required return on capital is not being met. At this higher wage rate, the firm will not be able to attract the capital necessary to continue operating in the long run. The long-run impact of the increase in the minimum wage could be a loss of all such jobs at the firm.

P16.10 ***Internal Labor Markets.*** *In 2005, insurance industry giant American International Group reported that it may had overstated its net worth by more than \$2.7 billion through a variety of questionable transactions. So-called finite-risk reinsurance transactions were apparently used by AIG and others to disguise losses that would have otherwise hurt net income, and cost top executives millions of dollars in incentive compensation. AIG's longtime chairman and chief executive, Maurice R. "Hank" Greenberg, was forced to give up those titles in a shakeup that shook the company to its core.*

A. *Do recent scandals at energy trading giant AIG and elsewhere suggest a breakdown in the functioning of the internal labor market and some inefficiency in two-way managerial monitoring within the firm? Explain.*

B.   *Does the presence of asymmetric information concerning managerial performance provide an important motivation for outside monitoring by corporate watchdogs, security analysts, and investors? Explain.*

P16.10   **SOLUTION**

A.   Yes, recent scandals at insurance industry AIG and elsewhere suggest a breakdown in the functioning of the internal labor market and some inefficiency in two-way managerial monitoring within the firm. Of course, evidence of managerial self-dealing in information management constitutes necessary but not sufficient evidence against the managerial labor market efficiency hypothesis. The functioning of the managerial labor market internal to the firm, and two-way managerial monitoring, has the theoretical potential to ensure efficiency in the face of asymmetric information among insiders and outsiders. However, the hierarchical structure of management within firms argues against the possibility of perfectly informed and unbiased two-way monitoring. When managers within an organization are organized or classified according to rank, authority, or capacity ("talent"), the efficiency of internal two-way monitoring becomes distinctly one-sided. As we proceed from the bottom to the top of an organization, the level of managerial talent or effectiveness can be expected to rise. By virtue of their past success in scaling the corporate ladder, top managers can be presumed relatively more efficient than lesser managers in the management of firm assets and information. "Survival of the fittest" argues for superior top-down versus bottoms-up internal two-way monitoring, and therefore against the notion of perfect monitoring symmetry.

B.   Yes, the presence of asymmetric information concerning managerial performance provides an important motivation for outside monitoring by corporate watchdogs, security analysts, and investors. Asymmetric information concerning target firm managerial performance gives an important motivation for unfriendly buyouts in that the capabilities that allow an individual to evaluate the skills of managers within a given organization, and thereby successfully climb the corporate ladder to the top, also lend themselves to the evaluation of competing management teams. Successful managers are especially well equipped to detect the failures of inefficient management, and to seize the opportunity provided by that inefficiency. It follows that the unfriendly buyout phenomenon will reflect, at least in part, the manager catalyst with insider (nonpublic) information concerning target firm managerial inefficiency.

             In the presence of firm-specific human capital, acquiring firm management will also possess strong economic incentives to spread its expertise over broader economic resources. As the firm grows, management becomes able to spread its firm-specific human capital over greater related assets and thereby obtain larger, but still only partial, economic rentals. With growth, management also becomes able to enhance its tools and techniques through greater experience or learning. Growth in the scale and/or scope of the enterprise will cause the firm-specific component of management human capital to shrink in relative terms. The nonfirm-specific component, and management opportunity cost, will rise. Therefore, unfriendly buyouts, especially conglomerate mergers, have the potential to enhance management's more marketable nonfirm-specific component of human capital and thereby provide a further motive for unfriendly buyouts.

Chapter 17

RISK ANALYSIS

Managers of successful companies incorporate risk analysis into everyday decision making. The certainty equivalent method converts expected risky profit streams into certain sum equivalents to eliminate value differences that result from different risk levels. For risk-averse decision makers, the value of a risky stream of payments is less than the value of a certain stream, and the application of certainty equivalent adjustment factors results in a downward adjustment to the value of expected returns. For risk-seeking decision makers, the value of a risky stream of payments is greater than that of a certain stream, and application of certainty equivalent adjustment factors results in an upward adjustment in the value of expected returns. In both cases, risky dollars are converted into certain-sum equivalents. Another method used to reflect uncertainty in the basic valuation model is the risk-adjusted discount rate approach. In this technique, the interest rate used in the denominator of the basic valuation model depends on the level of risk associated with a given cash flow. For highly risk-averse decision makers, higher discount rates are implemented; for less risk-averse decision makers, lower discount rates are employed. Using this technique, discounted expected profit streams reflect risk differences and become directly comparable.

This chapter is an essential component of managerial economics because it shows how managers deal effectively with risk. Attitudes toward risk taking are a matter of personal and corporate preferences. As such, they cannot be derived through economic analysis. However, in light of personal and corporate risk preferences, managerial economics can be effectively employed to determine an appropriate course of action.

CHAPTER OUTLINE

I. **CONCEPTS OF RISK AND UNCERTAINTY**

    A. **Economic Risk and Uncertainty:** To make effective investment decisions, managers must appreciate the difference between risk and uncertainty.

        1. Economic risk is the chance of loss because all possible outcomes and their probability of occurrence are unknown.

        2. Uncertainty exists when the outcomes of managerial decisions cannot be predicted with absolute accuracy but all possibilities and their associated probabilities are known.

    B. **General Risk Categories:** Risk analysis is facilitated when economic risk can be categorized and quantified.

1. Business risk is the chance of loss associated with a given managerial decision.

2. Market risk is the chance that a portfolio of investments can lose money because of overall swings in the financial markets.

3. Inflation risk is the danger that a general increase in the price level will undermine the real economic value of corporate agreements or assets.

4. Interest-rate risk is another type of market risk that can severely affect the value of corporate investments and obligations.

5. Credit risk is the chance that another party will fail to abide by contractual obligations.

6. Liquidity risk is the difficulty of selling corporate assets or investments at favorable prices under typical market conditions.

7. Derivative risk is the chance that volatile financial derivatives such as commodities futures and index options could create losses by increasing rather than decreasing price volatility.

C. **Special Risks of Global Operations:** Special risks are borne by companies that pursue a global rather than just a domestic investment strategy.

1. Cultural risk is the chance of loss due to product market differences derived from distinctive social customs.

2. Currency risk is the chance of loss due to price swings in the relative value of domestic and foreign currencies.

3. Global investors experience government policy risk because foreign government grants of monopoly franchises, tax abatements, and favored trade status can be tenuous.

4. Expropriation risk is the chance that business property located abroad might be seized by host governments.

II.   PROBABILITY CONCEPTS

A. **Probability Distribution:** The probability of an event is the chance, or odds, that the incident will occur.
1. Business risk is the chance of loss associated with a managerial decision.

2. If the probability of occurrence is assigned to each possible event, the listing is called a probability distribution.

3. A payoff matrix illustrates the dollar outcome associated with each possible state of nature.

B. Expected Value: Expected value is the anticipated realization from a given payoff matrix and probability distribution.

1. Expected-profit is expressed by the equation:

$$\text{Expected Profit} = E(\pi) = \sum_{i=1}^{n} \pi_i \times p_i,$$

where π_i is profit and p_i is probability.

C. Absolute Risk Measurement: Tight probability distributions imply low risk because the chance that actual outcomes will differ from expected values is small.

1. Absolute risk is measured by the standard deviation and is the square root of the variance:

$$\text{Standard Deviation} = \sigma = \sqrt{\sum_{i=1}^{n} [\pi_i - E(\pi)]^2 p_i}.$$

D. Relative Risk Measurement: Relative risk is the variation in possible returns compared to the expected payoff amount.

1. A popular measure of relative risk is the coefficient of variation:

$$\text{Coefficient of Variation} = v = \frac{\sigma}{E(\pi)}.$$

2. When comparing decision alternatives with costs and benefits that are not of approximately equal size, the coefficient of variation measures relative risk better than the standard deviation.

E. Other Risk Measures: The contribution of a single investment project to the overall return variation of the firm's asset portfolio is measured by beta.

1. Beta is a measure of the systematic variability or covariance of one asset's returns with returns on a portfolio of assets.

III. STANDARD NORMAL CONCEPT

A. Normal Distribution: A normal distribution has a symmetrical distribution about the mean or expected value.

1. The smaller the standard deviation, the smaller the probability of an outcome that is very different from the expected value.

2. For a normal distribution:

   a. Actual outcomes lie within ±1 standard deviation of the mean roughly 68 per cent of the time.

   b. The probability that actual outcomes will be within two standard deviations of the expected outcome is approximately 95 per cent.

   c. There is greater than a 99 per cent probability that actual outcomes occur within three standard deviations of the mean.

B. Standardized Variables: A standardized variable has a mean of zero and a standard deviation equal to one.

1. Any distribution of revenue, cost, or profit data can be standardized with the following formula:

$$z = \frac{x - \mu}{\sigma},$$

   where z is the standardized variable, x is the outcome of interest, and μ and σ are the mean and standard deviation of the distribution, respectively.

2. When $z = 1.0$, the point of interest is 1σ away from the mean; when $z = 2$, the value is 2σ away from the mean, and so on.

3. The probability of an outcome falling within two standards of the mean is 95.46 per cent; 99.74 per cent of all outcomes fall within three standard deviations of the mean.

C.   **Use of the Standard Normal Concept: An Example:** The standard normal concept is often used to estimate the probability of profitable operations.

IV.   **UTILITY THEORY AND RISK ANALYSIS**

A.   **Possible Risk Attitudes:** Three possible attitudes toward risk are present.

1.   Risk aversion characterizes individuals who seek to avoid or minimize risk.

2.   Risk neutrality describes decision makers who focus on expected returns and disregard the dispersion of returns (risk).

3.   Risk seeking portrays decision makers who prefer risk.

B.   **Relation Between Money and its Utility:** At the center of the risk aversion concept is the notion of diminishing marginal utility for money.

1.   Risk aversion implies that the total utility of money rises at a diminishing pace for additional increments of money (marginal utility of money is falling).

2.   Those who are indifferent to risk perceive a strictly proportional relationship between total utility and money (marginal utility of money is constant).

3.   Risk seekers perceive a more-than-proportional relation between total utility and money (marginal utility of money is rising).

C.   **An Example of Risk Aversion:** Utility theory dictates that investments are chosen on the basis of their ability to enhance decision-maker utility or well-being.

V.   **ADJUSTING THE VALUATION MODEL FOR RISK**

A.   **Basic Valuation Model:** The basic valuation model states that the value of the firm equals the discounted present worth of future profits:

$$V = \sum_{t=1}^{n} \frac{\pi_t}{(1 + i)^t}.$$

1.   Under conditions of certainty, the numerator of this expression is profit, and the denominator is a time-value adjustment using the risk-free rate of return i.

2. Under conditions of uncertainty, profits shown as π equal the expected value of profits during each future period.

B. **Certainty Equivalent Adjustments:** Any expected risky amount can be converted to an equivalent certain sum using the certainty equivalent adjustment factor, α, calculated as the ratio of a certain sum divided by an expected risky amount, where both dollar values provide the same level of utility:

$$\begin{matrix} \text{Certainty} \\ \text{Equivalent} \\ \text{Adjustment} \\ \text{Factor} \end{matrix} = \alpha = \frac{\text{Equivalent Certain Sum}}{\text{Expected Risky Sum}}.$$

1. $\alpha < 1$ implies risk aversion.

2. $\alpha = 1$ implies risk indifference.

3. $\alpha > 1$ implies risk preference.

4. The basic valuation model can be converted into a risk-adjusted valuation model that explicitly accounts for risk:

$$V = \sum_{t=1}^{n} \frac{\alpha E(\pi_t)}{(1 + i)^t}.$$

In this risk-adjusted valuation model, expected future profits, $E(\pi_t)$, are converted to their certainty equivalents, $\alpha E(\pi_t)$, and are discounted at a risk-free rate, i.

C. **Certainty Equivalent Adjustment Example:** If a potential project's required investment and risk levels are known, the α implied by a decision to accept the investment project can be calculated.

1. Risk-averse individuals should invest in projects if calculated α's are *less* than or equal to those for accepted projects in the same risk class.

D. **Risk-Adjusted Discount Rates:** Another way to incorporate risk in managerial decision making is to adjust the discount rate or denominator of the basic valuation model.

1. As risk increases, higher expected returns on investment are required to compensate investors for the additional risk.

2. The basic valuation model can be adapted to account for risk through adjustment of the discount rate, k, where:

$$V = \sum_{t=1}^{n} \frac{E(\pi_t)}{(1 + k)^t},$$

3. The risk-adjusted discount rate k is the sum of the risk-free rate of return, R_F, plus the required risk premium, R_p:

$$k = R_F + R_P$$

E. **Risk-Adjusted Discount Rate Example:** Investment projects with higher as opposed to lower risk-adjusted value should be chosen to maximize the value of the firm.

VI. **DECISION TREES AND COMPUTER SIMULATION**

A. **Decision Trees:** A decision tree is a visual mapping of the sequential decision-making process.

1. Decision trees are designed for analyzing decision problems that involve a series of choice alternatives that are constrained by previous decisions.

   a. Decision points are instances when management must select among several choice alternatives.

   b. Chance events are possible outcomes following each decision point.

2. The decision that offers the largest risk-adjusted net present value is the optimal choice.

3. The expected value and risk of each decision alternative must be calculated to help arrive at an appropriate managerial decision.

B. **Computer Simulation:** Computer simulation involves the use of computer software and sophisticated desktop computers to create a variety of decision outcome scenarios.

1. Using computer simulation, hypothetical "what if?" questions can be asked and answered on the basis of measurable differences in underlying assumptions.

2. Computer simulations require probability distribution estimates for investment outlays, unit sales, product prices, input prices, and asset lives.

    a. Full-scale simulations are expensive and time consuming, and restricted to projects such as major plant expansions or new-product decisions.

    b. Limited-scale simulations are used to project outcomes for projects or strategies.

C. **Computer Simulation Example:** Computer simulation randomly selects revenue and cost levels from each relevant distribution, and uses this information to estimate future profits, net present values, or the rate of return on investment.

    1. The simulation process is repeated a large number of times to identify the central tendency or expected value of projected returns.

    2. Computer simulation illustrates the frequency pattern and range of future returns that can be plotted and analyzed.

VII.   **USES OF GAME THEORY IN RISK ANALYSIS**

A. **Game Theory and Auction Strategy:** Mathematician John von Neuman and economist Oskar Morgenstern discovered that deciding when to bluff, fold, stand pat, or raise is not only relevant when playing cards, but also when opposed by aggressive competitors in the market place.

    1. One of the most interesting business uses of game theory is to analyze bidder strategy in auctions.

    2. The most familiar type of auction is an English auction where an auctioneer keeps raising the price until a single highest bidder remains.

        a. The advantage of an English auction is that it is widely regarded as a fair and open process.

        b. It is an effective approach for obtaining high winning bid prices.

    3. The winner's curse results when overly aggressive bidders pay more than the economic value of auctioned off items.

4.   Another commonly employed auction method is a sealed-bid auction where all bids are secret, and the highest bid wins.

    a.   A compelling advantage of the sealed-bid approach is that it is relatively free from the threat of collusion.

    b.   The downside to the approach is that it often encourages bidders to act cautiously.

5.   A relatively rare sealed-bid auction method is a Vickrey auction, where the highest sealed bid wins, but the winner pays the price of the second-highest bid.

    a.   A disadvantage of the technique is that it creates the perception that the buyer is taking advantage of the seller by paying only the second highest price.

6.   Another uncommon auctioning method is the so-called reverse or Dutch auction.

    a.   In a Dutch auction, the auctioneer keeps lowering a very high price until a winning bidder emerges.

    b.   The winning bidder is the first participant willing to pay the auctioneer's price.

    c.   A disadvantage of this approach is that bidders tend to act cautiously out of fear of overpaying for auctioned items.

B.   Maximin Decision Rule: The maximin (or secure strategy) criterion states that the decision maker should select the alternative that provides the best of the worst possible outcomes.

1.   This criterion instructs one to maximize the minimum possible outcome.

C.   Minimax Regret Decision Rule: The minimax regret criterion states that the decision maker should minimize the maximum possible regret (opportunity loss) associated with a wrong decision *after the fact*.

1.   This criterion instructs one to minimize the difference between possible outcomes and the best outcome for each state of nature.

D. **Cost of Uncertainty:** An unavoidable opportunity loss is the cost associated with uncertainty.

1. The cost of uncertainty is measured by the minimum expected opportunity loss.

   a. Using this concept, it is possible to assess the value of gaining additional information before choosing among decision alternatives.

2. Firms often engage in activities aimed at reducing the uncertainty of various alternatives before making an irrevocable decision.

VIII. SUMMARY

PROBLEMS & SOLUTIONS

P17.1   **Expected Value.** *Harrison Ford Motors, Inc., estimates that three out of every fifty individuals who take demonstration test drive will actually purchase a Ford Explorer. The firm's gross profit margin per vehicle is $500 and the cost of a test ride is $10.*

       A.   *What is the expected profit of each test ride given?*

P17.1   **SOLUTION**

       A.   The probability of an individual who takes a test ride actually purchasing a car is $3/50 = 0.06$. Because Harrison Ford's gross profit margin is $500, the expected gross profit margin per test drive is:

$$\begin{array}{c} \text{Expected} \\ \text{Profit} \end{array} = \begin{array}{l} \text{Purchase probability} \times \\ \text{Gross margin} - \text{Test ride cost} \end{array}$$

$$= 0.06(\$500) - \$10$$

$$= \$20$$

P17.2   **Probability Concepts.**   *The Cellular Telephone Corporation has just completed development work on a new line of cellular telephones. Preliminary market research indicates two feasible marketing strategies: (a) concentration on developing general consumer acceptance by advertising through newspapers, television, and other media; or (b) concentration on distributor acceptance of the cellular telephone through intensive sales calls by company representatives, extensive development of software support (user programs), and so forth. Eleanor Rigby, Celluar Telephone's marketing manager, has developed sales estimates under each alternative plan, and has arranged rough payoff matrices according to her assessment of likely product acceptance under each plan. These data are illustrated below:*

Strategy 1: Consumer-Oriented Promotion

Probability	Sales Outcome
0.1	*$500,000*
0.4	*1,500,000*
0.4	*2,500,000*
0.1	*3,500,000*

Strategy 2: Distributor-Oriented Promotion	
Probability	*Sales Outcome*
0.3	$1,000,000
0.4	1,500,000
0.3	2,000,000

A.   Assume that the company has a 50% profit margin on sales. Calculate the expected profit for each plan.

B.   Construct a simple bar graph of the possible profit outcomes for each plan. On the basis of the appearance of the two graphs, which plan appears more risky?

C.   Calculate the standard deviation and coefficient of variation associated with the profit distribution of each plan.

D.   Assume that management of Celluar Telephone has a utility function like the one illustrated below. Which marketing strategy should Rigby recommend?

Cellular Telephone Utility and Profit

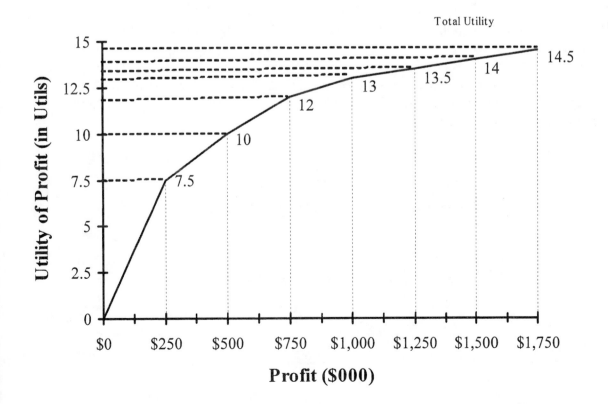

P17.2 SOLUTION

A.

Strategy 1: Consumer-Oriented Promotion

Probability (1)	Sales Outcomes (2)	Profit (3) = (2) × 0.5	Expected Profit (4) = (3) × (1)
0.1	$500,000	$250,000	$25,000
0.4	1,500,000	750,000	300,000
0.4	2,500,000	1,250,000	500,000
0.1	3,500,000	1,750,000	<u>175,000</u>
			$E(\pi_1) = \$1,000,000$

Strategy 2: Distributor-Oriented Promotion

Probability (1)	Sales Outcomes (2)	Profit (3) = (2) × 0.5	Expected Profit (4) = (3) × (1)
0.3	$1,000,000	$500,000	$150,000
0.4	1,500,000	750,000	300,000
0.3	2,000,000	1,000,000	<u>300,000</u>
			$E(\pi_2) = \$750,000$

B.

Cellular Telephone

Strategy 1: Consumer-Oriented Promotion

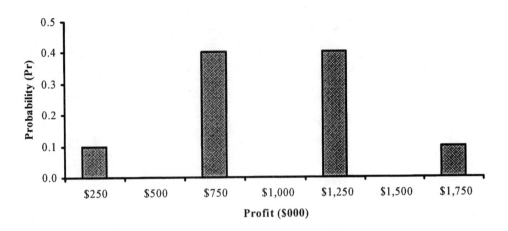

Strategy 2: Distributor-Oriented Promotion

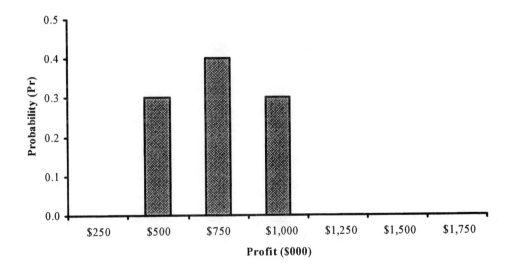

Strategy 1 appears to be more risky than strategy 2 due to the greater variability of outcomes.

C.

Strategy 1:

Probability (1)	Deviations (2)	(Deviations)^2 (3)	(1) × (3) = (4)
0.1	-750,000	5.625×10^{11}	5.625×10^{10}
0.4	-250,000	6.250×10^{10}	2.5×10^{10}
0.4	250,000	6.250×10^{10}	2.5×10^{10}
0.1	750,000	5.625×10^{11}	5.625×10^{10}
			$\sigma_1^2 = 16.25 \times 10^{10}$

$$\sigma_1 = \sqrt{\$16.25 \times 10^{10}} = \$4.0311 \times 10^5 = \$403,110$$

$$V_1 = \frac{\$403,110}{\$1,000,000} = 0.403$$

Strategy 2:

Probability (1)	Deviations (2)	(Deviations)^2 (3)	(1) × (3) = (4)
0.3	-250,000	6.25×10^{11}	1.875×10^{10}
0.4	0	0	0
0.3	250,000	6.25×10^{10}	1.875×10^{10}
			$\sigma^2 = 3.75 \times 10^{10}$

$$\sigma_2 = \sqrt{\$3.75 \times 10^{10}} = \$1.9365 \times 10^5 = \$193,650$$

$$V_2 = \frac{\$193,650}{\$750,000} = 0.258$$

These calculations make more precise the conclusion reached in part B that strategy 1 is the more risky marketing approach.

D.

Strategy 1:			
Probability **(1)**	**Profits** **(2)**	**Utils** **(3)**	**Expected Utility** **(4) = (3) × (1)**
0.1	$250,000	7.50	0.75
0.4	750,000	12.00	4.80
0.4	1,250,000	13.50	5.40
0.1	1,750,000	14.50	<u>1.45</u>

$$E(U_1) = 12.40 \text{ utils}$$

Strategy 2:			
Probability **(1)**	**Profits** **(2)**	**Utils** **(3)**	**Expected Utility** **(4) = (3) × (1)**
0.3	$500,000	10	3.0
0.4	750,000	12	4.8
0.3	1,000,000	13	<u>3.9</u>

$$E(U_2) = 11.7 \text{ utils}$$

Rigby should recommend strategy 1 because of its higher expected utility. In this case, the higher expected profit of strategy 1 more than offsets its greater riskiness.

P17.3 **Expected Utility.** *Penny Lane is considering two alternative investments, each costing $7,000. Present values of possible outcomes and their probabilities of occurrence are:*

Investment A			
	Outcome		
	1	*2*	*3*
Present Value	*$6,000*	*$8,000*	*$10,000*
Probability of occurrence	*0.25*	*0.50*	*0.25*

	Investment B		
	Outcome		
	1	*2*	*3*
Present Value	*$5,000*	*$9,000*	*$10,000*
Probability of occurrence	*0.30*	*0.50*	*0.20*

A. Calculate the expected present values of the two investments.

B. Calculate the standard deviation for each investment. Which alternative is riskier?

C. If Lane has a constant marginal utility of income as indicated by the utility function $U = 30 + 2X$, where X is thousands of dollars of present value, which investment should she choose? Why?

D. If Lane's utility of income is given by the function $U = 30X - X^2$, which investment should she select? Why?

P17.3   SOLUTION

A.

INVESTMENT A		
Present Value (1)	**Probability (2)**	**Expected Present Value (3) = (1) × (2)**
$6,000	0.25	$1,500
8,000	0.50	4,000
10,000	0.25	2,500
		$E(PV_A) = \$8,000$

INVESTMENT B		
Present Value (1)	**Probability (2)**	**Expected Present Value (3) = (1) × (2)**
$5,000	0.3	$1,500
9,000	0.5	4,500

$$10,000 \qquad 0.2 \qquad \underline{2,000}$$
$$E(PV_B) = \$8,000$$

B. $\sigma_A = \sqrt{0.25(\$6,000 - \$8,000)^2 + 0.50(\$8,000 - \$8,000)^2}$
$$\overline{+\ 0.25(\$10,000 - \$8,000)^2}$$

$$= \sqrt{\$2,000,000}$$

$$= \$1,414.21$$

$\sigma_B = \sqrt{0.3(\$5,000 - \$8,000)^2 + 0.5(\$9,000 - \$8,000)^2}$
$$\overline{+\ 0.2(\$10,000 - \$8,000)^2}$$

$$= \sqrt{\$4,000,000}$$

$$= \$2,000$$

Investment B is more risky than investment A.

C. When $U = 30 + 2X$, expected utility is:

INVESTMENT A

Probability (1)	PV (2)	X (3)	Utility ($U = 30 + 2X$) (4)	Expected Utility (5) = (4) × (1)
0.25	$6,000	6	42	10.5
0.50	8,000	8	46	23.0
0.25	10,000	10	50	12.5
				$E(U_A) = 46$ utils

INVESTMENT B

Probability (1)	PV (2)	X (3)	Utility (U = 30 + 2X) (4)	Expected Utility (5) = (4) × (1)
0.3	$5,000	5	40	12
0.5	9,000	9	48	24
0.2	10,000	10	50	<u>10</u>

$$E(U_B) = 46 \text{ utils}$$

With a linear utility function (constant marginal utility), Lane would be indifferent between the two investments. So long as the alternatives have equal expected dollar returns, they must provide the same expected utility to an individual exhibiting an indifference to risk.

D. When utility $U = 30X - X^2$, expected utility is:

INVESTMENT A

Probability (1)	PV (2)	X (3)	Utility (U = 30X - X²) (4)	Expected Utility (5) = (4) × (1)
0.25	$6,000	6	144	36
0.50	8,000	8	176	88
0.25	10,000	10	200	<u>50</u>

$$E(U_A) = 174 \text{ utils}$$

INVESTMENT B

Probability (1)	PV (2)	X (3)	Utility (U = 30X - X²) (4)	Expected Utility (5) = (4) × (1)
0.3	$5,000	5	125	37.5
0.5	9,000	9	189	94.5
0.2	10,000	10	200	<u>40.0</u>

$$E(U_A) = 172 \text{ utils}$$

Investment A should be selected because of its higher expected utility. In this case, Lane exhibits risk aversion (diminishing marginal utility), and, hence, with equal expected dollar returns, he prefers the alternative with less risk. We know

Lane has a diminishing marginal utility of income because marginal utility will fall as income grows.

P17.4 ***Certainty Equivalent Adjustment Factors.*** *Blue Chip Investors, Ltd. offers limited partnership investments to individual investors. A current $1.5 million offering consists of 25 equal shares priced at $60,000 each. Proceeds from the offering will be used to purchase and renovate a local apartment complex. BCI projects a total investment return for the project of $4 million, or $160,000 per share, to be paid in one lump sum at the end of 7 years.*

    A. *Using a 6% risk-free rate of return, calculate the discounted present value of projected returns for a single unit.*

    B. *Calculate and interpret the minimum certainty equivalent adjustment factor α necessary to justify investment in the project.*

P17.4 **SOLUTION**

    A. PV of future returns = Projected returns $\times$ (PVIF, n= 7, i = 6%)

                            = \$160,000(0.6651)

                            = \$106,416

    B. From the certainty equivalent adjustment factor formula note that:

$$\alpha = \frac{\text{Certain Sum}}{\text{Expected Risky Return}}$$

$$= \frac{\$60,000}{\$106,416}$$

$$= 0.56$$

In order for investors to justify investment in the project, each dollar of expected risky return must be worth at least 56¢ in certain dollars.

P17.5 ***Certainty Equivalents.*** *The Hungry Heifer, Inc., is considering opening a new restaurant in Hanover, Indiana. Projecting net profits for such an outlet is quite subjective, but Norm Peterson, Hungry Heifer's marketing director, estimates:*

Probability	Annual Net Profits
0.125	$135,000
0.750	225,000
0.125	315,000

During the past year, The Hungry Heifer opened new restaurants in four different markets. In analyzing these investment decisions, you discover the following:

Market	Certainty Equivalent	Coefficient of Variation
A	0.80	0.10
B	0.75	0.15
C	0.70	0.19
D	0.60	0.22

A. Calculate the expected return, standard deviation and coefficient of variation of annual net profits for the Hanover restaurant.

B. Given Hungry Heifer's historical decisions, calculate the range for the maximum acceptable investment requirement for the Hanover restaurant given an anticipated ten-year project life, and a 6% risk-free rate of return.

P17.5 **SOLUTION**

A. $E(R) = \$135,000(0.125) + \$225,000(0.750) + \$315,000(0.125) = \$225,000.$

$$\sigma = \sqrt{(\$135,000 - \$225,000)^2(0.125)}$$

$$\overline{+ (\$225,000 - \$225,000)^2(0.750)}$$

$$\overline{+ (\$315,000 - \$225,000)^2(0.125)}$$

$$= \sqrt{\$1.0125 \times 10^9 + \$1.0125 \times 10^9}$$

$$= \$45,000$$

$$V = \frac{\sigma}{E(R)} = \frac{\$45,000}{\$225,000} = 0.2$$

B.   By definition,

$$\alpha = \frac{\text{Certain sum}}{\text{Expected risky return}}$$

$$= \frac{\text{Investment requirement}}{E(R)}$$

Therefore, it is obvious that an acceptable investment requirement for an investment with a one year life would be:

$$\text{Investment Requirement} = \alpha \times E(R)$$

For the Hanover restaurant, which has a life span of more than one year, the range within which an acceptable investment requirement will be found using the relation:

$$\text{Investment Requirement} = \sum_{t=1}^{n} \frac{\alpha \times E(R)}{(1 + i)^t}$$

The Hanover restaurant has a $V = 0.2$, which is between $V_C = 0.19$ and $V_D = 0.22$. This implies that an acceptable certainty equivalent lies between $\alpha_C = 0.70$ and $\alpha_D = 0.60$.

In this instance, an acceptable investment requirement is found within the range:

$$\text{"High" Investment Limit} = \sum_{t=1}^{n} \frac{\alpha_C \times E(R)}{(1 + i)^t}$$

$$= \sum_{t=1}^{10} \frac{0.70(\$225,000)}{(1.06)^{10}}$$

$$= (\text{PVIFA, n=10, i=6\%})(0.70)(\$225,000)$$

$$= (7.3601)(0.70)(\$225,000)$$

$$= \$1,159,216.$$

$$\text{"Low" Investment Limit} = \sum_{t=1}^{n} \frac{\alpha_D \times E(R)}{(1 + i)^t}$$

$$= \sum_{t=1}^{10} \frac{0.60(\$225,000)}{(1.06)^{10}}$$

$$= (\text{PVIFA, n=10, i=6\%})(0.60)(\$225,000)$$

$$= (7.3601)(0.60)(\$225,000)$$

$$= \$993,614.$$

Thus, the maximum acceptable investment requirement which would be consistent with Hungry Heifer's past management decisions will be found within the range $993,614 to $1,159,216.

P17.6   ***The Standard Normal.*** *Dan Cooper, is owner-operator of D.B. Cooper's Sky Diving School, Inc., in Portland, Oregon. Cooper is considering a boost in advertising to increase sales. Cooper plans to make his media decision using the following data on the expected success of television versus newspaper promotions:*

	Market Response	*Probability*	*Revenues*
Newspaper	*Poor*	*0.18*	*$3,400*
	Good	*0.64*	*5,000*
	Very good	*0.18*	*6,600*
Television	*Poor*	*0.245*	*4,000*
	Good	*0.51*	*6,500*
	Very good	*0.245*	*9,000*

Assume that the returns from each promotion are normally distributed, and that net revenues are before advertising expenses.

A.   *Calculate the expected return, standard deviation, and coefficient of variation for each promotion.*

B.   *Which promotion is most risky? Why?*

C. *If the newspaper promotion costs $3,752 while the television promotion costs $2,825, what is the probability each will generate a profit?*

D. *Which promotion should be chosen?*

P17.6 **SOLUTION**

A. Newspaper Promotion

$$E(R_N) = \$3,400(0.18) + \$5,000(0.64) + \$6,600(0.18)$$

$$= \$5,000$$

$$\sigma_N = \sqrt{(\$3,400 - \$5,000)^2(0.18) + (\$5,000 - \$5,000)^2(0.64)}$$

$$\overline{+ (\$6,600 - \$5,000)^2(0.18)}$$

$$= \$960$$

$$V_N = \frac{\sigma_N}{E(R_N)} = \frac{\$960}{\$5,000} = 0.192$$

Television Promotion

$$E(R_{TV}) = \$4,000(0.245) + \$6,500(0.51) + \$9,000(0.245)$$

$$= \$6,500$$

$$\sigma_{TV} = \sqrt{(\$4,000 - \$6,500)^2(0.245) + (\$6,500 - \$6,500)^2(0.51)}$$

$$\overline{+ (\$9,000 - \$6,500)^2(0.245)}$$

$$= \$1,750$$

$$V_{TV} = \frac{\sigma_{TV}}{E(R_{TV})} = \frac{\$1,750}{\$6,500} = 0.269$$

B. The television promotion has a higher standard deviation and coefficient of variation than does the newspaper promotion, and is thus the more risky of the two promotion alternatives.

C.   To calculate the probability that each promotion will generate a profit one must consider the normal curve and relevant values of the standard normal. In graphic terms, one must calculate the share of the total area under the normal curve which is to the right of each breakeven point, the relevant point of interest.

Newspaper v. TV AD Revenue Distribution

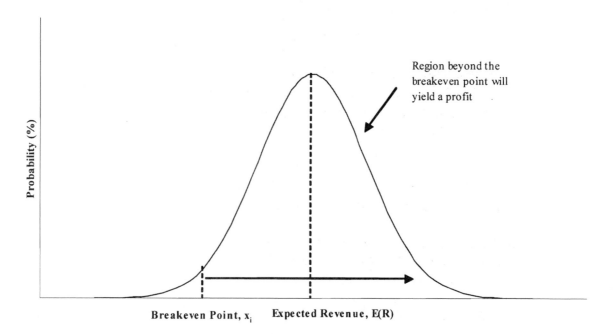

Newspaper Promotion Profit Probability

$$z = \frac{x_N - E(R_N)}{\sigma_N}$$

$$= \frac{\$3,752 - \$5,000}{\$960}$$

$$= -1.3$$

The standard normal distribution function value for $z = -1.3$ is 0.4032. This means that 0.4032 or 40.32% of the total area under the normal curve lies between x_N and $E(R_N)$, and implies a profit probability for the newspaper promotion of 0.4032 + 0.5 = 0.9032 or 90.32%.

Television Promotion Profit Probability

$$z = \frac{x_{TV} - E(R_{TV})}{\sigma_{TV}}$$

$$= \frac{\$2,825 - \$6,500}{\$1,750}$$

$$= -2.1$$

The standard normal distribution function value for $z = -2.1$ is 0.4821. This means that 0.4821 or 48.21% of the total area under the normal curve lies between x_{TV} and $E(R_{TV})$, and implies a profit probability for the television promotion of $0.4821 + 0.5 = 0.9821$ or 98.21%.

D. Without evidence on the firm's risk attitudes, we can't say which promotion should be undertaken. Although the TV promotion has a higher expected profit and profit probability, it is the more risky of the two promotion possibilities.

P17.7 **Game Theory.** *Jim Carey, owner of Universal Cinema, Inc., must decide between two alternative bookings. The first is a new movie called "Grouch," and features a cartoon character who seeks to ruin the holidays by stealing Christmas presents from little children. Despite featuring an established star in the leading role, Carey fears the movie may "bomb" (fail) because the subject matter may prove controversial. Thus, Carey expects only a 50% chance of "Grouch" proving to be a hit. If the movie is a hit, Carey anticipates $500,000 in weekly revenue during the initial booking. Only $100,000 in revenue is expected if it proves to be a bomb.*

As an alternative to booking "Grouch," Carey can rebook the second run of an action packed thriller called "Castaway." Because "Grouch" will be featured by other theaters in the Universal Cinema market area, Carey projects revenue for "Castaway" of $50,000 if "Grouch" is a hit, and $75,000 if "Grouch" bombs. Both movies would be rented by Universal Cinema from regional distributors on a fixed fee basis of $200,000 per week for "Grouch," and $40,000 for "Castaway."

A. *Construct a net profit (revenues minus fixed fee) payoff matrix for the two alternatives. Which would be chosen using the maximin criterion?*

B. *Construct a net profit regret or opportunity loss matrix for the two alternatives. Which would be chosen using the minimax regret criterion?*

C. *Which alternative would be chosen if Universal Cinema solely wished to maximize its expected net profit?*

D.   *Calculate the cost of uncertainty in this problem.*

E.   *Briefly describe when the choices made in parts A, B and C would be appropriate.*

P17.7   **SOLUTION**

     A.

Payoff Matrix

	States of Nature	
Decision Alternatives	**1. "Grouch" is a hit**	**2. "Grouch" bombs**
A. Book "Grouch"	$300,000 (=$500,000-$200,000)	-$100,000 (=$100,000-$200,000)
B. Book "Castaway"	$10,000 (=$50,000-$40,000)	$35,000 (=$75,000-$40,000)

Booking "Grouch" exposes Carey to the possibility of a $100,000 loss which would be incurred if the movie bombs. This worst payoff outcome can be avoided by choosing to book "Castaway" instead. Thus, decision B is the maximin strategy.

     B.

Regret Matrix

	States of Nature	
Decision Alternatives	**1. "Grouch" is a hit**	**2. "Grouch" bombs**
A. Book "Grouch"	$0 (=$300,000-$300,000)	$135,000 (=$35,000-(-$100,000))
B. Book "Castaway"	$290,000 (=$300,000-$10,000)	$0 (=$35,000-$35,000)

Booking "Castaway" exposes Carey to the possibility of a $290,000 opportunity loss in the event "Grouch" proves to be a hit. This worst opportunity loss outcome can be avoided by booking "Grouch" instead. Thus, decision A is the minimax strategy.

   C.   Using an expected profit criterion suggests:

$$E(\pi_A) = \$300,000(0.5) + (-\$100,000)(0.5) = \$100,000$$

$$E(\pi_B) = \$10,000(0.5) + \$35,000(0.5) = \$22,500$$

Thus, decision A is the preferred alternative based upon a criterion of simply choosing the alternative with the highest expected net profit.

D. The expected opportunity loss under each alternative is:

$$E(Loss_A) = \$0(0.5) + \$135,000(0.5) = \$67,500$$

$$E(Loss_B) = \$290,000(0.5) + \$0(0.5) = \$145,000$$

The cost of uncertainty is the minimum or unavoidable expected opportunity loss of $67,500.

E. If Carey is extremely risk averse, as would be true if a $100,000 loss would be a disastrous outcome for Universal Cinema, then the maximin strategy B would be most appropriate. A less risk averse decision maker would choose A, the minimax strategy. Decision making based on an expected profit criterion, part C, is most appropriate in the case of risk neutral decision makers.

Any of these three alternative individual decision strategies might prove appropriate depending on decision maker risk attitudes. It is always necessary to examine *both* decision maker attitudes and decision alternatives prior to making any recommendation regarding the "best" alternative.

P17.8 **Probability Concepts.** *Kung Fu Exports, Ltd., is faced with a very uncertain market for next summer's ginseng root harvest. Kung Fu has the opportunity to contract now for purchase of 1,000 pounds of ginseng root at $80 per pound. Alternatively, they can wait until summer and pay the current market rate at that time. With a good harvest, ginseng will sell for $70 per pound. With a poor harvest, ginseng will sell for $100 per pound.*

A. *Assuming risk indifference, at what probability of a good harvest would the firm contract now for 1,000 pounds of ginseng root?*

B. *If there is a 90% probability of a good harvest, what would the firm pay for an option to purchase 1,000 pounds at $80?*

P17.8 **SOLUTION**

A. Let X equal the probability of a good harvest needed to induce the firm to contract now. For indifference, the expected cost of waiting to purchase must be equal to the expected cost of a current purchase.

$$\begin{array}{c} \text{Expected} \\ \text{Cost of Waiting} \end{array} = \begin{array}{c} \text{Expected Cost} \\ \text{of Current} \\ \text{Purchase} \end{array}$$

$$X(\$70,000) + (1 - X)(\$100,000) = \$80,000$$

$$70,000X + 100,000 - 100,000X = 80,000$$

$$30,000X = 20,000$$

$$X = 0.67 \text{ or } 67\%$$

B. The option described would allow the firm to wait until all uncertainty had been resolved before making its purchase decision. Assuming risk indifference, the cost of uncertainty measures the maximum amount the manager would pay for such an option.

The cost of uncertainty is measured as the minimum expected opportunity loss associated with the two alternatives.

$$E(Loss_{\text{Current purchase}}) = \$0(0.1) + \$10,000(0.9)$$

$$= \$9,000$$

$$E(Loss_{\text{Wait to purchase}}) = \$20,000(0.1) + \$0(0.9)$$

$$= \$2,000$$

Therefore, the firm should be willing to pay up to $2,000 for the option.

P17.9 *Cost of Uncertainty. The Doodle Pen Company has just priced a new fiber tip pen at 50¢ each. The firm is trying to decide whether to use method A or method B for production. Under method A, the fixed costs of producing the pen are $1,000 and variable costs are 30¢ per unit. With method B, fixed costs are $3,000, and variable costs per unit are 20¢. The estimated probability distribution for sales volume is:*

Unit Sales	Probability
5,000	0.25
30,000	0.50
50,000	0.25

A.   *Construct the payoff matrix for this problem.*

B.   *Calculate the expected payoff for each alternative.*

C.   *Calculate the expected opportunity loss for each alternative.*

D.   *What is the cost of uncertainty in this problem?*

E.   *Should Doodle be willing to spend an amount equal to the cost of uncertainty to remove all uncertainty in this case? Why or why not?*

P17.9   **SOLUTION**

A.   Profits using method A are given by the equation:

$$\pi_A = P \times Q - TC_A$$

$$= \$0.50Q - \$1,000 - \$0.30Q$$

$$= \$0.20Q - \$1,000$$

Profits under the three possible states of nature will be:

$$\pi_{A1} = \$0.2(5,000) - \$1,000 = \$0$$

$$\pi_{A2} = \$0.2(30,000) - \$1,000 = \$5,000$$

$$\pi_{A3} = \$0.2(50,000) - \$1,000 = \$9,000$$

Profits using method B are:

$$\pi_B = P \times Q - TC_B$$

$$= \$0.50Q - \$3,000 - \$0.20Q$$

$$= \$0.30Q - \$3,000$$

Profits under the three states of nature will be:

$$\pi_{B1} = \$0.3(5,000) - \$3,000 = -\$1,500$$

$$\pi_{B2} = \$0.3(30,000) - \$3,000 = \$6,000$$

$$\pi_{B3} \quad = \quad \$0.3(50,000) - \$3,000 = \$12,000$$

The payoff matrix for the problem is:

Payoff Matrix

Decision Alternatives	States of Nature		
	$Q = 5,000$	$Q = 30,000$	$Q = 50,000$
Method A	$0	$5,000	$9,000
Method B	-$1,500	$6,000	$12,000

B.   The expected payoff for method A is:

$$E(\pi_A) \quad = \quad \$0(0.25) + \$5,000(0.50) + \$9,000(0.25)$$

$$= \quad \$4,750$$

The expected payoff for method B is:

$$E(\pi_B) \quad = \quad (-\$1,500)(0.25) + \$6,000(0.5) + \$12,000(0.25)$$

$$= \quad \$5,625$$

C.   The opportunity loss or regret matrix for the problem is:

Regret Matrix

Decision Alternatives	States of Nature		
	$Q = 5,000$	$Q = 30,000$	$Q = 50,000$
Method A	$0	$1,000	$3,000
Method B	$1,500	$0	$0

The expected opportunity loss for each alternative is:

$$E(\text{Loss}_A) \quad = \quad \$0(0.25) + \$1,000(0.5) + \$3,000(0.25)$$

$$= \quad \$1,250$$

$$E(\text{Loss}_B) \quad = \quad \$1,500(0.25) + \$0(0.5) + \$0(0.25)$$

= $375

D. The cost of uncertainty is equal to the minimum expected opportunity loss of $375, which is the expected opportunity loss associated with production method B.

E. The cost of uncertainty is the expected gain associated with making the right decision after the fact. A firm attempting to maximize expected profits without regard to risk should be willing to spend precisely that amount to remove all uncertainty. A risk-averse individual would spend at least that amount, and possibly significantly more, to remove the potential variation in profits.

P17.10 ***Decision Tree Analysis.*** *Klingon Vulcan, Inc., produces electronic equipment that readily lends itself to design alternatives. Layout changes under consideration would have an effect on both the expected demand and costs of an important product. Klingon Vulcan managers expect a major reaction from competitors during the first year if any design innovations are successful, but none thereafter. If design changes are undertaken, the firm has estimated the following relevant data for the next two years (the firm's planning horizon):*

YEAR 1

Design	Success	Competitor	Total Incremental Revenue	Total Incremental Cost
A	Yes (0.85)	Yes (0.75)	$50,000	$40,000
	No (0.15)	No (0.85)	20,000	30,000
	Yes (0.85)	No (0.25)	55,000	42,000
	No (0.15)	Yes (0.15)	17,000	29,000
B	Yes (0.75)	Yes (0.55)	60,000	48,000
	No (0.25)	No (0.80)	18,000	30,000
	Yes (0.75)	No (0.45)	65,000	50,000
	No (0.25)	Yes (0.20)	15,000	28,000

YEAR 2

Design	Probability	Total Inc. Rev.	Total Inc. Cost
A	0.65 given "successful" 1st year	$70,000	$55,000
	0.35 given "successful" 1st year	10,000	25,000
	1.0 given "failure" in 1st year	0	0
B	0.70 given "successful" 1st year	$80,000	$60,000
	0.30 given "successful" 1st year	5,000	20,000
	1.0 given "failure" in 1st year	0	0

A. Construct a decision tree for the problem.

B. Assume that incremental revenues come in at the end of the year, costs are incurred at the beginning of the year, and a 12% discount rate. Compute the NPV of each alternative at each branch terminal.

C. Which is the more risky alternative in terms of potential variation in total return?

D. Which design should Klingon Vulcan select?

P17.10   **SOLUTION**

A. Decision trees for design A and design B can be drawn as:

	(1) NPV	(2) Probability	(3) = (1) x (2)

Success	$A_1 = \$11,340$	0.42	$4,763

Yes

| **Success** | $A_2 = -\$9,707$ | 0.22 | -$2,136 |

Success

No

| **Sucess** | $A_3 = \$13,804$ | 0.14 | $1,933 |

| **Success** | $A_4 = -\$7,242$ | 0.07 | -$507 |

A

Failure

| **Failure** | $A_5 = -\$13,821$ | 0.02 | -$276 |

Yes

No

| **Failure** | $A_6 = -\$12,143$ | 0.13 | $\underline{-\$1,579}$ |

$$NPV_A = \$2,198$$

	(1) NPV	(2) Probability	(3) = (1) x (2)

B_1 = $15,776   0.29 $4,575

B_2 = -$8,300   0.12   -$996

B_3 = $18,240   0.24 $4,378

B_4 = -$5,835   0.10   -$584

B_5 = -$14,607   0.05   -$730

B_6 = -$13,929   0.20   -$2,786

NPV_B = $3,857

B. Net Present Value calculations:

Design A

$$NPV_{A1} = \frac{\$50,000}{(1.12)^1} - \$40,000 + \frac{\$70,000}{(1.12)^2} - \frac{\$55,000}{(1.12)^1}$$

$$= \$11,340$$

$$NPV_{A2} = \frac{\$50,000}{(1.12)^1} - \$40,000 + \frac{\$10,000}{(1.12)^2} - \frac{\$25,000}{(1.12)^1}$$

$$= -\$9,707$$

$$NPV_{A3} = \frac{\$55,000}{(1.12)^1} - \$42,000 + \frac{\$70,000}{(1.12)^2} - \frac{\$55,000}{(1.12)^1}$$

$$= \$13,804$$

$$NPV_{A4} = \frac{\$55,000}{(1.12)^1} - \$42,000 + \frac{\$10,000}{(1.12)^2} - \frac{\$25,000}{(1.12)^1}$$

$$= -\$7,242$$

$$NPV_{A5} = \frac{\$17,000}{(1.12)^1} - \$29,000 = -\$13,821$$

$$NPV_{A6} = \frac{\$20,000}{(1.12)^1} - \$30,000 = -\$12,143$$

$$E(NPV_A) = 0.42(\$11,340) + 0.22(-\$9,707) + 0.14(\$13,804)$$

$$+ 0.07(-\$7,242) + 0.02(-\$13,821) + 0.13(-\$12,143)$$

$$= \$2,198$$

Design B

$$NPV_{B1} = \frac{\$60,000}{(1.12)^1} - \$48,000 + \frac{\$80,000}{(1.12)^2} - \frac{\$60,000}{(1.12)^1}$$

$$= \$15,776$$

$$NPV_{B2} = \frac{\$60,000}{(1.12)^1} - \$48,000 + \frac{\$5,000}{(1.12)^2} - \frac{\$20,000}{(1.12)^1}$$

$$= -\$8,300$$

$$NPV_{B3} = \frac{\$65,000}{(1.12)^1} - \$50,000 + \frac{\$80,000}{(1.12)^2} - \frac{\$60,000}{(1.12)^1}$$

$$= \$18,240$$

$$NPV_{B4} = \frac{\$65,000}{(1.12)^1} - \$50,000 + \frac{\$5,000}{(1.12)^2} - \frac{\$20,000}{(1.12)^1}$$

$$= -\$5,835$$

$$NPV_{B5} = \frac{\$15,000}{(1.12)^1} - \$28,000 = -\$14,607$$

$$NPV_{B6} = \frac{\$18,000}{(1.12)^1} - \$30,000 = -\$13,929$$

$$E(NPV_B) = 0.29(\$15,776) + 0.12(-\$8,300) + 0.24(\$18,240)$$

$$+ 0.10(-\$5,835) + 0.05(-\$14,607) + 0.20(-\$13,929)$$

$$= \$3,857$$

C. The risk of these two alternatives can be examined by calculating the coefficient of variation for each.

Design A

Outcome (1)	Deviation from mean (2)	(Deviation)^2 (3)	Probability (4)	(3) × (4) = (5)
$11,340	$9,142	$83,576,164	0.42	$35,101,989
-9,707	-11,905	141,729,030	0.22	31,180,387
13,804	11,606	134,699,240	0.14	18,857,894
-7,242	-9,440	89,113,600	0.07	6,237,952
-13,821	-16,019	256,608,360	0.02	5,132,167
-12,143	-14,341	205,664,280	0.13	26,736,356
				$\sigma_A^2 = \$123,246,745$

$$\sigma_A = \sqrt{\$123,246,745} = \$11,102$$

$$V_A = \frac{\sigma_A}{E(NPV_A)} = \frac{\$11,102}{\$2,198} = 5.051$$

Design B

Outcome (1)	Deviation from mean (2)	(Deviation)^2 (3)	Probability (4)	(3) × (4) = (5)
$15,776	$11,919	$142,062,560	0.29	$41,198,142
-8,300	-12,157	147,792,650	0.12	17,735,118
18,240	14,383	206,870,690	0.24	49,648,966
-5,835	-9,692	93,934,864	0.10	9,393,486
-14,607	-18,464	340,919,300	0.05	17,045,965
-13,929	-17,786	316,341,800	0.20	63,268,360
				$\sigma_B^2 = \$198,290,037$

$$\sigma_B = \sqrt{\$198,290,037} = \$14,082$$

$$V_B = \frac{\sigma_B}{E(NPV_B)} = \frac{\$14,082}{\$3,857} = 3.651$$

Design B's coefficient of variation is approximately 28% smaller than that of design A, indicating that it is a considerably less risky alternative.

D.   Typically, it is difficult to determine what choice a decision maker should make between risky alternatives without explicit information concerning their risk aversion or utility function. However, in this case, design B has both a greater expected return and a lower risk. Therefore, design B it dominates design A and would be chosen regardless of the decision maker's degree of risk aversion. Note, however, that this does not preclude the possibility that a very risk averse individual might decline both projects, because they are quite risky. Design B, although superior to design A, still entails a good deal of risk relative to the expected return. One cannot say for sure that Klingon Vulcan would choose to go ahead with design B without more knowledge about the risk-return tradeoff function used in such decision problems.

Chapter 18

CAPITAL BUDGETING

To derive and manage an optimal capital budget, economically sound capital budgeting decision rules must be developed and employed. Such rules consistently lead to the acceptance of projects that will increase the value of the firm. When the discounted present-value of expected future cash flows exceeds the cost of investment, the project represents a worthy use of scarce resources and should be accepted. When the discounted present-value of expected future cash flows is less than the cost of investment, the project represents an inappropriate use of scarce resources and should be rejected. In other words, an investment project is attractive and should be pursued as long as the discounted net present-value (NPV) of cash inflows is greater than the discounted net present-value of the investment requirement, or net cash outlay. Because the attractiveness of individual projects increases with the magnitude of this difference, high NPV projects are inherently more appealing and are preferred to low NPV projects. Any investment project that is incapable of generating sufficient cash inflows to cover necessary cash outlays, when both are expressed on a present-value basis, should not be undertaken. NPV analysis represents a practical application of the marginal concept, in which the marginal revenues and marginal costs of investment projects are considered on a present-value basis. Use of the NPV technique in the evaluation of alternative investment projects allows managers to apply the principles of marginal analysis in a simple and clear manner. The widespread practical use of the NPV technique also lends support to the view of value maximization as the prime objective pursued by managers in the capital budgeting process.

CHAPTER OUTLINE

I. **CAPITAL BUDGETING PROCESS**

    A. **What is Capital Budgeting?:** Capital budgeting is the process of planning expenditures that generate cash flows expected to stretch beyond one year.

        1. Capital refers to financial resources used to fund production.

        2. A budget is a detailed plan of projected cash inflows and outflows over future periods.

        3. Well-managed firms go to great lengths to develop good capital budgeting proposals.

    B. **Project Classification Types:** Firms generally classify projects into a number of categories, and analyze projects in each category somewhat differently.

1.   Replacement projects consist of expenditures necessary to replace worn-out or damaged equipment.

2.   Cost reduction projects include expenditures to replace serviceable but obsolete plant and equipment.

3.   Safety and environmental projects are mandatory investments that are often nonrevenue-producing in nature.

4.   Expansion projects increase the availability of existing products and services.

II.   STEPS IN CAPITAL BUDGETING

A.   Sequence of Project Valuation: In theory, the capital budgeting process involves six logical steps.

1.   The cost of the project must be determined.

2.   Management must estimate the expected cash flows from the project, including the value of the asset at a specified terminal date.

3.   The riskiness of projected cash flows must be estimated.

4.   Given the riskiness of projected cash flows and the cost of funds under prevailing economic conditions as reflected by the riskless rate, R_F, the firm must determine the appropriate discount rate, or cost of capital, at which the project's cash flows are to be discounted.

5.   Expected cash flows must be converted to a present-value to obtain a clear estimate of the investment project's value to the firm.

6.   The present-value of expected cash inflows is compared with the required outlay, or cost, of the project.

   a.   If the present-value of cash flows derived from a project exceeds the cost of investment, the project should be accepted.

B.   Cash Flow Estimation: The most important and difficult step in capital budgeting is cash flows estimation.

1.   For the capital budgeting process to be successful, expected cash inflows and outflows must be estimated within a consistent and unbiased framework.

C. **Incremental Cash Flow Evaluation:** In capital budgeting, it is critical that decisions be based strictly on cash flows, the actual dollars that flow into and out of the company during each time period.

1. Relevant cash flows for capital budgeting purposes are the incremental cash flows attributable to a project.

   a. Incremental cash flows are the period-by-period changes in net cash flows due to an investment project:

$$Project\ CF_t = \begin{array}{c} CF_t\ for\ Corporation \\ with\ Project \end{array} - \begin{array}{c} CF_t\ for\ Corporation \\ without\ Project \end{array}.$$

2. Accounting income statements provide a crucial basis for estimating the relevant cash flows from investment projects.

   a. Accounting information must be adjusted to reflect the economic pattern of inflows and outflows so that value-maximizing investment decisions can be made.

III. CASH FLOW ESTIMATION EXAMPLE

A. **Project Description:** This example illustrates several important aspects of cash flow analysis and shows how they relate to one another.

1. Cash flow analysis involves estimating cash inflows and investment outlays associated with a project.

B. **Cash Flow Estimation and Analysis:** Computer spreadsheet software makes sophisticated cash flow analysis possible for even highly complex projects.

IV. CAPITAL BUDGETING DECISION RULES

A. **Net Present-value Analysis:** NPV analysis measures the current-dollar difference between the marginal revenues and marginal costs for individual investment projects:

$$NPV_i = \sum_{t=1}^{n} \frac{E(CF_{it})}{(1 + k_i)^t} - \sum_{t=1}^{n} \frac{C_{it}}{(1 + k_i)^t}$$

where NPV_i is the NPV of the *i*th project, $E(CF_{it})$ represents the expected cash inflows in the *t*th year, k_i is the risk-adjusted discount rate, and C_{it} is cash outflows.

1. If NPV > 0, the project should be accepted.

2. If NPV < 0, the project should be rejected.

B. **Profitability Index or Benefit/Cost Ratio Analysis:** The PI or B/C ratio shows the *relative* profitability of any project, or the present-value of benefits per dollar of cost:

$$PI = \frac{PV \text{ of Cash Inflows}}{PV \text{ of Cash Outflows}} = \frac{\sum_{t=1}^{n} [E(CF_{it})/(1 + k_i)^t]}{\sum_{t=1}^{n} [C_{it}/(1 + k_i)^t]}.$$

1. PI > 1 indicates a desirable investment project and NPV > 0.

2. PI < 1 indicates an undesirable investment project and NPV < 0.

3. For alternative projects of unequal size, PI and NPV criteria can give different project rankings.

C. **Internal Rate of Return Analysis:** The internal rate of return is the discount rate that equates the present-value of future receipts to the initial cost of a project. To calculate the internal rate of return k_i^*, simply set the NPV formula equal to zero:

$$NPV_i = 0 = \sum_{t=1}^{n} \frac{E(CF_{it})}{(1 + k_i^*)^t} - \sum_{t=1}^{n} \frac{C_{it}}{(1 + k_i^*)^t}.$$

1. The discount rate that produces a zero net present-value is the internal rate of return earned by the project.

2. Projects should be accepted when IRR > k, and rejected when IRR < k.

3. When capital is scarce, the IRR can be used to derive a project rank ordering from most desirable to least desirable projects.

D. **Payback Period Analysis:** The payback period is the expected number of years of operation required to recover an initial investment:

Payback Period = Number of Years to Recover Investment.

1. The payback period is the breakeven time period.

2. The shorter the payback period, the more desirable the investment project.

V. PROJECT SELECTION

A. **Decision Rule Conflict Problem:** Appropriate decision criteria consider the time value of money, and rank projects according to their impact on the value of the firm.

    1. Ranking consistency is a feature of relevant capital budgeting criteria.

B. **Reasons for Decision Rule Conflict:** NPV, PI and IRR criteria consider time value and valuation effects, but each incorporate assumptions that differently affect project rankings.

    1. NPV is an *absolute* measure of project attractiveness.

        a. NPV analysis can create a bias for larger as opposed to smaller projects.

    2. PI is a *relative* measure of project attractiveness.

        a. When capital is scarce, the PI method can lead a better project mix.

    3. In the IRR method, excess cash flows are reinvested at the IRR.

        a. The IRR can overstate project attractiveness when reinvestment of excess cash flows at the IRR is not possible.

C. **Ranking Reversal Problem:** A conflict can arise between NPV and IRR rankings when projects differ in the size and timing of cash flows.

    1. Changes in the appropriate discount rate can lead to reversals in project rankings.

    2. A ranking reversal occurs when a switch in project standing occurs with an increase in the relevant discount rate.

    3. The crossover discount rate is an interest factor that equates NPV for two or more projects. It is a ranking reversal point.

D. **Making the Correct Investment Decision:** Many comparisons between alternative investment projects involve neither crossing NPV profiles nor crossover discount rates.

1. Logic suggests that the NPV ranking should dominate because that method results in a value maximizing selection of projects.

2. For a firm with limited resources, the PI approach allocates scarce resources to projects with the greatest relative effect on value.

VI. **COST OF CAPITAL**

A. **Component Cost of Debt Financing:** The component cost of debt is the interest rate that investors require on debt, adjusted for taxes.

1. The after-tax cost of debt financing is:

$$k_d = \text{(Interest Rate)} \times (1.0 - \text{Tax Rate}).$$

B. **Component Cost of Equity Financing:** The component cost of equity is the rate of return stockholders require on common stock.

1. The cost of equity consists of a risk-free rate of return, R_F, plus a risk premium, R_P:
$$k_e = R_F + R_P.$$

2. k_e and R_P are sometimes estimated using the capital asset pricing model (CAPM). Risk is measured by the variability of return relative to the variability of returns on all stocks, or the beta coefficient, ß:

$$R_i = \alpha_i + \text{ß}_i R_M + e$$

where R_i is the weekly or monthly return on a given stock, and R_M is a similar market return

a. Low-risk stocks have betas less than 1.0; high-risk stocks have betas greater than 1.0.

b. The CAPM estimate of the required rate of return on any given stock is:

$$k_e = R_F + \text{ß}(k_M - R_F),$$

where k_M - R_F is the market risk premium.

3. Another common technique estimates the required return on equity as four or five percent plus the risk premium paid on a firm's long-term bonds.

4. A further method for determining the cost of equity is to use a constant growth model. If earnings, dividends, and the stock price all grow at the same rate, then:

$$\text{Required Return on Equity} = \frac{\text{Expected Dividend}}{\text{Current Stock Price}} + \text{Expected Growth Rate},$$

$$k_e = \frac{D_1}{P_0} + g.$$

C. **Weighted Average Cost of Capital:** The firm should be viewed as an ongoing concern, and the cost of capital should be calculated as a weighted average of the various types of funds it uses.

1. The weighted average cost of capital is the marginal cost of a composite dollar of debt and equity financing.

2. The proper set of weights to employ in computing the weighted average cost of capital is determined by the firm's optimal capital structure.

3. The optimal capital structure is the combination of debt and equity financing that minimizes the firm's overall weighted average cost of capital.

VII. OPTIMAL CAPITAL BUDGET

A. **Investment Opportunity Schedule:** The optimal capital budget is the funding level required to underwrite a value-maximizing level of new investment.

1. The investment opportunity schedule (IOS) shows the pattern of returns for all of the firm's potential investment projects.

2. To define the optimal capital budget, both the returns *and* costs of potential projects must be considered.

B. **Marginal Cost of Capital:** The marginal cost of capital (MCC) is the extra financing cost necessary to fund an additional investment project, expressed on a percentage basis.

1. When IOS = MCC, all profitable investment projects have been accepted.

C. **Postaudit:** The postaudit is a careful examination of actual and predicted results, coupled with a detailed reconciliation of any differences.

1. In the postaudit process, conscious or subconscious biases can be observed and eliminated; new forecasting methods can be sought as their need becomes apparent.

VIII. **SUMMARY**

PROBLEMS & SOLUTIONS

P18.1 *Decision Rule Criteria.* *Indicate whether the net present-value, profitability index, and/ or internal rate of return method of capital budget evaluation is most appropriate in each of the following decision situations. Explain your answer.*

A. *Access to capital is strictly limited.*

B. *Cash flows obtained during the life of the project can only be reinvested at the cost of capital rate.*

C. *The company's entire capital budget is just sufficient to fund its most attractive investment opportunity.*

D. *The company has easy access to ample capital resources.*

E. *Capital is scarce and the size of investment projects tends to vary widely.*

P18.1 *SOLUTION*

A. Profitability index method. When access to capital is strictly limited, use of the profitability index method will insure that projects with the highest relative net payoff are undertaken first.

B. Net present-value and/or profitability index methods. If cash flows obtained during the life of the project can only be reinvested at the cost of capital rate, then use of the NPV or PI method will result in the most accurate representation of the value of alternate investment projects. Use of the IRR method, which is based on an assumption of reinvestment at the IRR rate, would result in an overstatement of the attractiveness of the firm's most attractive investment projects.

C. Internal rate of return method. When the company's entire capital budget is required to fund its most attractive investment opportunity, project cash flows can be reinvested at the IRR rate, and use of the IRR method is most appropriate.

D. Net present-value and/or the internal rate of return methods. Depending on cash flow reinvestment opportunities, when a company has easy access to ample capital resources, either the NPV or IRR method can be relied upon to provide a useful ranking of the relative desirability of various projects.

E. Profitability index method. When capital is scarce and the size of investment projects tends to vary widely, use of the profitability index method will insure that projects with the highest relative net payoff are undertaken first.

P18.2 **Project Ranking**. *Indicate whether each of the following statements is true or false. Explain why.*

A. *By accepting all projects with NPV > 0, the value of the firm is maximized.*

B. *The IRR of a project equals the cost of capital when PI = 1.*

C. *Under capital rationing, the NPV approach is preferred to the PI for ranking project attractiveness.*

D. *Holding all else equal, doubling the size of project revenues and costs leaves the IRR unaffected.*

E. *When NPV > 0, the IRR is below the cost of capital.*

P18.2 **SOLUTION**

A. True. By definition, value maximization requires undertaking all NPV > 0 projects.

B. True. When the IRR equals the cost of capital, the PV of cash flows equals the cost of the project, and PI = 1.

C. False. With capital rationing, use of the PI criterion ensures that projects with the highest return per dollar of investment will be adopted.

D. True. Holding all else equal, changes in the size of projects leave the IRR unaffected.

E. False. When the IRR is below the cost of capital, NPV < 0.

P18.3 **NPV Analysis**. *Dr. Robert Romano, chief of staff at County General Hospital, is contemplating the purchase of additional magnetic resonance imaging (MRI) equipment. Romano's staff has generated the following projections for a five-year planning horizon:*

	Model 911 Targa	**Model 911 GT2**
Cost	*$2 million*	*$2.75 million*
PV of expected cash flow when k = 12%	*$3 million*	*$4 million*

A.   Calculate the net present-value for each type of equipment. Which is more desirable according to the NPV criterion?

B.   Calculate the profitability index for each. Which is more desirable according to the PI criterion?

C.   Under what conditions would either or both pieces of equipment be purchased?

P18.3 Solution

   A.   Model 911 Targa

$$\text{NPV}_{\text{Targa}} = \text{PV Cash Flow - Cost}$$

$$= \$3,000,000 - \$2,000,000$$

$$= \$1,000,000$$

                                 Model 911 GT2

$$\text{NPV}_{\text{GT2}} = \text{PV Cash Flow - Cost}$$

$$= \$4,000,000 - \$2,750,000$$

$$= \$1,250,000$$

Because $\text{NPV}_{\text{GT2}} > \text{NPV}_{\text{Targa}}$ the GT2 is ranked ahead of the Targa alternative, using the NPV criterion. However, because NPV > 0 for each, both are highly acceptable and would be profitable.

B.   <u>Model 911 Targa</u>

$$PI_{Targa} = \frac{PV\ Cash\ Flow}{Cost}$$

$$= \$3,000,000/\$2,000,00$$

$$= 1.50$$

<u>Model 911 GT2</u>

$$PI_{GT2} = \frac{PV\ Cash\ Flow}{Cost}$$

$$= \$4,000,000/\$2,750,000$$

$$= 1.45$$

Because $PI_{Targa} > PI_{GT2}$, the Targa is ranked ahead of the GT2 alternative using the PI criterion. However, because PI > 1 for each service, both are acceptable and would be profitable.

C. Should the company have relatively abundant capital resources, or at least $4.75 million available for investment, both types of equipment would be purchased. However, when capital resources are scarce, use of the PI criterion, and purchase of the Targa would result in scarce funds being used where their relative impact on value is greatest.

P18.4 **NPV Analysis.** *The Three's Company is considering two mutually exclusive capital budgeting projects. These projects have equal lives of 2 years, and similar costs of $8,000. Relevant cash flow data for the two projects are as follows:*

Project 1			
Year 1		Year 2	
Pr	*Cash Flow*	*Pr*	*Cash Flow*
0.35	$4,000	0.25	$5,000
0.40	5,000	0.50	6,000
0.25	6,000	0.25	7,000

Project 2

	Year 1		Year 2
Pr	**Cash Flow**	**Pr**	**Cash Flow**
0.20	$(200)	0.10	$1,000
0.30	4,000	0.30	4,500
0.30	5,000	0.35	6,500
0.20	7,000	0.25	8,000

A. What is the expected value of the annual cash flows from each project?

B. Using 10% for the more risky project and 8% for the other, and using variability of cash flows as an indicator of risk, what is the risk-adjusted NPV of each project?

C. Which project should Three's accept?

P18.4 **SOLUTION**

A.

Project 1

Year 1:			Year 2:		
0.35(4,000)	=	$1,400	0.25(5,000)	=	$1,250
0.40(5,000)	=	2,000	0.50(6,000)	=	3,000
0.25(6,000)	=	1,500	0.25(7,000)	=	1,750
$E(CF_{11})$	=	$4,900	$E(CF_{12})$	=	$6,000

Project 2

Year 1:			Year 2:		
0.20(-200)	=	$ -40	0.10(1,000)	=	$ 100
0.30(4,000)	=	1,200	0.30(4,500)	=	1,350
0.30(5,000)	=	1,500	0.35(6,500)	=	2,275
0.20(7,000)	=	1,400	0.25(8,000)	=	2,000
$E(CF_{21})$	=	$4,060	$E(CF_{22})$	=	$5,725

B. Project 2 appears to be more risky because by inspection the variability of cash flows is obviously higher. Thus, project 1 will be discounted at 8% and project 2 will be discounted at 10%.

Project 1

$$NPV_1 = E(CF_{11}) \times (PVIF, N = 1, i = 8\%)$$

$$+ E(CF_{12}) \times (PVIF, N = 2, i = 8\%) - C$$

$$= \$4,900(0.926) + \$6,000(0.857) - \$8,000$$

$$= \$1,679.40$$

Project 2

$$NPV_2 = E(CF_{21}) \times (PVIF, n = 1, i = 10\%)$$

$$+ E(CF_{22}) \times (PVIF, n = 2, i = 10\%) - C$$

$$= \$4,060(0.909) + \$5,725(0.826) - \$8,000$$

$$= \$419.39$$

C.   Project 1 should be chosen because it has the higher risk-adjusted NPV.

P18.5   ***Investment Project Choice.***   *Boris Badenov is a management trainee with Rocky & Bullwinkle, Inc. Badenov has been asked to evaluate two innovative pieces of machinery that might be used to replace obsolete equipment. The following annual cost savings (cash flows) will be generated over the four-year useful lives of the new machines:*

	Probability	*Cash Flow*
Alternative 1	*0.3*	*$2,900*
	0.5	*3,500*
	0.2	*4,100*
Alternative 2	*0.3*	*$0*
	0.5	*4,000*
	0.2	*8,000*

Whichever piece of machinery is chosen, the total investment cost is the same, $4,000.

A. *Badenov uses a discount rate of 12% for cash flows with a high degree of dispersion and a 10% rate for less risky cash values. Which machine has the highest expected net present-value?*

P18.5   SOLUTION

A.   The expected values of cash flows for each alternative are:

	Alternative 1	
Probability	Cash Flow	Expected Cash Flow (1) × (2)
0.3	$2,900	$ 870
0.5	3,500	1,750
0.2	4,100	820
		$E(CF_1) = \$3,440$

	Alternative 2	
Probability	Cash Flow	Expected Cash Flow (1) × (2)
0.3	$ 0	$ 0
0.5	4,000	2,000
0.2	8,000	1,600
		$E(CF_2) = \$3,600$

Alternative 2 is riskier because it has the greater variability in its cash flows. This is obvious from an inspection of the distributions of possible returns and could be verified by calculating the standard deviations of each alternative.

Alternative 1

$$\sigma_1 = \sqrt{(\$2{,}900 - \$3{,}440)^2(0.3) + (\$3{,}500 - \$3{,}440)^2(0.5)}$$

$$\overline{+ (\$4{,}100 - \$3{,}440)^2(0.2)}$$

$$= \$420$$

$$V_1 \;=\; \frac{\sigma_1}{E(CF_1)} \;=\; \frac{\$420}{\$3,440} \;=\; 0.122$$

Alternative 2

$$\sigma_2 \;=\; \sqrt{(\$0 - \$3,600)^2(0.3) + (\$4,000 - \$3,600)^2(0.5)}$$

$$\overline{+ (\$8,000 - \$3,600)^2(0.2)}$$

$$=\; \$2,800$$

$$V_2 \;=\; \frac{\sigma_2}{E(CF_2)} \;=\; \frac{\$2,800}{\$3,600} \;=\; 0.778$$

Obviously, Alternative 2 is to be evaluated at the 12% cost of capital, while alternative 1 requires only a 10% cost of capital.

$$NPV_1 \;=\; \sum_{t=1}^{4} \frac{\$3,440}{(1.10)^t} - \$4,000$$

$$=\; \$3,440(PVIFA, n = 4, i = 10\%) - \$4,000$$

$$=\; \$3,440(3.170) - \$4,000$$

$$=\; \$6,905$$

$$NPV_2 \;=\; \sum_{t=1}^{4} \frac{\$3,600}{(1.12)^t} - \$4,000$$

$$=\; \$3,600(PVIFA, n = 4, i = 12\%) - \$4,000$$

$$=\; \$3,600(3.037) - \$4,000$$

$$=\; \$6,933$$

Because alternative 2 has the higher risk adjusted net present-value, it is the appropriate investment.

P18.6   ***NPV Analysis.*** *Louie De Palma, cab dispatcher for Sunshine Cab Company, must choose between two mutually exclusive investment projects. Each project costs $6,000 and has an expected life of four years. Annual net cash flows from each project begin one year after the initial investment is made and have the following characteristics:*

	Annual Net Probability	**Cash Flow**
Project A	*0.05*	*$2,200*
	0.40	*3,300*
	0.25	*3,800*
	0.30	*3,600*
Project B	*0.15*	*$ 300*
	0.35	*3,700*
	0.22	*6,900*
	0.28	*6,200*

De Palma has decided to evaluate the riskier project at a 14% cost of capital and the less risky project at 12%.

A.   *What is the expected value of the annual net cash flows from each project?*

B.   *What is the risk-adjusted NPV of each project?*

P18.6   ***SOLUTION***

A. $E(CF_A)$ = $2,200(0.05) + $3,300(0.40) + $3,800(0.25) + $3,600(0.30)$

= $3,460

$E(CF_B)$ = $300(0.15) + $3,700(0.35) + $6,900(0.22) + $6,200(0.28)$

= $4,594

B.   Project B is the riskier project because it has the greater variability in its expected cash flows. Accordingly, project B is evaluated at a 14% cost of capital versus 12% for project A. The net present-values for each project are:

NPV_A = $3,460(PVIFA, n = 4, i = 12%) - $6,000

= $3,460(3.037) - $6,000

$$= \quad \$4,508$$

$$\text{NPV}_\text{B} \quad = \quad \$4,594(\text{PVIFA}, n = 4, i = 14\%) - \$6,000$$

$$= \quad \$4,594(2.914) - \$6,000$$

$$= \quad \$7,387$$

The above calculations indicate that De Palma should accept project B despite its higher risk.

P18.7   ***Cash Flow Estimation.*** *The ASU Co-op, a nonprofit student organization, runs a Laundromat located in the main dormitory complex at a large southwestern university. The latest monthly operating statement for the Laundromat is presented below.*

Revenues		
5,000 loads at $1.50 per load		*$7,500*
Costs:		
Rent	*$750*	
Maintenance	*500*	
Depreciation	*500*	
Electricity	*2,500*	
Water	*1,500*	
Miscellaneous Expenses	*1,000*	*$6,750*
Profit		*$ 750*

The month represented by this statement is typical, although there is considerable variation from month to month. Of the expenses incurred in the operation of the Laundromat, only electricity, water, and miscellaneous expenses are directly related to the level of output. These variable cost average $1 per load (=($2,500 + $1,500 + $1,000)/1,000). (Note: Maintenance is done under a service contract for a fixed fee).

Currently, the Co-op is considering the purchase of dry-cleaning equipment for the Laundromat. The dry-cleaning equipment costs $50,000 and has an expected life of three years with a zero salvage value. At a price of $3 per load, it is estimated that 1,000 loads of dry-cleaning per month will be the average use factor for the equipment. Cleaning fluid and electricity costs per load are 50¢ and 20¢, respectively. Additional annual maintenance costs of $500 are also expected. And finally, it is expected that by installing dry-cleaning equipment overall usage of laundry equipment will fall by 500 loads per month.

A.   *Develop the relevant cash flows for an analysis of this decision.*

B. *Assume the Co-op has the capital necessary to purchase the dry-cleaning equipment and that it places a 6% opportunity cost on those funds. Should the equipment be purchased? Why or why not?*

P18.7 **SOLUTION**

A.

<u>Initial Investment</u>:	$50,000
<u>Incremental Annual Revenues</u>:	
(1,000 loads/mo. × 12 × $3)	$36,000
<u>Incremental Annual Costs</u>:	
Cleaning Fluid: (1,000 loads/mo. × 12 × $0.50)	6,000
Electricity (1,000 loads/mo. × 12 × $0.20)	2,400
Maintenance	500
Loss of profit contribution from laundry (500 loads/mo. × 12 × $0.50)	<u>3,000</u>
	<u>$1,900</u>
<u>Incremental Annual Cash Flows</u>	<u>$24,100</u>

B.
$$\text{NPV} = \sum_{t=1}^{3} \frac{\text{Incremental Annual Cash Flows}}{(1.06)^t} - \text{Initial Investment}$$

$$= \sum_{t=1}^{3} \frac{\$24,100}{(1.06)^t} - \$50,000$$

$$= \$24,100(\text{PVIFA}, n = 3, i = 6\%) - \$50,000$$

$$= \$24,100(2.673) - \$50,000$$

$$= \$14,419.30$$

The dry-cleaning equipment has a positive net present-value and, therefore, should be purchased.

P18.8 ***NPV and PI***. *Z-Best Corporation is a small and rapidly growing company that specializes in carpet-cleaning and restoring fire- and flood-ravaged buildings. The company has the opportunity to complete the following services contracts:*

	Project A: *Hotel del* *Coronado* *Restoration*	*Project B:* *DBL-Miraman* *Station* *Cleanup*
Cost	*$ 500,000*	*$200,000*
PV of expected cash flow *@ k = 15%*	*1,000,000*	*500,000*

A. Calculate the net present-value for each service. Which is more desirable according to the NPV criterion?

B. Calculate the profitability index for each service. Which is more desirable according to the PI criterion?

C. Under what conditions would either or both of the services be undertaken?

P18.8   **SOLUTION**

A.   <u>Project A</u>

NPV_A = PV Cash Flow - Cost

= $1,000,000 - $500,000

= $500,000

<u>Project B</u>

NPV_B = PV Cash Flow - Cost

= $500,000 - $200,000

= $300,000

Because $NPV_A > NPV_B$, Project A service is ranked ahead of the Project B alternative, using the NPV criterion. However, because NPV > 0 for each service, both are acceptable and profitable.

B.

Project A

$$PI_A = \frac{PV \ Cash \ Flow}{Cost}$$

$$= \$1,000,000/\$500,000$$

$$= 2$$

Project B

$$PI_B = \frac{PV \ Cash \ Flow}{Cost}$$

$$= \$500,000/\$200,000$$

$$= 2.5$$

Because $PI_B > PI_A$, the project B alternative is ranked ahead of the project A alternative using the PI criterion. However, because $PI > 0$ for each service, both are acceptable and profitable.

C. Should the company have relatively abundant capital resources, or at least $700,000 available for investment, both services should be initiated. However, when capital resources are scarce, use of the PI criterion, and initiation of project B first, would result in scarce funds being used where their relative impact on value is greatest.

P18.9 **Project Ranking.** *Dr. Elizabeth Corday is considering three investment alternatives for expanding her medical practice. Project A, involves expanding her waiting room to speed the flow of patients. Project B, involves the purchase of new diagnostic equipment, thereby allowing her to handle patients faster. Project C, involves opening a new office in a suburban mall location. Expected net cash flows (before investment costs) over the next five years and investment requirements for each project are given below:*

	Project		
	A	*B*	*C*
Annual Net Cash Flows	*$8,000*	*$20,000*	*$35,000*
Investment Cost	*20,000*	*50,000*	*100,000*

A.   Rank each project according to the NPV criterion using an 8% cost of capital.

B.   Using the same cost of capital, rank each project according to the PI criterion.

C.   Rank each project according to the IRR criterion.

P18.9   **SOLUTION**

A.   In the NPV approach, NPV = PV cash flows - Cost. Therefore,

$$NPV_A = \$8,000(PVIFA, n = 5, i = 8\%) - \$20,000$$

$$= \$8,000(3.9927) - \$20,000$$

$$= \$11,941.60$$

$$NPV_B = \$20,000(PVIFA, n = 5, i = 8\%) - \$50,000$$

$$= \$20,000(3.9927) - \$50,000$$

$$= \$29,854$$

$$NPV_C = \$35,000(PVIFA, n = 5, i = 8\%) - \$100,000$$

$$= \$35,000(3.9927) - \$100,000$$

$$= \$39,744.50$$

Because $NPV_C > NPV_B > NPV_A$, a project rank ordering using the NPV criterion is C > B > A.

B.   In the PI approach, PI = PV cash flows/Cost. Therefore,

$$PI_A = \$8,000(3.9927)/\$20,000$$

$$= 1.597$$

$$PI_B = \$20,000(3.9927)/\$50,000$$

$$= 1.597$$

$$PI_C = \$35,000(3.9927)/\$100,000$$

$$= 1.397$$

Because $PI_A = PI_B > PI_C$, a project rank ordering using the PI criterion is A = B > C.

It is interesting to note how project B, which is 2.5 times larger than project A, is preferred to project A using the NPV criterion despite their equivalence using the PI approach. Note also how the relatively large size of project C causes it to be preferred using the NPV approach despite the fact that it is the least attractive project on a PI basis.

C. The IRR is the interest rate which equates the PV of cash flows and investment costs. Thus,

$$PV \text{ cash flows} = Cost$$

$$CF(PVIFA, n = 5, i = IRR) = Cost$$

$$(PVIFA, n = 5, i = IRR) = \frac{Cost}{CF}$$

$$\text{For project A: } (PVIFA, n = 5, i = IRR) = \frac{\$20,000}{\$8,000}$$

$$= 2.5$$

From the present-value tables, notice that this interest factor falls between 28% and 32%. Interpolating finds:

i	PVIFA(n = 5)
28%	2.5320
28% + ?	2.5000
32%	2.3452

because this factor covers 0.171 or 17.1% (= 320/1,868) of the distance between 28% and 32%, the relevant $IRR_A = 28.6\%$ [$= 28\% + 0.171(4\%)$].

The IRR for project B is the same as above because:

For project B: $(\text{PVIFA}, n = 5, i = \text{IRR}) = \dfrac{\$50,000}{\$20,000}$

$$= 2.5000$$

And finally,

For project C: $(\text{PVIFA}, n = 5, i = \text{IRR}) = \dfrac{\$100,000}{\$35,000}$

$$= 2.857$$

From the present-value tables, one can see that this interest factor falls between 20% and 24%. By interpolation:

i	PVIFA(n = 5)
20%	2.9906
20% + ?	2.8570
24%	2.7454

because this factor covers 0.545 or 54.5% (= 1,336/2,452) of the distance between 20% and 24%, the relevant $\text{IRR}_A = 22.2\%$ [= 20% + 0.545(4%)].

Therefore, because $\text{IRR}_A = \text{IRR}_B > \text{IRR}_C$, a project rank ordering using the IRR criterion is A = B > C.

P18.10   ***Cost of Capital.*** *Nirvana Products, Inc., is a rapidly growing chain of retail outlets offering brand-name merchandise at discount prices. A security analyst's report issued by a national brokerage firm indicates that debt yielding 13%, composes 50% of Nirvana's overall capital structure. Furthermore, both earnings and dividends are expected to grow at a rate of 12% per year.*

Currently, common stock in the company is priced at $20 and it should pay $0.60 per share in dividends during the coming year. This yield compares favorably with the 6% return currently available on risk-free securities and the 12% average for all common stocks, given the company's estimated beta of 1.5.

A.   *Calculate Nirvana's component cost of equity using both the capital asset pricing model and the dividend yield plus expected growth model.*

B.   *Assuming a 40% marginal federal-plus-state income tax rate, calculate Nirvana's weighted average cost of capital.*

P18.10   SOLUTION

A.   In the capital asset pricing model (CAPM) approach, the required return on equity is:

$$k_e = R_F + b(k_M - R_F)$$

where k_e is the cost of equity, R_F is the risk-free rate, b is stock-price beta, and k_M is the return on the market as a whole. Therefore,

$$k_e = 6\% + 1.5(12\% - 6\%)$$

$$= 15\%$$

In the dividend yield plus expected growth model approach, the required return on equity is:

$$k_e = \frac{D}{P} + g$$

Where D is the expected dividend during the coming period, P is the current price of the firm's common stock, and g is the expected growth rate.
Therefore,

$$k_e = \frac{\$0.60}{\$20} + 0.12$$

$$= 0.15 \text{ or } 15\%$$

B.   Given a 40% state plus federal income tax rate, the after-tax component cost of debt is:

$$\text{After-tax component cost of debt, } k_d = \text{Interest rate} \times (1.0 - \text{tax rate})$$

$$= 0.13 \times (1.0 - 0.4)$$

$$= 0.078 \text{ or } 7.8\%$$

Therefore,

$$\text{Weighted average} \atop \text{cost of capital} = {\text{Debt percentage} \times k_d \atop + \text{ Equity percentage} \times k_e}$$

$$= 0.5(0.078) + 0.5(0.15)$$

$$= 0.114 \text{ or } 11.4\%$$

Chapter 19

ORGANIZATION STRUCTURE AND CORPORATE GOVERNANCE

Problems in corporate governance exist to the extent that there are unresolved material conflicts between the self-seeking goals of (agent) managers and the value maximization goal of (principal) stockholders. "Agency costs" incurred by stockholders are reflected in expenses for managerial monitoring, excessive managerial compensation, the over-consumption of perquisites by managers, and lost opportunities due to excessive risk avoidance. Questions about corporate effectiveness are ultimately questions about corporate governance. Corporate governance is the system of controls that helps the corporation effectively manage, administer and direct economic resources. If a corporation fails to effectively command its economic resources, this corporate failure can often be blamed on a similar failure of its corporate governance mechanism.

In some instances, corporate internal control systems at giant U.S. corporations have failed to deal effectively with economic changes, especially slow growth and the requirement for exit from declining industries. However, in many parts of the economy, new and smaller organizations are emerging to take the place of giant corporations. In these agile organizations, management incentives are closely tied to performance, decentralization is common, and obligations to creditors and stockholders are clearly specified.

Thus, although it is entirely valid to express concerns with the adaptive capability of some specific corporations, pronouncements concerning the "death" of the modern corporation seem premature. The corporate form has endured and flourished because it is a useful and effective means for gathering and deploying economic resources. Don't bet against it.

CHAPTER OUTLINE

I.   ORGANIZATION STRUCTURE

      A.   What is Organization Structure? The optimal design of the firm is the organization type that most successfully meets customer demands.

           1.   Organization structure is described by the vertical and horizontal relationships among the firm, its customers and suppliers.

                 a.   A vertical relation is a business connection between companies at *different* points along the production-distribution chain from raw materials, to finished goods, to delivered products, e.g. GM and U.S. Steel.

b.   A horizontal relation is a business affiliation between companies at the *same* point along the production-distribution chain, e.g., GM and Toyota.

2.   The optimal boundaries and structure of the firm are not static, they are dynamic and responsive to the changing needs of the marketplace.

a.   If economiies of scale are important, large corporations evolve to minimize production costs.

b.   If economies of scale are slight to nonexistent, small and nimble corporations evolve to exploit niche markets.

c.   When economies of scope are relevant, it becomes attractive to offer customers bundles of related products and services.

B.   **Transaction Costs and the Nature of Firms:** The firm is a collection of contractual agreements among owners, managers, workers, suppliers and customers. It has no physical presence; it exists only as a legal device.

1.   The efficiency of firms depends upon the ability of participants to find effective means to minimize the transactions costs of coordinating productive activity.

2.   Transaction costs include:

a.   information costs,

b.   decision costs,

c.   enforcement costs.

3.   Search or information costs encompass expenses encountered in discovering the type and quality of goods and services demanded by consumers.

4.   Bargaining or decision costs include expenditures involved with successfully negotiating production agreements.

5.   Policing or enforcement costs include charges necessary to make sure that all parties live up to their contractual commitments.

C. **Coase Theorem:** According to Coase, firms exist as an economic force because they are an effective means of minimizing transaction costs.

    1. It would be prohibitively expensive for each of us to organize production of all goods and services that we desire.

    2. According to what is now referred to as the Coase Theorem, resource allocation will be efficient so long as transaction costs remain low and property rights can be freely assigned and exchanged.

II. AGENCY PROBLEMS: SOURCES OF CONFLICT WITHIN FIRMS

A. **What is the Firm's Agency Problem?** An agency problem is present to the extent that unresolved material conflicts exist between the self-seeking goals of (agent) managers and the value maximization goal of (principal) stockholders.

    1. Agency costs are the explicit and implicit transaction costs necessary to overcome the natural divergence of interest between agent managers and principal stockholders.

    2. Agency problems exist because of conflicts between the incentives and rewards that face owners and managers. Such conflicts commonly arise given owner-manager differences in:

        a. risk exposure,

        b. investment horizons,

        c. familiarity with investment opportunities.

B. **Risk Management Problems**: Significant differences in the risk exposure of managers and stockholders often leads to problems.

    1. When employees share in gains but not in losses, an excessive risk-taking problem can emerge.

    2. When employees do not share in gains but are penalized for losses, a risk-avoidance problem can emerge.

    3. An "other peoples' money" problem can occur because employees tend to be less vigilant with corporate resources than with their own money (apologies to Danny DeVito).

4.   To combat managerial myopia, more and more companies are insisting that managerial compensation be directly tied to long-term performance.

C.   **Investment Horizon Problems:** Investment horizon problems can occur because top executives and many other managers tend to have fairly short careers.

1.   Any tendency toward focusing on short-term results is reenforced by compensation plans that rely on near-term corporate performance.

2.   To combat the potential for shortsighted operating and investment decisions, sometimes referred to as the managerial myopia problem, most corporations tie a significant portion of total compensation to the company's long-term stock price performance.

a.   Stock options and other payments tied to stock-price appreciation now account for 30 per cent to 35 per cent of top executive pay.

3.   Given the advanced age of most top executives and many senior managers, firms must be on guard against what is sometimes referred to as the end-of-game problem.

a.   The end-of-game problem is the most serious manifestation of myopic decision making, or inefficient risk avoidance.

D.   **Information Asymmetry Problems:** Another source of agency problems is tied to management's inherently superior access to information inside the firm, or the information asymmetry problem.

1.   Knowledgeable critics of managerial inefficiency are troubled about the inherent difficulty of gauging excess compensation, unprofitable empire building, and other elements of managerial malfeasance when managers control the flow of information about firm and managerial performance.

III.   ORGANIZATION DESIGN

A.   **Resolving Unproductive Conflict Within Firms**: Successful firms are an effective means for collecting and processing a vast array of sometimes conflicting information about customer demands, technology, input prices, raw material supplies, and so on.

1. The design of the organization is appropriate if it facilitates constructive communication. Major functions that need to be performed are:

    a. allocate decision making authority,

    b. monitor and evaluate performance,

    c. reward productive behavior.

2. An effective organization design is one that allocates decision authority to that person or team of persons best able to perform a given task or influence a particular outcome.

B. Centralization Versus Decentralization: A fundamental question facing management of all companies is the basic issue of when and how to centralize versus decentralize decision making authority.

1. With centralized decision authority, detailed judgments concerning how to best manage corporate resources, deal with suppliers and customers, and so on, are handled by top-line executives within a "top down" organization.

2. With decentralized decision authority, front-line employees, often those in direct communication with customers, are empowered to make fundamental judgments concerning how to best serve customer needs in a "flat" organization.

C. Assigning Decision Rights: The question of centralization versus decentralization focuses on defining the appropriate numbers of levels within the organization.

1. A flat organization has few or a single level of decision making authority.

2. A vertical organization features multiple ascending levels of decision making authority.

3. At its most basic level, the production process encompasses a sequence of related tasks, or assignments necessary to effectively meet customer needs.

4. In turn, related tasks are bundled into jobs, when such packaging facilitates cost savings and a more productive use of firm resources.

5. Many larger organizations facing the need to successfully deal with increasingly complex tasks have turned to team concepts.

D.   **Decision Management and Control:** Decision management is the vital process of generating, choosing and implementing management decisions. Decision control is the essential process of assessing how well the decision management process functions.

1.   It is useful to characterize the decision management and control process as consisting of four distinct steps:

a.   generate attractive decision proposals,

b.   choose the best decision,

c.   implement the best decision,

d.   assess decision success.

2.   Constructive management demands an ongoing assessment of the decision making process and the success, or lack thereof, of past decisions.

a.   Correct investment and operating decisions are made on the basis of economic expectations, or a reasonable before-the-fact forecast of monetary implications.

b.   Judging the wisdom of past decisions involves much more than a simple after-the-fact analysis of economic realizations, or financial outcomes.

IV.   **CORPORATE GOVERNANCE**

A.   **Role Played by Boards of Directors:** The most important and closely monitored corporate governance mechanism is the company board of directors.

1.   Corporate governance is the system of controls that helps the corporation effectively manage, administer and direct economic resources.

B.   **Corporate Governance Inside the Firm:** Corporate control mechanisms inside the firm are useful means for helping alleviate the potential divergence of interests between managers and stockholders.

1. Organization design, including the degree of vertical integration and the horizontal scope of the corporation, are examples of essential corporate governance mechanisms inside the firm.

2. Another useful means for controlling the flow of corporate resources is provided by internal markets established among divisions to better balance the supply and demand conditions for divisional goods and services.

V. OWNERSHIP STRUCTURE AS A CORPORATE GOVERNANCE MECHANISM

A. **Dimensions of Ownership Structure:** Ownership structure of the firm is the complex array of divergent claims on the value of the firm.

1. In financial economics, the capital structure of the firm has been traditionally described in terms of the share of total financing obtained from equity investors versus lenders (debt).

2. Today, interest has shifted from capital structure to ownership structure, as measured along a number of important dimensions, including:

   a. inside equity,

   b. institutional equity,

   c. widely-dispersed outside equity,

   d. bank debt,

   e. widely-dispersed outside debt.

3. Inside equity is the share of stock closely held by the firm's chief executive officer (CEO), other corporate insiders including top managers, and members of the board of directors.

4. When ownership is concentrated among a small group of large and vocal institutional shareholders, called institutional equity, managers often have strong incentives to maximize corporate performance.

B. **Is Ownership Structure Endogenous?** The probability that outside investors will discover evidence of managerial inefficiency or malfeasance is increased when institutional ownership is substantial. Managers of firms with high institutional ownership are relatively more susceptible to unfriendly takeover bids.

1.   Fiduciary responsibility and the dynamics of ownership concentration have the potential to make institutional stockholders especially effective in the managerial monitoring process.

2.   Insider and institutional stock ownership represent alternative forms of ownership concentration that combine to form an effective method for monitoring managerial decisions.

3.   Four general forces affecting corporate ownership structure are:

   a.   amenity potential,

   b.   regulatory potential,

   c.   quality control potential,

   d.   ownership control potential.

4.   Amenity potential is derived from the ability to influence the type of goods produced. Such benefits can be derived from ownership of mass media and professional sports teams, for example.

5.   Extensive rate-of-return regulation, or regulatory potential, limits the capacity of managers to influence firm performance.

6.   In the case of firms that produce goods and services with the potential for high quality variation, or quality control potential, a more concentrated ownership structure may be required to give shareholders the amount of control necessary to mollify other suppliers and customers.

7.   The ownership control potential of the firm is the wealth gain achievable through more effective monitoring of managerial performance.

VI.   **AGREEMENTS AND ALLIANCES AMONG FIRMS**

   A.   **Franchising:** Franchise agreements are prime examples of voluntary contractual arrangements outside the firm that can be viewed as corporate governance mechanisms.

1. Franchise agreements give local companies the limited right to offer goods or services developed or advertised on a national basis.

B. **Strategic Alliances:** Strategic alliances are formal operating agreements between independent companies that also can be viewed as corporate governance mechanisms.

1. These combinations are increasingly used to improve foreign marketing.

2. Strategic alliances also arise when participating companies enjoy complementary capabilities.

VII. **LEGAL AND ETHICAL ENVIRONMENT**

A. **Sarbanes-Oxley Act:** Sarbanes-Oxley radically redesigns federal regulation of corporate governance and corporate reporting obligations.

1. Corporate audit committees must now comply with a new list of requirements affecting auditor appointment, compensation and oversight.

2. Each company must disclose current information about the company's financial condition, and the audit committee appointed by the board of directors must consist solely of independent directors.

3. CEOs and chief financial officers (CFOs) also must personally certify that corporate financial reports fully comply with SEC requirements and fairly represents the company's financial condition and operating results.

B. **Business Ethics**: Economic theory and methodology can offer important insight concerning business ethics.

1. Economics provides a theory of how individuals make choices; including choices that have ethical dimensions.

2. Business ethics and the structure of the organization are inextricably linked and they establish important incentives for those individuals who together compose the firm.

3. A corporation's reputation for ethical behavior is part of the company's brand-name capital.

        a.   Calculated or inadvertent violations of federal laws have the potential to impose significant costs on shareholders and other residual claimants.

VIII.   SUMMARY

PROBLEMS & SOLUTIONS

P19.1 **Organization Structure.** *Determine whether each of the following statements is true or false. Explain why.*

A. *A horizontal relation is a business connection between companies at the same point along the production-distribution chain.*

B. *The unintended loss of valued employees to competitors is a type of decision cost.*

C. *A merger between Internet content provider America Online, Inc., and Internet access provider AT&T WorldNet, Inc., would be horizontal in nature.*

D. *When a corporation fires an underperforming CEO, it is an admission that the organization was unable to minimize transactions costs.*

E. *Effective pay for performance requires that all employees retain an equity interest in the firm.*

P19.1 SOLUTION

A. True. A vertical relation is a business connection between companies at *different* points along the production-distribution chain.

B. True. Bargaining or decision costs include expenditures involved with successfully negotiating production agreements, including implicit or explicit labor agreements.

C. False. A horizontal relation is a business affiliation between companies at the *same* point along the production-distribution chain.

D. True. The efficiency of firms is defined by the ability of participants to find effective means to minimize the transactions costs of coordinating productive activity. The firing of an underperforming CEO implies a coordination failure.

E. False. Pay for performance requires that all employees be compensated according to how well they have achieved specific tasks. Profit sharing and gain sharing, for example, are two effective means for motivating employees. Employee stock ownership can be an effective motivating device, but it is not the only means for providing needed performance incentives.

P19.2   *Agency costs.*   *Indicate whether each of the following transaction costs is explicit or implicit, and describe how it is a manifestation of a particular type of agency problem.*

   A.   *A CEO with an options-laden compensation plan pursues a risky and value-reducing merger plan in the hope for short-term stock gains.*

   B.   *A manager fails to achieve optimum efficiency by engaging workers in a long and acrimonious strike.*

   C.   *Senior executives propose an overly generous pension benefits plan during their last few years of employment.*

   D.   *Value-reducing new product introductions are adopted in order to boost near-term accounting performance.*

   E.   *Executives switch from the tax-saving LIFO to FIFO inventory accounting method in order to boost short-term accounting profit performance and managerial compensation.*

P19.2   SOLUTION

   A.   Explicit. Significant differences in the risk exposure of managers and stockholders can lead to an excessive risk-taking problem on the part of overly ambitious empire-building managers.

   B.   Explicit. This and other examples of the "other peoples' money" problem arise when decision makers control resources that they do not own.

   C.   Explicit. To guard against the end-of-game problem, boards of directors often set long-term goals, compensation and benefits for senior managers.

   D.   Implicit. To combat shortsighted operating and investment decisions, the managerial myopia problem, most corporations tie a significant portion of total compensation to long-term performance.

   E.   Explicit. The information asymmetry problem is tied to management's inherently superior access to information inside the firm. When managers smooth or boost accounting performance to increase compensations, shareholders suffer an explicit cost.

P19.3 **Ownership structure.** *Describe each of the following factors as being responsible for increasing, decreasing, or having no effect on the amount of concentrated inside equity. Explain why.*

  A. *High national media advertising requirements.*

  B. *A corporate history of sterling operating performance.*

  C. *Intense product-market competition.*

  D. *Intense security analyst coverage of corporate performance.*

  E. *A relaxation of antitrust policy.*

P19.3 **SOLUTION**

  A. Increase the amount of concentrated inside equity. High advertising requirements are apt to increase the amount of concentrated inside equity. In the case of firms that produce goods and services with the potential for high quality variation, or quality control potential, a more concentrated ownership structure may be required to give shareholders the amount of control necessary to give high quality assurance to suppliers and customers.

  B. Decrease the amount of concentrated inside equity. A corporate history of good operating performance means that the management team in place is capable of providing effective stewardship of shareholder assets. Because there is little to be gained by winning control of efficiently run corporations, there is little so-called ownership control potential for efficient firms, and scant potential wealth gain achievable through more effective monitoring of managerial performance.

  C. Decrease the amount of concentrated inside equity. When product-market competition is intense, the loss potential due to managerial malfeasance is small, and the need to further align managerial and owner incentives is slight. Vigorous competition is a quick and effective check on underperforming management.

  D. Decrease the amount of concentrated inside equity. Intense security analyst coverage of corporate activities is apt to decrease the need for concentrated inside equity. Independent auditors, security analysts, and journalists all provide a watchdog function that can be an effective monitoring device.

  E. Increase the amount of concentrated inside equity. Antitrust and regulatory policy is a type of external monitoring device. Any reduction in external monitoring increases the need for the type of internal monitoring provided by high levels of inside equity. For example, diffuse ownership structures are common for utilities because their regulatory potential limits the capacity of managers to influence firm performance. Concentrated ownership is more common in the case of unregulated monopolies.

P19.4 *Excessive risk taking/investment horizon problems. Pfizer, Inc., is known for producing exciting new products, including drugs to treat migraine headaches, heart rhythm disorders, arthritis, and treatments for sexual dysfunction. The pace of Pfizer's research productivity has jumped sharply from the early 1990s, when it introduced an average of one product a year. By 2002, for example, Pfizer had literally hundreds of projects in the works. The company also plans to enter new therapeutic areas, such as cancer, obesity and age-related conditions, that it hopes will yield new products further into the future.*

> **A.** *Explain how the design and execution of corporate R&D programs has the potential to create excessive risk-taking and investment horizon problems.*

> **B.** *R&D managers typically have huge personal incentives to turn in favorable year-to-year growth in the revenues and earnings derived from specific projects. This can sometimes have the unfortunate effect of focusing managerial attention on near-term accounting performance to the detriment of long-term value maximization. Explain how managerial compensation can be designed to avoid such myopic behavior.*

P19.4 SOLUTION

> **A.** Significant differences in the risk exposure of managers and stockholders has the potential to create an excessive risk-taking problem. In Pfizer's case, the company continues to rapidly grow an impressive and broad pipeline of new product developments. Upbeat presentations regarding the company's R&D programs have clearly impressed investors and helped lift Pfizer's stock price.
>
> The risk is, of course, that the pursuit of short-term stock gains might lead the company to launch risky R&D projects where expected rewards fail to justify reasonable estimates of costs in light of the risk entailed. Although it is obviously enticing to attack such dreaded diseases as cancer, obesity, and other diseases of aging, the company must ensure that projects can be justified on a risk-reward basis. In addition, long term problems and unanticipated side effects are sometimes ignored when managers adopt an overly short-run perspective. In the case of Pfizer, for example, the company had to temper its amazing success with Viagra, a male impotence drug, with product labeling that states some users of the

drug have experienced priapism, a painful, prolonged erection that can cause serious damage.

B. Agency problems tied to differences between the investment horizons of stockholders and management can emerge when salary and bonus payments are tied to short-term rather than long-term performance. This can be especially troublesome when the payoffs to hard-to-predict R&D efforts are considered. To combat such myopic behavior, more and more companies are insisting that managerial compensation be directly tied to long-term performance. An efficient means for establishing this link is to demand that top management hold a significant stock position that cannot be sold until some time *after* retirement. In Pfizer's case, the company might be well advised to encourage or demand that R&D managers and top executives make open market purchases of the firm's common stock. This is a trend that seems to be spreading in the pharmaceuticals industry, and for good reason. Information about Pfizer, Inc., can be found on the company Web Site. (http://www.pfizer.com)

P19.5   *Coase Theorem. On February 18, 2002, United Airlines announced a tentative contract agreement with the International Association of Machinists and Aerospace Workers, the union representing its 12,800 mechanics and aircraft cleaners. The agreement came on the fourth day of urgent talks, and less than 36 hours before a strike deadline. Notwithstanding assurances that an agreement would be reached, United experienced a steep decline in passenger bookings, reflecting public fears of a shutdown. Despite enormous costs in terms of lost business, labor strife between management, pilots, mechanics, and other employees seems to be a way of life at United and other major airlines.*

     A.   *Use the Coase Theorem to explain why labor-management standoffs in the airline industry reflect failures in corporate governance due to flawed organization structures.*

     B.   *Suggest a permanent means for resolving ongoing labor disputes between airline management and worker unions.*

P19.5   SOLUTION

A. According to Coase, firms exist as an economic force because they are an effective means for minimizing transaction costs. It would be prohibitively expensive for each of us to organize production of all goods and services that we desire. According to what is now referred to as the Coase Theorem, resource allocation will be efficient so long as transaction costs remain low and property rights can be freely assigned and exchanged.

Company management in the airline industry struggles to contain fixed costs and improve razor-thin margins. At the same time, uncontrollable fuel and capital acquisition costs often change in ways that make it difficult, if not impossible, to estimate and control these important variable cost categories. This makes labor costs one of the few controllable costs in the industry, and an obvious target of cost-conscious management during ties of weak revenues or high operating expenses.

Periodic standoffs between airline management and various worker unions are examples of organization failure, or the inability of such firms to effectively resolve fundamental disputes within the organization concerning the division of revenues and profits.

B. The airline industry offers an integral service that is relied upon heavily by both business and leisure travelers. Through the air freight part of the business, the airline industry also becomes part of dozens of industries that do everything from build computers to ship expensive drugs and consumer products. If a major airline like United stops operating normally for even a few days at a time, some of the most advanced sectors of the U.S. economy take a terrific blow. Customers demand reliability, and the airline business and its customers suffer greatly without dependable service from the pilots, mechanics, and other workers.

Work stoppages that strand business and leisure customers have enormous economic costs. United Airlines, like any airline, needs the cooperation of the pilots, mechanics, and other workers. At the same time, all workers need aircraft to fly. As a result, workers need management. Perhaps the clearest and simplest means of ensuring a convergence of worker and management interests in the airline industry is to require all parties to take on a significant ownership interest in the company.

P 19.6 ***Organization Design.*** *BTG, Plc., is an unusual company that acquires the rights to important inventions and hustles for patent royalties. BTG executives call themselves "merchant scientists." The company holds 8,500 patents covering nearly 300 different technologies. For example, it owns patents on the basic cholesterol test done using blood samples, and magnetic resonance imaging (MRI) technology. Because all patents expire, BTG is constantly scrambling for new ones. BTG once counted heavily on academia for new inventions, but universities and research labs are increasingly doing their own licensing. BTG now looks to corporate America, and offers its services to help companies exploit underused intangible assets.*

Created as an agency of the British government in 1949 after U.S. companies patented penicillin, a British discovery, BTG once had monopoly rights on any publicly funded research in Britain. It lost those rights in the 1980s, was privatized in 1992 and became a publicly-owned corporation in 1995.

A.   *BTG has engineered and patented an innovative Torotrak transmission that cuts fuel consumption by 20%, but faces resistance from the auto industry which has big investments in traditional transmissions. Explain how BTG might overcome such resistence and make its invention a commercial success.*

B.   *BTG's business lends itself to endless patent disputes. Explain how the company might favorably resolve such problems.*

P19.6   SOLUTION

A.   To overcome auto industry resistence and make its invention a commercial success, BTG was forced to build a production facility in northern England to manufacture its new transmissions. This was a costly move that contributed to BTG's decision to spin off its entire Torotrak transmission operation. "Had we not invested in it, it would have died," BTG executives acknowledge. Meanwhile, the company continues in its quest to get industry adoptions. So far, the news on this front has not been promising. In January 2002, Torotrak announced that General Motors (GM) have given notice that they will not exercise their option for a production licence for Torotrak's Infinitely Variable Transmission (IVT) technology. The IVT demonstrator vehicles that GM reviewed successfully proved that the technology works, but commercial considerations led GM to decide not to undertake any further internal development work for the foreseeable future.

B.   BTG's business lends itself to endless patent disputes, but the company strives to work out cross-licensing deals rather than pay lawyers. In 1982, for example, BTG filed for patents on the discovery by Oxford University scientists of the gene for a rare form of hemophilia. With a gene-replacement drug in mind, the company filed world-wide rights for both the gene and a protein derived from it. As it turns out, the Washington Research Foundation, a nonprofit institute in Seattle representing researchers at the University of Washington, had already filed patents in the U.S. for the gene.

To avoid lengthy litigation and court costs, BTG approached the foundation and worked out a revenue-sharing agreement under which it took over all licensing. BTG then secured American Home Products Corp. as an exclusive licensee for the new drug, called BeneFix., which it began marketing in 1997. Further information can be obtained at the BTG Web Site. (http://www.btgplc.com)

P 19.7   *Contracting Issues. The country's largest book retailer, Barnes & Noble, Inc., sparked a wave of criticism with its $600 million buyout bid for Ingram Book Group, the largest book wholesaler in the United States, in November 1998. Ingram Books, based in Nashville, Tenn., had annual sales in excess of $1 billion from the distribution of consumer books, books-on-tape, textbooks and specialty magazines to a wide variety of* *customers, including Barnes & Noble, Borders, independent bookstores, libraries and Internet bookseller, Amazon.com, Inc.*

   News of the proposed deal pushed up Barnes & Noble stock price almost 11% on heavy trading volume, but critics called the acquisition anti-competitive. In June 1999, under heavy fire from independent booksellers and negative signals from the Federal Trade Commission, Barnes & Noble withdrew its bid. Independent booksellers rejoiced over their victory. Barnes and Noble announced plans to build new distribution channels, presumably with the $600 million in cash and stock left over from the failed bid. Meanwhile, Ingram grumbled that the FTC didn't understand the company, and Barnes & Noble continued to shrug off suggestions that the deal would hurt competition.

A.   *Explain economic differences among a vertical merger, strategic alliance and a long-term contractual relationship between Borders and Ingram Book Group.*

B.   *Does the fact that Borders and Ingram Book Group sought a merger agreement imply significant contracting costs in the industry?*

P19.7   SOLUTION

A.   Economic differences among a vertical merger, strategic alliance and a long-term contractual relationship between Borders and Ingram Book Group are matters of degree and formality. A vertical merger between the two would minimize subsequent contracting costs because all such negotiations become internal and all parties have the same objective: to maximize total net profits going forward. A vertical merger, combined with an effective transfer pricing policy within the firm, would result in an elimination of the costs and risk involved with dividing up the total profit contribution earned.

   Strategic alliances and a long-term contractual relationships are alternative and less formal methods of contracting among legal entities. In this case, a merger with Ingram would have expanded the size of Barnes & Noble's book-distribution system and sharply increased the speed with which Barnes & Noble gets copies of books to customers. Speed in distribution is not a small matter when competition with Internet bookseller Amazon.com is considered. In fact, the "need for speed" was the prime driver behind this failed merger proposal. With eleven strategically located distribution centers, more than 80% of the combined company's online and retail-store customers would have been eligible for overnight delivery.

   In commenting on the merger proposal, Barnes & Noble noted that independent booksellers constitute a substantial portion of Ingram's business and are responsible for a major share of its profits. The company argued that it would have been foolhardy for Barnes & Noble to do anything but try to increase its business with other independent booksellers.

B.   Yes, the fact that Borders and Ingram Book Group sought a merger agreement implies that contracting costs in the industry are significant. Although a vertical merger between the two would minimize contracting costs, a less formal and less comprehensive strategic alliance or long-term contractual relationship is subject to the risk of third-part intervention. For example, if Amazon.com were to buy Ingrams, Borders might rightfully fear an interruption in its beneficial supplier-retailer relationship with Ingrams.

To be sure, Ingrams has an incentive to maximize profits going forward whether or not it is independent or part of a larger organization that includes Borders, Amazon.com, or some other retailer. If the wholesale market for books were perfectly competitive, there would be no reason to fear negative competitive consequences from vertical relationships. Indeed, with perfectly competitive supply, there would be no reason to pursue long-term vertical relationships. (Notice that McDonald's sells milk but doesn't own dairy farms.) At a minimum, the fact that Borders sought a long-term vertical relationship with Ingrams implies a close strategic fit between the two. A merger may or may not have led to a durable competitive advantage over rivals such as Amazon.com.

Interestingly, in March 2001, Borders Group announced that it has signed an agreement to make Ingram the primary provider of book fulfillment services for Borders Group's special order and online sales. The transaction included the sale to Ingram of a large percentage of the book inventory housed in Borders Group's Fulfillment Center in La Vergne, Tenn., which previously handled the function assumed by Ingram. In this case, a strategic alliance may achieve many of the benefits sought in their failed merger proposal.

P19.8   *Incentive Compensation. Consumer-products juggernaut Procter & Gamble, Inc., shook up the advertising industry when it introduced a revolutionary compensation method that rewards advertising agencies for increases in company sales. Under P&G's historical compensation system, advertising agencies were paid roughly 13% to 15% of the amount P&G spent through them on advertising. Under the traditional system, critics contended that there was a big incentive to favor television. That's because agencies got a lot bigger paycheck for a $150,000 television commercial than for a $2,000 to $20,000 billboard.*

P&G wants a "media-neutral" advertising expenditure policy without any inherent advantage for network TV at the expense of other media such as the Internet, billboards, magazines and public-relations events.

A.   *Is there any necessary conflict between advertising expenditure efficiency and a commission-based compensation plan for advertising agencies?*

B.   *Can changes in technology explain why P&G might alter its method of compensating advertising agencies?*

P19.8   SOLUTION

A.   No. Of course, it's true that advertising agencies got a lot bigger paycheck for a $150,000 television commercial than for a $2,000 to $20,000 billboard. However, it's worth remembering that ad rates are set in a competitive market based upon advertising effectiveness. A $100,000 television commercial can be expected to generate far more customer awareness and sales revenue than an ad on a $2,000 to $20,000 per month billboard. In fact, in an efficient advertising market, the television ad would generate 5 to 50 times the value of such a billboard. Similarly, the amount paid in advertising agency commissions can be expected to vary proportionately with the amount of value added at the margin.   The fact that P&G wants a "media-neutral" advertising expenditure policy without any inherent advantage for network TV at the expense of other media such as the Internet, billboards, magazines and public-relations events makes good economic sense. So too do traditional forms of ad agency compensation.

B.   Yes. Effective people meters, price-tracking technology, scanner data, and computer software suited to measuring advertising effectiveness on the Internet all make it easier than ever before for P&G and other advertisers to effectively track advertising effectiveness. In fact, measurement technology now makes a significant contribution to advertising effectiveness, and thereby reduces the relative importance of the creative input traditionally provided by advertising agencies. Changes in advertising technology help explain why the traditional commission system is increasingly losing ground as advertisers gravitate toward base fees to cover fixed costs, plus various incentives. As the commission system has faded, agency profit margins have been squeezed. Traditional ad agencies grumble that it's tough to make a living churning out online ads, for example, because a commission-based system makes it less than lucrative to devote much time and effort to online-ad efforts.

P19.9   *Information Asymmetry Problem. Global Crossing, Ltd., a Bermuda-based telecom giant, was putting the finishing touches on its 100,000-mile fiber-optic network in 2001 when it entered into a series of transactions that many now regard as deceptive. For example, a small Orlando, Florida, company called EPIK Communications Inc. paid $40 million for the right to divert some of its telephone and data traffic through Global's Latin American fiber routes. Exactly offsetting that payment, Global spent $40 million for unspecified future use of EPIK's facilities, which include a 1,850-mile fiber network linking Atlanta and Miami. Using a series of such transactions with other telecom carriers, Global's revenues soared to $3.79 billion by 2000 from $419.9 million in 1998. Global also became a regular fixture in Washington, DC. The company and its executives donated $2.6 million in the 2000 presidential campaign, surpassing even notorious Enron Corp. in that regard.*

Unfortunately, in the wake of the dwindling revenue growth, soaring costs, and growing investor skepticism concerning the company's accounting practices, Global was forced to file for bankruptcy court protection in January, 2002. At the time, it was the fourth-largest bankruptcy filing in U.S. history. It also marked a stunning collapse for shareholders who saw the stock price steadily decline from a high of $61.06 per share, and a market capitalization of $47.6 billion in February 2000.

A. *Explain how the rise and fall of Global Crossing, Ltd., Inc., might be described as a manifestation of the information asymmetry problem.*

B. *How could this problem have been avoided?*

P19.9 SOLUTION

A. Accounting methods always leave room for managerial interpretation, and this flexibility can and has been used to understate expenses and inflate reported earnings. When CEO compensation and stock-based rewards are tied to various accounting performance targets, it's a bit like asking students to fill out their own final grade report. At a minimum, shareholder's shouldn't be surprised when accounting data places firm and managerial performance in a favorable light. Shareholder's must take steps to guard against significant manipulation of accounting standards and/or accounting bias that results in a meaningful distortion of accounting performance.

B. The most obvious and simplest corporate governance mechanisms used to guard against manipulation of the firm's accounting statements are corporate practices that insure independence on the part of auditors and members of the board of directors. Perhaps the best corporate practice is to have the independent auditor report to the board itself, or to a subcommittee comprised of independent board members (not members of top management). Boards of directors also tend to be most independent when the chairman of the board is not a member of top management, but rather an independent board member.

Independent security analysts also have a role to play in monitoring the quality of information reported by the firm. Though security analysts often do a good job of keeping shareholders informed, they obviously dropped the ball, or globe in the case of Global Crossing. See Dennis K. Berman and Deborah Solomon, "Global Crossing's Use of Swaps To Boost Revenue Wasn't Unusual," *The Wall Street Journal Online*, February 13, 2002 (http://online.wsj.com)

P19.10 Corporate Governance. *In March 2002, an unrepentant Jeffrey Skilling, former Enron Corp. chief executive, testified before Congress that the company had tight controls on financial risk but that he couldn't be expected to oversee everything and "close out the* *cash drawers... every night." Skilling, whose testimony to Congress was severely challenged by lawmakers, even sought to defend himself in an interview on CNN's "Larry King Live." "I think the Congress is acting as judge and jury," he said, and "that is to be expected in an election year." Meanwhile, from company computers obtained by Justice Department prosecutors, evidence was obtained that Enron paid its executives one-time bonuses totaling some $320 million. The stock targets, ending in 2000, were reached at the same time investigators say Enron officials were improperly inflating company profits by as much as $1 billion, thereby buoying the stock price.*

A. *Explain how the design and administration of state and federal laws can be seen as a means of outside monitoring designed to ensure a coincidence of managerial incentives, stockholder interests, and broader social objectives.*

B. *Explain how the economic effects of law enforcement actions on the value of the firm can be expected to differ according to the relative importance of intangible factors in firm valuation.*

P19.10 SOLUTION

A. Calculated or inadvertent violations of state and federal laws have the potential to impose significant costs on shareholders and other residual claimants. The pursuit of illegal short-term strategies can represent a form of self-dealing by managers who seek to reap short-term personal gain while escaping detection. Actual or suspected violations of federal laws have the potential to result in significant costs measured in terms of investigation expenditures, litigation expenses, fines and seizures, and lost reputational capital for the firm--all of which can measurably reduce future cash flows and current market values. Within this context, laws can be seen as part of the institutional framework that contributes to the range of control mechanisms that originate inside and outside the firm to comprise an effective system of corporate governance. Because short-term "hit and run" managers may possess incentives to "cut" legal and ethical corners, the design and administration of laws and regulations can be seen as a means of outside monitoring designed to ensure a coincidence of managerial incentives, stockholder interests, and broader social objectives. Law enforcement activities can be viewed as an important element in the institutional framework of corporate governance.

B. Economic effects of federal law enforcement actions on the value of the firm can be expected to differ across firms according to the relative importance of intangible factors in firm valuation. The value of the firm is derived from assets in place and growth opportunities stemming from research and development (R&D), advertising, and other such expenditures. Firms whose value stems mainly from growth opportunities, or complex trading strategies such as in the case of Enron, may be especially susceptible to law enforcement actions because of the enhanced potential to adversely impact the firm's reputational capital and growth options.

Chapter 20

GOVERNMENT IN THE MARKET ECONOMY

Government regulation is a compelling subject because the ability to regulate, tax, subsidize or otherwise compel economic activity is a potent force that shapes the competitive environment. The process and results of government regulation are controversial because regulatory policy often makes some trade-off between efficiency and equity considerations. Appropriate government regulation is based on a balancing of costs and benefits to society in general, taking into account both administrative expenses and hidden obligations borne by the private sector. Recent changes in the method and scope of government regulation, reflect this fact.

As trustees of valuable public resources, managers in the public sector must administer economic resources in a responsible manner. This task is made difficult by problems involved with assessing the true levels of demand and cost for government-administered goods and services. Because individuals not paying for many public goods cannot be excluded from consumption, there is a tendency for consumers to avoid payment responsibility. A so-called free-rider problem emerges because each consumer believes that public goods will be provided irrespective of his or her contribution towards covering their costs. Consumers of public goods are also reluctant to reveal strong personal demand for public goods because they fear correspondingly high payment demands. Like the free-rider problem, this hidden preferences problem makes assessing the true demand for public goods difficult. As a result, a variety of nonmarket-based mechanisms have evolved that can be used to effectively administer government programs in light of relative marginal social benefits and costs.

CHAPTER OUTLINE

I. **EXTERNALITIES**

    A. **Negative Externalities:** If economic activity among producers and consumers harms the well-being of a third party who is not compensated for any resulting damages, a negative externality is said to exist.

        1. Air, noise, and water pollution are the most familiar types of negative externalities.

        2. In the absence of externalities, the competitive market equilibrium maximizes consumer surplus, which is the difference between the total value received by consumers and the amount paid to producers.

        3. Negative externalities give rise to an overproduction problem because sellers need not reflect the full social costs of production in the prices charged to buyers.

B. **Positive Externalities:** If economic activity among producers and consumers helps the well-being of a third party who does not pay for any resulting benefits, a positive externality is created.

    1. Education is perhaps the most famous type of positive externality.

    2. Positive externalities give rise to an underproduction problem because sellers cannot reflect the full social value of production in the prices charged to buyers.

II. SOLVING EXTERNALITIES

A. **Government Solutions:** Government has a variety of means that can be used to make producers and/or consumers internalize the externality.

    1. Taxes are often used to correct the effects of negative externalities.

    2. Government sometimes controls the effects of externalities by forbidding certain types of conduct, while requiring other types of behavior.

        a. An advantage of command-and-control regulation is that it is consistent with the principle that all persons are equal before the law.

        b. An important disadvantage is that such regulation often fails to provide efficient incentives.

B. **Market Solutions:** Markets often provide effective penalties to moderate the production of negative externalities, and efficient incentives for the production of goods and services with positive externalities.

    1. A simple market solution is often capable of ensuring sufficient production of goods and services with significant externalities provided that information is freely available and transactions costs are moderate.

    2. A transaction cost is an expense that buyers and sellers incur in the process of arriving at and carrying through on a bargain.

    3. According to the Coase Theorm, if property rights are complete and private parties can bargain freely over the allocation of resources, then markets are capable of solving the problems posed by externalities and will operate efficiently.

III. PUBLIC GOODS

A. Rivalry and Exclusion: If the consumption of a product by one individual does not reduce the amount available for others, and if nonpaying customers cannot be prevented from consumption, the product is a public good.

1. A distinguishing characteristic of public goods is that they share the attribute of nonrival consumption.

    a. Use by certain individuals does not reduce availability for others.

2. A private good is one where consumption by one individual precludes or limits consumption by others.

    a. All private goods share the characteristic of rival consumption because one person's use diminishes another person's ability to use it.

    b. A good or service is nonexclusionary if it is impossible or prohibitively expensive to confine the benefits of consumption to paying customers.

    c. The tendency to overexploit common resources is often called the tragedy of the commons.

B. Free Riders and Hidden Preferences: Because individuals not paying for public goods cannot be excluded from consumption, there is a tendency for consumers to avoid payment responsibility.

1. A free-rider problem emerges because each consumer believes that the public good will be provided irrespective of his or her contribution toward covering its costs.

2. A hidden preferences problem also emerges in the provision of public goods because individuals have no economic incentive to accurately reveal their true demand.

IV. BENEFIT-COST CONCEPTS

A. Pareto Improvement: Nonmarket-based mechanisms have evolved that can be used to effectively administer government programs and investment expenditures.

1.   If investment in a public project makes at least one individual better off and no one worse off, then the project is described as Pareto satisfactory, after the noted Italian economist Vilfredo Pareto.

2.   When all such projects have been undertaken, the situation is deemed Pareto optimal.

3.   In practice, most public expenditures increase the welfare of some individuals while reducing the welfare of others. A potential Pareto improvement requires that there be positive net benefits.

4.   The marginal social costs of any good or service equal the marginal cost of production plus any marginal external costs, such as air pollution, that are not directly borne by producers or their customers.

5.   Marginal social benefits are the sum of marginal private benefits plus marginal external benefits. Marginal private benefits are enjoyed by those who directly pay for any good or service; marginal external benefits are enjoyed by purchasers and non-purchasers alike and are not reflected in market prices. When no externalities are present, marginal social benefits equal marginal private benefits.

    a.   When the ratio MSB/MSC > 1, the value of marginal social benefits exceeds the value of marginal social costs.

    b.   When the ratio MSB/MSC < 1, then the value of marginal social benefits is less than the value of marginal social costs.

    c.   Only when MSB/MSC = 1 for the marginal public-sector project and private-sector project are resources effectively allocated between the public and private sectors.

B.   Benefit-Cost Methodology: Benefit-cost analysis is often used when the economic consequences of a project or a policy change are apt to extend beyond 1 year.

1.   The guiding principle of benefit-cost analysis is economic efficiency in a global sense.

2.   The purpose of benefit-cost analysis is to determine if a given public expenditure would produce greater benefits than if such funds were invested in an alternative public program, or if they were instead left in the private sector.

C.   **Social Rate of Discount:** Determining the appropriate social rate of discount, or interest-rate cost of public funds, is critical to the selection of appropriate alternatives.

    1.   A low rate favors long-term investments with substantial future benefits.

    2.   A higher rate favors short-term projects with benefits that accrue soon after the initial investment.

    3.   The average pretax rate of return on government securities is a very conservative estimate of the opportunity cost of private-sector consumption that is diverted to public use.

V.   **BENEFIT/COST CRITERIA**

A.   **Social Net Present-Value :** Under the social net present-value criterion, marginal social benefits and marginal social costs are discounted back to the present using an appropriate social discount rate.

    1.   Like net present-value analysis in private-sector project evaluation, the social net present-value criterion establishes a rank-order of acceptable projects according to the magnitude of the net present-value of resulting benefits.

        a.   Whenever SNPV < 0, program funding is unwise on an economic basis.

        b.   A judicious use of social resources requires that SNPV > 0 for every public program or public investment project.

B.   **Benefit-Cost Ratio:** A variant of SNPV analysis that is often used in complex capital budgeting situations is called benefit-cost (B/C) ratio analysis.

    1.   The B/C ratio shows the relative attractiveness of any social program or public-sector investment project, or the present value of marginal social benefits per dollar of marginal social cost.

    2.   SNPV > 0 implies a desirable investment program and a B/C ratio > 1.

    3.   Any social program with B/C ratio > 1 should be accepted; any program with *B/C ratio* < 1 should be rejected.

C.   **Social Internal Rate of Return:** The social internal rate of return (SIRR) is the interest or discount rate that equates the present value of future receipts to the initial cost or outlay.

   1.   Because the social net present-value equation is complex, it is difficult to solve for the actual social internal rate of return on an investment without a computer spreadsheet.

   2.   Social internal rate of return analysis suggests that programs should be accepted when the SIRR > k and rejected when the SIRR < k.

   3.   As in the case of programs with an SNPV > 0 and B/C ratio > 1, the acceptance of all investment programs with SIRR > k will lead public-sector managers to maximize net social benefits.

D.   **Limitations of Benefit-Cost Analysis:** Although the benefit-cost analysis is conceptually appealing, it has several limitations that must be considered.

   1.   Without competitive markets for public goods and services, it is difficult to ascertain the social value placed on public programs.

   2.   Evaluation problems also occur when a nonefficiency objective, such as reducing the level of highway noise pollution around a schoolyard, must be considered alongside an efficiency objective, such as increasing business activity along a new highway corridor.

VI.   **ADDITIONAL METHODS FOR IMPROVING PUBLIC MANAGEMENT**

A.   **Cost-Effectiveness Analysis:** The purpose of cost-effectiveness analysis is to determine how to best employ resources in a given social program or public-sector investment project.

   1.   Cost-effectiveness analysis is useful when output can be identified and measured in qualitative terms but is difficult to express in monetary terms.

   2.   Cost-effectiveness studies are also useful in situations where significant externalities or other intangibles exist that cannot be easily measured in dollar terms.

B.   **Privatization:** With privatization, public-sector resources are transferred to the private sector in the hope that the profit motive might spur higher product quality, better customer service, and lower costs.

1. In the United States, privatization has failed to generate the type of enthusiasm seen in many foreign countries.

2. The economic justification for privatization is that cheaper and better goods and services result when the profit motive entices firms to improve quality and cut costs.

3. Opponents of privatization argue that the transfer of government programs to the private sector does not necessarily lead to smaller government and fewer budget deficits.

VII. **REGULATORY REFORM IN THE NEW MILLENNIUM**

A. **Promoting Competition in Electric Power Generation:** The electric power industry comprises three different components: the generation of electric power, the transmission of electric power from generators to local utilities, and the distribution of electricity by local utilities to commercial and residential customers.

   1. All three segments of the industry are currently subject to some state and federal regulation.

   2. Competition has emerged in the wholesale generation of electric power, and regulators now face the question of how to foster and encourage such competition.

B. **Fostering Competition in Telecommunications:** The FCC struggles to prevent antiquated monopoly regulations from the analog era from hampering the progress of emerging telecommunications technologies.

   1. To facilitate competition, FCC rules were changed in 2004 to allow consumers to keep their cell phone numbers when switching carriers.

   2. State and local regulators face similarly daunting challenges to make local phone companies and cable TV companies more price sensitive and responsive to consumer demands.

C. **Reforming Environmental Regulation:** Environmental regulation expanded greatly during the 1970s and 1980s.

1. By requiring firms and consumers to account for pollution costs, the Clean Air Act, the Clean Water Act, and the Resource Conservation and Recovery Act have all limited environmental waste.

2. At the same time, each of these environmental regulations imposes significant costs on the private economy.

D. **Improving Regulation of Health and Safety:** Proponents of expanded government health and safety regulation assert that consumers and employees either do not have sufficient information or are incapable of making appropriate health and safety decisions.

1. Just as firms and individuals must balance risk and benefits when making decisions, so too must regulators.

VIII. HEALTH-CARE REFORM

A. **Managed Competition:** Uncontrolled increases in health-care expenditures and a growing number of uninsured, especially among the poor, have led to a proliferation of proposals for U.S. health-care reform.

1. The most promising health-care reform proposals involve market-based reforms designed to expand access to health insurance and to improve the private markets for health-care services.

2. Market-based plans would expand health insurance coverage by promoting the use of health insurance networks to act as group purchasing agents for smaller employers, thus obtaining more favorable premiums and reducing administrative costs.

B. **Outlook for Health-Care Reform:** No plan for health-care reform is without its pluses and minuses, costs and benefits.

1. Reforms that give consumers, insurers, and providers appropriate incentives are likely to be most effective in controlling costs, improving access, and giving consumers the quality of healthcare that they want.

IX. SUMMARY

PROBLEMS & SOLUTIONS

P20.1   ***Public Versus Private Goods.*** *Publicly-funded educational television provides a valuable service across the United States and Canada. Innovative children's programming, award-winning environmental and nature telecasts and imaginative historical documentaries are all delivered free on "ultra high frequency" (UHF) television stations across America.*

    A.   *Give a public good argument in favor of public funding for educational television.*

    B.   *Does educational television display both nonrival consumption and nonexclusion characteristics?*

    C.   *Explain how private-sector providers of educational television might operate profitably in the United States*

P20.1   *SOLUTION*

    A.   The distinguishing characteristic of public goods is the concept of nonrival consumption. In the case of public goods, use by certain individuals does not reduce availability for others. For example, when an individual watches a network broadcast of a popular TV program such as *The Nightly Business Report*, this does not interfere with the enjoyment of that same TV program by others. In contrast, if an individual consumes a 12 ounce can of *Diet Coke*, this same can of soda is not available for others to consume.

        Educational television clearly displays the nonrival consumption concept. Moreover, education is typically regarded a public good because of tangible and intangible external social benefits. Social benefits of a more highly educated populace include higher income tax revenues, reduced crime, higher voter participation, and so on.

    B.   No. Because educational television programs can be enjoyed equally by more than one person at the same point in time, they display the nonrival consumption attribute and represent a type of public good. This is despite the fact that public television does not exhibit the characteristic of nonexclusion because access to educational television programming can be restricted. Educational TV is not exclusive because such programs could be provided by cable TV operators that charge subscribers a fee for watching.

    C.   A great number of public goods are not typified by the nonexclusion concept. Examples include public support for educational television, National Public Radio, recreational services provided by national parks and forests, weather forecasts by the National Weather Service, and so on. In these and many other instances, use by nonpaying customers can be easily precluded by private-sector providers. For example, public television's popular *Nightly Business Report* program could be easily restricted to paying sponsors, much like cable television restricts viewing to paying subscribers.

P20.2   ***Public vs Private Goods.*** *Use the nonrival concept to classify each of the following goods and services as public goods or private goods. Also indicate whether or not the good or service in question can be characterized by the nonexclusion concept. Explain your answer.*

    A.   *Fire protection.*

    B.   *Major league baseball game attendance.*

    C.   *National defense.*

    D.   *Long-distance phone service.*

    E.   *The "Wall $treet Week" public television program provided on "free" broadcast TV.*

P20.2   **SOLUTION**

    A.   Public good that is nonexclusionary. Enjoyment of fire protection by one consumer does not reduce its enjoyment by others. Hence, it is nonrival in consumption and a public good. It is also nonexclusionary because it would be impossible or prohibitively expensive to confine the benefits of fire protection to paying customers.

    B.   Private good that is not nonexclusionary. In the case of major league baseball games, attendance by certain individuals can in fact reduce availability for others, especially during the pennate race when attendance is high. Baseball games are, therefore, a private good. Because attendance is restricted to paying customers, baseball games cannot be described as nonexclusionary.

    C.   Public good that is nonexclusionary. Enjoyment of national defense by one consumer does not reduce its enjoyment by others. Hence, it is nonrival in consumption and a public good. It is also nonexclusionary because it would be impossible or prohibitively expensive to confine the benefits of national defense to paying customers.

D. Private good that is not nonexclusionary. In the case of long-distance telephone service, use by certain individuals can in fact reduce availability for others, especially during the peak periods when telephone usage is high. It is, therefore, a private good. Because long-distance phone service is in fact restricted to paying customers, it cannot be described as nonexclusionary.

E. Public good that is nonexclusionary. When an individual watches a "free" over-the-air (UHF or VHF) broadcast of a popular PBS program this does not interfere with the enjoyment of that same PBS program by others. As a result, PBS and all other over-the-air broadcasts are a type of nonexclusionary public good. The enjoyment of TV broadcasts can be made exclusive by restricting viewing to cable TV customers.

P20.3 *Market Failure. Water run-off from agricultural crops washes fertilizer, pesticides, and other chemicals into streams, rivers, and lakes. In some instances, the ground water itself becomes contaminated. Concerned citizens are appalled at the aesthetic and environmental implications of such pollution, as well as the potential health hazard to the local population.*

    A. *Pollution is a negative production externality and an example of market failure. What reasons might you cite for why markets fail?*

    B. *In analyzing remedies to the current situation, consider three general types of controls to limit pollution:*

- *Regulations -- licenses, permits, compulsory standards, and so on.*

- *Payments -- various types of government aid to help companies install pollution-control equipment. Aid can take the form of forgiven local property taxes, income tax credits, special accelerated depreciation allowances for pollution-control equipment, low-cost government loans, and so on.*

- *Charges -- excise taxes on polluting fuels (coal, oil, and so forth), pollution discharge taxes, and others.*

Review each of these methods of pollution control and do the following:

    (1) *Determine the incentive structure for the polluter under each form of control.*

(2) *Decide who pays for a clean environment under each form of control. (Note that each form of control has definite implications about who owns the property rights to the environment.)*

(3) *Defend a particular form of control on the basis of your analysis, including both efficiency and equity considerations.*

P20.3   SOLUTION

A.   Markets can fail due to:

(i) Structural problems: Fewness in the number of buyers and/or sellers.

(ii) Incentive problems: If some product benefit (cost) is not reflected in firm revenues (costs), then non-optimal production quantities and output prices will result due to improper firm incentives.

B.   Methods of pollution control:

(i) Incentive structure:

(a) Regulation: Incentive is to avoid regulation, or be made a "special case."

(b) Payments: Incentive is to reduce pollution to earn subsidy.

(c) Charges: Incentive is to reduce pollution to avoid charges.

(ii) Who pays for the clean environment?

(a) Regulation: Industry customers, employees, and stockholders pay to reduce pollution. Society's right to a clean environment is implied.

(b) Payments: Society pays to reduce pollution, implying that the company has a right to pollute.

(c) Charges: Industry customers, employees, and stockholders pay to reduce pollution. Again, society's right to a clean environment is implied.

(iii) Defense of the alternatives:

Efficiency considerations favor payments and charges as more efficient methods of pollution control.

Equity or "ability to pay" considerations make the choice among pollution control methods less certain.

(a) Regulation: Insures due process, a day in court, for the polluter.

(b) Payments: Avoids penalty to polluters with "sunk" investment costs.

(c) Charges: Polluter should pay full costs of production consumption.

P20.4 **Benefits of Regulation.** *Each of the following problems illustrate instances where unregulated market activity might result in suboptimal market outcomes. Indicate whether the problem identified reflects market failure caused by a structural problem, or market failure caused by an incentive (enforcement) problem. Explain your answer.*

A. Price-gouging by a pharmaceutical manufacturer protected by patents on an important medicine used to treat a major infectious disease.

B. Acid rain caused by factory pollution.

C. Excess profits for domestic manufacturers protected by import tariffs.

D. Excessive automobile insurance policy prices due to a lack of competition in the local market.

E. Excessive noise levels due to freeway traffic.

P20.4 **SOLUTION**

A. Structural problem. Price-gouging by a pharmaceutical manufacturer protected by patents on an important medicine used to treat a major infectious disease is an example of market failure caused by structural problems. When too few competitors are present in a given market, high prices and excess profits can result.

B. Incentive (enforcement) problem. Acid rain caused by factory pollution is an example of market failure due to incentive problems. When factories emit excessive sulphur dioxide pollution they cause some of the environmental costs of producing output to be borne by third parties.

C.   Structural problem. Excess profits for domestic manufacturers protected by import tariffs are an example of the social costs that result from limiting foreign competition.

D.   Structural problem. Excessive automobile insurance policy costs due to a lack of sufficient competition in the local market reflects a structural problem in the market for insurance services.

E.   Incentive (enforcement) problem. Excessive noise due to freeway traffic is an example of market failure due to a lack of proper incentives in the marketplace to reduce the level of noise pollution.

P20.5   ***Demand Estimation for Public Goods.*** *Assume that ardent concert goers and casual concert goers have revealed their demands for summertime classical concerts in the park, a public good, as follows:*

$$P_1 = \$4,000 - \$100Q \qquad \text{(Ardent concert goers demand)}$$

$$P_2 = \$500 - \$50Q \qquad \text{(Casual concert goers demand)}$$

where P is price and Q is the number of concerts per year in the local park.

A.   Calculate the total or aggregate demand for summertime concerts.

B.   The marginal cost of summertime concerts is $3,000 each. Determine the socially optimal amount of publicly-supported summertime concerts.

P20.5   SOLUTION

A.   Total or aggregate demand for public goods is determined by a vertical summation of ardent concert goer and casual concert goer demand curves:

$$\text{Total demand} = P_1 + P_2$$

$$= \$4,000 - \$100Q + \$500 - \$50Q$$

$$= \$4,500 - \$150Q$$

B.   The socially optimal amount of summertime classical concerts in the park is determined by the intersection of demand and supply:

$$\text{Demand} = \text{Supply}$$

$$P_1 + P_2 = MC$$

$$\$4,500 - \$150Q = \$3,000$$

$$150Q = 1,500$$

$$Q = 10$$

And,

$$P = \$4,500 - \$150(10) = \$3,000 \qquad \text{(Demand)}$$

$$P = \$3,000 \qquad \text{(Supply)}$$

P20.6 ***Demand Estimation for Public Goods.*** *Assume that students and nonstudents have revealed their group demands for junior college education, a public good, as follows:*

$$Q = 1,500 - 0.25P, \qquad \text{(Student demand)}$$

$$Q = 4,000 - P, \qquad \text{(Nonstudent demand)}$$

where Q is the number of students educated per year and P is the price of tuition at the local 2-year junior college.

A. *Calculate the total or aggregate demand for secondary education.*

B. *The marginal cost of college education is given by the expression:*

$$MC = \$1,000 + Q,$$

where MC is marginal cost and Q is again the number of students.
   Determine the socially optimal amount of publicly-supported college education.

P20.6 **SOLUTION**

A. Total or aggregate demand for public goods such as college education is determined by a vertical summation of individual student and nonstudent demand curves. First, it is necessary to express student and nonstudent demand in terms of Q as a function of P.

For student demand:

$$Q = 1,500 - 0.25P$$

$$-0.25P = Q - 1,500$$

$$P = \$6,000 - \$4Q$$

For nonstudent demand:

$$Q = 4,000 - P$$

$$-P = Q - 4,000$$

$$P = \$4,000 - Q$$

Then,

$$\text{Total demand} = \text{Student demand} + \text{Nonstudent demand}$$

$$= \$6,000 - \$4Q + \$4,000 - Q$$

$$= \$10,000 - \$5Q$$

B. The socially optimal amount of publicly-supported college education is determined by the intersection of demand and supply:

$$\text{Demand} = \text{Supply}$$

$$\text{Student demand} + \text{Nonstudent demand} = MC$$

$$\$10,000 - \$5Q = \$1,000 + Q$$

$$6Q = 9,000$$

$$Q = 1,500$$

And,

$$P = \$10,000 - \$5(1,500) = \$2,500 \qquad \text{(Demand)}$$

$$P = \$1{,}000 + \$1(1{,}500) = \$2{,}500 \qquad\qquad \text{(Supply)}$$

P20.7   ***Consequences of Regulation.*** *The Lawn Fertilizer Company takes raw mineral phosphate and converts it into a phosphate-based fertilizer. During the production process, fluoride gas is released into the air. This pollutant then settles on the citrus crops and grass in a wide area surrounding production facilities, retards the growth of crops and results in an inferior fruit product. The pollutant also settles on grass eaten by cattle, and produces an arthritic condition retarding their growth. As a result, agriculture and cattle interests have petitioned the State Environmental Protection Agency for pollution controls on LFC's conversion process. These controls would affect annual fixed and variable costs of the fertilizer industry, and add $30 million to their total asset base of $210 million.*

LFC and other firms in the fertilizer industry agree that something needs to be done to stop the pollution. However, caution is necessary because these changes could reduce the 10% "fair" rate of return on investment earned by the industry. Although they agree with the idea of pollution control, the fertilizer industry argues that an immediate pollution abatement program would lower industry profits, hamper future capital expansion, lower output, and force layoffs. The fertilizer industry advocates a slower program with a major emphasis on new facilities. This more gradual process will have a smaller impact on profits, output, and employment; and add only $5 million to the total asset base of the industry.

An independent committee acceptable to both sides was established to analyze relevant economic data. As a result of their analysis, the following industry demand, revenue and cost curves were discovered:

$$P = \$35{,}000 - \$0.5Q \qquad\qquad \textit{(Demand)}$$

$$MR = \partial TR/\partial Q = \$35{,}000 - \$1Q \qquad\qquad \textit{(Marginal Revenue)}$$

$$TC = \$100{,}000{,}000 + \$8{,}000Q + \$1Q^2 \qquad\qquad \textit{(Total cost)}$$

$$MC = \partial TC/\partial Q = \$8{,}000 + \$2Q \qquad\qquad \textit{(Marginal Cost)}$$

where P is price in dollars per hundred tons, Q is hundreds of tons of fertilizer, MR is marginal revenue, TC is total cost in dollars (before capital costs), and MC is marginal cost in dollars (before capital costs).

If controls advocated by the agriculture and cattle interests were immediately implemented, fertilizer industry cost curves would be adjusted to:

$$TC_1 = \$106{,}000{,}000 + \$8{,}200Q + \$1.1Q^2$$

$$MC_1 = \partial TC_1/\partial Q = \$8,200 + \$2.2Q$$

If controls advocated by the fertilizer industry were implemented, the cost curves would be adjusted to:

$$TC_2 = \$101,000,000 + \$8,050Q + \$1Q^2$$

$$MC_2 = \partial TC_2/\partial Q = \$8,050 + \$2Q$$

A. *What is the current profit-maximizing price/output combination, level of profits, and rate of return on investment in the fertilizer industry?*

B. *What would be the profit-maximizing price/output combination, level of profits, and rate of return on investment in the fertilizer industry if the agriculture and cattle interests' recommendations were implemented?*

C. *What would be the profit-maximizing price/output combination, level of profits, and rates of return on investment in the fertilizer industry if their own recommendations were adopted?*

D. *Which recommendation should be implemented?*

P20.7 SOLUTION

A. Set $M\pi = MR - MC = 0$ to find the current profit-maximizing output level:

$$M\pi = MR - MC$$

$$0 = \$35,000 - \$1Q - \$8,000 - \$2Q$$

$$0 = 27,000 - 3Q$$

$$3Q = 27,000$$

$$Q = 9,000(00) \text{ or } 900,000 \text{ tons}$$

$$P = \$35,000 - \$0.5Q$$

$$= \$35,000 - \$0.5(9,000)$$

$$= \$30,500 \text{ per hundred tons (or } \$305/\text{ton)}$$

$$\pi \;=\; -\$100,000,000 + \$27,000(9,000)$$

$$-\$1.5(9,000^2)$$

$$=\; \$21,500,000$$

$$\text{Return on investment} \;=\; \frac{\pi}{\text{Total assets}}$$

$$=\; \frac{\$21,500,000}{\$210,000,000}$$

$$=\; 0.102 \text{ or } 10.2\%$$

(*Note*: Profit is falling for Q > 9,000, so Q = 9,000 is a point of maximum profits.)

B. Based on the assumption that agriculture and cattle industry interests are adopted, set relevant $M\pi = MR - MC = 0$ to find the profit-maximizing output level:

$$M\pi \;=\; MR - MC_1$$

$$0 \;=\; \$35,000 - \$1Q - \$8,200 - \$2.2Q$$

$$0 \;=\; 26,800 - 3.2Q$$

$$3.2Q \;=\; 26,800$$

$$Q \;=\; 8,375(00) \text{ or } 837,500 \text{ tons}$$

$$P \;=\; \$35,000 - \$0.5Q$$

$$=\; \$35,000 - \$0.5(8,375)$$

$$=\; \$30,813 \text{ per hundred tons (or } \$308.13/\text{ton)}$$

$$\pi \;=\; TR - TC_1$$

$$=\; -\$106,000,000 + \$26,800(8,375)$$

$$-\$1.6(8,375^2)$$

$$=\; \$6,225,000$$

$$\frac{\text{Return on}}{\text{investment}} = \frac{\pi}{\text{Total assets}}$$

$$= \frac{\$6,225,000}{\$240,000,000}$$

$$= 0.0259 \text{ or } 2.59\%$$

(*Note*: Profit is falling for $Q > 8,375$, so $Q = 8,375$ is a point of maximum profits).

C. Based on the assumption that fertilizer industry interests are adopted, set relevant $M\pi = MR - MC = 0$ to find the profit-maximizing output level:

$$M\pi = MR - MC_2$$

$$0 = \$35,000 - \$1Q - \$8,050 - \$2Q$$

$$0 = 26,950 - 3Q$$

$$3Q = 26,950$$

$$Q = 8,983.33(00) \text{ or } 898,333 \text{ tons}$$

$$P = \$35,000 - \$0.5Q$$

$$= \$35,000 - \$0.5(8,983.33)$$

$$= \$30,508 \text{ per hundred tons (or } \$305.08/\text{ton)}$$

$$\pi = TR - TC_2$$

$$= -\$101,000,000 + \$26,950(8,983.33)$$

$$- \$1.5(8,983.33^2)$$

$$= \$20,050,417$$

$$\frac{\text{Return on}}{\text{investment}} = \frac{\pi}{\text{Total assets}}$$

$$= \frac{\$20,050,417}{\$215,000,000}$$

$$= \ 0.093 \ or \ 9.3\%$$

(*Note*: Profit is falling for Q > 8,983.33, so Q = 8,983.33 is a point of maximum profits).

D.   Obviously, there is no easy answer. Pollution abatement is not free; it will result in higher prices and/or lower profits. Importantly, after pollution abatement costs, industry profits may no longer be adequate. Although several issues might be raised, some of the more important considerations include:

1.   Output and Price: As a result of implementing the agriculture and cattle interests' recommendations, price per ton would be $3.05 higher and industry output would be 60,800 tons lower than if the fertilizer industry's recommendations were implemented.

2.   Because output would be much lower with TC_1 than with TC_2, the increase in unemployment in the fertilizer industry would probably be less with the fertilizer industry proposal.

3.   The return on investment with TC_1 would fall to less than 3%, while TC_2 would fall to only 9.3%. The former decrease could substantially hamper necessary investment in the fertilizer industry.

4.   What is the difference in the short-term and long-run effectiveness of the two pollution abatement programs recommended by the opposing industries?

P20.8   ***Severance Taxes.*** *Rocky Mountain Natural Resources, Inc., processes enriched ore to extract silver and lead. Each ton of processed ore yields one ounce of silver and one pound of lead. Marginal processing costs equal $5 per ton. After insurance, transportation and other marketing costs, the net price and marginal revenue of silver received by Rocky Mountain are:*

$$P_S \ = \ \$10 - \$0.00025Q_S$$

$$MR_S \ = \ \partial TR_S/\partial Q_S = \$10 - \$0.0005Q_S$$

and for lead are:

$$P_L \ = \ \$2 - \$0.0001Q_L$$

$$MR_L \ = \ \partial TR_L/\partial Q_S = \$2 - \$0.0002Q_L$$

Q_S is ounces of silver and Q_L is pounds of lead.

A.   Calculate Rocky Mountain's optimal sales quantities and prices for silver and lead.

B.   Calculate Rocky Mountain's optimal sales quantities and prices in the event of a 5% state silver revenue tax.

C.   Calculate Rocky Mountain's optimal sales quantities and prices in the event of a 5% state lead revenue tax.

D.   Which state tax is preferable in terms of minimizing short-run employment effects in the mining industry?

P20.8   **SOLUTION**

A.   Because each unit of production generates revenue from both metals, the optimal activity level is reached when aggregate marginal revenue (silver plus lead) is equated with marginal cost:

$$MR = MR_S + MR_L \;\; = \;\; MC$$

$$\$10 - \$0.0005Q + \$2 - \$0.0002Q \;\; = \;\; \$5 \;\; \text{(Because } Q_S = Q_L = Q)$$

$$12 - 0.0007Q \;\; = \;\; 5$$

$$0.0007Q \;\; = \;\; 7$$

$$Q \;\; = \;\; 10{,}000$$

and

$$P_S \;\; = \;\; \$10 - \$0.00025(10{,}000) = \$7.50 \text{ per ounce}$$

$$P_L \;\; = \;\; \$2 - \$0.0001(10{,}000) = \$1 \text{ per pound}$$

To be optimal, marginal revenues for each joint output must be greater than or equal to zero. At this activity level:

$$MR_S \;\; = \;\; \$10 - \$0.0005(10{,}000) = \$5$$

$$MR_L \;\; = \;\; \$2 - \$0.0002(10{,}000) = \$0$$

Therefore, the quantities and prices derived above are optimal. The marginal revenue from silver covers all marginal production costs. The marginal revenue from lead equals zero, which is the marginal production cost of lead given ore processing for silver production.

B. The effect of a silver revenue tax is to reduce MR_S. As in Part A, consider:

$$MR = MR_S + MR_L = MC$$

$$(1 - 0.05)(\$10 - \$0.0005Q) + \$2 - \$0.0002Q = \$5 \text{ (Because } Q_S = Q_L = Q)$$

$$9.50 - 0.000475Q + 2 - 0.0002Q = 5$$

$$11.50 - 0.000675Q = 5$$

$$0.000675Q = 6.50$$

$$Q = 9,630$$

and

$P_S = \$10 - \$0.00025(9,630) = \$7.59$ (Price paid by consumers)

$P_S = (1 - 0.05)\$7.59 = \$7.21$ (Price received by Rocky Mountain)

$P_L = \$2 - \$0.0001(9,630) = \$1.037$

To be optimal, marginal revenues to Rocky Mountain for each joint output must be nonnegative at this activity level.

$MR_S = \$9.50 - \$0.000475(9,630) = \$4.93$

$MR_L = \$2 - \$0.0002(9,630) = \$0.07$

Because the marginal revenues from each joint product are positive, each contributes toward covering marginal processing costs of $5, and the prices and quantities derived above are optimal.

C. The effect of a lead revenue tax is to reduce MR_L. As above, set:

$$MR_S + MR_L = MC$$

$$\$10 - \$0.0005Q + (1 - 0.05)(\$2 - \$0.0002Q) \quad = \quad \$5 \ (\text{Because } Q_S = Q_L = Q)$$

$$10 - 0.0005Q + 1.90 - \$0.00019Q \quad = \quad 5$$

$$11.90 - 0.00069Q \quad = \quad 5$$

$$0.00069Q \quad = \quad 6.90$$

$$Q \quad = \quad 10,000$$

and

$$P_S \quad = \quad \$7.50 \qquad\qquad (\text{As in part A})$$

$$P_L \quad = \quad \$1 \qquad\qquad (\text{Paid by consumers})$$

$$P_L \quad = \quad (1 - 0.05)\$1 = \$0.95 \qquad (\text{Received by Rocky Mountain})$$

Marginal revenues to Rocky Mountain at this activity level are again nonnegative because:

$$MR_S \quad = \quad \$10 - \$0.0005(10,000) = \$5$$

$$MR_L \quad = \quad \$1.90 - \$0.00019(10,000) = \$0$$

As in Part A, the marginal revenue from silver covers all marginal production costs. The marginal revenue from lead again equals zero, which is the marginal production cost of lead given ore processing for silver production. Prices and quantities shown above are optimal.

D. The lead revenue tax will have no short-run effect on output and employment, and is therefore preferable to a silver revenue tax.

In general, a tax on byproduct revenues affects neither output nor employment in the short-run. Such a tax on primary product revenues will always reduce both. Unlike a byproduct tax, a primary product revenue tax always causes consumer prices to rise for each product.

P20.9 **Size of Government.** *Over the past several decades, the scope and magnitude of government activity has increased dramatically in the United States and in many foreign countries. In the United States, the Federal government has built dams and highways, conducted research, expanded the arts, and increased it's regulatory authority over many facets of the economy. Through the federal revenue sharing program, the Federal* *government has also directed millions of dollars to state and local governments to support education, crime-prevention programs and highway construction.*

In the United States, the purchase of goods and services by all levels of government exceeds 20% of GDP, with a budget in excess of $2 trillion and more than 3 million employees. Spreading taxpayer resistance, to the growth in government has spawned increasing efforts to curb the size of government while improving the quality and efficiency of government services.

A.   *Discuss the primary strengths of the unregulated private- sector allocation of economic resources.*

B.   *Discuss how the presence of positive external social benefits give rise to a demand for government.*

P20.9   **SOLUTION**

A.   Private markets can identify and be responsive to individual preferences through the interaction of supply and demand. In the absence of important externalities, marginal social benefits associated with any good or service are directly reflected in equilibrium prices and quantities. At the same time, marginal social costs of production are reflected in the market supply curve.

Perfectly functioning competitive markets yield output prices and quantities that exactly balance marginal social benefits and marginal social costs. In terms of demand, consumers dictate the strength of their preferences to producers. In terms of supply, production is allocated among the most efficient marginal producers.

In sum, perfectly functioning competitive markets provide customers *what* they want in a least-cost fashion.

B.   Positive external social benefits give rise to a demand for government because private markets are unable to ensure cooperative allocations that maximize social welfare. When positive marginal social benefits are enjoyed following the consumption or production activity of others, the failure to reward those responsible for positive externalities leads to underconsumption or to underproduction. Conversely, when negative marginal social costs are suffered following the consumption or production activity of others, the failure to penalize those responsible for negative externalities leads to overconsumption or to overproduction.

P20.10   ***Benefit-cost Analysis.*** *AIDS, acquired immune deficiency syndrome, is the final stage of the disease caused by the human immunodeficiency virus (HIV). In most victims, HIV causes a deterioration in the immune system by killing a class of white blood cells called*

"T4 helpers." After a period of five to ten years, too few of these T4 helper cells remain, and the HIV victim succumbs to an opportunistic infection such as pneumonia. During the period between HIV infection and the onset of AIDS, victims are infectious, asymptomatic carriers. Because HIV alters the victim's genetic material and is highly prone to mutation, finding a cure is extremely difficult and any vaccine is likely to be ineffective in a substantial minority of those vaccinated. Moreover, no natural immunity has been observed. So far, the disease is fatal for nearly everyone who gets it. For all of these reasons, AIDS has become the most dreaded disease in the world today.

Since the AIDS outbreak during the 1980s, public sector managers have been confronted with a complex social and economic problem in the field of epidemiology, the study of epidemics and epidemic diseases. Even under "optimistic" scenarios, AIDS is expected to remain a leading cause of death for persons in the 25 to 44 age group for the forseeable future. In the United States, treatment cost estimates run as high as $50 billion per year, and will continue to have a dramatic influence on the cost and availability of hospital care, health and life insurance, employee benefits, and public services. Although the dreadful personal cost of the AIDS epidemic in terms of lost life and personal suffering is immeasurable, the fact that AIDS strikes primarily young people in their most productive years intensifies its economic and social impact. To mitigate these costs, public-sector managers must evaluate the benefits associated with a number of alternative means of focusing current research efforts and treatment methods designed to control the human suffering and economic costs of the AIDS epidemic.

A. *From an economic standpoint, the value of a human life is sometimes measured as the discounted present-value of a person's expected lifetime earnings. Is this a reasonable basis for public-sector managers to use in placing a dollar value on the lives saved through finding a cure for AIDS?*

B. *The "willingness to pay" approach, bases life value estimates on the payments one would require to accept a small risk of death or, alternatively, the payments one would be willing to make to reduce the risk of death. Is this a reasonable basis for public-sector managers to use in placing a dollar value on the lives saved through finding a cure for AIDS?*

C. *Which approach, the human capital approach of part A or the willingness to pay approach of part B, is likely to yield higher life value estimate? Explain.*

P20.10   SOLUTION

A.   In a general sense, money spent on the prevention, treatment and cure of AIDS cannot be used in other areas, such as in the treatment of cancer or to improve the safety of air traffic control facilities. Therefore, to evaluate the efficacy of public expenditures and public policies aimed to save human lives, public-sector managers must make some determination, using either subjective or objective criteria, of the value of human life.

The human capital approach, determines the value of a human life as the discounted present-value of a person's expected lifetime earnings. An obvious disadvantage of this approach is that it is one-dimensional. By focusing only on earning power it implies that the lives of nonworkers have no economic value.

B. The "willingness to pay" approach, bases life value estimates on the payments one would require to accept a small risk of death or, alternatively, the payments one would be willing to make to reduce the risk of death. In implementing this approach, questionnaires have been used to determine the amount people would be willing to pay to participate in a program that would reduce the risk of death due to a given disease. It is worth mentioning that the results of these surveys are not totally reliable because the hypothetical nature of the questions makes it difficult for people to answer truthfully and accurately.

C. Without specific information on disease incidence and the distribution of income it is not possible to say which approach, the human capital approach or the willingness to pay approach, is likely to yield higher life value estimate.

Obviously, if one has contracted AIDS, he or she would pay whatever it takes to obtain a cure. The only obvious limit is the amount of income or wealth available. If AIDS were most common among the wealthy, then a willingness to pay approach would suggest relatively high life value estimates. If AIDS were most common among the poor, then a willingness to pay approach would suggest relatively low life value estimates.

Similarly, if AIDS were most common among the highly educated, then a human capital approach would suggest relatively high life value estimates. If AIDS were most common among the uneducated, then a human capital approach would suggest relatively low life value estimates.

(*Note:* This topic was purposely chosen to be thought provoking. No one can be so presumptuous as to value something so sacred as human life. Nevertheless, everyday public policy decisions are based on economic values that must be debated and understood.)